IMMEDIATE AND PROGRESSIVE REALISATION IN INTERNATIONAL HUMAN RIGHTS LAW

This book makes a new and original contribution to the old debate about differences between socio-economic and civil and political rights, which has engaged human rights discourse over several decades.

Although scholars and practitioners now agree that these categories are more alike than originally assumed, they continue to delineate them based on the alleged difference between immediate and progressive realisation. This book asks whether this differentiation is still valid by exploring the historical and theoretical background, the text of relevant UN human rights treaties and the practice of the UN human rights committees. By so doing, it shows that the standards of realisation converge more than diverge and that this last remaining distinction should be abandoned.

Human rights lawyers, advocates, practitioners and policy makers will find this book invaluable as it brings much needed clarification to this key question.

Volume 31: Human Rights Law in Perspective

Human Rights Law in Perspective

General Editor: Colin Harvey
Professor of Human Rights Law
School of Law
Queen's University Belfast

The language of human rights figures prominently in legal and political debates at the national, regional and international levels. In the UK the Human Rights Act 1998 has generated considerable interest in the law of human rights. It will continue to provoke much debate in the legal community and the search for original insights and new materials will intensify.

The aim of this series is to provide a forum for scholarly reflection on all aspects of the law of human rights. The series will encourage work which engages with the theoretical, comparative and international dimensions of human rights law. The primary aim is to publish over time books which offer an insight into human rights law in its contextual setting. The objective is to promote an understanding of the nature and impact of human rights law. The series is inclusive, in the sense that all perspectives in legal scholarship are welcome. It will incorporate the work of new and established scholars.

Human Rights Law in Perspective is not confined to consideration of the UK. It will strive to reflect comparative, regional and international perspectives. Work which focuses on human rights law in other states will therefore be included in this series. The intention is to offer an inclusive intellectual home for significant scholarly contributions to human rights law.

Recent titles in this series

The Times and Temporalities of International Human Rights Law
Edited by Kathryn McNeilly and Ben Warwick

Social Rights and the Constitutional Moment: Learning from Chile and International Experiences
Edited by Koldo Casla, Magdalena Sepúlveda, Vicente Silva, and Valentina Contreras

Article 8 ECHR, Family Reunification and the UK's Supreme Court: Family Matters?
Helena Wray

Rethinking Human Rights: Critical Insights from Palestinian Youth
Erika Jiménez

Immediate and Progressive Realisation in International Human Rights Law
Tobias Wirthle

For the complete list of titles in this series, see 'Human Rights Law in Perspective' link at www.bloomsbury.com/uk/series/human-rights-law-in-perspective/

Immediate and Progressive Realisation in International Human Rights Law

Tobias Wirthle

•HART•
OXFORD • LONDON • NEW YORK • NEW DELHI • SYDNEY

HART PUBLISHING

Bloomsbury Publishing Plc

Kemp House, Chawley Park, Cumnor Hill, Oxford, OX2 9PH, UK

1385 Broadway, New York, NY 10018, USA

Bloomsbury Publishing Ireland Limited, 29 Earlsfort Terrace, Dublin 2, D02 AY28, Ireland

HART PUBLISHING, the Hart/Stag logo, BLOOMSBURY and the Diana logo are trademarks of Bloomsbury Publishing Plc

First published in Great Britain 2025

A catalogue record for this book is available from the British Library.

A catalogue record for this book is available from the Library of Congress.

Library of Congress Control Number: 2024949835

ISBN: HB: 978-1-50998-247-9
ePDF: 978-1-50998-249-3
ePub: 978-1-50998-248-6

Typeset by Compuscript Ltd, Shannon

For product safety related questions contact productsafety@bloomsbury.com

To find out more about our authors and books visit www.hartpublishing.co.uk. Here you will find extracts, author information, details of forthcoming events and the option to sign up for our newsletters.

Acknowledgements

THERE ARE MANY people to thank for their support during the time of writing this book which started as a PhD thesis at the University of Münster. My thanks go to my supervisor and first reader, James Fowkes, who provided precise and carefully thought-out answers to all my questions throughout the years – always with a refreshing sense of humour. The second reader of my thesis, Nora Markard, enabled a very swift review process and provided valuable feedback on my text. Together with Michaela Hailbronner, they made the oral exam feel like a pleasant conversation between colleagues. During my time as a research assistant at the University of Münster, Frank Zimmermann and his team offered a welcoming atmosphere, inspiring discussions, and restorative lunch-breaks. I also want to thank Pierre Thielbörger and his team at the IFHV Bochum for facilitating many useful colloquiums which helped steer me in the right direction, particularly at the beginning of the project.

Of course, my most heartfelt expressions of gratitude go to the individuals that accompanied me as my personal and social circle. I give thanks to my parents and family who enabled and encouraged my academic career from the start and offered me comfort and support during the more arduous stretches of the way. I am also grateful for my friends who provided welcome distraction and a wonderful time in Münster, particularly in connection with our orchestra. But the – at least in this regard – dubious fortune of being my closest companion fell to my partner, who modestly wants to remain unnamed but carried what sometimes felt like more than half of the burden of this project while always retaining her loving and cheerful disposition. Lastly, I must not forget my feline friend Harhour, who kept me company during many hours in home office.

D 6 – This book is based on the author's PhD thesis accepted at the University of Münster, Faculty of Law, 2023.

Table of Contents

PART III
TREATY INTERPRETATION

Abbreviations and Acronyms

ACHPR	African Commission on Human and Peoples' Rights
ATM	Automatic teller machine
CAT	Convention against Torture and Other Cruel, Inhuman or Degrading Treatment or Punishment
CAT-Com	Committee against Torture
CED	Committee on Enforced Disappearances
CEDAW	Convention on the Elimination of All Forms of Discrimination Against Women
CEDAW-Com	Committee on the Elimination of Discrimination against Women
CEDAW-OP	Optional Protocol to the Convention on the Elimination of All Forms of Discrimination against Women
CERD	Committee on the Elimination of Racial Discrimination
CESCR	Committee on Economic, Social and Cultural Rights
CMW	Committee on the Protection of the Rights of All Migrant Workers and Members of their Families
CRC	Convention on the Rights of the Child
CRC-Com	Committee on the Rights of the Child
CRC-OP3	(Third) Optional Protocol to the Convention on the Rights of the Child on a Communications Procedure
CRPD	Convention on the Rights of Persons with Disabilities
CRPD-Com	Committee on the Rights of Persons with Disabilities
CRPD-OP	Optional Protocol to the Convention on the Rights of Persons with Disabilities
CSW	Commission on the Status of Women
ECHR	European Convention of Human Rights
EComHR	European Commission of Human Rights
ECOSOC	United Nations Economic and Social Council

ECSR	European Committee of Social Rights
ECtHR	European Court of Human Rights
ESC	European Social Charter
ETS	European Treaty Series
HRC	Human Rights Committee
IACtHR	Inter-American Court of Human Rights
ICCPR	International Covenant on Civil and Political Rights
ICCPR-OP1	(First) Optional Protocol to the International Covenant on Civil and Political Rights
ICERD	International Convention on the Elimination of All Forms of Racial Discrimination
ICESCR-OP	Optional Protocol to the International Covenant on Economic, Social and Cultural Rights
ICJ	International Court of Justice
ICJ Rep	Annual Reports of the International Court of Justice
IComJ	International Commission of Jurists
ICRMW	International Convention on the Protection of the Rights of All Migrant Workers and Members of their Families
ILA	International Law Association
ILC	International Law Commission
IFHP	Interim Federal Health Program
NGO	Non-governmental organisation
NHRIs	National human rights institutions
OHCHR	United Nations Office of the High Commissioner for Human Rights
OP	Optional Protocol
PCIJ	Permanent Court of International Justice
Res	Resolution
UDHR	Universal Declaration of Human Rights
UN	United Nations

UNHRC	United Nations Human Rights Council
UNCHR	United Nations Commission on Human Rights
UNGA	United Nations General Assembly
UNHCHR	United Nations High Commissioner for Human Rights
UNSG	United Nations Secretary-General
UNTS	United Nations Treaty Series
VCLT	Vienna Convention on the Law of Treaties

Judicial Decisions and Individual Communications

International Courts

European Commission of Human Rights

Greece v the United Kingdom ('Cyprus') (1958)
2 Yearbook of the European Convention on Human Rights 172

European Court of Human Rights

Lawless v Ireland Series A No 3 (1961)
1 EHRR 15
National Union of Belgian Police v Belgium Series A No 19 (1975)
1 EHRR 578
Airey v Ireland Series A No 32 (1979)
2 EHRR 305
Petrovic v Austria ECHR 1998-I 21 (1998)
33 EHRR 14
Osman v the United Kingdom ECHR 1998-VIII 3124 (1998)
29 EHRR 245
Kiliç v Turkey ECHR 2000-III 75 (2000)
33 EHRR 1357
Frăsilă and Ciocîrlan v Romania (2012)
App No 25329/03

Inter-American Court of Human Rights

Villagrán Morales et al v Guatemala (1999)
Series C No 63
Sawhoyamaxa Indigenous Community v Paraguay (2006)
Series C No 146

International Court of Justice

Interpretation of Peace Treaties with Bulgaria, Hungary and Romania (Second Phase, Advisory Opinion)
[1950] ICJ Rep 221
Reservations to the Convention on the Prevention and Punishment of the Crime of Genocide (Advisory Opinion)
[1951] ICJ Rep 15

Legal Consequences for States of the Continued Presence of South Africa in Namibia (South West Africa) Notwithstanding Security Council Resolution 276 (1970) (Advisory Opinion)
[1971] ICJ Rep 16
Land, Island and Maritime Frontier Dispute (El Salvador v Honduras, Nicaragua intervening) (Merits, Judgment)
[1992] ICJ Rep 351
LaGrand (Germany v USA) (Merits, Judgment)
[2001] ICJ Rep 2001
Legal Consequences of the Construction of a Wall in the Occupied Palestinian Territory (Advisory Opinion)
[2004] ICJ Rep 136
Application of the Convention on the Prevention and Punishment of the Crime of Genocide (Bosnia and Herzegovina v Serbia and Montenegro) (Merits, Judgment)
[2007] ICJ Rep 43
Certain Questions of Mutual Assistance in Criminal Matters (Djibouti v France) (Merits, Judgment)
[2008] ICJ Rep 177
Ahmadou Sadio Diallo (Republic of Guinea v Democratic Republic of the Congo) (Merits, Judgment)
[2010] ICJ Rep 639
Pulp Mills on the River Uruguay (Argentina v Uruguay) (Merits, Judgment)
[2010] ICJ Rep 14
Application of the International Convention on the Elimination of All Forms of Racial Discrimination (Georgia v Russian Federation) (Preliminary Objections, Judgment)
[2011] ICJ Rep 70
Territorial and Maritime Dispute (Nicaragua v Colombia) (Application by Costa Rica for Permission to Intervene, Judgment)
[2011] ICJ Rep 420
Questions relating to the Obligation to Prosecute or Extradite (Belgium v Senegal) (Merits, Judgment)
[2012] ICJ Rep 422
Alleged Violations of Sovereign Rights and Maritime Spaces in the Caribbean Sea (Nicaragua v Colombia) (Preliminary Objections, Judgment)
[2016] ICJ Rep 3
Maritime Delimitation in the Indian Ocean (Somalia v Kenya) (Preliminary Objections, Judgment)
[2017] ICJ Rep 3
Application of the International Convention on the Elimination of All Forms of Racial Discrimination (Qatar v United Arab Emirates) (Preliminary Objections, Judgment)
[2021] ICJ Rep 71

Permanent Court of International Justice

Case of the SS 'Wimbledon'
[1923] Series A No 1, 14

UN Human Rights Treaty Bodies

Committee on Economic, Social, and Cultural Rights

Djazia and Bellili v Spain [Adoption of Views] (20 June 2017)
E/C.12/61/D/5/2015
López Albán v Spain [Adoption of Views] (11 October 2019)
E/C.12/66/D/37/2018
Goumari and Tidli v Spain [Adoption of Views] (18 February 2021)
E/C.12/69/D/85/2018

Committee on the Elimination of Discrimination against Women

OG v Russian Federation [Adoption of Views] (6 November 2017)
CEDAW/C/68/D/91/2015
JI v Finland [Adoption of Views] (5 March 2018)
CEDAW/C/69/D/103/2016

Committee on the Elimination of Racial Discrimination

Er v Denmark [Adoption of Views] (8 August 2007)
CERD/C/71/D/40/2007
Zentralrat Deutscher Sinti und Roma et al v Germany [Adoption of Views] (22 February 2008)
CERD/C/72/D/38/2006
Dawas and Shava v Denmark [Adoption of Views] (6 March 2012)
CERD/C/80/D/46/2009
VS v Slovakia [Adoption of Views] (4 December 2015)
CERD/C/88/D/56/2014
Belemvire v Republic of Moldova [Adoption of Views] (24 November 2017)
CERD/C/94/D/57/2015

Committee on the Rights of Persons with Disabilities

Nyusti and Takács v Hungary [Adoption of Views] (16 April 2013)
CRPD/C/9/D/1/2010
Bacher v Austria [Adoption of Views] (16 February 2014)
CRPD/C/19/D/26/2014
X v Argentina [Adoption of Views] (11 April 2014)
CRPD/C/11/D/8/2012

F v Austria [Adoption of Views] (21 August 2015) CRPD/C/14/D/21/2014
Beasley v Australia [Adoption of Views] (1 April 2016) CRPD/C/15/D/11/2013
Lockrey v Australia [Adoption of Views] (1 April 2016) CRPD/C/15/D/13/2013
Noble v Australia [Adoption of Views] (2 September 2016) CRPD/C/16/D/7/2012
Makarova v Lithuania [Adoption of Views] (18 August 2017) CRPD/C/18/D/30/2015
X v Tanzania [Adoption of Views] (18 August 2017) CRPD/C/18/D/22/2014
Given v Australia [Adoption of Views] (16 February 2018) CRPD/C/19/D/19/2014
JH v Australia [Adoption of Views] (31 August 2018) CRPD/C/20/D/35/2016
Y v Tanzania [Adoption of Views] (31 August 2018) CRPD/C/20/D/23/2014
Al Adam v Saudi Arabia [Adoption of Views] (20 September 2018) CRPD/C/20/D/38/2016
Doolan v Australia [Adoption of Views] (30 August 2019) CRPD/C/22/D/18/2013
Leo v Australia [Adoption of Views] (30 August 2019) CRPD/C/22/D/17/2013
Vela v Mexico [Adoption of Views] (6 September 2019) CRPD/C/22/D/32/2015
Z v Tanzania [Adoption of Views] (19 September 2019) CRPD/C/22/D/24/2014
JM v Spain [Adoption of Views] (21 August 2020) CRPD/C/23/D/37/2016
Sahlin v Sweden [Adoption of Views] (21 August 2020) CRPD/C/23/D/45/2018
Calleja Loma and Calleja Lucas v Spain [Adoption of Views] (28 August 2020) CRPD/C/23/D/41/2017

Human Rights Committee

Hertzberg v Finland [Adoption of Views] (2 April 1982) CCPR/C/15/D/61/1979
Mukong v Cameroon [Adoption of Views] (21 July 1994) CCPR/C/51/O/458/1991
Prutina et al v Bosnia and Herzegovina [Adoption of Views] (28 March 2013) CCPR/C/107/D/1917,1918,1925/2009&1953/2010
Rizvanović v Bosnia and Herzegovina [Adoption of Views] (21 March 2014) CCPR/C/110/D/1997/2010

Selimović et al v Bosnia and Herzegovina [Adoption of Views] (17 July 2014)
CCPR/C/111/D/2003/2010
Hero v Bosnia and Herzegovina [Adoption of Views] (28 October 2014)
CCPR/C/112/D/1966/2010
Kožljak v Bosnia and Herzegovina [Adoption of Views] (28 October 2014)
CCPR/C/112/D/1970/2010
Bhandari v Nepal [Adoption of Views] (29 October 2014)
CCPR/C/112/D/2031/2011
Castillo v Venezuela [Adoption of Views] (10 November 2017)
CCPR/C/121/D/2610/2015
Toussaint v Canada [Adoption of Views] (24 July 2018)
CCPR/C/123/D/2348/2014
Carrero et al v Venezuela [Adoption of Views] (11 March 2020)
CCPR/C/128/D/3018/2017

National Jurisprudence

South Africa (Constitutional Court)

Rail Commuters Action Grp. v Transnet Ltd. t/a Metrorail
2005 (2) SA 359 (CC)
August and Another v Electoral Commission and Others
(1999) 4 BCLR 363 (CC)
Government of the Republic of South Africa v Grootboom
(2000) 11 BCLR 1169 (CC)

India (Supreme Court)

Navtej Singh Johar and Others v Union of India through Secretary Ministry of Law and Justice
Writ Petition No 76 of 2016

General Comments and Recommendations

Committee on Economic, Social, and Cultural Rights

'General Comment No 1: Reporting by States Parties' (1981)
E/1989/22
'General Comment No 3: The Nature of States Parties' Obligations (art. 2, para. 1, of the Covenant)' (1990)
E/1991/23 para 9
'General Comment No 4: The Right to Adequate Housing (Art 11(1) of the Covenant)' (1991)
E/1992/23
'General Comment No 5: Persons with Disabilities' (1994)
E/1995/22
'General Comment No 6: The Economic, Social and Cultural Rights of Older Persons' (1995)
E/1996/22
'General Comment No 7: The Right to Adequate Housing (art. 11 (1) of the Covenant): Forced Evictions' (1997)
HRI/GEN/1/Rev.7 at 46
'General Comment No 11: Plans of Action for Primary Education (Article 14 of the International Covenant on Economic, Social and Cultural Rights)' (1999)
E/C.12/1999/4
'General Comment No 12: The Right to Adequate Food (art. 11)' (1999)
E/C.12/1999/5
'General Comment No 13: The Right to Education (Article 13 of the Covenant)' (1999)
E/C.12/1999/10
'General Comment No 14: The Right to the Highest Attainable Standard of Health (Article 12 of the International Covenant on Economic, Social and Cultural Rights)' (2000)
E/C.12/2000/4
'General Comment No 15: The Right to Water (arts. 11 and 12 of the International Covenant on Economic, Social and Cultural Rights)' (2003)
E/C.12/2002/11
'General Comment No 16: The Equal Right of Men and Women to the Enjoyment of all Economic, Social and Cultural Rights (art. 3 of the International Covenant on Economic, Social and Cultural Rights)' (2005)
E/C.12/2005/4

'General Comment No 17: The Right of Everyone to Benefit from the Protection of the Moral and Material Interests Resulting from any Scientific, Literary or Artistic Production of which He or She is the Author (Article 15, Paragraph 1 (c), of the Covenant)' (2006)
E/C.12/GC/17

'General Comment No 18: The Right to Work (Article 6 of the International Covenant on Economic, Social and Cultural Rights' (2006)
E/C.12/GC/18

'General Comment No 19: The Right to Social Security (art. 9)' (2008)
E/C.12/GC/19

'General Comment No 21: Right of Everyone to Take Part in Cultural Life (art. 15, para 1 (a) of the International Covenant on Economic, Social and Cultural Rights)' (2009)
E/C.12/GC/21

'General Comment No 22 on the Right to Sexual and Reproductive Health (Article 12 of the International Covenant on Economic, Social and Cultural Rights)' (2016)
E/C.12/GC/22

'General Comment No 23 on the Right to Just and Favourable Conditions of Work (Article 7 of the International Covenant on Economic, Social and Cultural Rights)' (2016)
E/C.12/GC/23

'General Comment No 25 on Science and Economic, Social and Cultural Rights (Article 15 (1) (b), (2), (3) and (4) of the International Covenant on Economic, Social and Cultural Rights)' (2020)
E/C.12/GC/25

Committee on the Elimination of Discrimination against Women

'General Recommendation No 3: Education and Public Information Campaigns' (1987)
HRI/GEN/1/Rev.7 at 234

'General Recommendation No 5: Temporary Special Measures' (1988)
A/43/38 at 109

'General Recommendation No 6: Effective National Machinery and Publicity' (1982)
HRI/GEN/1/Rev.7 at 235

'General Recommendation No 9: Statistical Data Concerning the Situation of Women' (1989)
HRI/GEN/1/Rev.7 at 237

'General Recommendation No 13: Equal Remuneration for Work of Equal Value' (1989)
A/44/38 at 76

'General Recommendation No 14: Female Circumcision' (1990)
HRI/GEN/1/Rev.7 at 241
'General Recommendation No 17: Measurement and Quantification of the Unremunerated Domestic Activities of Women and their Recognition in the Gross National Product' (1991)
HRI/GEN/1/Rev.7 at 245
'General Recommendation No 19: Violence against Women' (1992)
A/47/38
'General Recommendation No 23: Political and Public Life' (1997)
A/52/38 at 61
'General Recommendation No 24: Article 12 of the Convention (Women and Health)' (1999)
HRI/GEN/1/Rev.7 at 274
'General Recommendation No 25: Article 4, Paragraph 1, of the Convention (Temporary Special Measures)' (2004)
HRI/GEN/1/Rev.7 at 282
'General Recommendation No 28 on the Core Obligations of States Parties under Article 2 of the Convention on the Elimination of All Forms of Discrimination against Women' (2010)
CEDAW/C/GC/28
'General Recommendation No 29 on Article 16 of the Convention on the Elimination of All Forms of Discrimination against Women (Economic Consequences of Marriage, Family Relations and their Dissolution)' (2013)
CEDAW/C/GC/29
'General Recommendation No 30 on Women in Conflict Prevention, Conflict and Post-conflict Situations' (2013)
CEDAW/C/GC/30
'General Recommendation No 31 on Harmful Practices' (2014)
CEDAW/C/GC/31
'General Recommendation No 32 on the Gender-related Dimensions of Refugee Status, Asylum, Nationality and Statelessness of Women' (2014)
CEDAW/C/GC/32
'General Recommendation No 33 on Women's Access to Justice' (2015)
CEDAW/C/GC/33
'General Recommendation No 34 on the Rights of Rural Women' (2016)
CEDAW/C/GC/34
'General Recommendation No 35 on Gender-based Violence Against Women, Updating General Recommendation No 19' (2017)
CEDAW/C/GC/35
'General Recommendation No 38 on Trafficking in Women and Girls in the Context of Global Migration' (2020)
CEDAW/C/GC/38

Committee on the Elimination of Racial Discrimination

'General Recommendation No 15 on Article 4 of the Convention' (1993)
HRI/GEN/1/Rev.7

'General Recommendation No 20 on Article 5 of the Convention' (1996)
A/51/18

'General Recommendation No 25 on Gender-related Dimensions of Racial Discrimination' (2000)
A/55/18

'General Recommendation No 27 on Discrimination Against Roma' (2000)
HRI/GEN/1/Rev.7 at 219

'General Recommendation No 29 on Article 1, Paragraph 1, of the Convention (Descent)' (2002)
HRI/GEN/1/Rev.7 at 226

'General Recommendation No 30 on Discrimination Against Non-citizens (2005)
A/59/18 at 93

'General Recommendation No 31 on the Prevention of Racial Discrimination in the Administration and Functioning of the Criminal Justice System' (2005)
A/60/18 at 98

'General Recommendation No 32: The Meaning and Scope of Special Measures in the International Convention on the Elimination of All Forms Racial Discrimination' (2009)
CERD/C/GC/32

'General Recommendation No 34: Racial Discrimination Against People of African Descent' (2011)
CERD/C/GC/34

'General Recommendation No 35: Combating Racist Hate Speech' (2013)
CERD/C/GC/35

Committee on the Rights of the Child

'General Comment No 1: Article 29 (1): The Aims of Education' (2001)
CRC/GC/2001/1

'General Comment No 2: The Role of Independent National Human Rights Institutions in the Promotion and Protection of the Rights of the Child' (2002)
CRC/GC/2002/2

'General Comment No 3: HIV/AIDS and the Rights of the Child' (2003)
CRC/GC/2003/3

'General Comment No 4: Adolescent Health and Development in the Context of the Convention on the Rights of the Child' (2003)
CRC/GC/2003/4

'General Comment No 5: General Measures of Implementation of the Convention on the Rights of the Child (arts. 4, 42 and 44, para. 6)' (2003)
CRC/GC/2003/5

'General Comment No 6: Treatment of Unaccompanied and Separated Children Outside their Country of Origin' (2005)
CRC/GC/2005/6

'General Comment No 7: Implementing Child Rights in Early Childhood' (2006)
CRC/C/GC/7/Rev.1

'General Comment No 8: The Right of the Child to Protection from Corporal Punishment and Other Cruel or Degrading Forms of Punishment (arts. 19; 28, para. 2; and 37, inter alia)' (2007)
CRC/C/GC/8

'General Comment No 9: The Rights of Children with Disabilities' (2007)
CRC/C/GC/9

'General Comment No 11: Indigenous Children and their Rights under the Convention' (2009)
CRC/C/GC/11

'General Comment No 12: The Right of the Child to be Heard' (2009)
CRC/C/GC/12

'General Comment No 13: The Right of the Child to Freedom from All Forms of Violence' (2011)
CRC/C/GC/13

'General Comment No 14 on the Right of the Child to have his or her Best Interests Taken as a Primary Consideration (art. 3, para. 1)' (2013)
CRC/C/GC/14

'General Comment No 15 on the Right of the Child to the Enjoyment of the Highest Attainable Standard of Health (art. 24)' (2013)
CRC/C/GC/15

'General Comment No 16 on State Obligations Regarding the Impact of the Business Sector on Children's Rights' (2013)
CRC/C/GC/16

'General Comment No 18 on Harmful Practices' (2019)
CRC/C/GC/18/Rev.1

'General Comment No 19 on Public Budgeting for the Realization of Children's Rights (art. 4)' (2016)
CRC/C/GC/19

'General Comment No 21 on Children in Street Situations' (2017)
CRC/C/GC/21

'General Comment No 22 on the General Principles Regarding the Human Rights of Children in the Context of International Migration' (2017)
CRC/C/GC/22

'General Comment No 23 on State Obligations Regarding the Human Rights of Children in the Context of International Migration in Countries of Origin, Transit, Destination and Return' (2017)
CRC/C/GC/23

'General Comment No 24 on Children's Rights in the Justice System' (2019)
CRC/C/GC/24
'General Comment No 25 on Children's Rights in Relation to the Digital Environment' (2021)
CRC/C/GC/25
'General Comment No 26 on Children's Rights and the Environment with a Special Focus on Climate Change' (2023)
CRC/C/GC/26

Committee on the Rights of Persons with Disabilities

'General Comment No 1: Article 12: Equal Recognition before the Law' (2014)
CRPD/C/GC/1
'General Comment No 2: Article 9: Accessibility' (2014)
CRPD/C/GC/2
'General Comment No 3: Article 6: Women and Girls with Disabilities' (2016)
CRPD/C/GC/3
'General Comment No 4 on the Right to Inclusive Education' (2016)
CRPD/C/GC/4
'General Comment No 5 on Living Independently and being Included in the Community' (2017)
CRPD/C/GC/5
'General Comment No 6 on Equality and Non-discrimination' (2018)
CRPD/C/GC/6
'General Comment No 7 on the Participation of Persons with Disabilities, including Children with Disabilities, through their Representative Organizations, in the Implementation and Monitoring of the Convention' (2018)
CRPD/C/GC/7
'General Comment No 8 on the Right of Persons with Disabilities to Work and Employment' (2022)
CRPD/C/GC/8

Human Rights Committee

'General Comment No 6: Article 6 (Right to Life)' (1982)
HRI/GEN/1/Rev.7 at 128
'General Comment No 9: Article 10 (Humane Treatment of Persons Deprived of their Liberty)' (1982)
HRI/GEN/1/Rev.7 at 131
'General Comment No 12: Article 1 (Right to Self-determination)' (1984)
HRI/GEN/1/Rev.7 at 134

'General Comment No 17: Article 24 (Rights of the Child)' (1989)
HRI/GEN/1/Rev.1
'General Comment No 18: Non-discrimination' (1989)
HRI/GEN/1/Rev.1
'General Comment No 21: Article 10 (Humane Treatment of Persons Deprived of their Liberty)' (1992)
HRI/GEN/1/Rev.7 at 153
'General Comment No 23: Article 27 (Rights of Minorities)' (1994)
HRI/GEN/1/Rev.7 at 158
'General Comment No 24 on Issues Relating to Reservations Made upon Ratification or Accession to the Covenant or the Optional Protocols thereto, or in Relation to Declarations under Article 41 of the Covenant' (1994)
CCPR/C/21/Rev.1/Add.6
HRC, 'General Comment No 25: Article 25 (Participation in Public Affairs and the Right to Vote)' (1996)
HRI/GEN/1/Rev.7 at 167
'General Comment No 28: Article 3 (The Equality of Rights Between Men and Women)' (2000)
HRI/GEN/1/Rev.9
'General Comment No 31: The Nature of the General Legal Obligation Imposed on States Parties to the Covenant' (2004)
CCPR/C/21/Rev.1/Add.13
'General Comment No 34: Article 19: Freedoms of Opinion and Expression' (2011)
CCPR/C/GC/34
'General Comment No 36: Article 6: Right to Life' (2019)
CCPR/C/GC/36
'General Comment No 37 on the Right to Peaceful Assembly (Article 21)' (2020)
CCPR/C/GC/37

Other UN Documents

Commission on Human Rights

'Drafting Committee on an International Bill of Rights, First Session: Report of the Drafting Committee to the Commission on Human Rights' (1 July 1947) E/CN.4/21

'Summary Record of the 125th Meeting' (13 June 1949) E/CN.4/SR.125

'Report of the 5th Session' (23 June 1949) E/CN.4/350

'Summary Record of the 178th Meeting' (12 May 1950) E/CN.4/SR.178

'Report of the 6th Session' (29 May 1950) E/CN.4/507

'Report of the 7th Session' (24 May 1951) E/CN.4/640

'Summary Record of the 233rd Meeting' (2 July 1951) E/CN.4/SR.233

'Summary Record of the 271st Meeting' (14 May 1952) E/CN.4/SR.271

'Summary Record of the 273rd Meeting' (14 May 1952) E/CN.4/SR.273

'Summary Record of the 308th Meeting' (6 June 1952) E/CN.4/SR.308

'Summary Record of the 307th Meeting' (9 June 1952) E/CN.4/SR.307

'United Kingdom: Amendments to Article 2 of the Draft Convention on the Elimination of All Forms of Racial Discrimination' (1 January 1964) E/CN.4/L.689 contained in E/3873

'Summary Record of the 787th Meeting' (21 April 1964) E/CN.4/SR.787

'Summary Record of the 788th Meeting' (21 April 1964) E/CN.4/SR.788

'The Limburg Principles on the Implementation of the International Covenant on Economic Social and Cultural Rights' (8 January 1987) E/CN.4/1987/17

'Report on the Right to Adequate Food as a Human Right Submitted by Mr. Asbjørn Eide, Special Rapporteur' (7 July 1987) E/CN.4/Sub.2/1987/23

'Draft Convention on the Rights of the Child: Text of the Draft Convention as Adopted by the Working Group' (24 February 1988)
E/CN.4/1988/WG.1/WP.1/Rev.1

'Report of the Working Group on a Draft Convention on the Rights of the Child on its 10th Session' (6 April 1988)
E/CN.4/1988/28

'Technical Review of the Text of the Draft Convention on the Rights of the Child' (20 October 1988)
E/CN.4/1989/WG.1/CRP.1

'Report of the Working Group on a Draft Convention on the Rights of the Child on its 11th Session' (2 March 1989)
E/CN.4/1989/48

'Final Report on Enhancing the Long-term Effectiveness of the United Nations Human Rights Treaty System by the Independent Expert Philip Alston' (27 March 1997)
E/CN.4/1997/74

'Status of the International Covenants on Human Rights: Report of the Secretary General on the Draft Optional Protocol to the International Covenant on Economic, Social and Cultural Rights' (16 March 1998)
E/CN.4/1998/84/Add.1

'Status of the International Covenants on Human Rights: Report of the Independent Expert on the Question of a Draft Optional Protocol to the International Covenant on Economic, Social and Cultural Rights' (12 February 2002)
E/CN.4/2002/57

'Report of the Open-ended Working Group to Consider Options Regarding the Elaboration of an Optional Protocol to the International Covenant on Economic, Social and Cultural Rights on its 1st Session' (15 March 2004)
E/CN.4/2004/44

'Elements for an Optional Protocol to the International Covenant on Economic, Social and Cultural Rights: Analytical Paper by the Chairperson-Rapporteur, Catarina de Albuquerque' (30 November 2005)
E/CN.4/2006/WG.23/2

'Report of the Open-ended Working Group to Consider Options Regarding the Elaboration of an Optional Protocol to the International Covenant on Economic, Social and Cultural Rights on its 3rd Session' (14 March 2006)
E/CN.4/2006/47

Commission on the Status of Women

'Summary Record of the 661st Meeting' (8 December 1976)
E/CN.6/SR.661

'Summary Record of the 662nd Meeting' (8 December 1976)
E/CN.6/SR.662

'Summary Record of the 665th Meeting' (10 December 1976)
E/CN.6/SR.665
'Summary Record of the 666th Meeting' (13 December 1976)
E/CN.6/SR.666
'Summary Record of the 667th Meeting' (13 December 1976)
E/CN.6/SR.667
'Summary Record of the 672nd Meeting' (15 December 1976)
E/CN.6/SR.672
'Summary Record of the 673rd Meeting' (16 December 1976)
E/CN.6/SR.673
'Report on the 26th and Resumed 26th Sessions' (1 January 1977)
E/CN.6/608

Committee on Economic Social and Cultural Rights

'An Evaluation of the Obligation to Take Steps to the "Maximum of Available Resources" under an Optional Protocol to the Covenant' (21 September 2007)
E/C.12/2007/1
'Report on the 44th and 45th Sessions' (3 May 2011)
E/2011/22

Committee on the Rights of the Child

'Treaty-specific Guidelines Regarding the Form and Content of Periodic Reports to be Submitted by States Parties under Article 44, Paragraph 1 (b), of the Convention on the Rights of the Child' (3 March 2015)
CRC/C/58/Rev.3
'Rules of Procedure' (1 March 2019)
CRC/C/4/Rev.5

Economic and Social Council

Res 5 (I) 'Commission on Human Rights with a Sub-Commission on the Status of Women' (16 February 1946)
E/RES/5(I)
'Summary Record of the 378th Meeting' (1950)
E/SR.378
Res 303 (XI) 'Report of the Commission on Human Rights (Sixth Session)' (9 August 1950)
E/Res/303(XI)

'Report of the Economic and Social Council Covering the Period from 16 August 1950 to 21 September 1951' (1951)
A/1884

Res 384 (XIII) 'Report of the Commission on Human Rights (Seventh Session)' (29 August 1951)
E/RES/384(XIII)

Res 1985/17, 'Review of the Composition, Organization and Administrative Arrangements of the Sessional Working Group of Governmental Experts on the Implementation of the International Covenant on Economic, Social and Cultural Rights' (28 May 1985)
E/RES/1985/17

General Assembly

Res 217 A (III) 'Universal Declaration of Human Rights' (10 December 1948)
A/RES/217(III)

Res 421 (V) 'Draft International Covenants on Human Rights and Measures of Implementation: Future Work for the Commission on Human Rights' (4 December 1950)
A/RES/421(V)

Res 543 (VI) 'Preparation of two Draft International Covenants on Human Rights' (5 February 1952)
A/RES/543(VI)

'Draft International Covenants on Human Rights: Annotation Prepared by the Secretary-General' (1 July 1955)
A/2929

'Draft International Covenants on Human Rights: Observations by Governments' (13 October 1955)
A/2910/Add.6

'Summary Record of the 1495th Plenary Meeting' (16 December 1966)
A/PV.1495

Res 2200 (XXI) 'International Covenant on Economic, Social and Cultural Rights, International Covenant on Civil and Political Rights and Optional Protocol to the International Covenant on Civil and Political Rights' (16 December 1966)
A/RES/2200(XXI)

Res 38/117 'Reporting Obligations of the States Parties to the International Covenants on Human Rights' (16 December 1983)
A/RES/38/117

'Vienna Declaration and Programme of Action' (12 July 1993)
A/CONF.157/23

Res 49/178 'Effective Implementation of International Instruments on Human Rights, including Reporting Obligations under International Instruments on Human Rights' (23 December 1994)
A/RES/49/178

'Report of the Ad Hoc Committee on a Comprehensive and Integral International Convention on the Protection and Promotion of the Rights and Dignity of Persons with Disabilities on its 4th Session' (14 September 2004)
A/59/360

'Report of the Chairs of the Human Rights Treaty Bodies on their 23rd Meeting' (22 July 2011)
A/66/175

Res 68/268 'Strengthening and Enhancing the Effective Functioning of the Human Rights Treaty Body System' (9 April 2014)
A/RES/68/268

'Report of the Chairs of the Human Rights Treaty Bodies on their 31st Annual Meeting' (30 July 2019)
A/74/256

'Report of the Chairs of the Human Rights Treaty Bodies on their 32nd Annual Meeting' (14 September 2020)
A/75/346

'Report on the Process of the Consideration of the State of the United Nations Human Rights Treaty Body System' (17 November 2020)
A/75/601

'Report of the Chairs of the Human Rights Treaty Bodies on their 33rd Annual Meeting' (30 July 2021)
A/76/254

'Report of the Chairs of the Human Rights Treaty Bodies on their 34th Meeting' (26 July 2022)
A/77/228

General Assembly – Third Committee

'Draft International Declaration of Human Rights and Measures of Implementation: Memorandum Presented by Israel' (8 January 1952)
A/C.3/565

'Summary Record of the 395th Meeting' (19 January 1952)
A/C.3/SR.395

'Summary Record of the 410th Meeting' (29 January 1952)
A/C.3/SR.410

'Summary Record of 1181st meeting' (13 November 1962)
A/C.3/SR.1181

'Summary Record of the 1202nd Meeting' (5 December 1962)
A/C.3/SR.1202

'Summary Record of the 1203rd Meeting' (5 December 1962)
A/C.3/SR.1203
'United Kingdom: Amendments to Article 2 of the Draft Covenant on Civil and Political Rights' (7 November 1963)
A/C.3/L.1167
'Summary Record of the 1257th Meeting' (8 November 1963)
A/C.3/SR.1257
'Report on the 18th Session' (10 December 1963)
A/5655
'Summary Record of the 1427th Meeting' (18 November 1966)
A/C.3/SR.1427
'Report on the 21st Session' (13 December 1966)
A/6546

High Commissioner for Human Rights

'Plan of Action Submitted by the United Nations High Commissioner for Human Rights, Louise Arbour' (26 May 2005)
A/59/2005/Add.3
'Concept Paper on the High Commissioner's Proposal for a Unified Standing Treaty Body' (22 March 2006)
HRI/MC/2006/2
'Report of the United Nations High Commissioner for Human Rights on Progressive Realization' (25 June 2007)
E/2007/82
'Report of UN High Commissioner for Human Rights Navi Pillay on the Strengthening of Human Rights Treaty Bodies Pursuant to General Assembly Resolution 66/254' (26 June 2012)
A/66/860

Human Rights Committee

'Report on the 19th Session' (15 September 1963)
A/38/40(SUPP)
'Summary Record of the Meeting Held on 27 July 1982' (27 July 1982)
CCPR/C/SR.378/Add.1
'Draft General Comment No. 33: The Obligations of States Parties under the Optional Protocol to the International Covenant on Civil and Political Rights, 2nd Version' (25 August 2008)
CCPR/C/GC/33/CRP.3
'The Relationship of the Human Rights Committee with Nongovernmental Organizations' (4 June 2012)
CCPR/C/104/3

Human Rights Council

'Report of the Open-ended Working Group on an Optional Protocol to the International Covenant on Economic, Social and Cultural Rights on its 4th Session' (30 August 2007)
A/HRC/6/8

'Report of the Open-ended Working Group on an Optional Protocol to the International Covenant on Economic, Social and Cultural Rights on its 5th Session' (6 May 2008)
A/HRC/8/7

'Report of the Open-ended Working Group on an Optional Protocol to the Convention on the Rights of the Child to Provide a Communications Procedure on its 2nd Session' (24 May 2011)
A/HRC/17/36

International Law Commission

'Second Report on Reservations to Treaties by Alain Pellet, Special Rapporteur' (13 June 1996)
A/CN.4/477/ADD.1

'Fourth Report on Subsequent Agreements and Subsequent Practice in Relation to the Interpretation of Treaties by Georg Nolte, Special Rapporteur' (7 March 2016)
A/CN.4/694

Office of the High Commissioner on Human Rights

'Human Rights Indicators: A Guide to Measurement and Implementation' (2012)
HR/PUB/12/5

Security Council

'Report of the Secretary-General on the Rule of Law and Transitional Justice in Conflict and Post-Conflict Societies' (23 August 2004)
S/2004/616

International Treaties and Instruments

Convention against Torture and Other Cruel, Inhuman or Degrading Treatment or Punishment (adopted 10 December 1984, entered into force 26 June 1987) 1465 UNTS 85.

Convention on the Elimination of All Forms of Discrimination Against Women (adopted 18 December 1979, entered into force 3 September 1981) 1249 UNTS 13.

Convention on the Rights of Persons with Disabilities (adopted 13 December 2007, entered into force 3 May 2008) 2515 UNTS 3.

Convention on the Rights of the Child (adopted 20 November 1989, entered into force 2 September 1990) 1577 UNTS 3.

European Convention of Human Rights (adopted 4 November 1950, entered into force 3 September 1953) ETS 5.

European Social Charter (adopted 3 May 1996, entered into force 1 July 1999) ETS 163.

Inter-American Convention on the Prevention, Punishment and Eradication of Violence against Women ('Convention of Belém Do Pará') (adopted 9 June 1994, entered into force 3 February 1995) available at www.oas.org/juridico/english/treaties/a-61.html.

International Convention on the Elimination of All Forms of Racial Discrimination (adopted 21 December 1965, entered into force 4 January 1969) 660 UNTS 195.

International Convention on the Protection of the Rights of All Migrant Workers and Members of their Families (adopted 18 December 1990, entered into force 1 July 2003) 2220 UNTS 3.

International Covenant on Civil and Political Rights (adopted 16 December 1966, entered into force 23 March 1976) 999 UNTS 171.

International Covenant on Economic, Social and Cultural Rights (adopted 16 December 1966, entered into force 3 January 1976) 993 UNTS 3.

Optional Protocol to the Convention on the Elimination of All Forms of Discrimination against Women (adopted 6 October 1999, entered into force 22 December 2000) 2131 UNTS 83.

(Third) Optional Protocol to the Convention on the Rights of the Child on a Communications Procedure (adopted 19 December 2011, entered into force 14 April 2014) 2983 UNTS 157.

Optional Protocol to the Convention on the Rights of Persons with Disabilities (adopted 13 December 2006, entered into force 3 May 2008) 2518 UNTS 283.

(First) Optional Protocol to the International Covenant on Civil and Political Rights (adopted 16 December 1966, entered into force 23 March 1976) 999 UNTS 171.

Optional Protocol to the International Covenant on Economic, Social and Cultural Rights (adopted 10 December 2008, entered into force 5 May 2013) 2922 UNTS 29.

Vienna Convention on the Law of Treaties (adopted 23 May 1969, entered into force 27 January 1980) 1155 UNTS 331.

Introduction

BACKGROUND

IN ITS PREAMBLE, the Universal Declaration of Human Rights (UDHR) envisions 'a world in which human beings shall enjoy freedom of speech and belief and freedom from fear and want'.[1] This formulation was inspired by then US President Roosevelt's conception of the 'four essential human freedoms' which he famously presented in a speech before the US Congress in 1941. Roosevelt spoke of freedom of speech and expression, freedom of religion, freedom from want (meaning conditions where States secure a 'healthy peacetime life' to every person), and freedom from fear of war.[2]

Like Roosevelt, the UDHR acknowledges that a range of conditions must exist to provide real freedom to any individual. Accordingly, the substantive provisions of the UDHR continue to set out a range of inalienable rights including the rights to life, liberty, freedom of thought, conscience, and religion, as well as the rights to social security, education, and a standard of living adequate for health and wellbeing. All of these rights are presented on an equal footing. No difference is made between the categories of socio-economic[3] and civil and political rights; a divide which would later play a significant role. The text protects both categories indiscriminately.[4]

When it came to translating the UDHR into binding human rights commitments, however, fault lines started to develop along the boundaries of these categories. The differentiation between socio-economic and civil and political rights suddenly gained legal relevance as discussions arose about alleged differences between the two categories. It was frequently argued that different methods of implementation were required for each category. Socio-economic rights were thought of as requiring substantial State action and resources and were thus considered programmatic rights, their realisation being a matter of policy rather than adjudication. Civil and political rights, on the other hand, were considered to be immediately applicable negative rights demanding judicial remedies in cases of violations.[5] Cold war ideologies certainly also played a

[1] UNGA Res 217 A (III) 'Universal Declaration of Human Rights' (1 January 1948) A/RES/217(III).

[2] See WA Schabas, 'Introduction Essay: The Drafting and Significance of the Universal Declaration of Human Rights' in WA Schabas (ed), *The Universal Declaration of Human Rights: The Travaux Préparatoires* (Cambridge, Cambridge University Press, 2013) lxxi–cxxv, Ixxii-Ixxv.

[3] The term socio-economic rights here is intended to also include cultural rights.

[4] See S Fredman, *Comparative Human Rights Law* (Oxford, Oxford University Press, 2018) 59.

[5] See JA King, *Judging Social Rights* (Cambridge, Cambridge University Press, 2012) 1.

role in this context.[6] A statement by Maurice Cranston concerning the inclusion of so-called social rights in the UDHR illustrates this point: 'What the modern communists have done is to appropriate the word "rights" for the principles that they believe in.'[7]

Although States generally agreed that socio-economic rights are human rights, the perception that this category was somehow different or even inferior had a pivotal influence on the development of binding instruments in the UN human rights system. In 1966, the categories of civil and political and socio-economic rights were formally separated by the adoption of two distinct instruments:[8] the International Covenant on Civil and Political Rights (ICCPR) and the International Covenant on Economic, Social and Cultural Rights (ICESCR).[9] Specific features in the design of the treaties reflect the idea that there are differences between the two categories of rights, particularly regarding the nature of States parties' obligations.

The ICESCR sets out that States parties must take steps to the maximum of available resources with a view to progressively realising the rights within this treaty.[10] No such provision is contained in the ICCPR. This difference in the treaties has ever since been used as a basis to claim that there is a legal difference between immediately realisable civil and political rights and progressively realisable socio-economic rights. The treaty regimes furthermore originally set out different methods of implementation on the UN level, based on the idea that socio-economic rights are not suitable for adjudication. The Human Rights Committee (HRC) was established and authorised to receive to receive interstate and individual complaints in the year of the ICCPR's adoption.[11] The ICESCR regime, on the other hand, did originally not establish an associated Committee and only set out a reporting procedure.

Many aspects of this traditional differentiation between the categories have since been contested. On the institutional level, the 'historical asymmetry' between the two categories has been corrected:[12] the ICESCR regime received its own treaty body in 1985, the Committee on Economic, Social and Cultural

[6] Although this role might not be as one-dimensional as sometimes claimed, see DJ Whelan and J Donnelley, 'The West, Economic and Social Rights, and the Global Human Rights Regime: Setting the Record Straight' (2007) 29 *Human Rights Quarterly* 908.

[7] MW Cranston, *Human Rights To-day* (London, Ampersand, 1962) 38–39.

[8] See C de Albuquerque, 'Chronicle of an Announced Birth: The Coming into Life of the Optional Protocol to the International Covenant on Economic, Social and Cultural Rights – the Missing Piece of the International Bill of Human Rights' (2010) 32 *Human Rights Quarterly* 144, 147.

[9] International Covenant on Civil and Political Rights (adopted 16 December 1966, entered into force 23 March 1976) 999 UNTS 171; International Covenant on Economic, Social and Cultural Rights (adopted 16 December 1966, entered into force 3 January 1976) 993 UNTS 3.

[10] Article 2 (1) of the ICESCR; the same standard of progressive realisation of socio-economic rights was later introduced into other treaties in the UN system, see further 1.2.2.

[11] Optional Protocol to the International Covenant on Civil and Political Rights (adopted 16 December 1966, entered into force 23 March 1976) 999 UNTS 171.

[12] L Chenwi, 'Correcting the Historical Asymmetry Between Rights: The Optional Protocol to the International Covenant on Economic, Social and Cultural Rights' (2009) 9 *African Human Rights Law Journal* 23.

Rights (CESCR).[13] In 2013, the CESCR was finally endowed with the power to receive Individual Communications and interstate complaints by the Optional Protocol to the ICESCR (ICESCR-OP).[14] On the occasion of the ICESCR-OP's adoption, then United Nations High Commissioner for Human Rights (UNHCHR), Louise Arbour, expressed her hopes that this instrument would enable the UN system to overcome cold war ideological ballast and promote the ideal of 'human rights made whole' by finally placing the two categories of rights on an equal footing.[15]

On the theoretical level, too, the majority of scholars and practitioners soon started to embrace the view that the divide between socio-economic and civil and political rights is largely artificial. Not only has it been stressed repeatedly that socio-economic and civil and political rights are indivisible and interdependent,[16] it is also increasingly accepted that the categories might not be so different after all. This modern understanding of human rights recognises that all rights require State action as well as omission and, therefore, all rights require resources. What somehow stubbornly remains to this day, however, is the notion that the categories create obligations for States parties which are different as to their pace of realisation. The UN human rights Committees, as well as literary commentators, continuously insist that civil and political rights require immediate realisation while socio-economic rights are 'only' progressively realisable.

This last remaining aspect of the historic divide, the differentiation between immediately and progressively realisable rights, will be the main focus of this book. The central question asked here is the following: Are there any valid reasons why the long process of convergence between the two categories must end at this last dichotomy? This book will show that neither theoretical nor normative reasons require differentiating between immediate and progressive realisation and that, in practice, both standards converge. This means that the process of convergence of socio-economic and civil and political rights should and does extend to the dichotomy of immediate and progressive realisation.

COURSE OF THE ARGUMENT, METHODOLOGY, AND SELECTION OF MATERIALS

The argument is divided into three parts. Part I (chapters 1 and 2) will engage with human rights history and theory, illustrating that giving up the

[13] ECOSOC Res 1985/17, 'Review of the Composition, Organization and Administrative Arrangements of the Sessional Working Group of Governmental Experts on the Implementation of the International Covenant on Economic, Social and Cultural Rights' (28 May 1985) E/RES/1985/17.

[14] Optional Protocol to the International Covenant on Economic, Social and Cultural Rights (adopted 24 September 2009, entered into force 5 May 2013) 2922 UNTS 29.

[15] L Arbour, 'Human Rights Made Whole' (Project Syndicate, 26 June 2008), www.project-syndicate.org/commentary/human-rights-made-whole.

[16] See, for example, UNGA, 'Vienna Declaration and Programme of Action' (12 July 1993) A/CONF.157/23.

immediate/progressive realisation divide is a logical consequence of abandoning the positive/negative rights divide. This part will also explore the concept of progressive realisation of socio-economic rights in order to provide a point of comparison for the analysis of UN human rights Committee jurisprudence in part II (chapters 3–6). Part II will show that the standard of realisation applied to civil and political rights by the UN human rights treaty bodies converges with progressive realisation. Part III (chapters 7–9) then argues that this convergence is in accordance with the UN human rights treaties by conducting an interpretation according to the rules of the Vienna Convention on the Law of Treaties (VCLT). In a last step, the book will provide a conclusion as well as some practical recommendations for the Committees and an outlook.

In general, this book will employ a doctrinal or black letter methodological approach, focusing on classical legal sources such as the text of relevant international treaties, the preparatory work of those treaties, pertinent international law literature, and the pronouncements of the UN human rights treaty bodies.[17]

Part I will first explore the rise and fall of different dichotomies between socio-economic and civil and political rights as well as the relationship between these alleged traits. This will reveal that the differentiation between progressive and immediate realisation was originally based on the idea that socio-economic rights create only positive obligations while civil and political rights create only negative obligations. With the latter dichotomy long since abandoned, logic dictates also abandoning the dichotomy between immediate and progressive realisation which depends upon it. From this first conclusion follows a hypothesis of convergence regarding the standards of realisation: if all rights create negative and positive obligations, it is plausible that all rights are interpreted to entail both immediate and progressive obligations. Thus, it is suspected that the standards for socio-economic and civil and political rights converge in the practice of the Committees.

Part I will continue by laying out the concept of progressive realisation as it has been developed in the context of socio-economic rights. Progressive realisation, as understood by scholars and practitioners today, does not allow States parties to drag their feet but requires immediate action to the fullest of a State party's capabilities. Progressiveness – in the strict sense of the word – only applies to those obligations which are simply impossible to realise at once. Accordingly, progressive realisation – in an umbrella sense – encompasses both immediate and progressive obligations, giving it the necessary flexibility to cover both negative and positive obligations. Clearly, this dual nature of the concept is often overlooked when progressive realisation is contrasted with the alleged immediacy of civil and political rights.

[17] *cf* S Kilcommins, 'Doctrinal Legal Method (Black Letterism): Assumptions, Commitments and Shortcomings' in L Cahillane and J Schweppe (eds), *Legal Research Methods: Principles and Practicalities* (Dublin, Clarus Press, 2016).

In order to confirm the other side of the hypothesis of convergent standards of realisation, it is necessary to explore whether the – allegedly immediate – realisation of civil and political rights functions in a similar way. Therefore, part II of this book explores whether civil and political rights are also interpreted to create not only immediate but also progressive obligations. The appropriate material to inspect here is the work of the UN human rights treaty bodies (the Committees) because these bodies were established by the States parties as the primary interpreters of the treaties. While the legal effects of their pronouncements are debated in detail,[18] those documents are envisioned as a common point of reference for all States parties to the UN human rights treaties.

The Committees produce a number of different documents. The most interpretational value can be gained from the Committees' General Comments and General Recommendations. These are documents concerned with a range of issues regarding the somewhat authoritative interpretation of certain provisions and the clarification of States parties' obligations.[19] The evaluation of General Comments and Recommendations will be exhaustive. An analysis has been conducted of all General Comments and Recommendations adopted until June 2024.[20]

Most Committees are also mandated to receive Individual Communications on alleged human rights violations.[21] Decisions in Individual Communications cases will be utilised to illustrate the results found in the analysis of General Comments and Recommendations. The cases have been selected after certain relevant rights or doctrinal concepts have been identified in the analysis of the General Comments and Recommendations.[22] As such, many of the HRC's Individual Communications decisions regarding the right to life under Article 6 of the ICCPR have been analysed because the HRC has interpreted this right to entail extensive positive obligations. The analysis of the General Comments of the Committee on the Rights of Persons with Disabilities shows that there are certain doctrinal concepts which are related to progressive realisation, namely accessibility and reasonable accommodation. This is why an extensive analysis has been conducted of those Individual Communications which reference these concepts. Individual Communications also play an important role when determining the self-ascribed role of the Committees, eg, concerning the margin of appreciation doctrine and the standard of review. Accordingly, ample reference will be made to the views adopted in Individual Communications which (implicitly) refer to these concepts.

[18] See further 8.4.2.

[19] See D McGrogan, 'On the Interpretation of Human Rights Treaties and Subsequent Practice' (2014) 32 *Netherlands Quarterly of Human Rights* 347, 365.

[20] While all General Comments and Recommendations have been analysed by the author, not all of them have been deemed to contain statements relevant for this book, which is why some of them are not referenced in part II.

[21] See further 1.2.2.

[22] The Committees' jurisprudence data bank allows for a search for keywords or certain provisions which is how the relevant case law has been found.

Because General Comments are the most suitable source of information for this analysis, those treaty bodies that have produced a sufficient number of these documents have been chosen for the analysis: the HRC, the CESCR, the Committee on the Elimination of Racial Discrimination (CERD), the Committee on the Elimination of Discrimination against Women (CEDAW-Com), the Committee on the Rights of the Child (CRC-Com), and the Committee on the Rights of Persons with Disabilities (CRPD-Com).[23] Another reason for selecting these Committees was that they all make explicit statements regarding the differentiation between immediate civil and political and progressive socio-economic rights.

The immediate dimension of civil and political rights is not disputed, which is why part II will focus on potentially progressive elements read into the positive dimension of civil and political rights. As suspected, the Committees implicitly accept that positive obligations pursuant to civil and political rights must be subject to available resources and that States parties will, in some cases, require time to fulfil them. Consequently, the standard of realisation applied to civil and political rights is constructed in a way which combines immediate and progressive aspects. This result confirms the hypothesis of convergence; immediate and progressive realisation have converged into a single de facto uniform standard of realisation.

These findings lead to the third and last issue of this book which is addressed in part III, namely the question whether the convergence of immediate and progressive realisation is permitted by the treaties. While parts I and II illustrate that a uniform treatment of all rights makes sense from a theoretical perspective and takes place in practice, it is commonly claimed that the treaties legally require a differential treatment of socio-economic and civil and political rights. Arguments for the adherence to the immediate/progressive rights divide usually refer to the treaties which are read to set out such a differentiation. Accordingly, it is necessary to conduct an interpretation of the treaties in light of the rules of treaty interpretation under international law in order to determine whether a uniform application of a standard analogous to progressive realisation to all rights is in line with the requirements set out in this context.

The relevant rules are laid down in the Vienna Convention on the Law of Treaties (VCLT). Even though the details of the correct approach to human rights treaty interpretation are debated,[24] the VCLT is an appropriate point of departure. This is so because it is commonly accepted that the VCLT reflects the customary law on treaty interpretation.[25] On the basis of the rules of

[23] At the time of writing, the HRC has drafted 37 General Comments, the CESCR 26, the CERD 36 (currently working on No 37), the CEDAW-Com 39, the CRC-Com 26, and the CRPD-Com 8; see www.ohchr.org/en/treaty-bodies/general-comments.

[24] See further 7.2.

[25] See, eg, ICJ, *LaGrand (Germany v USA)* (Merits, Judgment) [2001] ICJ Rep 2001, 466 para 99; see also A Orakhelashvili, *The Interpretation of Acts and Rules in Public International Law* (Oxford, Oxford University Press, 2008) 313.

interpretation laid down in Articles 31 and 32 of the VCLT, a detailed engagement not only with the text of the treaties but also with State practice and the preparatory materials will be conducted. After the last chapter, the book ends with a conclusion, including recommendations for the Committees and an outlook.

GAPS IN THE EXISTING LITERATURE

This book intends to fill two major gaps in literature. The first gap concerns human rights theory. While extensive literature exists regarding the argument that socio-economic rights are not inherently different from civil and political rights, the differentiation between progressive and immediate realisation in international human rights law did not and still does not receive much attention. To the author's knowledge, no other account exists which exclusively deals with this issue. Most relevant contributions discuss the nature of human rights obligations in general and only briefly touch upon immediate and progressive realisation. The present book takes up these fragments and sets them in the context of a rigorous interpretation of the treaty text.

The second gap concerns the engagement with human rights practice, particularly the work of the UN human rights Committees. There is no detailed analysis of the UN Committees' practice regarding the question whether their concepts of immediate and progressive realisation are different. Literary commentators have mostly viewed progressive realisation in isolation; there are no detailed accounts which explore whether there is a consistent differentiation between immediate and progressive categories of rights. This book is also unique because it adopts a cross-cutting approach by analysing the jurisprudence of several Committees instead of focusing on one treaty body. The following paragraphs will present the landscape of adjacent literary accounts and further specify the two gaps they leave for the present book.

After the Covenants had been adopted, a small number of contemporaneous publications discussed whether the ICCPR and ICESCR demand different standards of realisation. Most authors answered this question in the affirmative.[26] On the other side, Farrokh Jhabvala argued for a uniform standard of realisation, practically alone for a long time.[27] The contributions on both sides of the discussion addressed only a very limited number of sources of treaty interpretation. At the centre of discussion stood the

[26] See, eg, E Schwelb, 'The Nature of the Obligations of the States Parties to the International Covenant on Civil and Political Rights' in R Cassin (ed), *Amicorum Discipulorumque Liber: Problèmes de Protection Internationale des Droits de l'Homme* (Paris, Pédone, 1969) 301; JP Humphrey, 'Letter to the Editor' (1984) 6 *Human Rights Quarterly* 539.

[27] See, eg, F Jhabvala, 'Domestic Implementation of the Covenant on Civil and Political Rights' (1985) 32 *Netherlands International Law Review* 461.

wording of Article 2 of the ICCPR in comparison to Article 2 of the ICESCR and thus the popular *argumentum e contrario*. There was no engagement with treaties other than the ICCPR and ICESCR, as many of them were adopted only later on.

Over the years, the discussion occasionally resurfaced as a marginal problem in contributions concerned with the nature of human rights obligations more generally. Scholars did not add many new aspects to it but instead revisited arguments about the wording of Articles 2 and 40 of the ICCPR, the comparison to Article 2 of the ICESCR, as well as some limited aspects of the drafting history.[28] Most of these contributions do recognise that there is a requirement for some sort of flexibility in the realisation of civil and political rights but still insist that these rights are 'immediate' in contrast to progressively realisable socio-economic rights.[29] While scholars thereby indirectly accept some sort of progressive element for civil and political rights, they do not draw the connection to progressive realisation and thus fail to mark the convergence of both standards. For example, in the most recent edition of a leading commentary, William Schabas acknowledges that the full scope of civil and political rights cannot be realised immediately, but still adheres to the differentiation between immediate and progressive realisation.[30]

Only a handful of authors reject the traditional differentiation. However, their remarks on this topic are cursory and refer only to selected aspects of treaty interpretation or remain entirely vague regarding the normative background of their claims. As mentioned above, one of these authors is Farrokh Jhabvala who published a number of relevant articles during the 1980s, focusing on selected textual and contextual aspects as well as parts of the drafting history. More recently, Eva Brems explicitly argued for extending progressive realisation to civil and political rights. Analogous to the argument made in this book, Brems considers the immediate/progressive rights divide to depend upon the positive/negative rights divide and argues that the recognition of progressiveness can improve the acceptance of positive obligations.[31] However, beyond these points, Brems does not provide more factual or normative support for the thesis that progressive realisation should be a uniform standard of obligations.

[28] See, eg, C Tomuschat, 'National Implementation of International Standards on Human Rights' (1984–1985) 31 *Canadian Human Rights Yearbook* 31 and A Seibert-Fohr, 'Domestic Implementation of the International Covenant on Civil and Political Rights Pursuant to its Article 2 Para. 2' in JA Frowein, R Wolfrum and CE Philipp (eds), *Max Planck Yearbook of United Nations Law Volume 5* (The Hague, Kluwer Law International, 2001) 406–07.

[29] See, eg, MM Sepúlveda, *The Nature of the Obligations Under the International Covenant on Economic, Social and Cultural Rights* (Antwerp, Intersentia, 2003) 130–31.

[30] WA Schabas, *U.N. International Covenant on Civil and Political Rights: Nowak's CCPR Commentary*, 3rd edn (Kehl, NP Engel, 2019) 893.

[31] E Brems, 'Human Rights: Minimum and Maximum Perspectives' (2009) 9 *Human Rights Law Review* 349, 365–69.

Other authors present similar arguments but stay even more vague when supporting it. Katherine Young acknowledges that the divide between immediately and progressively realisable rights is dubious at best.[32] Rolf Künnemann similarly explains that Article 2 of the ICCPR and Article 2 of the ICESCR emphasise two different parts of a uniform spectrum of human rights obligations, arguing that full realisation in a substantive sense must be progressive for all rights.[33] In the context of the Convention on the Rights of Persons with Disabilities (CRPD), Gauthier de Beco argues for applying progressive realisation to all rights by stressing that the categories cannot be clearly distinguished. Additionally, he considers that all rights require positive action which he also connects to progressive realisation.[34] Frédéric Mégret makes a related argument and briefly inspects the wording of the Convention.[35] Regarding the International Convention on the Elimination of All Forms of Racial Discrimination (ICERD), Joshua Castellino argues that progressive realisation is 'more realistic' than immediate realisation with regard to the obligations flowing from this treaty.[36] None of these authors, however, apply the whole canon of treaty interpretation under the VCLT. More importantly, none of them offers a book-length study, establishing the detailed evidence such a suggestion demands.

Most other contributions on the nature of international human rights obligations do not discuss in detail how progressive and immediate realisation are different. This includes relevant commentaries on the UN human rights treaties, which mostly reiterate the traditional divide without further discussion. John Tobin, in his commentary on the Convention on the Rights of the Child (CRC), acknowledges that resource considerations play a role for all rights without addressing the consequences this has for immediacy and progressiveness.[37] In another CRC commentary, Mervat Rishmawi acknowledges that the rights in the Convention are not easily categorised but still insists that only socio-economic rights are subject to progressive realisation.[38] Two commentaries on the CRPD argue that civil and political rights are immediate because progressive

[32] KG Young, 'Waiting for Rights: Progressive Realization and Lost Time' in KG Young (ed), *The Future of Economic and Social Rights* (Cambridge, Cambridge University Press, 2019) 673–75.

[33] R Künnemann, 'A Coherent Approach to Human Rights' (1995) 17 *Human Rights Quarterly* 323, 330.

[34] G de Beco, 'The Indivisibility of Human Rights and the Convention on the Rights of Persons with Disabilities' (2019) 68 *International and Comparative Law Quarterly* 141.

[35] F Mégret, 'The Disabilities Convention: Towards a Holistic Concept of Rights' (2008) 12 *The International Journal of Human Rights* 261, 271–72.

[36] J Castellino, 'How Effective has CERD been in Protecting Minorities?' in D Keane and A Waughray (eds), *Fifty Years of the International Convention on the Elimination of All Forms of Racial Discrimination: A Living Instrument* (Manchester, Manchester University Press, 2017) 233.

[37] J Tobin, 'Article 4: A State's General Obligation of Implementation' in J Tobin (ed), *The UN Convention on the Rights of the Child: A Commentary* (Oxford, Oxford University Press, 2019) 130–31.

[38] M Rishmawi, *Article 4: The Nature of States Parties' Obligations*, A Commentary on the United Nations Convention on the Rights of the Child Series 4 (Leiden, Nijhoff, 2005) 17–18.

realisation is set out only for socio-economic rights.[39] Both commentaries do not discuss further how this can work in light of mixed rights and the ubiquity of positive obligations. Two commentaries on the non-discrimination treaties do not utilise the terms of immediate and progressive realisation at all. Instead, they simply reiterate that States parties need to immediately adopt a policy of non-discrimination, without discussing what this means for the timeframe establishing full equality.[40]

An even larger gap in scholarship exists with regard to the analysis of UN Committee practice. While many contributions engage with progressive realisation in isolation, there is a noticeable lack of studies exploring how this standard is different from the 'immediate' realisation of civil and political rights. Accordingly, this book's analysis fills a gap by exploring what 'immediacy' means in the context of positive civil and political rights obligations. There appears to exist only one contribution which explicitly recognises that the HRC treats civil and political rights as progressively realisable, and it neither presents concrete evidence from Committee practice nor considers other UN treaty bodies.[41]

[39] V Della Fina, 'Article 4: General Obligations' in V Della Fina, R Cera and G Palmisano (eds), *The United Nations Convention on the Rights of Persons with Disabilities: A Commentary* (Cham, Springer, 2017) 147 and A Broderick, 'Article 4: General Obligations' in I Bantekas, MA Stein, and D Anastasiou (eds), *The UN Convention on the Rights of Persons with Disabilities: A Commentary* (Oxford, Oxford University Press, 2018) 131.

[40] AC Byrnes, 'Article 2' in MA Freeman, CM Chinkin and B Rudolf (eds), *The UN Convention on the Elimination of All Forms of Discrimination against Women: A Commentary*, 1st edn (Oxford, Oxford University Press, 2012) 76–77 and N Lerner, *The UN Convention on the Elimination of All Forms of Racial Discrimination*, Nijhoff Classics in International Law 3 (Leiden, Nijhoff, 2015) 41.

[41] See D McGoldrick, *The Human Rights Committee: Its Role in the Development of the International Covenant on Civil and Political Rights* (Oxford, Clarendon Press, 1991) 346, 347.

Part I

History and Theory

1

The Rise and Fall of the Historic Divide between Socio-economic and Civil and Political Rights

1.1. INTRODUCTION

PART I OF this book will provide the necessary historical and theoretical background for the analysis and treaty interpretation carried out in parts II and III. This chapter will start out by tracing the historical development of arguments about conceptual differences between socio-economic and civil and political rights, illustrating a turn from divergence towards convergence. During the earlier decades of the twentieth century, there was a widespread belief that socio-economic rights are different from civil and political rights because they require positive State action and resources, exhibit vagueness and polycentricity, and, overall, are not amenable to judicial review. While this notion of conceptual dichotomies had numerous supporters in earlier times, the tides turned towards the end of the last century and, now, the majority of commentators reject the idea of a conceptual differentiation.

The whole discussion has rightfully been described as a 'quiet echo from the past'.[1] As early as 1989, Craig Scott held that the rejection of generalised dichotomies is 'almost trite'.[2] More recently, Ida Elisabeth Koch noted that arguments against traditional dichotomies are mainly concerned with points raised during the 1970s.[3] And yet, it is useful for this present inquiry to recount the most important elements of this discussion. Particularly, because inspecting the argument illustrates that one aspect of the divide stubbornly remains in the heads of practitioners and literary commentators: the idea that civil and political rights are immediately realisable while socio-economic rights are progressively

[1] M Scheinin, 'Justiciability and the Indivisibility of Rights' in J Squires, M Langford and B Thiele (eds), *The Road to a Remedy: Current Issues in the Litigation of Economic, Social and Cultural Rights* (Sydney, Australian Human Rights Centre, 2005) 17.

[2] C Scott, 'The Interdependence and Permeability of Human Rights Norms: Towards a Partial Fusion of the International Covenants on Human Rights' (1989) 27 *Osgoode Hall Law Journal* 769, 834.

[3] IE Koch, 'Dichotomies, Trichotomies or Waves of Duties?' (2005) 5 *Human Rights Law Review* 81, 101–02 with reference to Sepúlveda, *The Nature of the Obligations*.

realisable. This chapter will argue that this last dichotomy is dubious because the idea of two different standards of realisation was based on other dichotomies which have since been abandoned. This logic gives rise to the hypothesis that, in practice, immediate and progressive realisation might converge because the basis for this differentiation has fallen away.

The second section of the present chapter will trace the origins of the idea that socio-economic and civil and political rights are somehow different from each other (1.2). The third section will then continue to show how most of these alleged dichotomies between the categories have been called into question over the last decades, illustrating a process of convergence (1.3). Lastly, this chapter will address the last remaining dichotomy between immediately and progressively realisable rights, arguing that it is highly dubious from a theoretical perspective (1.4), before ending with a conclusion (1.5).

1.2. THE HISTORIC DIVIDE BETWEEN SOCIO-ECONOMIC AND CIVIL AND POLITICAL RIGHTS

While the UDHR does not differentiate between the categories of socio-economic and civil and political rights, the process of drafting the ICESCR and ICCPR sparked a discussion about the different nature of these two categories and the implications these alleged differences would have for the creation of legally binding State obligations. The decision to separate the categories into two independent instruments was mainly due to 'implementation-based reasons'.[4] Socio-economic rights were thought to entail challenges regarding their implementation in general and adjudication in particular which were thought not to exist in the civil and political rights context. Underlying this argument was the assumption that socio-economic rights display a number of features which delimit them from civil and political rights (and make them non-justiciable), namely that these rights require State action and resources and that their associated duties are difficult to define.

The drafters of the ICCPR and the ICESCR included in these treaties specific features aimed at accommodating these differences between the categories. Most importantly, the general obligation provision of the ICESCR acknowledges that the realisation of these rights can only be undertaken within the limit of available resources and, therefore, necessarily takes place progressively.[5] This textual differentiation carried over into other instruments in the UN human rights treaty system. The codification of progressive realisation for socio-economic rights cemented the idea that there is a fundamental legal difference between the categories and therefore constituted both a culmination of the historic divide and a reference point for later arguments in this context.

[4] Scott, 'Interdependence and Permeability', 794.

[5] See Article 2 (1) of the ICESCR.

In a first step, this section will explore the background of the decision to bifurcate the UDHR into two Covenants in order to illustrate the conception of the division between the categories at that time (1.2.1). It will then continue to map out the way in which the alleged dichotomies found their way into the treaty texts of not only the ICCPR and ICESCR, but also later UN human rights instruments (1.2.2). In a third and last step, this section will summarise the alleged dichotomies between socio-economic and civil and political rights, their role in international human rights theory, and their interrelationship (1.2.3).

1.2.1. The Bifurcation Decision

While the decision to formally separate rights into two Covenants may not have been the origin of the conceptual divide between the two categories, it certainly plays a central role in the debate as a point of reference for many arguments in the following decades. It is therefore appropriate to briefly explore the sequence of events and the reasoning behind the bifurcation decision. Because there have been other extensive analyses in this regard, this subsection will be limited to an overview of the matter.[6]

On 16 February 1946, the Commission on Human Rights (UNCHR) was established by the UN Economic and Social Council (ECOSOC) in pursuance of Article 68 of the UN Charter and tasked with submitting proposals, recommendations and reports to the Council regarding an international bill of rights, as well as '[i]nternational declarations or conventions on civil liberties, the status of women, freedom of information and similar matters'.[7] Upon request of the chairman of the newly established Commission, ECOSOC approved the appointment of a drafting committee which would undertake to prepare a preliminary draft of the international bill of rights.[8] In its first session, the drafting committee discussed whether the international bill of rights should take the form of a declaration or an international convention and ultimately decided to prepare both documents.[9] This notion was adopted by the Commission; it was decided that the international bill of rights should be comprised of a declaration as well as a convention or covenant and measures of implementation.[10]

[6] See, eg, UNGA, 'Draft International Covenants on Human Rights: Annotation Prepared by the Secretary-General' (1 July 1955) A/2929, ch I; F Jhabvala, 'On Human Rights and the Socio-Economic Context' (1984) 31 *Netherlands International Law Review* 149; Scott, 'Interdependence and Permeability'.

[7] ECOSOC Res 5 (I) 'Commission on Human Rights with a Sub-Commission on the Status of Women' (16 February 1946) E/RES/5(I).

[8] See UNGA, 'Draft International Covenants on Human Rights', ch I para 3.

[9] UNCHR, 'Drafting Committee on an International Bill of Rights, 1st Session: Report of the Drafting Committee to the Commission on Human Rights' (1 July 1947) E/CN.4/21, ch I para 12.

[10] See UNGA, 'Draft International Covenants on Human Rights', ch I para 5.

While the draft declaration was quickly revised, completed and adopted as the UDHR by the General Assembly (UNGA) in 1948, the drafting of the covenant would take more time. Notably, at this point in time, the Commission had only prepared draft provisions on civil and political rights, even though the UDHR contained a range of rights from both categories.[11] During its fifth session, the Commission revised the draft articles it had already prepared and then turned towards the question of implementation of these civil and political rights. It was debated whether or not an international court, ad hoc committees, or other permanent organs should be established in order to supervise the observance of these rights.[12] While some parties argued that this would undermine the sovereignty and independence of States, a majority of the Commission agreed that there should be some form of implementation procedure, as became clear during the sixth session.[13] The decision was made to establish the HRC as a permanent body which would be competent to receive interstate complaints concerning violations of the civil and political rights already established.[14]

Also at the sixth session, the Commission discussed proposals of socio-economic rights provisions and the question whether these rights should be incorporated into the present draft covenant. Some representatives supported this idea, arguing that socio-economic rights are 'a prerequisite for the enjoyment of the other rights already included in ... the draft covenant' and that 'the Commission should not give the impression that it had overlooked them'.[15] The majority of representatives argued, however, that the sixth session of the Commission did not provide enough time to discuss these rights.[16] Consequently, the Commission decided that it would prepare an additional Covenant which would deal with 'economic, social, cultural, political and other categories of human rights' and which would provide additional measures of implementation, requesting ECOSOC to confirm this decision.[17] The foundation for the bifurcation was thereby laid. ECOSOC approved of the approach to create a separate Covenant and requested a decision by the UNGA regarding '[t]he desirability of including articles on economic, social and cultural rights' into the first Covenant.[18] It is at this point that arguments emerged regarding differences between the categories concerning their method of implementation, as several representatives expressed concern that the inclusion of socio-economic rights would complicate implementation procedures for the treaty as a whole.[19]

[11] See also Jhabvala, 'Socio-Economic Context', 153.

[12] UNCHR, 'Report of the 5th Session' (23 June 1949) E/CN.4/350, ch V paras 16–18.

[13] UNCHR, 'Summary Record of the 178th Meeting' (12 May 1950) E/CN.4/SR.178, para 45.

[14] UNCHR, 'Report of the 6th Session' (30 June 1950) E/CN.4/507, ch IV para 36.

[15] ibid, ch IV para 30.

[16] ibid.

[17] ibid, ch IV para 31.

[18] ECOSOC Res 303 (XI) 'Report of the Commission on Human Rights (Sixth Session)' (9 August 1950) E/Res/303(XI).

[19] ECOSOC, 'Summary Record of the 378th Meeting' (4 July 1950) E/SR.378, paras 5–12.

However, this first attempt to bifurcate the drafting procedure remained fruitless. The UNGA adopted a resolution which commanded the creation of a single binding instrument including all rights by deciding 'to include in the Covenant on Human Rights economic, social and cultural rights'.[20] The UNGA did so recalling the basic importance of all rights to the free person in the sense of the declaration and declaring that 'the enjoyment of civic and political freedoms and of economic, social and cultural rights are interconnected and interdependent'.[21]

Thus, during its seventh session, the Commission continued to draft articles on socio-economic rights in the framework of a single international treaty. In substance, however, the trench between the two categories continued to deepen as the Commission developed a separate method of implementation for socio-economic rights, namely the reporting procedure. No decision was reached regarding the question which implementation procedure would apply to which category of rights.[22] However, the issue of implementation led to some representatives clearly disagreeing with the UNGA's decision to create a single instrument. While it was generally recognised that all rights were equally important, the concern was voiced that socio-economic rights were not justiciable and therefore required a different method of implementation. In light of these differences in implementation, a proposal was introduced to call on the UNGA to reconsider non-bifurcation. This proposal was, however, not adopted.[23] Furthermore, an umbrella clause specific to socio-economic rights was introduced which is very similar to the current form of Article 2 (1) of the ICESCR.[24]

Clearly, the ambiguities concerning implementation constituted a leverage point to reopen the discussion about separate instruments in ECOSOC.[25] The question whether a separate treaty should be established was discussed at its thirteenth session in 1951. On this level, too, a proposal was introduced to reconsider its decision for a uniform treaty.[26] The general opinion was that the draft Covenant was an 'imperfect document' due to disagreements about the inclusion of socio-economic rights and questions of implementation.[27] While some members rejected a bifurcation because it 'would be a step backwards and that these categories were equally fundamental', others insisted that there is a fundamental difference between the two categories of rights which demands different methods of implementation. This difference was argued to lie in the amount of State action required to fulfil the respective categories: some drafters declared

[20] UNGA Res 421 (V) 'Draft International Covenants on Human Rights and Measures of Implementation: Future Work for the Commission on Human Rights' (4 December 1950) A/RES/421(V).
[21] ibid.
[22] UNCHR, 'Report of the 7th Session' (24 May 1951) E/CN.4/640, ch III para 22.
[23] ibid, ch III para 67.
[24] ibid, ch III para 54.
[25] See also Jhabvala, 'Socio-Economic Context', 155.
[26] ECOSOC, 'Report of the Economic and Social Council Covering the Period from 16 August 1950 to 21 September 1951' (1951) A/1884, para 771.
[27] ibid, para 773.

that 'civic and political rights could be implemented by the adoption of legislative measures' while socio-economic rights would only be realised 'through the creation of conditions conducive to their progressive achievement'.[28] Furthermore, difficulties regarding the question which method of implementation to apply to which category were used as an argument to support a division.[29] Finally, a resolution was adopted requesting the UNGA to reconsider its decision in light of the circumstance that both categories are set up with different methods of implementation and '*conscious* of the difficulties which may flow from embodying in one covenant two different kinds of rights and obligations'.[30]

After support from the General Assembly's Third Committee,[31] the plenum, this second time around, agreed on two separate Covenants. The consequent bifurcation resolution requested the Commission to draft two Covenants while declaring that unity shall be emphasised by including 'as many similar provisions as possible' and by opening both treaties for signature at the same time.[32] A general survey of UNGA debates in this context conducted by Craig Scott illustrates that, besides pragmatic and ideological reasons, the principle motivation for the bifurcation decision was implementation-based.[33] According to this survey, representatives were convinced that the two categories of rights were inherently different in nature and exhibited a number of differentiating features which in turn were perceived to render those rights not included into the ICCPR non-justiciable.[34] Thus, the same arguments which tilted the scales towards a bifurcation in the UNCHR and ECOSOC also decided the matter in the UNGA.

After this decision, the drafting of the two Covenants continued in the Commission. Although there were further proposals to request the UNGA to reconsider its decision of bifurcating the Covenants, they were rejected and the bifurcation decision remained final.[35] The ICCPR and ICESCR where adopted by the UNGA on 16 December 1966.[36]

1.2.2. The Divide in the Treaties

Subsequent to the bifurcation decision, a number of legally binding human rights instruments were adopted in the UN human rights system. The treaties

[28] ibid, para 775.

[29] ibid.

[30] ECOSOC Res 384 (XIII) 'Report of the Commission on Human Rights (Seventh Session)' (29 August 1951) E/RES/384(XIII).

[31] UNGA Third Committee, 'Summary Record of the 395th Meeting' (19 January 1952) A/C.3/SR.395.

[32] UNGA Res 543 (VI) 'Preparation of two Draft International Covenants on Human Rights' (5 February 1952) A/RES/543(VI).

[33] Scott, 'Interdependence and Permeability', 794–98.

[34] ibid, 794.

[35] See UNGA, 'Draft International Covenants on Human Rights', ch I para 37.

[36] UNGA Res 2200 (XXI) 'International Covenant on Economic, Social and Cultural Rights, International Covenant on Civil and Political Rights and Optional Protocol to the International Covenant on Civil and Political Rights' (16 December 1966) A/RES/2200(XXI).

subject to this inquiry are the ICCPR and ICESCR (both adopted in 1966), the International Convention on the Elimination of All Forms of Racial Discrimination (ICERD, adopted in 1965),[37] the Convention on the Elimination of All Forms of Discrimination Against Women (CEDAW, adopted in 1979),[38] the Convention on the Rights of the Child (CRC, adopted in 1989)[39] and the Convention on the Rights of Persons with Disabilities (CRPD, adopted in 2006).[40] The perception that the two categories of rights are different, which also influenced the bifurcation decision, has led to some specific features in some of these treaties. These features are usually the point of attachment for later arguments about the different nature of rights. This subsection will only lay out the text of the treaties. More details regarding the drafting history and the precise reasoning for including these provisions will be discussed later on in this book.[41]

For socio-economic rights, the ICESCR, CRC and CRPD explicitly prescribe that States parties must realise them progressively and to the maximum of available resources, while provisions aimed at civil and political rights do not contain such a specific approach. The ICESCR, only concerned with rights which are traditionally called socio-economic, prescribes that each State party 'undertakes to take steps … to the maximum of its available resources, with a view to achieving progressively the full realisation of the rights recognised in the present Covenant …'.[42] The ICCPR, in contrast, does not provide for progressive realisation and the relevance of available resources but instead demands that '[e]ach State Party to the present Covenant undertakes to respect and to ensure to all individuals … the rights recognized in the present Covenant'.[43] It must be noted, however, that, while there is no recognition of progressive realisation in the ICCPR, there is also no explicit reference to immediate realisation either. Instead, the ICCPR remains silent on the timeframe of realisation.[44]

This difference between the ICCPR and ICESCR is mirrored in the CRPD and the CRC, two instruments which combine both categories of rights.[45] These treaties were established later on and the drafting parties explicitly referenced the divide established by the Covenants.[46] According to the CRC, 'States Parties shall

[37] International Convention on the Elimination of All Forms of Racial Discrimination (adopted 21 December 1965, entered into force 4 January 1969) 660 UNTS 195.

[38] Convention on the Elimination of All Forms of Discrimination Against Women (adopted 18 December 1979, entered into force 3 September 1981) 1249 UNTS 13.

[39] Convention on the Rights of the Child (adopted 20 November 1989, entered into force 2 September 1990) 1577 UNTS 3.

[40] Convention on the Rights of Persons with Disabilities (adopted 13 December 2007, entered into force 3 May 2008) 2515 UNTS 3.

[41] See further 9.3.

[42] Article 2 (1) of the ICESCR; progressive realisation is also referenced in some substantive rights provisions of the ICESCR, for example Article 13 (2) (b) of the ICESCR which demands 'the progressive introduction of free education'.

[43] Article 2 (1) of the ICCPR.

[44] See further 7.3.1.

[45] See also de Beco, 'The Indivisibility of Human Rights', 150.

[46] See further 9.3.4. and 9.3.5.

respect and ensure the rights [ie, all rights] set forth in the present Convention to each child within their jurisdiction without discrimination of any kind'.[47] After prescribing that States parties shall undertake 'all appropriate legislative, administrative, and other measures', the CRC continues to specify that '[w]ith regard to economic, social and cultural rights, States Parties shall undertake such measures to the maximum extent of their available resources'.[48] While this provision only references resource constraints, it is commonly accepted that this reference introduces a progressive mode of realisation.[49] The CRPD also differentiates between the two categories:

> With regard to economic, social and cultural rights, each State Party undertakes to take measures to the maximum of its available resources … with a view to achieving progressively the full realization of these rights, without prejudice to those obligations contained in the present Convention that are immediately applicable according to international law.[50]

What is new in this treaty is the explicit recognition of immediately applicable obligations in the field of socio-economic rights in the last part of Article 4 (2) of the CRPD. The CRPD is the first treaty in the UN system to include such a provision.[51]

The ICERD and CEDAW, like the ICCPR, do not set out any reference to progressive realisation or the maximum of available resources. Yet, both treaties concern the elimination of discrimination in the enjoyment of human rights from both categories.[52] The reason why there is no differentiation in these treaties perhaps lies in the common perception that non-discrimination is a civil and political right. However, the fact that the treaties still indirectly concern both categories of rights leads to some difficulties regarding their delimitation, as will be argued later on.[53] In both treaties, the relevant provisions speak of realisation 'without delay'. The general obligation provision of the CEDAW is the following: 'States Parties condemn discrimination against women in all its forms,

[47] Article 2 (1) of the CRC; the CRC, too, reiterates the standard of progressive realisation in some substantive provisions concerning socio-economic rights, for example in Article 24 (4) of the CRC concerning the right to the highest attainable standard of health or Article 28 (1) of the CRC concerning the right to education.

[48] Article 4 of the CRC.

[49] See CRC-Com, 'General Comment No 5: General Measures of Implementation of the Convention on the Rights of the Child (arts. 4, 42 and 44, para. 6)' (2003) CRC/GC/2003/5, para 7: 'The second sentence of article 4 reflects a realistic acceptance that lack of resources – financial and other resources – can hamper the full implementation of economic, social and cultural rights in some States; this introduces the concept of "progressive realization"'; CRC-Com, 'General Comment No 19 on Public Budgeting for the Realization of Children's Rights (art. 4)' (2016) CRC/C/GC/19, para 29; see also Tobin, 'Article 4', 131–32.

[50] Article 4 (2) of the CRPD.

[51] W Ringel, 'Non-discrimination, Accommodation, and Intersectionality under the CRPD: New Trends and Challenges for the UN Human Rights System' (2017) 20 *Max Planck Yearbook of United Nations Law* 98, 104–05.

[52] See Articles 7–16 of the CEDAW and Article 5 of the ICERD.

[53] See further 8.2.1.2.

agree to pursue by all appropriate means and without delay a policy of eliminating discrimination against women …'.[54] The ICERD similarly prescribes that 'States Parties condemn racial discrimination and undertake to pursue by all appropriate means and without delay a policy of eliminating racial discrimination in all its forms and promoting understanding among all races …'.[55]

The second type of difference in the treaties concerns the standard of review to be applied by the Committees when examining Individual Communications. By now, all treaty regimes explored in this study establish the competence of the Committees to receive Individual Communications. This assimilation, however, took several decades. During the drafting of the ICCPR and ICESCR, the Commission on Human Rights remained firm in its opinion that socio-economic rights were different and not justiciable. Thus, the HRC was furnished with the competence to consider interstate complaints and Individual Communications only regarding civil and political rights, the latter by way of the Optional Protocol to the International Covenant on Civil and Political Rights (ICCPR-OP1), which was adopted in 1966.[56]

It was not until 1985 that ECOSOC established the CESCR which was tasked with carrying out the monitoring functions assigned to the Council in Part IV of the ICESCR, namely those in the context of the reporting procedure.[57] It would take several more decades for the competences of the CESCR to be adapted to those of the HRC. In 2008, the Optional Protocol to the International Covenant on Economic, Social and Cultural Rights (ICESCR-OP) was adopted which establishes the competence of the CESCR to receive interstate complaints and Individual Communications.[58] An Individual Communications procedure was established for the CEDAW by the Optional Protocol to the Convention on the Elimination of All Forms of Discrimination against Women (CEDAW-OP, adopted 1999),[59] for the CRPD by the Optional Protocol to the Convention on the Rights of Persons with Disabilities (CRPD-OP, adopted 2006)[60] and for the CRC by the Third Optional Protocol to the Convention on the Rights of the Child (CRC-OP3, adopted 2011).[61] Only in the case of the ICERD, the

[54] Article 2 of the CEDAW.

[55] Article 2 (1) of the ICERD.

[56] Optional Protocol to the International Covenant on Civil and Political Rights (adopted 16 December 1966, entered into force 23 March 1976) 999 UNTS 171.

[57] ECOSOC Res 1985/17; for further details on the development of the CESCR, see also P Alston, 'Out of the Abyss: The Challenges Confronting the New U. N. Committee on Economic, Social and Cultural Rights' (1987) 9 *Human Rights Quarterly* 332, 340–49.

[58] Optional Protocol to the International Covenant on Economic, Social and Cultural Rights (adopted 10 December 2008, entered into force 5 May 2013) 2922 UNTS 29.

[59] Optional Protocol to the Convention on the Elimination of All Forms of Discrimination against Women (adopted 6 October 1999, entered into force 22 December 2000) 2131 UNTS 83.

[60] Optional Protocol to the Convention on the Rights of Persons with Disabilities (adopted 13 December 2006, entered into force 3 May 2008) 2518 UNTS 283.

[61] (Third) Optional Protocol to the Convention on the Rights of the Child on a Communications Procedure (adopted 19 December 2011, entered into force 14 April 2014) 2983 UNTS 157.

Committee's competence to hear individual complaints was established by the treaty itself.[62]

However, there is one notable difference remaining, namely the standard of review for individual complaints concerning socio-economic rights. During the drafting process of the ICESCR-OP, '[s]ome delegations expressed doubts as to whether all economic, social and cultural rights were equally justiciable'.[63] In order to reconcile the divergent opinions on justiciability and save the Individual Communications mechanism, a compromise was included into the text of the ICESCR-OP.[64] The working group agreed on a reasonableness standard for the review of individual complaints, which was to serve as a 'safeguard against undue interference with national policymaking'.[65]

Article 8 (4) of the ICESCR-OP sets out that

> [w]hen examining communications under the present Protocol, the Committee shall consider the reasonableness of the steps taken by the State Party in accordance with part II of the Covenant. In doing so, the Committee shall bear in mind that the State Party may adopt a range of possible policy measures for the implementation of the rights set forth in the Covenant.

A similar provision has been included in the CRC-OP3, explicitly limiting the applicability of the reasonableness standard to communications alleging the violation of socio-economic rights.[66] No such specification regarding the standard of review is contained in the OP-ICCPR, CEDAW-OP or ICERD.

1.2.3. Alleged Dichotomies between the Categories

The perception that socio-economic rights are different in nature compared to civil and political rights not only was the basis for the bifurcation decision,[67] but it also continued to shape discussions about categories of rights and their

[62] See Article 14 of the ICERD.

[63] UNCHR, 'Report of the Open-ended Working Group to Consider Options Regarding the Elaboration of an Optional Protocol to the International Covenant on Economic, Social and Cultural Rights on its 1st Session' (15 March 2004) E/CN.4/2004/44, para 65.

[64] See B Porter and S Liebenberg, 'Consideration of Merits Under the OP-ICESCR: Reasonableness Review under 8(4) and the Maximum of Available Resources Standard: Notes for Discussion at the Workshop on Strategic Litigation under the OP-ICESCR' 1 (with the author).

[65] UNCHR, 'Report of the Open-ended Working Group to Consider Options Regarding the Elaboration of an Optional Protocol to the International Covenant on Economic, Social and Cultural Rights on its 3rd Session' (14 March 2006) E/CN.4/2006/47, para 92.

[66] Article 10 (4) of the CRC-OP3: 'When examining communications alleging violations of economic, social or cultural rights, the Committee shall consider the reasonableness of the steps taken by the State party in accordance with article 4 of the Convention. In doing so, the Committee shall bear in mind that the State party may adopt a range of possible policy measures for the implementation of the economic, social and cultural rights in the Convention.' While no such rule can be found in the CRPD, a similar standard is applied by the CRPD-Com in the context of the rights of persons with disabilities see further 6.3.1.

[67] See, eg, UNGA, 'Draft International Covenants on Human Rights', ch II paras 9, 10.

implementation afterwards. While the interconnected and interdependent nature of all rights was frequently stressed during the discussions in the UN,[68] as well as ever since,[69] a number of alleged differences between the two categories has accumulated over time.[70] This delimitation of rights has taken place not only in the context of the drafting of the Covenants but has also been applied by the UN Committees and many literary commentators after the treaties have entered into force. At least up until the 1980s, the emphasis in the discussion has been on differences between the categories rather than commonalities.

First and foremost, there was the assumption that socio-economic rights are positive rights, ie, rights requiring State action, while civil and political rights are negative, meaning they require only abstention by the State party. The drafting parties of the Covenants argued that the former are 'rights which the State would have to take positive action to promote', while the latter were understood as 'rights of the individual "against" the State, ie, against unlawful and unjust action of the State'.[71] In the literature, too, duties of restraint have traditionally been attributed to civil and political rights, while socio-economic rights were said to entail positive duties for the State.[72] Connected to this alleged structure of obligations was the assertion that socio-economic rights are resource-intensive while civil and political rights are mostly free. Mostly based on this reasoning, it was further assumed that civil and political rights are 'immediately applicable', while socio-economic rights are 'to be progressively implemented'.[73] Accordingly, progressive realisation was and is commonly understood as 'a recognition of the fact that full realization of all economic, social and cultural rights will generally not be able to be achieved in a short period of time'.[74]

Another argument often invoked to support the claim that socio-economic rights are different is the accusation of vagueness. The argument can be broken down into the following proposition: It is easier to define what States should not do than it is to define what they should do. For instance, it has been argued that the obligation of a State not to restrict a citizen's freedom of movement is relatively clear, while the obligation to provide sufficient housing is vague because

[68] See ibid, ch II para 7; see also UNGA Res 421 (V).

[69] See, eg, S Fredman, *Human Rights Transformed: Positive Rights and Positive Duties* (Oxford, Oxford University Press, 2008) 67.

[70] For a summary of these alleged dichotomies, see P Alston and G Quinn, 'The Nature and Scope of States Parties' Obligations under the International Covenant on Economic, Social and Cultural Rights' (1987) 9 *Human Rights Quarterly* 156, 159–60.

[71] UNGA, 'Draft International Covenants on Human Rights', ch II para 9.

[72] See, eg, Q Wright as cited in: SP Marks, 'Emerging Human Rights: A New Generation for the 1980s?' (1981) 33 *Rutgers Law Review* 435, 439; see also C Fried, *Right and Wrong* (Cambridge, Harvard University Press, 1979) 110; see also FB Cross, 'The Error of Positive Rights' (2001) 48 *UCLA Law Review* 857, 866.

[73] See UNGA, 'Draft International Covenants on Human Rights', ch II para 9; see also Alston and Quinn 'Obligations under the ICESCR', 159.

[74] CESCR, 'General Comment No 3: The Nature of States Parties' Obligations (art. 2, para. 1, of the Covenant)' (1990) E/1991/23, para 9.

there is no way clearly to delimit human rights obligations from unnecessary luxury.[75] Thus, this argument is at least partly based on the assumption that positive obligations are a unique feature of socio-economic rights. A similar point often brought up when talking about socio-economic rights (particularly regarding the rights to health, education, social security, or housing) is polycentricity.[76] The term polycentricity refers to subject areas, human rights claims, or other problems with a particularly complex system of interactions and interdependencies. In such a complicated interlocking system, a change in one dimension can cause changes in other relationships that can be difficult or even impossible to predict.[77] It was often argued that polycentricity is a unique feature of socio-economic rights because these rights require budget decisions with wide-ranging and unforeseeable consequences.

Lastly, it was frequently presumed that socio-economic rights, because of their specific nature, are not amenable to judicial review. During the drafting of the Covenants, a line was drawn between civil and political rights which were seen as 'enforceable, or justiciable, or of an "absolute" character' and socio-economic rights which 'were not or might not be'.[78] For implementation at the UN level, this was taken to mean that civil and political rights are 'legal rights' which could be supervised by a Committee, while socio-economic rights are 'programme rights' which would best be implemented by a periodic reports system.[79] This differentiation between legal and programmatic rights has since also been the focus of the general discussion about the two categories of rights.[80] The concern has long been whether it is possible to clarify the obligations under the ICESCR to such an extent that a violation thereof can be found by a Committee.[81] The idea was that socio-economic rights only entail the vague obligation of reaching an aspirational goal at some time in the more or less far future. Thus, it was argued by some critics, there are simply no workable criteria to assess compliance with these obligations.[82] Furthermore, the requirement of positive action and resource expenditure was argued to lead to the necessity

[75] D Kelley, *A Life of One's Own: Individual Rights and the Welfare State* (Washington, Cato Institute, 1998) 27; K Tomaševski, 'Justiciability of Economic, Social and Cultural Rights' (1995) 55 *ICJ Review* 203, 217.

[76] See JA King, 'The Pervasiveness of Polycentricity' (2008) 53 *Public Law* 101, 102.

[77] See, generally, LL Fuller, 'The Forms and Limits of Adjudication' (1978) 92 *Harvard Law Review* 353; Fuller referred back to the conception of polycentricity in M Polanyi, *The Logic of Liberty: Reflections and Rejoinders*, The International Library of Sociology, Political Sociology 11 (London, Routledge, 1951) 170–84.

[78] UNGA, 'Draft International Covenants on Human Rights', ch II para 9.

[79] ibid, ch II para 9–12.

[80] See L Henkin, 'Introduction' in L Henkin (ed), *The International Bill of Rights: The Covenant on Civil and Political Rights* (New York, Columbia University Press, 1981) 10.

[81] See UNCHR, 'Status of the International Covenants on Human Rights: Report of the Independent Expert on the Question of a Draft Optional Protocol to the International Covenant on Economic, Social and Cultural Rights' (12 February 2002) E/CN.4/2002/57, paras 16, 20.

[82] See, generally, MJ Dennis and DP Stewart, 'Justiciability of Economic, Social, and Cultural Rights: Should There Be an International Complaints Mechanism to Adjudicate the Rights to Food, Water, Housing, and Health?' (2004) 98 *American Journal of International Law* 462.

of prioritisation decisions which were often perceived as unsuitable for (quasi-) judicial review due to concerns about democratic legitimacy and competence.[83]

A useful way to think about these arguments for a conceptual divide is putting them into a logical sequence. Proponents of a different nature of obligations assumed that socio-economic rights are positive rights and therefore resource-intensive and vague. Because they are resource-intensive, they are progressively realisable. Because they are vague and progressively realisable, they are non-justiciable.[84] It becomes clear that all aspects of the legal differentiation between the categories were ultimately built upon the positive/negative rights divide which was then argued to create a number of follow-up problems which culminate in the overall assessment that socio-economic rights are non-justiciable. Thus, as proposed by Craig Scott, it is appropriate to refer to the justiciability argument as a 'meta-dichotomy', meaning that it is based on the combined effect of the various alleged dichotomies between the two categories of rights.[85] While non-justiciability was not seen as a feature of socio-economic rights as such, it was constructed as the consequence of certain features perceived to be inherent to socio-economic rights.[86] This interrelationship and logical correlation of the alleged dichotomies will play an important role when asking the question what happens when some of them are abandoned while others are upheld.

1.3. THE DISSOLUTION OF BOUNDARIES BETWEEN THE CATEGORIES

Starting not long after the adoption of the Covenants, many of the dichotomies between socio-economic and civil and political rights have been challenged in human rights theory and practice. By now, the vast majority of scholars and practitioners advocate the view, not only that socio-economic and civil and political rights are difficult to differentiate from each other, but also that the assumed conceptional divide between these categories is largely artificial.[87] This section will illustrate how human rights theory and practice have shown that many of the perceived specific features of socio-economic rights are really applicable to

[83] For an engagement with this sort of argument see E Felner, 'Closing the "Escape Hatch": A Toolkit to Monitor the Progressive Realization of Economic, Social, and Cultural Rights' (2009) 1 *Journal of Human Rights Practice* 402, 407; Koch, 'Waves of Duties?', 84; M Pieterse, 'Coming to Terms with Judicial Enforcement of Socio-economic Rights' (2004) 20 *South African Journal on Human Rights* 383, 390, 391.

[84] A similar logical sequence of arguments is observed in Alston and Quinn, 'Obligations under the ICESCR', 159; see also J Todres, 'Emerging Limitations on the Rights of the Child: The U. N. Convention on the Rights of Child and its Early Case Law' (1998) 30 *Columbia Human Rights Law Review* 159, 178 (fn).

[85] Scott, 'Interdependence and Permeability', 797 (fn).

[86] ibid, 832–34.

[87] For a popular example see GJH van Hoof, 'The Legal Nature of Economic, Social and Cultural Rights: A Rebuttal of Some Traditional Views' in P Alston and K Tomaševski (eds), *The Right to Food*, International Studies in Human Rights 4 (Boston, Nijhoff, 1984).

all rights: civil and political rights are also positive (1.3.1), costly (1.3.2), and no more or less vague or polycentric than socio-economic rights (1.3.3). It is now also commonly accepted that both categories of rights are justiciable (1.3.4).

1.3.1. All Rights Entail Positive and Negative Obligations

The last decades have shown a shift away from the positive/negative rights divide. Doubt has been cast on the idea that socio-economic rights only entail positive obligations while civil and political rights are purely negative. Keeping in mind the fact that the arguments for a special nature of socio-economic rights are of a sequential nature, the most important aspect of the modern understanding of human rights is rejecting the positive/negative rights divide. If the features of resource-intensity, progressiveness, vagueness and non-justiciability are ultimately predicated upon this dichotomy, the entire differentiation stands and falls with this initial assumption, as later subsections will show.[88]

The roots of this shift lie in the philosophical recognition that freedom of the individual does not only require abstention of the State but also active removal of barriers to the substantive enjoyment of rights (1.3.1.1). Accordingly, a tripartite structure of positive and negative obligations (respect, protect, fulfil) for all rights has gained more and more traction in international human rights theory (1.3.1.2). The notion of positive obligations for all rights is also clearly supported by the treaty texts (1.3.1.3).

1.3.1.1. Positive Freedom, Substantive Enjoyment, and Substantive Equality

Underlying the acceptance that all rights require positive State action is a shift from a negative towards a positive understanding of freedom. According to a negative understanding, a person's freedom depends only on the presence or absence of interference by the State. A lack of opportunities or means to seize those opportunities, however, is no detriment to freedom.[89] This conception of freedom is commonly based on an interpretation of Enlightenment individualism according to which the individual's primary need is to act without interference, freely speak their mind, be secure against assault, and keep the fruits of their labour.[90] What is deduced from this conception is a narrow interpretation of the role of the State. An individual's freedom is inevitably reduced when the State interferes with the individual's choices in any way. Adherents

[88] A similar argument is made in Sepúlveda, *The Nature of the Obligations*, 123.

[89] See, eg, I Berlin, *Four Essays on Liberty* (Oxford, Oxford University Press, 1969) 121; FA Hayek and R Hamowy (ed), *The Constitution of Liberty: The Definitive Edition*, The Collected Works of F.A. Hayek 17 (London, Routledge, 2012) 60; F Neumann, *The Democratic and the Authoritarian State: Essays in Political and Legal Theory* (Glencoe, Free Press, 1957) 201, 202.

[90] Kelley, *A Life of One's Own*, 16.

of the traditional concept of negative freedom will interpret civil and political rights as giving rise only to duties of restraint.[91]

A positive conception of freedom, on the other hand, argues that the crucial factor for freedom is not formal choice but a person's true capabilities to exercise this choice. Capabilities, in contrast to formal freedom of choice, express the extent to which a person can actually achieve their valued goals.[92] Recognising the value of capabilities over formal freedoms, and considering this substantive freedom as the central objective of the State, imposes on the State the duty to actively remove sources of 'un-freedom'.[93] This positive conception of freedom is also reflected in the Preamble to the UDHR and in Roosevelt's four freedoms address.[94] Freedom does not only mean being free from interference but also requires 'freedom from want', which means that the State must actively provide the preconditions the individual requires to thrive.[95] Connected to this substantive notion of rights is a shift towards a substantive notion of equality; inequality exists not only where the State actively engages in discriminatory practices but also where it omits to take action against existing structural disadvantages. In other words, individuals are not equal where they are treated equally (on paper) but where the State actively creates the circumstances which accord them the same opportunities.[96]

There are two simple reasons why the positive dimension of civil and political rights often remains unseen. Firstly, it becomes clear that the differentiation between positive and negative rights is simply founded on a skewed perspective. If the requirement of de facto enjoyment of rights is only applied in the context of socio-economic rights while a formal approach is taken with regards to civil and political rights, the latter category is necessarily perceived as only negative.[97] Secondly, there often exist misunderstandings about the delimitation of State action and inaction. Well-established systems of State action are often-times confused with non-interference or abstention because a 'largely unarticulated normative baseline' is assumed.[98] This normative baseline consists of assumptions about desirable or natural functions of government. For

[91] This line of argument has also been noted by Fredman, *Human Rights Transformed*, 67.

[92] Amartya Sen, *Development as Freedom* (New York, Alfred A. Knopf, 2001) 75; see also M Nussbaum, *Women and Human Development: The Capabilities Approach*, The Seeley Lectures 3 (Cambridge, Cambridge University Press, 2000).

[93] Sen, *Development*, 13–34; CA Gearty and V Mantouvalou, *Debating Social Rights*, Debating Law 2 (Oxford, Hart Publishing, 2011) 101–04; Fredman, *Human Rights Transformed*, 9–62.

[94] See A Eide, 'The Four Freedoms and Human Rights in the New International Order' in A Eide and J Helgesen (eds), *The Future of Human Rights Protection in a Changing World: 50 Years since the Four Freedoms Address. Essays in Honour of Torkel Opsahl* (Oslo, Norwegian University Press, 1991).

[95] See further Introduction.

[96] See, generally, A Sen, *Inequality Reexamined* (Oxford, Oxford University Press, 1995); see also Fredman, *Human Rights Transformed*, 176–80.

[97] Jhabvala, 'Socio-Economic Context', 165.

[98] C Scott and P Macklem, 'Constitutional Ropes of Sand or Justiciable Guarantees? Social Rights in a New South African Constitution' (1992) 141 *University of Pennsylvania Law Review* 1, 46–47.

example, the protection of property and freedom of contract seem to entail only duties of restraint because the positive dimension of those guarantees is taken for granted.[99]

1.3.1.2. A Tripartite Structure of Obligations for All Rights

There is now widespread agreement that socio-economic and civil and political rights cannot be distinguished by the nature of their correlative duties.[100] The current understanding of human rights demands that all rights should be interpreted to give rise to a range of duties from both the positive and the negative dimension.[101] On the one hand, there are obligations of the State to refrain from interference. On the other hand, human rights require positive action, resource allocation and the implementation of complex administrative and economical systems.[102]

There are some popular examples often used to illustrate that this also applies to civil and political rights: the traditional civil and political right of freedom of expression requires the State to take action, for example, by protecting protesters exercising this freedom from third persons interfering. Furthermore, the right to vote indisputably requires the establishment of a voting system allowing all citizens to take part in the political process. Therefore, the right to vote entails substantive positive duties for the State.[103] Similar arguments are made in relation to the rights to due process, procedural fairness and the assistance of counsel.[104] On the other hand, socio-economic rights also entail duties of

[99] See CR Sunstein, 'Lochner's Legacy' (1987) 87 *Columbia Law Review* 873, 889; DP Currie, 'Positive and Negative Constitutional Rights' (1986) 53 *University of Chicago Law Review* 864, 876.

[100] See, eg, IComJ, 'Maastricht Guidelines on Violations of Economic, Social and Cultural Rights' (1998) 20 *Human Rights Quarterly* 691, 693–94: 'Like civil and political rights, economic, social and cultural rights impose three different types of obligations on States: the obligations to respect, protect and fulfil'; B Porter, 'Reasonableness and Article 8(4)' in M Langford, B Porter, R Brown and J Rossi (eds), *The Optional Protocol to the International Covenant on Economic, Social and Cultural Rights: A Commentary* (Pretoria, Pretoria University Law Press, 2016) 175; see also Fredman, *Human Rights Transformed*, 67–68 and Gearty and Mantouvalou, *Debating Social Rights*, 110, 111, both providing examples from jurisprudence.

[101] H Shue, *Basic Rights: Subsistence, Affluence, and U.S. Foreign Policy*, 40th Anniversary edn (Princeton, Princeton University Press, 2020) 52–53; Fredman, *Human Rights Transformed*, 66–70; S Holmes and CR Sunstein, *The Cost of Rights: Why Liberty Depends on Taxes* (New York, Norton, 2000) 35–48; S Liebenberg, 'The International Covenant on Economic, Social and Cultural Rights and its Implications for South Africa' (1995) 11 *South African Journal on Human Rights* 359, 362; J Cavallaro and E Schaffer, 'Less as More: Rethinking Supernational Litigation of Economic and Social Rights in the Americas' (2004) 56 *Hastings Law Journal* 217, 252–54.

[102] Fredman, *Human Rights Transformed*, 2.

[103] Van Hoof, 'The Legal Nature', 103.

[104] See Scott and Macklem, 'Constitutional Ropes of Sand?', 48–53 (with many examples from domestic and international jurisprudence). For the concept of positive rights as a result of the Due Process Clause in US law, see A Cox, 'Foreword: Constitutional Adjudication and the Promotion of Human Rights' (1966) 80 *Harvard Law Review* 91, 110; see also S Bandes, 'The Negative Constitution: A Critique' (1990) 88 *Michigan Law Review* 2271.

restraint for the State.[105] The CESCR has recognised, for example, that the right to housing would clearly be incomplete without a negative obligation of the State to abstain from unlawful evictions.[106] In relation to the right to food, the State's obligation to respect the right entails refraining from expropriating land from people who rely on the access or control over that land as their primary means to acquire food.[107]

A tripartite structure of obligations, based on the ideas of Henry Shue,[108] has gained more and more support in the context of the UN human rights system.[109] The most commonly used terminology in this context stems from Asbjørn Eide, who established the triad of 'respect, protect and fulfil', originally in the context of the right to food.[110] The obligation to respect requires the State party to abstain from interfering with rights enjoyment, while the obligation to protect demands positive action by the State party aimed at preventing the interference of third parties. The obligation to fulfil, according to Eide, requires States parties to take those positive measures which are necessary to enable each person in its jurisdiction to satisfy those needs which are recognised in the relevant human rights instruments and which cannot be satisfied by the person's own efforts alone.[111]

Shue originally used the term 'duty to avoid depriving'[112] when referring to what was later renamed the duty to respect. With this terminology he intended to emphasise that even rights traditionally classified as positive involved negative duties.[113] Moreover, Shue chose the term 'to avoid depriving' instead of simply 'not depriving' to illustrate the positive aspects of traditional negative rights, since avoiding demands positive effort.[114] Changing the terminology to 'duty to respect', in Shue's mind, encompasses both aspects while being a more elegant phrase.[115]

The CESCR, on the basis of Eide's work, also introduced this tripartite structure into its jurisprudence.[116] Eide soon extended the tripartite approach to all

105 See M Langford, 'The Justiciability of Social Rights: From Practice to Theory' in M Langford (ed), *Social Rights Jurisprudence: Emerging Trends in International and Comparative Law* (Cambridge, Cambridge University Press, 2009) 31.

106 CESCR, 'General Comment No 4: The Right to Adequate Housing (Art 11(1) of the Covenant)' (1991) E/1992/23, para 18.

107 Van Hoof, 'The Legal Nature', 107.

108 See Shue, *Basic Rights*, 51–53.

109 See, generally, Sepúlveda, *The Nature of the Obligations*, 157–65.

110 See UNCHR, 'Report on the Right to Adequate Food as a Human Right Submitted by Mr. Asbjørn Eide, Special Rapporteur' (7 July 1987) E/CN.4/Sub.2/1987/23.

111 A Eide, 'Realization of Social and Economic Rights – the Minimum Threshold Approach' (1989) 43 *ICJ Review* 40, 42.

112 Shue, *Basic Rights*, 52–53.

113 H Shue, 'The Interdependence of Duties' in P Alston and K Tomaševski (eds), *The Right to Food*, International Studies in Human Rights 4 (Boston, Nijhoff, 1984) 83–85.

114 ibid, 84.

115 ibid, 85.

116 See CESCR, 'General Comment No 12: The Right to Adequate Food (art. 11)' (1999) E/C.12/1999/5, para 15.

rights, arguing that it is not possible to distinguish between socio-economic and civil and political rights along the axis of positive and negative obligations.[117] The HRC also recognises that civil and political rights have not only negative but also positive components.[118] Others soon followed suit and applied this structure to all rights,[119] thereby overcoming the positive/negative rights divide in favour of a common set of obligations.[120]

While this tripartite structure is sometimes called into question in favour of more nuanced continuous approaches,[121] or refined into systems of four or five types of obligations,[122] there is now general agreement about the fact that all rights have a range of obligations located somewhere on the spectrum from abstention to active engagement.[123] Shue himself explained that the tripartite structure was never intended to be a 'frozen abstraction' which would take the place of the previous positive/negative rights divide but instead was meant to serve as a rebuttal to those traditional views.[124]

1.3.1.3. *Positive Obligations in the Treaty Texts*

Little debate exists around the fact that all rights entail positive obligations. It is commonly assumed that the treaties clearly allow such an interpretation because neither the ICCPR nor the ICESCR contain any provisions limiting the respective category of rights to either negative or positive obligations.[125] Instead, the requirement to 'ensure' human rights in Article 2 (1) of the ICCPR implies positivity,[126] as does the obligation to 'undertake ... to take the steps ... to adopt such laws or other measures as may be necessary to

[117] Eide, 'Realization of Social and Economic Rights', 41.

[118] See, eg, HRC, 'General Comment No 31: The Nature of the General Legal Obligation Imposed on States Parties to the Covenant' (2004) CCPR/C/21/Rev.1/Add.13, para 6.

[119] See, eg, van Hoof, 'The Legal Nature', 107; M Langford and JA King, 'Committee on Economic, Social and Cultural Rights: Past, Present and Future' in M Langford (ed), *Social Rights Jurisprudence: Emerging Trends in International and Comparative Law* (Cambridge, Cambridge University Press 2009) 484.

[120] Van Hoof, 'The Legal Nature', 107.

[121] See, eg, Koch, 'Waves of Duties?'.

[122] See van Hoof, 'The Legal Nature', 106: 'In this regard four "layers" of State obligations may be discerned which, for lack of better terms, may be called: an obligation to respect, an obligation to protect, an obligation to ensure, and an obligation to promote'; see also the fivefold structure proposed in HJ Steiner, P Alston and R Goodman, *International Human Rights in Context: Law, Politics, Morals; Text and Materials*, 3rd edn (Oxford, Oxford University Press, 2008) 185–89.

[123] See Koch, 'Waves of Duties?', 86.

[124] Shue, *Basic Rights*, 160.

[125] See, eg, Whelan and Donnelley, 'Setting the Record Straight', 934 (fn).

[126] See Jhabvala, 'Socio-Economic Context', 161–62; A Nolan, B Porter and M Langford, 'The Justiciability of Social and Economic Rights: An Updated Appraisal' in MT Kamminga (ed), *Challenges in International Human Rights Law Volume III* (London, Routledge, 2014) 99.

give effect to the rights recognized in the present Covenant' in Article 2 (2) of the ICCPR. Similar wording is used in the CRC, without limiting this positive dimension to socio-economic rights.[127] The ICERD and CEDAW both proceed from a substantive notion of equality, acknowledging that full equality between all individuals will require States parties to work towards an elimination of prejudices by, for example, modifying social and cultural behaviour.[128]

The CRPD in particular sets out a wide array of positive and negative obligations for the range of rights contained in the treaty.[129] The duty to provide reasonable accommodation introduces positive aspects to all rights in the Convention, no matter which category it is traditionally ascribed to.[130] The treaty also combines both positive and negative duties in singular provisions.[131] This treaty is also the first one to explicitly set out specific positive obligations in provisions concerning civil and political rights, such as the right to equal recognition before the law.[132] The CRPD's point of departure is the social model of disability. This includes the acknowledgment that the inability of a person with disabilities to enjoy certain rights is not a personal medical problem but rather the result of an interaction with barriers created by society.[133] Consequently, the Convention lays a focus on the active removal of barriers to the equal enjoyment of all human rights, regardless of their category.[134]

[127] See Articles 2 and 4 of the CRC.

[128] See Article 5 (a) of the CEDAW: 'States Parties shall take all appropriate measures … [t]o modify the social and cultural patterns of conduct of men and women, with a view to achieving the elimination of prejudices and customary and all other practices which are based on the idea of the inferiority or the superiority of either of the sexes or on stereotyped roles for men and women'; Article 7 of the ICERD: 'States Parties undertake to adopt immediate and effective measures, particularly in the fields of teaching, education, culture and information, with a view to combating prejudices which lead to racial discrimination and to promoting understanding, tolerance and friendship among nations and racial or ethnical groups'.

[129] Article 4 (1) of the CRPD obligates States parties to 'ensure and promote the full realization' by adopting a range of positive and negative measures. These general obligations apply to all rights in the Convention, whatever their nature. Several individual rights expressly refer to positive duties on the States parties, eg, the duty in Article 21 of the CRPD to promote the use of sign language in order to ensure the right of disabled persons to exercise their freedom of expression and opinion or the frequent reference to the duty to take 'effective' or 'appropriate measures' regarding different kinds of rights.

[130] See A Lawson, *Disability and Equality Law in Britain: The Role of Reasonable Adjustment* (Oxford, Hart, 2008) 33; for more detail on the concept of reasonable accommodation, see 5.2.1.–5.2.3.

[131] See Mégret, 'The Disabilities Convention', 265–66.

[132] See Article 12 (3) of the CRPD; see also R Uerpmann-Wittzack, 'Die UN-Behindertenrechtskonvention in der Praxis des Ausschusses für die Rechte von Menschen mit Behinderungen' (2016) 54 *Archiv des Völkerrechts* 181, 198.

[133] CRPD, preamble (e); see also D Ferri, 'Reasonable Accommodation as a Gateway to the Equal Enjoyment of Human Rights: From New York to Strasbourg' (2018) 6 *Social Inclusion* 40, 41; Ringel, 'Non-discrimination', 126 with further references.

[134] See Ferri, 'Reasonable Accommodation', 41–42 with further references.

1.3.2. All Rights Cost Money

It is also widely accepted that having budgetary implications is not a unique characteristic of socio-economic rights. All rights cost money, as has famously been argued by Stephen Holmes and Cass R Sunstein.[135] This argument is a logical consequence of the shift towards a tripartite structure of obligations for all rights: because all rights entail positive duties, all rights require the allocation of resources in order to undertake these active steps.[136] Whether a human rights claim has budgetary implications does not depend on the underlying category of rights but rather on the nature of the duty in question.[137] Civil and political rights, just like socio-economic rights, can depend on resource allocation and budgetary decisions if the positive dimensions of 'protect' and 'fulfil' are concerned.[138] Conversely, negative duties associated with socio-economic rights can be performed mostly free of cost. For example, refraining from government-sanctioned evictions or from demolishing low-cost housing to make room for luxury apartments saves expenditure rather than creating new budgetary requirements.[139]

There exist many examples in international and domestic civil and political rights jurisprudence to support the above claim.[140] The European Court of Human Rights (ECtHR) found structural problems concerning the excessive length of proceedings in the Italian justice system in 2,183 identical cases, calling for extensive (and expensive) reforms.[141] In the case of *August and Another v Electoral Commission and Others* in the Constitutional Court of South Africa, the Court held prisoners to be eligible to vote and ordered the Electoral Commission to make arrangements for all prisoners to exercise their democratic rights.[142] More generally, the right to free speech calls not only for the protection of the speaker from disruption in a specific case,[143] but also for the provision of safe and open spaces for expressive activity, even though this requires positive action and resource allocation.[144]

[135] See Holmes and Sunstein, *The Cost of Rights*, 44; see also Gearty and Mantouvalou, *Debating Social Rights*, 111–13.

[136] See Nolan, Porter and Langford, 'Justiciability', 100–01.

[137] See UNCHR, 'Report on the Right to Adequate Food', para 115.

[138] See B Çalı and A Koch, 'Explaining Compliance: Lessons Learned from Civil and Political Rights' in M Langford, C Rodríguez-Garavito and J Rossi (eds), *Social Rights Judgements and the Politics of Compliance: Making it Stick* (Cambridge, Cambridge University Press, 2017) 48.

[139] See D Bilchitz, *Poverty and Fundamental Rights: The Justification and Enforcement of Socio-economic Rights* (Oxford, Oxford University Press, 2007) 129.

[140] For a number of examples, see UNCHR, 'Elements for an Optional Protocol to the International Covenant on Economic, Social and Cultural Rights: Analytical Paper by the Chairperson-Rapporteur, Catarina de Albuquerque' (30 November 2005) E/CN.4/2006/WG.23/2, paras 35–53.

[141] See Çalı and Koch, 'Explaining Compliance', 48 (fn).

[142] Constitutional Court of South Africa, *August and Another v Electoral Commission and Others* (1999) 4 BCLR 363 (CC), para 42.

[143] This is also recognised by M Tushnet, 'Social Welfare Rights and the Forms of Judicial Review' (2004) 82 *Texas Law Review* 1895, 1896.

[144] See Holmes and Sunstein, *The Cost of Rights*, 52.

There is a simple explanation why budgetary implications have been perceived as a specific feature of socio-economic rights for so long: the infrastructure and budgets for civil and political rights are often already established. While it is not true that civil and political rights do not require budget allocation, they might require less allocation of *new* budget, which may either be perceived as less intrusive or overlooked altogether.[145]

1.3.3. All Rights are Vague and Polycentric

The argument that socio-economic rights are inherently vague also rests on the distinction between positive and negative rights.[146] When acknowledging that all rights must be interpreted to entail a range of duties, it becomes clear that vagueness is not a feature of a particular category but rather of a layer in the system of obligations. The perceived imprecision of the right is not a result of differences between the rights themselves but instead a result of the comparison between different levels of duties. While the first two levels of obligations are relatively straight forward, the obligation to fulfil is subject to imprecision to a greater extent.[147]

The perception of vagueness also results from the fact that socio-economic rights are lacking behind in terms of judicial and scholarly interpretation.[148] The lack of precise definition is not only the reason but also a consequence of scepticism towards socio-economic rights.[149] The perception of an inherent imprecision and the normative underdevelopment are caught in a negative feedback loop, making the scepticism towards the justiciability of socio-economic rights a self-fulfilling prophecy.[150]

When adjusting for differences in the amount of scholarly and judicial interpretation, civil and political rights are revealed to also rely on inherently indeterminate standards.[151] Concepts like due process or equal protection under the law appear clearer than the right to housing or health care, not because

[145] See J Fowkes, 'Normal Rights, Just New: Understanding the Judicial Enforcement of Socioeconomic Rights' (2020) 68 *American Journal of Comparative Law* 722, 722–32; J Fowkes, *Building the Constitution: The Practice of Constitutional Interpretation in Post-Apartheid South Africa*, Cambridge Studies in Constitutional Law 16 (Cambridge, Cambridge University Press, 2016) 133–42; see also Nolan, Porter and Langford, 'Justiciability, 100.

[146] This is also implied by D Marcus, 'The Normative Development of Socioeconomic Rights Through Supranational Adjudication' (2006) 42 *Stanford Journal of International Law* 53, 60.

[147] See Scott and Macklem, 'Constitutional Ropes of Sand?', 76.

[148] See Alston, 'Out of the Abyss', 351–52.

[149] See Scott and Macklem, 'Constitutional Ropes of Sand?', 72–73; M Craven, *The International Covenant on Economic, Social, and Cultural Rights: A Perspective on Its Development* (Oxford, Clarendon, 1995) 10.

[150] Marcus, 'Normative Development', 54–55.

[151] See E Mureinik, 'Beyond a Charter of Luxuries: Economic Rights in the Constitution' (1992) 8 *South African Journal on Human Rights* 464, 469–70.

they are inherently less vague but because they have been interpreted by judges over decades.[152] Another inherently vague term central to many civil and political rights in the international and domestic context is the concept of human dignity.[153] Human dignity proves to be elusive to such a degree that it is applied without providing an express definition,[154] true to the motto 'I know it when I see it even if I cannot tell you what it is'.[155]

The same is true for polycentricity. In Fuller's opinion, it is the aspect of resource allocation which makes an issue polycentric.[156] If, however, all rights require resources because all rights are positive, then it becomes clear that polycentricity is not an inherent feature of socio-economic rights. Even though the concept of polycentricity is now firmly baked into the arguments critical of socio-economic rights, Fuller himself did not limit his argument of polycentricity to this category of rights.[157] He rather recognised that polycentric issues arise in 'almost all problems submitted to adjudication'.[158] Polycentric elements are just as present in issues regarding free speech, racial equality and procedural rights and tax law.[159]

1.3.4. All Rights are Justiciable

It is now also commonly accepted that the two categories of rights cannot be distinguished by their justiciability. There are two conceivable ways to make this argument. The first one is to acknowledge that justiciability is a 'meta-dichotomy' which means that it stands and falls with the primary dichotomies it is built upon.[160] When the underlying primary dichotomies are abandoned, justiciability ceases to function as a differentiating factor between categories of rights and the question becomes whether certain layers of the tripartite structure of obligations are suitable for judicial review.[161] It then makes more sense to ask whether positive obligations, particularly the 'fulfil' dimension, can be specified enough to be adjudicated and whether the adjudication of such resource-intensive aspects can be reconciled with democratic principles.

[152] See P Alston, 'International Law and the Human Right to Food' in P Alston and K Tomaševski (eds), *The Right to Food*, International Studies in Human Rights 4 (Boston, Nijhoff, 1984) 57.

[153] See O Schachter, 'Human Dignity as a Normative Concept' (1983) 77 *American Journal of International Law* 848, 848.

[154] eg, ECtHR, *Lawless v Ireland* Series A No 3 (1961) 1 EHRR 15 (individual opinion Maridakis).

[155] Schachter, 'Human Dignity', 849.

[156] Fuller, 'Adjudication'.

[157] See Fowkes, 'Normal Rights, Just New', 742–43.

[158] Fuller, 'Adjudication', 397.

[159] See O Fiss, 'Foreword: The Forms of Justice' (1979) 93 *Harvard Law Review* 1, 43; for an extensive argument concerning the resolution of polycentric issues in tax law, see King, 'Polycentricity'.

[160] See further 1.2.3.

[161] This was also noted by IE Koch, 'The Justiciability of Indivisible Rights' (2003) 72 *Nordic Journal of International Law* 3, 21.

However, one underlying primary dichotomy has not yet been abandoned: most commentators and practitioners adhere to the idea that socio-economic rights are progressively realisable while civil and political rights are immediately applicable.[162] Accordingly, the prevalent approach in literature and practice does not resolve the justiciability issue in this way. Instead, the most common argument made in this context views the justiciability of socio-economic rights in isolation, implicitly proceeding from the premise that justiciability concerns inherent to positive (and progressive) obligations are unique to this category of rights. In other words, socio-economic rights are perceived as different, at least regarding the timeframe of their realisation, but still as justiciable in their own right.

The primary argument for the justiciability of socio-economic rights usually is a factual one: socio-economic rights are justiciable because they are being adjudicated. Evidence from the domestic context is often provided to support this claim.[163] A prominent example used in this context is the Constitutional Court of South Africa and its engagement with socio-economic rights,[164] and often the *Grootboom* case stands at the centre of these comments.[165] Reference has also been made to the Supreme Court of India.[166] Another practical argument against the claim of non-justiciability refers to the UN system that has been adapted in a way which clearly shows that socio-economic rights are perceived as justiciable. The relevant Optional Protocols have largely eliminated differences in the implementation mechanisms existing between the treaties.[167] Accordingly, the argument is that there is no delimitation of justiciable and non-justiciable rights in the UN human rights system at the current point in time.[168] Arguably, a difference in implementation between the two categories of rights has never existed in the regime of the ICERD. From the moment of its adoption, this treaty has allowed individual complaints to the CERD regarding 'any of the rights set forth in this Convention', including socio-economic rights.[169]

[162] See, eg, 3.2.–3.4. and 7.4.2.

[163] See, for example, S Liebenberg, 'The Protection of Economic and Social Rights in Domestic Legal Systems' in A Eide, A Rosas and C Krause (eds), *Economic, Social, and Cultural Rights: A Textbook*, 2nd edn (Leiden, Nijhoff, 2001); see also F Coomans (ed), *Justiciability of Economic and Social Rights: Experiences from Domestic Systems* (Antwerp, Intersentia, 2006); see also Tobin, 'Article 4', 115–17 with further references.

[164] See MA Baderin and R McCorquodale, 'The International Covenant on Economic, Social and Cultural Rights: Forty Years of Development' in M Baderin and R McCorquodale (eds), *Economic, Social, and Cultural Rights in Action* (Oxford, Oxford University Press, 2007) 11–12.

[165] See Constitutional Court of South Africa, *Government of the Republic of South Africa v Grootboom* (2000) 11 BCLR 1169 (CC). In para 20 of this decision, Justice Yakoob explicitly declares socio-economic rights to be justiciable.

[166] See, eg, P Alston, 'No Right to Complain About Being Poor: The Need for an Optional Protocol to the Economic Rights Covenant' in A Eide and J Helgesen (eds), *The Future of Human Rights Protection in a Changing World: 50 Years since the Four Freedoms Address. Essays in Honour of Torkel Opsahl* (Oslo, Norwegian University Press, 1991) 97.

[167] See further 1.2.2.

[168] See Chenwi, 'Correcting the Historical Asymmetry'; see also de Beco, 'The Indivisibility of Human Rights', 145.

[169] See also Alston, 'No Right to Complain About Being Poor', 95.

On the theoretical side, too, extensive arguments have been made insisting that socio-economic rights are amenable to judicial review.[170] The claim that the adjudication of human rights claims based on positive (socio-economic) obligations would lead to the judiciary encroaching on areas reserved for the democratically elected institutions has been countered by more nuanced understandings of democracy. These conceptions have served to illustrate that positive human rights obligations are central in assuring equal participation as the central prerequisite for a functioning democratic society.[171] Positive obligations pursuant to both civil and political and socio-economic rights and their judicial enforcement are necessary in order to ensure that elections are held, that individuals are protected from third-party interference in this process, and that citizens are actually capable of making an informed decision.[172]

Considerable progress has also been achieved in clarifying *how* positive obligations can be adjudicated, namely by fleshing out the concepts of progressive realisation and reasonableness review.[173] One part of the argument has focused on immediate components of socio-economic rights.[174] It has become clear that progressive realisation must not be understood as some vague standard with realisation postponed to an indefinite point in the future. Rather, a number of immediate and justiciable positive obligations have been identified, namely to provide core entitlements and to take steps to the maximum of available resources.[175] Regarding the gradual improvement of conditions over time, indicators and benchmarks have been utilised as tools for measuring progress in rights implementation. These tools have enabled the determination of violations of socio-economic rights, including those aspects that cannot and must not be realised immediately.[176]

1.4. THE REMAINING DICHOTOMY AND THE HYPOTHESIS OF FULL CONVERGENCE

The one aspect of the historic divide which persists to this day is the differentiation between immediately and progressively realisable rights. The UN Committees explicitly differentiate between socio-economic and civil and

[170] See, eg, M Langford (ed), *Social Rights Jurisprudence: Emerging Trends in International and Comparative Law* (Cambridge, Cambridge University Press, 2009); Scheinin, 'Justiciability'.

[171] See Fredman, *Human Rights Transformed*, 32–40.

[172] Nolan, Porter and Langford, 'Justiciability', 102–03.

[173] See, generally, IComJ, 'Maastricht Guidelines' and UNCHR, 'The Limburg Principles on the Implementation of the International Covenant on Economic Social and Cultural Rights' (8 January 1987) E/CN.4/1987/17.

[174] See, eg, Scott and Macklem, 'Constitutional Ropes of Sand?', 77–84.

[175] See further 2.3.

[176] See, generally, A Chapman, 'A Violations Approach for Monitoring the International Covenant on Economic, Social and Cultural Rights' (1996) 18 *Human Rights Quarterly* 23.

political rights along the lines of immediate and progressive realisation.[177] Literary commentators usually do the same.[178]

From a theoretical standpoint, this insistence upon a clear line between immediately and progressively realisable rights is dubious. This is so because the divide is ultimately founded upon the differentiation between positive and negative rights which has now been abandoned. In the context of socio-economic rights, progressive realisation has been developed as an answer to the issues created by the positive and costly dimensions of these rights, which were thought to only appear in this category. Conversely, civil and political rights were held to be immediately realisable because they were thought to only require inaction from the State parties.[179] The differentiation between immediate and progressive realisation is thus inextricably linked to the perception of rights as either negative and free or positive and costly.[180]

Accordingly, it is often argued that that the temporally open-ended nature of socio-economic rights results, at least in part, from the fact that those rights require positive action from States parties.[181] This connection between positive action, resource implications and progressive realisation is also echoed in Article 2 (1) of the ICESCR which obligates each State party to undertake to take steps 'to the maximum of its available resources, with a view to achieving progressively the full realization' of the rights in the Covenant.[182] Just like justiciability, progressive realisation is constructed as a meta-feature of rights in the sense that it does not directly flow from the nature of the rights but instead from the fact that they are positive, costly and vague.[183]

Thus, if both categories of rights are now read to incorporate the whole spectrum of obligations from negative to positive, there is no reason to uphold differentiated methodologies for their realisation. The progressive/immediate rights divide is ultimately built upon the positive/negative rights divide. Abandoning the latter dichotomy means eradicating the basis for the former.[184] Further support for this conclusion lies in the fact that there is no way of drawing clear boundaries between the categories of socio-economic and civil and political rights, particularly in the context of the CRC and CRPD.[185]

In the mind of a sceptic, one possible excuse for upholding this differentiation might be that, while all kinds of rights require *some* amount of positive

[177] For the Committee pronouncements on this matter, see 3.2.–3.4.

[178] See, eg, the references in 7.4.2.

[179] See further 1.2.3.

[180] See also Alston and Quinn 'Obligations under the ICESCR', 173.

[181] See Young, 'Waiting for Rights', 664; see also Schabas, *Nowak's CCPR Commentary*, 893: 'The recognition of positive duties necessarily brings with it a relative or dynamic element in the realization of human rights.'

[182] See also Fredman, *Human Rights Transformed*, 80.

[183] *cf* 1.2.3.

[184] See also Sepúlveda, *The Nature of the Obligations*, 123.

[185] See further 8.2.1.

action and resource allocation, socio-economic rights are different in the aspect that they require *more* action and money. With a view to practical cases, this assumption is difficult to refute.[186] It is true that socio-economic rights often concern areas that demand relatively large State activity and/or allocation of large parts of the budget, for example health care or housing.[187] However, this admission does not mandate a categorical differentiation between the groups of rights as it only concerns a difference in degree.[188] Even though it is true that socio-economic aspects usually require larger parts of the States' budget, there are also aspects of civil and political rights which raise the same issues by creating obligations which cannot be fulfilled immediately for lack of resources.

These considerations represent the origin of the hypothesis of convergence which underlies this book: if all rights create both negative and cheap and positive and expensive obligations, their respective standards of realisation might have been adapted in a convergent way in order to address the same issues which now arise irrespective of the boundaries of the traditional categories. For socio-economic rights, this would entail acknowledging that progressive realisation comprises an immediate dimension for those obligations which are negative and/or free to perform. This part of the hypothesis is relatively easy to verify because it is now generally accepted and often explicitly stated that progressive realisation entails immediate obligations, as will be shown in chapter 2. Convergent tendencies on the side of civil and political rights are more difficult to establish. This is why chapters 4 to 7 will engage in a detailed examination of Committee practice in order to test for an implicit acceptance of this progressive dimension.

It is very uncommon to explicitly acknowledge progressive elements in the realisation of civil and political rights.[189] It appears that there exists a common concern that allowing the language of progressive realisation in the context of civil and political rights would weaken their protection by allowing States parties to take their time regarding those obligations which were immediate before. As accurately summed up by Jhabvala, any mention of the idea that certain aspects of civil and political rights might only be realised in time is suspected, without fail, of being 'a scarcely-veiled attempt at justifying arbitrary and repressive rule'.[190]

[186] This is also recognised by Fowkes, 'Normal Rights, Just New', 724; see also Koch, 'Waves of Duties?', 95–96.

[187] See King, *Judging Social Rights*, 7–8, who shows that social security, health, education, and housing accounted for 69% of the UK state budget in 2009–2010.

[188] See Nolan, Porter and Langford, 'Justiciability', 100–01; Alston and Quinn 'Obligations under the ICESCR', 183–84; E Riedel, 'The Right to Life and the Right to Health, in Particular the Obligation to Reduce Child Mortality' in C Tomuschat, E Lagrange and S Oeter (eds), *The Right to Life* (Leiden, Nijhoff, 2010) 354.

[189] This has also been noted by Koch, 'Justiciability', 21.

[190] Jhabvala, 'Socio-Economic Context', 151.

Only a handful of commentators explicitly recognise progressive elements of civil and political rights, although none provide extensive arguments regarding this point.[191] One of them is Eva Brems, who agrees that limiting progressive realisation to socio-economic rights is nothing more than a reflection of artificial and outdated dichotomies between the two categories.[192] Another author who agrees with this evaluation is Gauthier de Beco, who correctly argues that a logical consequence of abandoning the other dichotomies between the two categories is extending the methodology of progressive realisation to civil and political rights.[193]

The question then arises why there is still such a firm insistence upon this remaining dichotomy. Proponents of this view would presumably find an easy answer to the question: because the treaties say so; progressive realisation is explicitly set out only for socio-economic rights. The problem is that the positive/negative divide, which has now been overcome, has led to some specific features in the treaties which are interpreted to command a differentiation between immediately and progressively realisable rights.[194] Many examples illustrate how the insistence upon the immediate/progressive rights divide is based on this textual reason rather than conceptual grounds.[195] But whether the treaties really prescribe such a differentiation is a question which will be explored in detail in part III of this book.

1.5. CONCLUSION

This chapter has shown that the conceptual differentiation between socio-economic and civil and political rights has mostly been abandoned, except for the claim that socio-economic rights are progressively realisable while civil and political rights are immediately realisable. Because we have given up all the other dichotomies which constituted the basis for this last dichotomy, there should not be different standards of realisation. Due to this lack of theoretical rationale, the suspicion arises that, in practice, immediate and progressive realisation

[191] Progressive realisation of civil and political rights is explicitly recognised by the IComJ, 'Maastricht Guidelines', para 8; only a few literary commentators also make this point; see Young, 'Waiting for Rights', 673–75; Brems, 'Minimum and Maximum Perspectives', 365–69; regarding the ICCPR, see F Jhabvala, 'Domestic Implementation' (1985) 32 *Netherlands International Law Review* 461, 467–72; Künnemann, 'A Coherent Approach', 330; regarding the CRC, see Tobin, 'Article 4', 130–31; regarding the CRPD, see Mégret, 'The Disabilities Convention', 271–72 and de Beco, 'The Indivisibility of Human Rights', 156–57; regarding the ICERD, see Castellino, 'Protecting Minorities', 233.

[192] Brems, 'Minimum and Maximum Perspectives', 365.

[193] De Beco, 'The Indivisibility of Human Rights', 157.

[194] See ibid.

[195] For an analysis of the extensive reliance on differences in the treaty texts see 7.4.1.

could function in similar ways. It seems likely that both standards take into account negative as well as positive obligations by demanding both immediate and progressive realisation. Testing this hypothesis of convergence requires comparing how the UN Committees treat both categories. The next chapter will address the first half of the convergence hypothesis by exploring the concept of progressive realisation in the context of socio-economic rights.

2

The Concept of Progressive Realisation

2.1. INTRODUCTION

UNDERSTANDING PROGRESSIVE REALISATION is a necessary part of testing the hypothesis of convergence. This hypothesis suggests that the standards applied to both socio-economic and civil and political rights work in similar ways. Traditionally, socio-economic rights have been interpreted as programmatic rights which do not require immediate action but only create vague, long-term commitments. But because it is now accepted that all rights create a range of obligations from negative and/or free to positive and/or expensive, it appears likely that progressive realisation has been adapted in a way which accommodates this range. It is no secret that progressive realisation is now interpreted to create not only obligations which are progressive in the sense that they may be fulfilled in the future but also immediate obligations. Many detailed accounts of this concept already establish this aspect.[1] Accordingly, this part of the hypothesis will require only a brief overview of the structure of progressive realisation in this chapter.

The prescription of progressive realisation was first included in Article 2 (1) of the ICESCR and subsequently transferred to the CRC and CRPD. The latter treaties include both categories of rights and expressly limit the application of this standard of realisation to socio-economic rights because it was believed that only socio-economic rights created obligations which realistically take time to fulfil. On the basis of these provisions, the Committees, alongside literary commentators, have developed an intricate conception of progressive realisation of socio-economic rights. Because it was concerned with the earliest version of these provisions, the CESCR has been central in this endeavour and its jurisprudence has been a point of reference for academics and the CRC-Com and CRPD-Com.[2] Accordingly, the CESCR's remarks will be of particular importance for this chapter.

[1] See, eg, Porter, 'Reasonableness and Article 8(4)'; Alston and Quinn 'Obligations under the ICESCR'; B Saul, DH Kinley and J Mowbray, *The International Covenant on Economic, Social and Cultural Rights: Commentary, Cases, and Materials* (Oxford, Oxford University Press, 2016) 133–72; L Chenwi, 'Unpacking "Progressive Realisation", its Relation to Resources, Minimum Core and Reasonableness, and Some Methodological Considerations for Assessing Compliance' (2013) 46 *De Jure* 742.

[2] The CRC-Com declares that, due to the parallels of general obligation provisions in the treaties, the jurisprudence of the CESCR and General Comment No 3 in particular 'should be seen

Understanding progressive realisation first requires examining the general idea behind the concept and the terminology used in this context (2.2). The chapter will then continue to examine the concept in detail, first examining the immediate obligations flowing from progressive realisation (2.3). Next, this chapter will lay out how the overall goal of full realisation informs the concrete steps which must be taken by States parties (2.4). The following section will explore the requirement of utilising the maximum of available resources (2.5). The chapter then explains the specific role of the UN Committees and the standard of review connected to progressive realisation (2.6), before closing with a conclusion (2.7).

2.2. THE GENERAL CONCEPT OF PROGRESSIVE REALISATION

Progressive realisation has been described as 'a blend of pragmatism and principle',[3] the principle aspect being that States are required to provide full positive realisation of a right, while the pragmatic aspect recalls the fact that, realistically, this will take time. The CESCR similarly acknowledges that '[t]he concept of progressive realization constitutes a recognition of the fact that full realization of all economic, social and cultural rights will generally not be able to be achieved in a short period of time'.[4] It is a 'necessary flexibility device, reflecting the realities of the real world and the difficulties involved for any country in ensuring full realization' of these rights.[5] These difficulties include financial constraints, as evidenced by Article 2 (1) of the ICESCR which requires States parties to take measures to the maximum of available resources in order to provide for progressive realisation. However, deeply entrenched societal norms and habits are also recognised as a reason for accepting the progressive realisation of a right.[6]

But the recognition that limited resources may sometimes delay full realisation does not mean that socio-economic rights do not create immediate obligations. Commentators and practitioners are adamant in stating that there are certain obligations which apply immediately.[7] The CESCR in particular repeatedly stresses that, while socio-economic rights must be realised progressively due to

as complementary' to its own General Comments, CRC-Com, 'General Comment No 5', para 5; the experts of the CRPD-Com likewise reference this document when engaging with the concept of progressive realisation, see, eg, CRPD-Com, 'General Comment No 4 on the Right to Inclusive Education' (2016) CRPD/C/GC/4, para 40 (fn).

[3] Tobin, 'Article 4', 137.

[4] CESCR, 'General Comment No 3', para 9.

[5] ibid.

[6] See E Brems, 'Accommodating Diversity in International Human Rights: Legal Techniques' in Paul Meerts (ed), *Culture and International Law*, From Peace to Justice Series 2 (The Hague, Hague Academic Press, 2008) 73–78; see also Fowkes, 'Normal Rights, Just New' and his arguments regarding newness.

[7] See, eg, UNCHR, 'Limburg Principles', para 21; Langford and King, 'CESCR', 486; for further details, see 8.3.2.1.

resource constraints, a range of immediate obligations pursuant to these rights must be considered.[8] The immediate aspect of progressive realisation is usually tied to the phrase 'undertake to take steps' in Article 2 (1) of the ICESCR. The Limburg Principles accordingly declare that '[a]ll States parties have an obligation to begin immediately to take steps towards full realization of the rights contained in the Covenant'.[9] This immediate component of progressive realisation was later also included explicitly in Article 4 (2) of the CRPD which prescribes progressive realisation for socio-economic rights 'without prejudice to those obligations contained in the present Convention that are immediately applicable according to international law'.

The following subsections will describe in more detail the way in which progressive realisation can be conceptualised, showing that a useful parallel can be drawn with Robert Alexy's theory of rights as principles (2.2.1). Another important step in understanding progressive realisation is to differentiate between the umbrella and narrow sense of the term (2.2.2). Lastly, the concept of obligations of conduct and result is a useful distinction to better understand the structure of obligations pursuant to progressive realisation (2.2.3).

2.2.1. Human Rights as Principles and Optimisation Requirements

A useful way of conceptualising progressive realisation is to utilise Alexy's theory of rights as principles. Alexy famously considered rights to be principles rather than rules, describing principles as 'optimisation requirements'.[10] With this term he meant to express that, in contrast to rules which are either violated or not, principles prescribe not one fixed level of compliance but instead demand realisation of a right to the highest degree possible in light of legal and factual possibilities. Accordingly, principles demand the 'optimisation' of conditions to varying degrees while the precise level of realisation demanded by the right varies depending on the prevailing circumstances.[11]

This is in line with the modern interpretation of progressive realisation which requires States parties to do as much as possible at any point in time in order to realise the right in question. Sandra Fredman gains useful insights by relating the ideas behind progressive realisation to Alexy's theory of rights as principles.[12] She shows that progressive realisation establishes the obligation for States parties to optimise rights as far as possible according to factual and legal circumstances. She further explains that the factor of limited resources and the

[8] See, eg, CESCR, 'General Comment No 3', para 1 and CESCR, 'General Comment No 15', para 17.

[9] UNCHR, 'Limburg Principles', para 16.

[10] R Alexy and J Rivers (trans), *A Theory of Constitutional Rights* (Oxford, Oxford University Press, 2010).

[11] ibid, 47–48.

[12] See Fredman, *Human Rights Transformed*, 80–81.

prioritisation of other (expensive) competing principles constitute the pivotal limitations to the immediate realisation of rights. Constructing progressive realisation in this way also explains why immediate obligations are a necessary component of this concept. If a right is a principle which demands optimisation to the highest degree possible at any time, then this achievable degree of realisation is an immediate obligation. In other words, if there are no competing principles or resource constraints justifying a delay in realisation, this certain aspect is subject to an immediate obligation of realisation.[13]

This conceptualisation helps in understanding the combination of immediate and progressive obligations pursuant to progressive realisation. It clearly shows that States parties must immediately realise as much of the right as possible and may only delay the realisation of certain aspects if it is justifiable to give precedence to other competing principles. This means that progressiveness in the sense of a temporal delay of certain results is only allowed as far as this is justified by resource (or other) constraints. Accordingly, progressive realisation is a tool flexible enough to accommodate all dimensions of resource requirements, from absolutely free to very costly. If a right requires little or no resources, progressive realisation will allow little or no wriggle room regarding the timeframe of realisation.

Another useful insight which can be gained from this conceptualisation is that progressive realisation requires balancing interests or, more generally, an analysis of proportionality.[14] This recognition creates a synchronism between negative and positive obligations. Regarding the negative dimension of rights, it is generally recognised that conflicting interests can justify active interference by the State with the interests protected by these rights.[15] Resource dependency and progressive realisation serve the same purpose in the context of positive obligations. When a State must make decisions regarding the allocation of resources, it becomes necessary to balance different interests protected by human rights. In case of limited resources, it is possible that one positive aspect must stand back in favour of another, which makes the realisation of the former progressive.

2.2.2. The Umbrella and Narrow Meaning of Progressive Realisation

The finding that progressive realisation entails immediate obligations leads to ambiguities in terminology. Progressive realisation is used with two different

[13] See Fredman, *Human Rights Transformed*, 80–81.

[14] For an inquiry into the differences and similarities between reasonableness review and proportionality analysis, see KG Young, 'Proportionality, Reasonableness, and Economic and Social Rights' in VC Jackson and M Tushnet (eds), *Proportionality: New Frontiers, New Challenges*, Comparative Constitutional Law and Policy (Cambridge, Cambridge University Press, 2017).

[15] This is reflected, for example, in Article 12 (3) of the ICCPR which establishes that the right to liberty of movement is subject to restrictions which are necessary to protect, eg, 'the rights and freedoms of others'.

meanings. For example, the authors of one contribution state that '[t]he full scope of … rights in ICESCR is subject to progressive realization' but then continue to declare that 'this does not mean that all obligations have to be realized progressively: certain obligations are to be realized immediately'.[16] At first, this statement appears contradictory because the authors first state that all rights under the ICESCR are progressively realisable but then continue to say that not all obligations are to be realised progressively.

Here, it is useful to distinguish between what can be called the umbrella and the narrow understandings of progressive realisation. The key to untangling this terminological issue is to clarify whether one is talking about *rights* or *obligations*. The progressive realisation of *rights* encompasses both immediate and progressive *obligations*. In the umbrella sense, progressiveness refers to the realisation of rights as a whole. The complete realisation of the right is a process which takes time. It is this umbrella understanding that the authors refer to in the first sentence of the above quote. The umbrella concept of progressively realisable *rights* includes both immediate *obligations* and progressive *obligations*. On the level of obligations, progressiveness denotes those obligations which are progressive in the strict sense of the word, ie, those obligations in relation to which the State party is justified in delaying complete realisation. This meaning of the term becomes relevant in the second sentence of the above quote.

This duality of immediate and progressive obligations under the umbrella term of progressive realisation is also reflected in the text of the CRPD. Article 4 (2) of the CRPD prescribes that States undertake to progressively realise socio-economic rights to the maximum of their available resources 'without prejudice to those obligations contained in the present Convention that are immediately applicable according to international law'. The CRPD thereby utilises progressive realisation in its umbrella sense when referring to the full realisation of rights. On the level of obligations, however, Article 4 (2) of the CRPD implies a differentiation between immediate obligations and obligations which are progressive in the narrow sense of the word.

The ambiguity of the terminology contributes to the stubborn perception that progressive realisation is a weak standard. Some commentators only proceed from the narrow understanding, thinking that any action towards the realisation of the right may be delayed by the States parties, forgetting that the umbrella meaning of the term includes immediate obligations. Langford and King correctly note that the 'most persistent myth about the Covenant is that it does not give rise to the obligation to act in a particular way immediately'.[17] This misunderstanding is also the reason for the concern that progressive realisation could provide excuses for States parties to avoid putting in any work

[16] R O'Connell, A Nolan, C Harvey, M Dutschke and E Rooney, *Applying an International Human Rights Framework to State Budget Allocations: Rights and Resources* (London, Routledge, 2014) 79.

[17] Langford and King, 'CESCR', 486.

towards the realisation of socio-economic rights by pointing to the concept of progressive realisation. The insistence that progressive realisation is no excuse for inaction appears to not alleviate concerns that States *unwilling* to fulfil rights may invoke the term even though it only allows a delay regarding aspects which States are *unable* to realise at once.

2.2.3. Obligations of Conduct and Result

Another helpful way of explaining the coexistence of immediate and progressive obligations is to think about the concept of obligations of conduct and result.[18] Already in 1987, Philip Alston and Gerard Quinn (the former of whom would later become Chairperson of the CESCR) considered the rights under the ICESCR to create a combination of obligations of conduct and result.[19] According to Alston and Quinn, the obligation to take steps is one of conduct while the obligation of States parties 'to match their performance with their objective capabilities' is one of result.[20] This, in fact, implies a threefold set of obligations consisting of an immediate obligation of conduct to take steps, an immediate obligation of result, namely making the best of available resources at any point in time, and a long-term obligation to produce the result of full realisation.[21]

The CESCR later adopted General Comment No 3 on States Parties' Obligations which confirms this coexistence of obligations of conduct and result. Referencing the work of the International Law Commission (ILC), the experts state that the obligations under Article 2 (1) of the ICESCR include obligations of conduct as well as result.[22] The CESCR continues to clarify that States parties are generally under an obligation to immediately 'take steps', which is an obligation 'not qualified or limited by other considerations'.[23] Accordingly, while the full realisation of the right in question is to be achieved only progressively, those steps must be taken 'within a reasonably short time after the Covenant's entry into force for the States concerned'.[24] Regarding full

[18] See also Saul, Kinley and Mowbray, *The ICESCR*, 137; GS Goodwin-Gill, 'Obligations of Conduct and Result' in P Alston and K Tomaševski (eds), *The Right to Food*, International Studies in Human Rights 4 (Boston, Nijhoff, 1984).

[19] Alston and Quinn, 'Obligations under the ICESCR', 185.

[20] ibid.

[21] Regarding this last obligation, see also IComJ, 'Maastricht Guidelines', para 7; Craven, *The ICESCR*, 107.

[22] CESCR, 'General Comment No 3', para 1; the CRC-Com also mentions this differentiation, see CRC-Com, 'General Comment No 16 on State Obligations Regarding the Impact of the Business Sector on Children's Rights' (2013) CRC/C/GC/16, para 25.

[23] CESCR, 'General Comment No 3', para 2.

[24] ibid; see also CESCR, 'General Comment No 15: The Right to Water (arts. 11 and 12 of the International Covenant on Economic, Social and Cultural Rights)' (2003) E/C.12/2002/11, para 17; CESCR, 'General Comment No 13: The Right to Education (Article 13 of the Covenant)' (1999) E/C.12/1999/10, para 43.

realisation, the CESCR states that '[t]he principal obligation of result reflected in article 2 (1) is to take steps "with a view to achieving progressively the full realization of the rights recognized" in the Covenant'.[25] It becomes clear that the experts interpret Article 2 (1) of the ICESCR to impose upon States parties a progressive obligation of result concerning the full realisation of rights and an immediate obligation of conduct which is to take steps towards this goal.

It is important, however, not to overstate this delimitation between obligations of conduct and result.[26] Formulating an obligation of conduct always requires stating the long-term goal towards which the conduct must be targeted. Reversely, an obligation of result must always be formulated in terms of a specific course of action in order to provide tangible guidance for States parties.[27] For progressive realisation, this means that the obligation to take steps only receives its meaning when it is clarified that the steps must be targeted towards the long-term result of full realisation. The requirement of immediate steps implies progressiveness because the steps must promote a long-term goal. In relation to the long-term goal, this means that States parties' obligations must be concretised to specific steps in order to make this obligation tangible.

2.3. THE IMMEDIATE OBLIGATIONS

The experts of the CESCR state again and again that there are two obligations of immediate application in Article 2 (1) of the ICESCR: the obligation to 'take steps' and the obligation to guarantee rights without discrimination. In addition, there is another obligation which is treated as immediate even though the experts do not explicitly use this terminology: the CESCR considers that the duty to respect human rights only entails the obligation to abstain from certain behaviour, which is also constructed as an immediately applicable obligation. By now, this long-standing interpretation of progressive realisation as entailing immediate obligations has been explicitly included in the text of the CRPD as the newest of the treaties examined here. Article 4 (2) of the CRPD sets out that socio-economic rights are progressively realisable 'without prejudice to those obligations contained in the present Convention that are immediately applicable according to international law'.

The immediacy of the obligation to take steps (in contrast to the obligation of complete realisation) rests on the common assertion that '[t]he "availability of resources", although an important qualifier to the obligation to take steps, does not alter the immediacy of the obligation, nor can

[25] CESCR, 'General Comment No 3', para 9.

[26] See also S Leckie, 'Another Step Towards Indivisibility: Identifying the Key Features of Violations of Economic, Social and Cultural Rights' (1998) 20 *Human Rights Quarterly* 81, 92.

[27] See Craven, *The ICESCR*, 107.

resource constraints alone justify inaction'.[28] According to the experts, there is always something that can be done; 'even where the available resources are demonstrably inadequate, the obligation remains for a State party to strive to ensure the widest possible enjoyment of the relevant rights under the prevailing circumstances.'[29] This position is also taken by the CRC-Com and CRPD-Com.[30]

When the Committees and literary commentators lay out which steps must be taken immediately, they usually refer to the conception of a strategy targeted towards the full realisation of the right, which will be illustrated in the first subsection (2.3.1). As the second subsection will explain, the insistence upon the immediacy of non-discrimination is meant to refer only to de jure non-discrimination, while it is acknowledged that de facto equality requires time to realise (2.3.2). The third and last subsection will show that the obligation of States 'to match their performance with their objective capabilities'[31] at any point in time means that they may be under an immediate obligation of result when individual cases are concerned (2.3.3).

2.3.1. Strategies, Policies, and Plans of Action

It is generally agreed that one aspect which must be addressed immediately, regardless of resource constraints, is adopting a strategy, policy, or plan of action which is targeted towards the full realisation of the right in question and engages with the necessary measures and resources.[32] According to the interpretation of the CESCR, Article 14 of the ICESCR provides further guidance in this matter. This provision declares that States parties must develop 'a detailed plan of action for the progressive implementation, within a reasonable number of years, … of the principle of compulsory free education free of charge for all'.[33] This plan must be developed regardless of available resources, as this obligation only applies when a party 'has not been able to secure … compulsory primary education, free of charge', ie, when States parties are not able to fully realise the right immediately. The CESCR holds that this obligation of developing a plan 'applies, almost by definition, to situations characterized by inadequate financial resources'.[34] This obligation, although not mentioned explicitly elsewhere in the

[28] CESCR, 'An Evaluation of the Obligation to Take Steps to the "Maximum of Available Resources" under an Optional Protocol to the Covenant' (21 September 2007) E/C.12/2007/1, para 4.
[29] CESCR, 'General Comment No 3', para 11.
[30] See, for example CRC-Com, 'General Comment No 5', para 8 with reference to CESCR, 'General Comment No 3', para 11.
[31] Alston and Quinn, 'Obligations under the ICESCR', 185.
[32] See, eg, Saul, Kinley and Mowbray, *The ICESCR*, 166.
[33] Article 14 of the ICESCR.
[34] CESCR, 'General Comment No 11: Plans of Action for Primary Education (Article 14 of the International Covenant on Economic, Social and Cultural Rights)' (1999) E/C.12/1999/4, para 9.

Covenant, is held by the experts of the CESCR to be 'clearly implied by the obligation in article 2, paragraph 1 "to take steps ... by all appropriate means ..."'.[35]

Accordingly, the CESCR repeatedly places planning at the centre of the immediate obligation to take steps. States parties must immediately perform legislative review,[36] introduce monitoring mechanisms, and design and implement strategies, programmes, plans of action, and timeframes for the realisation of rights.[37] The same obligations apply in the context of striving for substantive equality: States parties must design and start to implement 'permanent policies and strategies undertaken to achieve equality of men and women'[38] and 'take concrete, deliberate and targeted measures' regarding the elimination of discrimination.[39] In the socio-economic rights jurisprudence of the CRPD, the experts likewise repeatedly declare that progressive realisation requires State parties to immediately design and adopt concrete strategies and plans of action.[40] The failure to take any such steps will therefore result in a violation of the treaties. This has been declared explicitly by the CESCR, for example, in cases where States parties fail to adopt a national policy in the area of health or water which is defined as a violation of the obligation to fulfil the right to the highest attainable standard of health under Article 12 of the ICESCR or the right to water under Articles 11, 12 of the ICESCR.[41]

Progressive realisation as a concept recognises that not every aspect of a right can be realised at once. Accordingly, strategies and policies in this regard must necessarily prioritise certain aspects over others. The Committees commonly require that policies for progressive realisation prioritise particularly vulnerable groups.[42] Processes of devising a strategy or a plan of action 'shall give particular attention to all vulnerable or marginalized groups'.[43] This is stressed in particular for cases where severe resource constraints exist.[44]

[35] CESCR, 'General Comment No 1: Reporting by States parties' (1981) E/1989/22, para 4.

[36] ibid, para 2.

[37] CESCR, 'General Comment No 3', para 11; CESCR, 'General Comment No 1', para 3; CESCR, 'General Comment No 15', para 46; CESCR, 'General Comment No 4', para 12; CESCR, 'General Comment No 12', para 21.

[38] CESCR, 'General Comment No 16: The Equal Right of Men and Women to the Enjoyment of all Economic, Social and Cultural Rights (art. 3 of the International Covenant on Economic, Social and Cultural Rights)' (2005) E/C.12/2005/4, para 35; see also ibid, para 32; CESCR, 'General Comment No 20: Nondiscrimination in Economic, Social and Cultural Rights (art. 2, para. 2, of the International Covenant on Economic, Social and Cultural Rights)' (2009) E/C.12/GC/20, para 38.

[39] CESCR, 'General Comment No 20', para 36.

[40] CRPD-Com, 'General Comment No 5 on Living Independently and being Included in the Community' (2017) CRPD/C/GC/5, paras 39, 42; CRPD-Com, 'General Comment No 4', para 42.

[41] CESCR, 'General Comment No 14: The Right to the Highest Attainable Standard of Health (Article 12 of the International Covenant on Economic, Social and Cultural Rights)' (2000) E/C.12/2000/4, para 52; CESCR, 'General Comment No 15', paras 43, 44 (c).

[42] See, eg, CESCR, 'General Comment No 3', para 12.

[43] CESCR, 'General Comment No 14', para 43 (f); see also CESCR, 'General Comment No 4', para 8 (e); CESCR, 'General Comment No 15', para 37 (h).

[44] CESCR, 'General Comment No 6: The Economic, Social and Cultural Rights of Older Persons' (1995) E/1996/22, para 17.

2.3.2. Non-discrimination

Another aspect which is often declared to be of immediate effect is non-discrimination.[45] According to the CESCR, States parties are under an obligation to immediately guarantee rights without discrimination in line with Articles 2 (2) and 3 of the ICESCR.[46] According to the CESCR, non-discrimination is a matter which 'does not necessarily require significant resource allocations' and which therefore is not subject to progressive realisation.[47]

However, it is important to differentiate between de jure and de facto equality. While de jure equality requires only the abolition of discrimination in law, de facto or substantive equality requires actively counteracting biases in society and reducing structural barriers to the equal enjoyment of rights. While the former concept is subject to immediate realisation, it is generally recognised that the creation of substantive equality takes time and, therefore, is subject to progressive realisation. The Limburg Principles on the Implementation of the ICESCR explicitly differentiate between these two components of the obligation of non-discrimination. Regarding de jure discrimination, the Principles hold that, upon signing the Covenant, States parties must abolish 'without delay any discriminatory laws, regulations and practices' which inhibit the equal enjoyment of socio-economic rights. De facto discrimination, according to the Principles, results from unequal enjoyment of rights due to a lack of resources or other reasons. This aspect of discrimination 'should be brought to an end as speedily as possible'.[48] While the terms 'without delay' and 'as speedily as possible' are not completely analogous to immediate and progressive realisation, it does appear that the Limburg Principles recognise a difference between aspects of discrimination which may be redressed relatively quickly by removing discriminatory legislation and other aspects which concern more complex inequalities and will require time to eradicate.

This conception of equality also becomes apparent in the CESCR's jurisprudence.[49] In the context of Article 3 ICESCR, the experts made the following statement:

> Guarantees of non-discrimination and equality in international human rights treaties mandate both de facto and de jure equality. De jure (or formal) equality and de facto

[45] See UNCHR, 'Limburg Principles', para 22, 35; A Chapman and S Russell, 'Introduction' in A Chapman and S Russell (eds), *Core Obligations: Building a Framework for Economic, Social and Cultural Rights* (Antwerp, Intersentia, 2002) 6.

[46] See CESCR, 'General Comment No 3', para 1; CESCR, 'General Comment No 15', para 17; CESCR, 'General Comment No 16', para 16.

[47] CESCR, 'Evaluation of the Obligation to Take Steps to the Maximum of Available Resources', para 7; see also CESCR, 'General Comment No 13', para 31.

[48] UNCHR, 'Limburg Principles', paras 37–38.

[49] For an analysis of the CESCR's jurisprudence in this context, see R Brown, L Chenwi and MA Stein, 'Equality and Non-Discrimination' in M Langford, B Porter, R Brown and J Rossi (eds), *The Optional Protocol to the International Covenant on Economic, Social and Cultural Rights: A Commentary* (Pretoria, Pretoria University Law Press, 2016) 254–57; see also Young, 'Waiting for Rights', 663–64.

> (or substantive) equality are different but interconnected concepts. Formal equality assumes that equality is achieved if a law or policy treats men and women in a neutral manner. Substantive equality is concerned, in addition, with the effects of laws, policies and practices and with ensuring that they do not maintain, but rather alleviate, the inherent disadvantage that particular groups experience.[50]

It becomes clear in the further jurisprudence of the Committee that the assertion of immediacy and unconditionality regarding non-discrimination only refers to the aspect of formal equality. One illustrative example are the CESCR's remarks on equal representation of women in the scientific field. According to the experts, the underrepresentation of women can depend either on 'situations of direct discrimination in access to education or professional employment and promotion' or on more subtle discrimination in the form of 'stereotypes or professional practices that discourage women's participation in scientific research'.[51]

In order to deal with these two dimensions of inequality, States parties must, on the one hand, 'immediately eliminate barriers' for the equal participation of women and girls in education, employment and scientific research. On the other hand, States must 'take steps to ensure women's substantive equality in access to scientific education and careers', for example by conducting public awareness campaigns which are targeted at eliminating stereotypes detrimental to the equal participation of women in science.[52] In general, States parties must 'make all necessary efforts to overcome persistent inequalities' in this regard, particularly through means of education and communication.[53]

These statements imply that States parties must immediately rescind laws and regulations hindering the equal enjoyment of human rights for certain groups, therefore creating de jure equality. The de facto equal enjoyment of these rights, however, is an aspect dependent on much more than the adoption of non-discrimination legislation and can, realistically, only be achieved over time. Accordingly, States parties must immediately undertake steps towards the progressive realisation of substantive or de facto equality. Therefore, States parties are under an immediate obligation of conduct regarding 'taking steps' towards substantive equality, while reaching this overall goal must be understood as a progressive obligation of result.

This is confirmed by the CESCR's conception of 'temporary special measures'. This term refers to measures which temporarily privilege a group of persons in order to compensate systemic disadvantages of these groups.[54] Temporary

[50] CESCR, 'General Comment No 16', para 7; see also CESCR, 'General Comment No 20', para 8.

[51] CESCR, 'General Comment No 25 on Science and Economic, Social and Cultural Rights (Article 15 (1) (b), (2), (3) and (4) of the International Covenant on Economic, Social and Cultural Rights)' (2020) E/C.12/GC/25, para 29.

[52] ibid, para 31.

[53] ibid, para 26.

[54] See CESCR, 'General Comment No 16', paras 35–36.

measures are clearly envisioned as part of a process for creating substantive equality as they are often described as being tailored 'to *accelerate* women's equal enjoyment of their rights' (emphasis added).[55] The temporal aspect also becomes apparent when the Committee declares that these measures must be 'discontinued when substantive equality has been sustainably achieved'.[56] A similar conceptualisation is conducted by the CERD and CEDAW-Com, which shows that these Committees also adopt a progressive understanding of realisation regarding substantive equality.[57]

2.3.3. Immediate Obligations of Result in Individual Cases

When speaking about State conduct in general, taking steps to the maximum of available resources is not tied to a specific result. Accordingly, this obligation is described as an obligation of conduct. However, when exchanging the variables of the equation with specific facts from an individual case, the situation changes. It is then possible to determine in detail which degree of realisation is mandated at a certain point by conducting an evaluation whether the denial of positive measures by the State party would be reasonable and proportionate. In individual cases, the precise extent of positive obligations required by States parties must thus be determined by an assessment of proportionality. In this way, the obligation to take steps can be pinned down to a specific obligation of result if the details of an individual case are known.[58]

This becomes clear in the CESCR's decisions in Individual Communications cases. In *Djazia and Bellili v Spain*, the CESCR adopted such an individual-oriented approach by holding that,

> [i]n the event that a person is evicted from his or her home without the State granting or guaranteeing alternative accommodation, the State party must demonstrate that it has considered the specific circumstances of the case and that, despite having taken all reasonable measures, to the maximum of its available resources, it has been unable to uphold the right to housing of the person concerned.[59]

A look at the CRPD-Com's socio-economic rights jurisprudence confirms this result. Rights which are generally progressively realisable under Article 4 (2) of the CRPD are interpreted to translate into immediate duties of result limited by disproportionality. In *Gröninger v Germany*, the Committee found that the

[55] ibid, paras 21, 35, 36; see also CESCR, 'General Comment No 20', para 38.

[56] CESCR, 'General Comment No 20', para 9.

[57] See further 4.4.2.

[58] Arguably, this is what Alston and Quinn meant when they argued that States parties are under an obligation of result which requires that they 'match their performance with their objective capabilities', see Alston and Quinn 'Obligations under the ICESCR', 185.

[59] CESCR, *Djazia and Bellili v Spain* [Adoption of Views] (20 June 2017) E/C.12/61/D/5/2015, para 15.5.

author's son's right to work and employment under Article 27 of the CRPD was violated not only due to a general failure to adopt sufficient legislative measures in general,[60] but also due to a failure to take sufficient specific measures in his case to integrate him into the labour market.[61] The State party failed not only to take the necessary steps in general but also to produce the required result in the case of the author.

2.4. ENSURING PROGRESS TOWARDS COMPLETE FULFILMENT

While the long-term goal of full realisation itself might be difficult to grasp in terms of State obligations, it has a direct influence on the concrete and immediate obligations incurred by States parties. The complete fulfilment of the right is the final aim of all measures taken in this context, and this target must also inform the way in which these measures are planned and executed. The efforts of a State party must always be modelled in a way which ensures that States parties 'move as expeditiously as possible' towards the complete fulfilment of the right,[62] thus establishing a dependable 'continuum of improvement'.[63] Scott Leckie aptly explains that this standard requires 'a constantly expanding web of legal protection for all right holders'.[64]

The Committees are likewise insistent that the ultimate goal of all measures by States parties in the context of human rights is to fully realise the rights in the treaties. According to the CESCR, all obligations in the context of progressive realisation must be interpreted in light of 'the overall objective, indeed the raison d'être, of the Covenant which is to establish clear obligations for States parties in respect of the full realization of the rights in question'.[65] Progressive realisation is thus interpreted to entail the 'constant and continuing duty'[66] to move as expeditiously and effectively as possible towards that goal.[67] States parties must, for example, take measures in order to allow everyone the enjoyment of the highest attainable standard of health 'as soon as possible'.[68]

This leads to a number of features in the system of obligations which are constructed in the context of progressive realisation. In order to ensure that full realisation is indeed furthered by States parties' conduct, the Committees commonly emphasise that, firstly, all measures must be targeted clearly towards

[60] CRPD-Com, *Gröninger v Germany* [Adoption of Views] (4 April 2010) E/C.12/61/D/5/2015, para 6.2.

[61] ibid, para 6.3.

[62] UNCHR, 'Limburg Principles', para 21.

[63] S Byrne, 'Reclaiming Progressive Realisation: A Children's Rights Analysis' (2020) 28 *International Journal of Children's Rights* 748, 767.

[64] Leckie, 'Another Step Towards Indivisibility', 94.

[65] CESCR, 'General Comment No 3', para 9.

[66] CESCR, 'General Comment No 15', para 18.

[67] CESCR, 'General Comment No 3', para 9; see also CESCR, 'General Comment No 13', para 44.

[68] CESCR, 'General Comment No 14', para 53.

the full realisation of human rights (2.4.1), secondly, progress towards that goal must be continuously monitored (2.4.2), and, thirdly, retrogressive steps are only permissible in exceptional circumstances (2.4.3).

2.4.1. Goal-driven Alignment of Immediate Measures

States parties must not just take any measures immediately but select those measures which are best suited to achieve the relevant long-term goal, ie, the full realisation of the right in question.[69] This means that the immediate measures laid out in the previous subsection 'should be deliberate, concrete and targeted as clearly as possible towards meeting the obligations recognized in the Covenant'.[70] For example, human rights strategies must clearly be aligned with the long-term goal of full realisation and, therefore, must 'define clear objectives' and 'set targets or goals to be achieved and the time-frame for their achievement'.[71] In the context of sexual and reproductive health, the experts of the CESCR hold that States parties must adopt measures to 'combat attitudes that perpetuate inequality and discrimination' and 'recognize, and take measures to rectify, entrenched social norms and power structures that impair the equal exercise' of rights under the Covenant.[72] The obligation to protect in the context of the right to equality between men and women under Article 3 of the ICESCR is interpreted to require States parties to 'take steps aimed directly at the elimination of prejudices, customary and all other practices that perpetuate the notion of inferiority or superiority of either of the sexes, and stereotyped roles for men and women'.[73]

2.4.2. Monitoring, Indicators, Benchmarks, Data

In order to ensure the goal-driven alignment set out in the previous subsection, States parties must at all times be aware of their level of progress in the fulfilment of rights and the effectiveness of the measures already taken. According to

[69] See O'Connell, Nolan, Harvey, Dutschke and Rooney, *Applying an International Human Rights Framework*, 67.

[70] CESCR, 'General Comment No 3', para 2; see also CESCR, 'Evaluation of the Obligation to Take Steps to the Maximum of Available Resources', paras 3, 8 (a); CESCR, 'General Comment No 15', para 17; CESCR, 'General Comment No 13', para 43; CESCR, 'General Comment No 14', para 30.

[71] CESCR, 'General Comment No 15', para 47; see also CRPD-Com, 'General Comment No 5', para 41.

[72] CESCR, 'General Comment No 22 on the Right to Sexual and Reproductive Health (Article 12 of the International Covenant on Economic, Social and Cultural Rights)' (2016) E/C.12/GC/22, para 35; see also CESCR, 'General Comment No 25', para 25.

[73] CESCR, 'General Comment No 16', para 19.

many commentators and practitioners, this requires monitoring the realisation of those rights by developing and applying criteria and indicators for assessing compliance.[74] The CESCR holds that States parties must immediately start and always continue 'monitor[ing] the extent of the realisation, or more especially of the non-realization, of economic, social and cultural rights' and draw from this consequences for their programmes of action.[75] Monitoring, according to the experts, 'is an integral part of any process designed to promote accepted goals of public policy'.[76] The same is true for the realisation of substantive equality; monitoring of policies aimed at promoting the equal enjoyment of socio-economic rights is described as an integral part of the obligation to fulfil the right to non-discrimination under Article 3 ICESCR.[77]

Frequently, benchmarks and indicators are recommended as tools for measuring progress. Regarding the monitoring of human rights compliance or, specifically, the progressive fulfilment of socio-economic rights, the CESCR holds that benchmarks or specific goals may prove useful in evaluating the level of progress made towards the full realisation of rights in the Covenant.[78] The UNHCHR, in the context of socio-economic rights, stated that, '[t]o assess progress over time in the implementation of rights, statistical human rights indicators must be combined with specific targets and benchmarks'.[79] Indicators, benchmarks, and disaggregated statistics are also set out as requirements for a policy in the context of pursuing substantive equality by the CESCR.[80] Guidance in the development of indicators and benchmarks can be obtained through cooperation with international organisations such as the World Health Organization, UNICEF, the International Labour Organization and others.[81]

Measuring progress with reference to indicators and benchmarks furthermore requires a reliable, available, and frequently updated set of data. States parties need to know which obligations are realised to which extent regarding which

[74] See UNCHR, 'Limburg Principles', para 89; IComJ, 'Maastricht Guidelines', para 15 (f); Craven, *The ICESCR*, 142; M Green, 'What We Talk About When We Talk About Indicators: Current Approaches to Human Rights Measurement' (2001) 23 *Human Rights Quarterly* 1062; J Heymann, K McNeill, and A Raub, 'Rights Monitoring and Assessment Using Quantitative Indicators of Law and Policy: International Covenant on Economic, Social and Cultural Rights' (2015) 37 *Human Rights Quarterly* 1071.

[75] CESCR, 'General Comment No 3', para 11; see also CESCR, 'General Comment No 4', para 13; CESCR, 'General Comment No 5: Persons with Disabilities' (1994) E/1995/22, para 13.

[76] CESCR, 'General Comment No 1', para 3.

[77] CESCR, 'General Comment No 16', para 21; see also CESCR, 'General Comment No 20', para 41.

[78] CESCR, 'General Comment No 1', para 6; see also CESCR, 'General Comment No 14', paras 43 (f), 57, 58; CESCR, 'General Comment No 15', para 47; CESCR, 'General Comment No 12', para 29.

[79] UNHCHR, 'Report of the United Nations High Commissioner for Human Rights on Progressive Realization' (25 June 2007) E/2007/82, para 53.

[80] CESCR, 'General Comment No 16', para 39; CESCR, 'General Comment No 20', para 41.

[81] CESCR, 'General Comment No 15', para 53.

group of persons, making data collection an 'inherent process requirement' of progressive realisation.[82] The Committees thus interpret their respective treaties to entail an obligation of accumulating the necessary data and making this data public for review.[83] Qualitative and quantitative data, according to the experts, are central in determining the 'progress over time' made by States parties.[84]

2.4.3. Non-retrogression

The previous subsection has shown that progressive realisation represents the idea of continuous improvement towards the goal of complete fulfilment. Accordingly, a major component of this standard of realisation is the prohibition of measures by States parties which reverse the process of expansion.[85] This enables States parties to 'lock in' progress which has been achieved, making regression the absolute exception.[86] Limited resources can generally not justify the active interference with existing levels of rights protection unless there are exceptional circumstances which necessitate such measures. Accordingly, retrogressive measures constitute prima facie violations of socio-economic rights through an act of commission.[87]

The CESCR considers that '[t]here is a strong presumption' that retrogressive measures regarding the enjoyment of rights under the ICESCR are in violation of the Covenant.[88] If States parties undertake such retrogressive steps and therefore reduce the current level of realisation,

> the burden of proof rests with the State party to show that such a course of action was based on the most careful consideration and can be justified by reference to the totality of the rights provided for in the Covenant and by the fact that full use was made of available resources.[89]

The same is true for the right to non-discrimination, ie, retrogressive steps concerning the progress of creating complete substantive equality.[90]

[82] O'Connell, Nolan, Harvey, Dutschke and Rooney, *Applying an International Human Rights Framework*, 69.

[83] CESCR, 'General Comment No 4', para 13.

[84] CESCR, 'General Comment No 1', para 7.

[85] See J Wills and B Warwick, 'Contesting Austerity: The Potential and Pitfalls of Socioeconomic Rights Discourse' (2016) 23 *Indiana Journal of Global Legal Studies* 629, 653.

[86] ibid; see also A Nolan, 'Two Steps Forward, No Steps Back?: Evolving Criteria on the Prohibition of Retrogression in Economic and Social Rights' in A Nolan (ed), *Economic and Social Rights after the Global Financial Crisis* (Cambridge, Cambridge University Press, 2014).

[87] See IComJ, 'Maastricht Guidelines', para 14 (e).

[88] CESCR, 'General Comment No 15', para 19; see also CESCR, 'General Comment No 13', para 45; CESCR, 'General Comment No 14', para 32.

[89] CESCR, 'Evaluation of the Obligation to Take Steps to the Maximum of Available Resources', para 9; see also CESCR, 'General Comment No 3', para 9; CESCR, 'General Comment No 13', para 45; CESCR, 'General Comment No 14', para 32.

[90] See CESCR, 'General Comment No 16', para 42.

In order to assist with the determination whether the State party has met its burden of proof when claiming that resource constraints require retrogressive steps, the CESCR has laid down a number of criteria. On a 'country-by-country basis', the experts will consider the country's level of development and current economic situation, including any particular 'serious claims on the State party's limited resources', and the severity of the alleged breach. Furthermore, the State party must show that it has 'sought to identify low-cost options' and cooperation and international assistance in order to prevent retrogression.[91]

2.5. THE MAXIMUM OF AVAILABLE RESOURCES

Article 2 (1) of the ICESCR, Article 4 (2) of the CRPD and Article 4 of the CRC further set out that, in relation to socio-economic rights, States parties are obliged to utilise the maximum of their available resources when undertaking progressive realisation. The concept of limited resources and the progressive realisation of rights are intertwined. Accepting that, at a certain point in time, not enough resources may be available to fully realise a right for everyone necessarily leads to the recognition that full realisation will take time.[92] Thus, limited resources determine how much a State party can and must do at a certain point in time while, at the same time, influencing the tempo at which full realisation can and must be progressively achieved.

This inextricable connection between resource dependency and progressive realisation becomes particularly clear in the CRC-Com's interpretation of Article 4 of the CRC. The provision sets out that '[w]ith regard to economic, social and cultural rights, States Parties shall undertake such measures to the maximum extent of their available resources'. Article 4 of the CRC thus refers to limited resources but not to progressive realisation. However, the CRC-Com considers progressive realisation to be implied by the acceptance of resource limitations:

> [A]rticle 4 reflects a realistic acceptance that lack of resources … can hamper the full implementation of economic, social and cultural rights in some States; this introduces the concept of 'progressive realization' of such rights.[93]

Firstly, the requirement to use the maximum of available resources is commonly read to mean that States parties are required to consider human rights obligations already during the phase of budgeting. In other words, available resources include not only those earmarked for a certain sector but all resources available to the State party (2.5.1). Furthermore, it has been made clear that the concept

[91] CESCR, 'Evaluation of the Obligation to Take Steps to the Maximum of Available Resources', para 10.

[92] See Alston and Quinn, 'Obligations under the ICESCR', 173.

[93] CRC-Com, 'General Comment No 5', para 7; CRC-Com, 'General Comment No 19', para 24.

of available resources also includes those resources available through international cooperation (2.5.2). Lastly, it is generally agreed that there are certain core elements of socio-economic rights which are not subject to the availability of resources (2.5.3).

2.5.1. Nature and Availability of Resources

Resources in the sense of the relevant provisions in the ICESCR, CRC and CRPD are not just money but encompass a range of 'financial, natural, human, technological, and informational' resources of the State party.[94] The CESCR clarifies that, when full realisation of a right is delayed due to resource constraints, States parties must demonstrate that they utilised all available resources:

> If resource constraints render it impossible for a State to comply fully with its Covenant obligations, it has the burden of justifying that every effort has nevertheless been made to use all available resources at its disposal in order to satisfy, as a matter of priority, the obligations outlined above.[95]

This burden of justification is a way to 'distinguish the inability from the unwillingness' of States parties to fulfil their rights.[96]

Since human rights obligations must be satisfied as a matter of priority, States parties cannot simply justify their pace or level of realisation based on the fact that resources are earmarked for other sectors and therefore not available in the sense of Article 2 (1) of the ICESCR and its sister provisions in the CRPD and CRC.[97] Consequently, human rights and efforts to move towards their full realisation must find expression already in States parties' budgets. The experts of the CESCR repeatedly stress that States parties must undertake budgetary measures as part of their strategies and policies aimed at progressive realisation.[98] Also, the goal of substantive equality should

[94] RE Robertson, 'Measuring State Compliance with the Obligation to Devote the "Maximum Available Resources" to Realizing Economic, Social, and Cultural Rights' (1994) 16 *Human Rights Quarterly* 693, 697; see also Saul, Kinley and Mowbray, *The ICESCR*, 144.

[95] CESCR, 'General Comment No 14', para 47.

[96] CESCR, 'General Comment No 12', para 17; see also CESCR, 'General Comment No 14', para 47.

[97] See Robertson, 'Measuring State Compliance', 698; Alston and Quinn 'Obligations under the ICESCR', 177–81.

[98] See CESCR, 'General Comment No 14', para 33; CESCR, 'General Comment No 17: The Right of Everyone to Benefit from the Protection of the Moral and Material Interests Resulting from any Scientific, Literary or Artistic Production of which He or She is the Author (Article 15, Paragraph 1 (c), of the Covenant)' (2006) E/C.12/GC/17, para 28; CESCR, 'General Comment No 18: The Right to Work (Article 6 of the International Covenant on Economic, Social and Cultural Rights' (2006) E/C.12/GC/18, para 22; CESCR, 'General Comment No 21: Right of Everyone to Take Part in Cultural Life (art. 15, para 1 (a), of the International Covenant on Economic, Social and Cultural Rights)' (2009) E/C.12/GC/21, para 48; CESCR, 'General Comment No 22', paras 33, 45; CESCR, 'General Comment No 25', para 23.

inform budgetary measures: 'Economic policies, such as budgetary allocations and measures to stimulate economic growth, should pay attention to the need to guarantee the effective enjoyment of the Covenant rights without discrimination.'[99] The CRC-Com even devoted an entire General Comment to the topic of children's rights and public budgeting.[100] In this General Comment, the experts of the CRC-Com explain that human rights obligations must be considered at any point in the fiscal procedure. States parties are required 'to demonstrate that they have made every effort to mobilize, allocate and spend budget resources to fulfil the economic, social and cultural rights of all children'.[101]

2.5.2. International Cooperation

The treaties prescribe that States parties must take steps towards the realisation of rights not only individually but, where needed, within a framework of international cooperation.[102] Accordingly, as the CESCR clarifies, the concept of utilising the maximum of available resources must be understood to refer to both 'the resources existing within a State and those available from the international community through international cooperation and assistance'.[103] States parties are under the obligation to actively secure international funding if they face difficulties in progressively realising rights due to limited national resources.[104] In order to claim the inability to provide a certain level of rights fulfilment on the basis of insufficient resources, a State party carries 'the burden of proving that this is the case and that it has unsuccessfully sought to obtain international support to ensure' the right in question.[105]

[99] CESCR, 'General Comment No 20', para 38.

[100] CRC-Com, 'General Comment No 19'.

[101] ibid, para 30.

[102] Article 2 (1) of the ICESCR: 'Each State Party to the present Covenant undertakes to take steps, *individually and through international assistance and co-operation*, especially economic and technical, to the maximum of its available resources, with a view to achieving progressively the full realization of the rights recognized in the present Covenant' (emphasis added); Article 4 (2) of the CRPD: 'With regard to economic, social and cultural rights, each State Party undertakes to take measures to the maximum of its available resources and, *where needed, within the framework of international cooperation*, with a view to achieving progressively the full realization of these rights' (emphasis added); Article 4 of the CRC: 'With regard to economic, social and cultural rights, States Parties shall undertake such measures to the maximum extent of their available resources and, *where needed, within the framework of international co-operation*' (emphasis added).

[103] CESCR, 'General Comment No 3', para 13; see also CESCR, 'Evaluation of the Obligation to Take Steps to the Maximum of Available Resources', para 5.

[104] CESCR, 'General Comment No 23 on the Right to Just and Favourable Conditions of Work (Article 7 of the International Covenant on Economic, Social and Cultural Rights)' (2016) E/C.12/GC/23, para 52.

[105] CESCR, 'General Comment No 12', para 17.

2.5.3. Minimum Core

It is widely accepted that a complete concept of progressive realisation sets certain limits to the relevance of resource scarcity for the necessary level of fulfilment. The so-called minimum core of rights describes a minimum level of subsistence which, as a general rule, is not subject to the availability of resources and therefore not subject to progressive realisation.[106] Alston argues that, if one wants to employ the terminology of rights, the normative content of these claims cannot be so indeterminate that 'the rightholders possess no particular entitlement to anything'.[107] He concludes that each human right must be read to establish an absolute minimum level of realisation which marks a boundary below which the State party must be considered to be in violation of its obligations.[108]

The experts of the CESCR agree, arguing that the raison d'être of the ICESCR demands the satisfaction of such minimum essential levels of each right.[109] In the context of the right to the highest attainable standard of health under Article 12 of the ICESCR, for example, the CESCR provided a list of 'core obligations' including (amongst others) the provision of 'access to the minimum essential food which is nutritionally adequate and safe, to ensure freedom from hunger to everyone', 'access to basic shelter, housing and sanitation, and an adequate supply of safe and potable water', and access to essential drugs.[110] Because minimum core obligations are not subject to progressive realisation, there is some overlap with the other immediate obligations set out above. This becomes clear, for example, when the CESCR holds that minimum core obligations regarding the right to water and the right to health include the duty to ensure non-discrimination, to adopt plans of action, and to monitor the extent of realisation.[111]

As a general rule, minimum core obligations must be fulfilled regardless of the current economic situation in the State party.[112] Situations of economic distress are generally not suited to justify the violation of these minimum levels of subsistence, as the experts of the CESCR clarify: '[D]espite externally caused problems, the obligations under the Covenant continue to apply and are perhaps even more pertinent during times of economic contraction.'[113] States parties not providing this minimum level of rights are, prima facie, in violation of the treaty.

[106] See, eg, A Chapman and S Russell (eds), *Core Obligations: Building a Framework for Economic, Social and Cultural Rights* (Antwerp, Intersentia, 2002); Byrne, 'Reclaiming Progressive Realisation', 753–54.

[107] Alston, 'Out of the Abyss', 352–53.

[108] ibid, 353.

[109] CESCR, 'General Comment No 3', para 10.

[110] CESCR, 'General Comment No 14', paras 43 (b), (c), (d).

[111] CESCR, 'General Comment No 15', paras 37 (b), (f), (g); CESCR, 'General Comment No 14', paras 43 (a), (e), (f).

[112] UNCHR, 'Limburg Principles', para 25.

[113] CESCR, 'General Comment No 4', para 11.

The burden of proof then lies on the State party to demonstrate that 'every effort has been made to use all resources that are at its disposition in an effort to satisfy, as a matter of priority, those minimum obligations'.[114] At other points, the CESCR even describes the minimum core of a right to be 'non-derogable', meaning that 'a State party cannot justify its non-compliance with the core obligations'.[115] In its newer jurisprudence, however, the CESCR has returned to its model of an intensified burden of proof.[116] The CRPD-Com and the CRC-Com have largely adopted this latter conception of the minimum core.[117]

2.6. ROLE OF THE COMMITTEES AND STANDARD OF REVIEW

The standard of progressive realisation also raises questions regarding the role of the Committees in reviewing State conduct and determining violations of Convention or Covenant rights. State conduct cannot simply be measured against a universally applicable standard due to the relative nature of progressive realisation. Rather, the Committees must determine whether the steps taken by States parties conform with the obligation to undertake sufficient steps towards full realisation. The solution to this problem adopted by the drafters of the ICESCR-OP is the so-called reasonableness standard, which originates from the jurisprudence of the Constitutional Court of South Africa.[118] This standard was explicitly included into the ICESCR-OP in order to deal with the difficulties arising from the judicial review of progressively realisable rights.[119] The concepts of progressive realisation and reasonableness are thus inextricably linked. Article 8 (4) ICESCR-OP sets out:

> When examining communications under the present Protocol, *the Committee shall consider the reasonableness* of the steps taken by the State Party in accordance with part II of the Covenant. In doing so, the Committee shall bear in mind that the *State Party may adopt a range of possible policy measures* for the implementation of the rights set forth in the Covenant. (emphases added)

A similar provision is set out in Article 10 (4) CRC-OP3. These provisions, on the one hand, stress that States parties are the primary decision-makers regarding the policy aimed at progressively realising socio-economic rights. On the other hand, the Committees are described as competent to evaluate the reasonableness

[114] CESCR, 'General Comment No 3', para 10; see also CESCR, 'Evaluation of the Obligation to Take Steps to the Maximum of Available Resources', para 6.
[115] CESCR, 'General Comment No 14', para 47; CESCR, 'General Comment No 15'.
[116] See CESCR, 'General Comment No 19: The Right to Social Security (art. 9)' (2008) E/C.12/GC/19, para 60.
[117] CRPD-Com, 'General Comment No 4', para 41; CRC-Com, 'General Comment No 21 on Children in Street Situations' (2017) CRC/C/GC/21, para 34; CRC-Com, 'General Comment No 19', para 31.
[118] See, generally, Porter, 'Reasonableness and Article 8(4)'.
[119] See ibid, 178–84.

of the States parties' conduct, thus striking a balance between the democratically legitimised authority of the State and the role of the Committee as a (quasi-) judicial body. In the jurisprudence of the CESCR, CRC-Com and CRPD-Com, this balance is further elaborated in the concepts of the margin of appreciation or discretion and the precise contours of the reasonableness standard. These two aspects are inextricably linked; the stricter the standard of review is constructed, the less room remains for a margin of appreciation.[120] They are separated only for taxonomical reasons in the following subsections.

2.6.1. Margin of Appreciation or Discretion

Article 8 (4) ICESCR-OP reflects the acceptance that there is a range of options and that States parties are primarily tasked with choosing the appropriate policy aimed at progressive realisation.[121] The CESCR recognises this primary 'authority vested in relevant State organs to adopt what it considers to be its most appropriate policies and to allocate resources accordingly' as a relevant factor for determining its own role in examining communications regarding this State party.[122]

The primary authority of States parties in policy matters eschewed, for example, in Article 8 (4) of the ICESCR-OP is usually recognised by granting a margin of appreciation or margin of discretion to States parties.[123] This concept, originally developed by the ECtHR,[124] describes a certain space of manoeuvre reserved for States parties in fulfilling their human rights obligations, denying (quasi-)judicial organs the authority to replace policy decisions with their own notion of what would be ideal.[125] Accordingly, the CESCR strictly delimits its own role and the role of the State party, utilising the margin of appreciation as a tool to achieve a balance between the two areas of competence:

> At all times the Committee bears in mind its own role as an international treaty body and the role of the State in formulating or adopting, funding and implementing laws and policies concerning economic, social and cultural rights. To this end, and in

[120] See D McGoldrick, 'A Defence of the Margin of Appreciation and an Argument for its Application by the Human Rights Committee' (2016) 65 *International and Comparative Law Quarterly* 21, 26.

[121] See Porter, 'Reasonableness and Article 8(4)', 187.

[122] CESCR, 'Evaluation of the Obligation to Take Steps to the Maximum of Available Resources', para 2.

[123] See IComJ, 'Maastricht Guidelines', para 8.

[124] For the first application of the concept by the former European Commission on Human Rights, see EComHR, *Greece v the United Kingdom* ('Cyprus') (1958) 2 *Yearbook of the European Convention on Human Rights* 172–97; see also HC Yourow, *The Margin of Appreciation Doctrine in the Dynamics of European Human Rights Jurisprudence*, International Studies in Human Rights 28 (Dordrecht, Nijhoff, 1996) 15–16. It is interesting to note that the ECtHR grants this margin of appreciation regardless of whether a civil and political or socio-economic right is concerned.

[125] See, generally, A Legg, *The Margin of Appreciation in International Human Rights Law: Deference and Proportionality* (Oxford, Oxford University Press, 2012).

> accordance with the practice of judicial and other quasi-judicial human rights treaty bodies, the Committee always respects the margin of appreciation of States to take steps and adopt measures most suited to their specific circumstances.[126]

In its General Comment on the Right to Health, the CESCR stresses that '[t]he most appropriate feasible measures to implement the right to health will vary significantly from one State to another', which is then held to necessarily entail a margin of discretion in assessing which measures are most suitable for each State party.[127] The experts consider that States are more competent particularly in the area of budgeting, declaring that they will respect the margin of appreciation regarding the States parties' decisions on the optimum use of resources and the prioritisation of resource demands in their budgeting decisions.[128]

This is in line with the structure of obligations set out above. It makes sense to explicitly refer to a margin of appreciation in the context of obligations of conduct, namely the obligation to take steps towards the realisation of rights, as obligations of result already imply leeway regarding the precise method of implementation.[129] The margin of appreciation is thus intertwined with progressive realisation and the reasonableness standard. This is at least true where the leeway pursuant to the margin refers to judicial deference regarding the implementation of the right rather than to normative flexibility regarding the end result.[130]

The CRPD-Com also makes ample use of the margin of appreciation doctrine. A first mention of this principle appears in its views on the case of *Jungelin v Sweden* which concerned reasonable accommodation measures in the context of the right to work under Article 27 of the CRPD.[131] According to the CRPD-Com, 'when assessing the reasonableness and proportionality of accommodation measures, State parties enjoy a certain margin of appreciation'.[132] Interestingly, in this case, the State party and the Committee reference several decisions on Individual Communications by the HRC.[133] In *DR v Australia*, the CRPD-Com refers to the jurisprudence of the CESCR regarding the margin of appreciation.[134]

[126] CESCR, 'Evaluation of the Obligation to Take Steps to the Maximum of Available Resources', para 11.

[127] CESCR, 'General Comment No 14', para 53; see also, regarding the right to water, CESCR, 'General Comment No 15', para 45 and, regarding the right to food, CESCR, 'General Comment No 12', para 21.

[128] CESCR, 'Evaluation of the Obligation to Take Steps to the Maximum of Available Resources', para 12.

[129] Y Shany, 'Toward a General Margin of Appreciation Doctrine in International Law?' (2005) 16 *European Journal of International Law* 907, 917.

[130] For this differentiation, see ibid, 909–10.

[131] CRPD-Com, *Jungelin v Sweden* [Adoption of Views] (2 October 2014) CRPD/C/12/D/5/2011, paras 10.1–11.

[132] ibid, para 10.5.

[133] ibid, para 8.11.

[134] CRPD-Com, *DR v Australia* [Adoption of Views] (24 March 2017) CRPD/C/17/D/14/2013, para 4.27 (fn).

The CRPD-Com also mentions the margin of appreciation in its General Comment No 5 on Living Independently and being Included in the Community under Article 19 of the CRPD, stating that, while there is a margin of appreciation of States parties regarding 'the programmatic implementation' of the switch from institutionalised settings to independent living support services, there is none regarding 'the question of replacement' itself.[135] Accordingly, the CRPD-Com clearly considers that the margin of appreciation has its boundaries. The margin does not mean that States parties can abandon their obligations altogether and also does not require the Committees to relinquish their role as (quasi-)judicial bodies. It is generally recognised that the leeway of States parties regarding their policy choices does not extend to the decision whether these choices are reasonable in light of the State party's obligations under the relevant treaty.[136] This decision remains firmly in the competence of the human rights treaty bodies.

The CESCR likewise sets limits to the leeway granted by the margin of appreciation, repeatedly emphasising in its General Comments that the margin of appreciation does not amount to an abdication of the Committee's jurisdiction: while States parties are primarily responsible for policy decisions and must provide reasoning as to why a measure taken is appropriate, 'the ultimate determination as to whether all appropriate measures have been taken remains one for the Committee to make'.[137] A similar argument is made by members of the CRPD-Com in the individual dissenting opinion on *Jungelin v Sweden*. Here, the experts declared that, while it is true that 'the Committee has no power to act as a third instance' and 'that States parties enjoy a certain margin of appreciation when assessing the reasonableness of accommodation measures', the majority decision of the other Committee members should have included a review of the criteria applied by the State party in its decision as to their reasonableness.[138] Accordingly, the limit of States parties' leeway is determined by the reasonableness standard.

2.6.2. Reasonableness

Respecting the State parties' principal competence and legitimacy to decide upon the appropriateness of policy measures entails that the Committees do not replace this evaluation with their own when testing for a violation of the Conventions and Covenants. This means that the Committees do not prescribe one definitive approach to the progressive realisation of rights which must be adhered to in order to comply with the obligations pursuant to

[135] CRPD-Com, 'General Comment No 5', para 42.
[136] See, eg, Porter, 'Reasonableness and Article 8(4)', 187.
[137] CESCR, 'General Comment No 3'.
[138] CRPD-Com, *Jungelin v Sweden*, Appendix paras 1–6.

socio-economic rights. Instead, the policy choices made by the States parties pursuant to their margin of appreciation are evaluated by the Committees as to their reasonableness. In its evaluation of obligations under Article 2 (1) of the ICESCR, the CESCR lays out precisely what the reasonableness test involves: reasonableness requires States parties to adopt measures which are 'deliberate, concrete and targeted towards the fulfilment' of socio-economic rights; those measures must be 'non-discriminatory and nonarbitrary' as well as the least restrictive choice when several policy options are available. Furthermore, the timeframe of action is relevant and, lastly, States parties must take into account the interests of disadvantaged and marginalised individuals, prioritising situations of high risk.[139] Further details regarding what makes out a reasonable policy can be deduced from the Committee's statements concerning the obligation to 'take steps' which are laid out above.[140] This is so because the normative determination of States parties' obligations largely overlaps with the standard employed to determine violations in Individual Communications cases.[141]

This standard of reasonableness, on the one hand, takes into account the interest of rights holders in an effective and equitable pursuit of fulfilling their human rights while, on the other hand, recognising States parties' limitations, particularly with a view to resources. Reasonableness review can thus be described as a 'contextual inquiry' into the precise obligations flowing from human rights which takes into account both the interests of the claimant and the restrictions faced by the State party.[142]

Another important part of the concept of reasonableness is the requirement of transparency and participation regarding the decision-making processes.[143] According to the experts of the CESCR, 'the right of individuals and groups to participate in decision-making processes, ... must be an integral component of any policy, programme or strategy developed to discharge governmental obligations' under the Covenant.[144] As a precondition for informed participation, reasonableness requires giving individuals and groups full and equal access to the relevant information regarding the right and its realisation as well as the decision-making process itself.[145]

[139] CESCR, 'Evaluation of the Obligation to Take Steps to the Maximum of Available Resources', para 8.
[140] See further 2.3.
[141] Accordingly, Bruce Porter engages in detail with the CESCR's statements regarding the obligation to take steps under Article 2 (1) of the ICESCR when laying out the Committee's interpretation of the reasonableness standard under Article 8 (4) of the ICESCR-OP, see Porter, 'Reasonableness and Article 8(4)', 195–200.
[142] ibid, 195.
[143] CESCR, 'Evaluation of the Obligation to Take Steps to the Maximum of Available Resources', para 11.
[144] CESCR, 'General Comment No 14', para 54.
[145] CESCR, 'General Comment No 15', para 48.

Because States parties are primarily competent to make policy choices, they are also burdened with providing the evidence for the reasonableness of their policies. This particularly applies when a State party blames delays in full realisation on resource limitations:

> If resource constraints render it impossible for a State party to comply fully with its Covenant obligations, it has the burden of justifying that every effort has nevertheless been made to use all available resources at its disposal in order to satisfy, as a matter of priority, the obligations outlined above.[146]

2.7. CONCLUSION

This chapter has shown that progressive realisation as an umbrella concept creates a wide range of different obligations on the spectrum from immediate to progressive. Understanding this structure is a necessary precondition for identifying the convergence between immediate and progressive realisation because a large part of the insistence upon the divide between those two standards is due to a terminological misunderstanding of progressive realisation. Arguments for differentiated standards often proceed from the notion that civil and political rights must be subject to a stricter standard because progressive realisation is seen as allowing indefinite postponement of realisation. The Committees and literary commentators regularly ignore the fact that the umbrella meaning of the term includes immediate obligations when they contrast this standard to immediate realisation, as parts II and III will show.

Part I has thus created a clear mission for the analysis of civil and political rights jurisprudence in part II: chapter 1 has provided the hypothesis, and chapter 2 has revealed precisely how to test it, ie, what features to look for in the Committees' civil and political rights jurisprudence. Accordingly, the next part of this book will identify parallels to progressive realisation in the structure of obligations which the Committees establish for civil and political rights.

[146] ibid, para 41.

Part II

Analysis of Committee Jurisprudence

3

The General Conception of the Divide between Categories

3.1. INTRODUCTION

THIS PART SETS out to confirm the second half of the hypothesis of convergence by determining whether the standard of realisation applied to civil and political rights is analogous to progressive realisation. In the context of socio-economic rights, progressive realisation has been conceived as an umbrella concept which incorporates both immediate and progressive obligations. This will serve as a point of comparison to the standard applied to civil and political rights. According to the traditional conception, civil and political rights are purely 'immediate'. Thus, the crucial question resulting from the convergence hypothesis is whether the standard of 'immediacy' applied to civil and political rights is not only immediate in the narrow sense but also includes progressive obligations in the sense of an umbrella concept analogous to progressive realisation.

Such progressive elements are most likely to be found wherever civil and political rights are interpreted to create positive obligations. This is so because the protect and fulfil dimensions of civil and political rights raise precisely those issues which led States to include progressive realisation for socio-economic rights, namely resource and other limitations which inhibit immediate realisation.[1] While commentators do acknowledge that civil and political rights have resource implications, they, at the same time, insist upon the immediacy of these rights without explaining why the logical connection between positivity, costliness, and progressive realisation does not apply here.[2] The Committees also accept that all rights create positive as well as negative obligations,[3] but

[1] A similar argument is made by Tobin, 'Article 4', 129.

[2] See, for example, UNHCHR, 'Report on Progressive Realization', paras 23–27, arguing this: it is true that CPR also require resources and might be realizable only over time. But the obligations regarding SER are still 'more flexible'. While a failure to ensure fair trial guarantees cannot be justified, violations of most SER obligations can be justified by demonstrating that all available resources have been utilized; see also Sepúlveda, *The Nature of the Obligations*, 130–31.

[3] See, eg, CRPD-Com, 'General Comment No 3: Article 6: Women and Girls with Disabilities' (2016) CRPD/C/GC/3, paras 7, 12; CRC-Com, 'General Comment No 6: Treatment of Unaccompanied and Separated Children Outside their Country of Origin' (2005) CRC/GC/2005/6, para 13;

none of them explicitly acknowledge progressive elements. For lack of any explicit engagement with the issue, it is necessary to conduct a detailed analysis which focuses on implicit parallels to progressive realisation.

This first chapter of part II explores the way in which the Committees address the divide between socio-economic and civil and political rights generally. An important question in this context is whether the Committees have developed a clear method of determining which right belongs to which category. Such a clear divide would be necessary because without it there would be no way for States parties to know the scope of their duties. This is particularly important for the regimes of the CRPD and CRC which combine rights from both traditional categories. But the issue of delimitation also arises in the context of the right to non-discrimination under the ICCPR, CEDAW and ICERD. Non-discrimination is generally interpreted to relate to all areas of life, which leads to the question whether this right is always civil and political or combines aspects from both categories and, consequently, whether it requires immediate or progressive realisation.

In a first step, it will be shown that the CRPD-Com and CRC-Com attach legal relevance to the categories in the traditional way, differentiating between immediately and progressively realisable rights. However, it will be seen that methods of delimitation are inconsistent (3.2). Secondly, it will be illustrated that the CEDAW-Com and CERD do not clarify whether their respective treaties are read to establish only civil and political rights or whether the categorisation depends on the area where equal treatment is sought. It appears, however, that they claim the immediacy of all relevant rights as often done in the context of civil and political rights (3.3). The fourth section will show that the HRC, on the surface, adheres to the traditional conception, arguing that the ICCPR entails only immediate civil and political rights but fails to provide a consistent approach to the categorisation of equality rights (3.4). In a last step, this chapter will illustrate the tendency of some Committees to ascribe one singular obligation to rights from both categories which further blurs the boundaries between them, making the categories factually indistinguishable (3.5).

3.2. THE CRPD-COM AND CRC-COM

The CRPD and CRC reiterate both socio-economic and civil and political rights from the ICCPR and ICESCR, place them in the specific context of the life of persons with disabilities and children respectively, and enrich the understanding of existing rights for these groups.[4] Accordingly, the treaties encompass

CEDAW-Com, 'General Recommendation No 19: Violence against women' (1992) A/47/38, para 4; CERD, 'General Recommendation No 32: The Meaning and Scope of Special Measures in the International Convention on the Elimination of All Forms Racial Discrimination' (2009) CERD/C/GC/32, para 14; HRC, 'General Comment No 31'.

[4] See Mégret, 'The Disabilities Convention'; Rishmawi, *Article 4*, 15–16.

both categories of rights. This also explains why Article 4 (2) of the CRPD and Article 4 of the CRC explicitly provide for the progressive realisation of only one category, namely socio-economic rights. If these provisions are understood to establish a legal differentiation between the two categories, the Committees must find a way to draw clear boundaries.

The CRPD-Com and CRC-Com appear to consider the relevant provisions to establish a legal differentiation between immediate civil and political rights and progressive socio-economic rights (3.2.1). However, they encounter considerable difficulties when trying to consistently determine which right belongs to which category. These difficulties arise when the Committees are faced with rights that bear resemblance to rights from both the ICCPR and ICESCR (3.2.2). Furthermore, the two Committees frequently set out States parties' obligations without explaining which right these obligations result from. Such an allocation would, however, be necessary to determine whether the obligation is immediately or progressively realisable (3.2.3).

3.2.1. Insistence on the Immediate/Progressive Rights Divide

Both the CRPD and the CRC-Com claim to adhere to the traditional understanding of immediately realisable civil and political rights and progressively realisable socio-economic rights. The CRPD-Com holds that '[t]he obligations of States parties must reflect the nature of human rights as either absolute and immediately applicable (civil and political rights) or progressively applicable (economic, social and cultural rights)'.[5] The Committee also engages with this issue in the context of several civil and political rights clarifying that this category entails only immediately realisable obligations, no matter whether those obligations are positive and/or costly. One example is the CRPD-Com's General Comment No 1 on Equal Recognition before the Law under Article 12 of the CRPD.[6] The CRPD-Com considers this right to fall into the category of civil and political rights.[7] Article 12 of the CRPD is also interpreted to contain a decidedly positive dimension.[8] However, the Committee considers all resulting positive duties to be immediate and unconditional. According to the Committee, 'the rights provided for in article 12 apply at the moment of ratification and are subject to immediate realization'.[9]

[5] CRPD-Com, 'General Comment No 5', para 39; the CESCR similarly states that the obligation under Article 2 (1) of the ICESCR 'differs significantly from that contained in article 2 of the International Covenant on Civil and Political Rights which embodies an immediate obligation to respect and ensure all of the relevant rights', CESCR, 'General Comment No 3', para 9.

[6] CRPD-Com, 'General Comment No 1: Article 12: Equal Recognition before the Law' (2014) CRPD/C/GC/1.

[7] ibid, para 30.

[8] ibid, paras 24, 29, 51.

[9] ibid, para 30.

The CRPD-Com seems to be aware that this strict categorisation might raise questions regarding the positive aspects included in Article 12 (3) of the CRPD, as it goes on to explicitly highlight that this is 'an obligation for the fulfilment of the civil and political right to equal recognition before the law. "Progressive realization" (Article 4, para. 2) does not apply to the provisions of article 12.'[10] Furthermore, the Committee does not consider the necessary positive measures under Article 12 (3) of the CRPD to be limited by resource constraints: 'The right to support in the exercise of legal capacity shall not be limited by the claim of disproportionate or undue burden. The State has an absolute obligation to provide access to support in the exercise of legal capacity.'[11]

The right to participation under Articles 4 (3) and 33 (3) of the CRPD is likewise interpreted to be immediate and unconditional. Although General Comment No 7 on this matter does not contain an explicit reference to Article 4 (2) of the CRPD, it restates the content of this provision when holding that '[t]he right to participate is a civil and political right and an obligation of immediate application, not subject to any form of budgetary restriction, to be applied to decision-making, implementation and monitoring processes related to the Convention'.[12]

The CRC-Com does not provide many statements regarding this issue. But it becomes clear that, even though the CRC-Com is aware of the difficulties in differentiating between rights,[13] the experts still adhere to a strictly traditional reading of Article 4 of the CRC. According to the CRC-Com's understanding, civil and political rights are 'immediate and unqualified',[14] while socio-economic rights must be realised 'to the maximum extent of … available resources' and thus 'progressively'.[15]

3.2.2. Uncertainties in the Categorisation of Mixed Rights

Instances of explicit categorisation are scarce in the jurisprudence of the CRPD-Com and CRC-Com, even though the Committees interpret Article 4 (2)

[10] ibid.

[11] ibid, para 34.

[12] CRPD-Com, 'General Comment No 7 on the Participation of Persons with Disabilities, including Children with Disabilities, through their Representative Organizations, in the Implementation and Monitoring of the Convention' (2018) CRPD/C/GC/7, para 28.

[13] According to the Committee, 'caution should be exercised in differentiating between economic, social and cultural rights on the one hand, and civil and political rights on the other', CRC-Com, 'General Comment No 19', para 30.

[14] Regarding the right of the child to freedom from all forms of violence, see CRC-Com, 'General Comment No 13: The Right of the Child to Freedom from All Forms of Violence' (2011) CRC/C/GC/13, para 65; see also, regarding the right of the child to protection from corporal punishment and other cruel or degrading forms of punishment, CRC-Com, 'General Comment No 8: The Right of the Child to Protection from Corporal Punishment and Other Cruel or Degrading Forms of Punishment (arts. 19; 28, para. 2; and 37, inter alia)' (2007) CRC/C/GC/8, para 22.

[15] CRC-Com, 'General Comment No 19', para 25.

of the CRPD and Article 4 of the CRC to prescribe a differentiation. The rare instances where a categorisation takes place reveal inconsistencies in the Committees' approaches. Neither the CRPD-Com nor the CRC-Com explicitly state whether there are any factors which inherently place rights in the category of socio-economic or civil and political rights. Instead, the Committees' approach to categorisation is characterised by attempts to draw parallels to the ICESCR and ICCPR. Regarding rights which constitute a close restatement of those 'root-rights', this method is relatively straightforward. However, it leads to difficulties regarding the categorisation of rights which bear a resemblance to rights from both Covenants.

In its General Comments Nos 1, 4, 5 and 7, the CRPD-Com builds on the bifurcation of rights in the ICCPR and ICESCR as a means of differentiation. According to the CRPD-Com, the right to equal recognition before the law under Article 12 of the CRPD 'has long been recognized as a civil and political right, with roots in the International Covenant on Civil and Political Rights'.[16] Indeed, Article 16 of the ICCPR establishes that '[e]veryone shall have the right to recognition everywhere as a person before the law'. Similarly, in General Comment No 7, the CRPD-Com simply states that '[t]he right to participate is a civil and political right'[17] and refers to Article 25 of the ICCPR (political rights, particularly participation in public affairs) as the underlying provision.[18] In relation to the right to education under Article 24 of the CRPD, the Committee explicitly considers Article 4 (2) of the CRPD to be applicable, thereby categorising this right as socio-economic.[19] The basis for this right is clearly seen in Article 13 of the ICESCR, as the CRPD-Com refers repeatedly to the CESCR's interpretation of this provision.[20]

Difficulties arise, however, in the CRPD-Com's General Comment No 5 on Living Independently and being Included in the Community under Article 19 of the CRPD. This text contains more detailed reasoning regarding the differentiation between the categories. While the rights subject to General Comments Nos 1, 4 and 7 can be more clearly ascribed to provisions in the ICESCR or the ICCPR, Article 19 of the CRPD is more ambiguous. The CRPD-Com recognises that this provision is 'one of the widest ranging and most intersectional articles of the Convention and has to be considered as integral to the full implementation of the Convention'.[21] As such, the Committee considers this right to have roots in civil and political as well as economic, social and cultural rights, such as the rights to liberty of movement and freedom to choose one's residence under

[16] CRPD-Com, 'General Comment No 1', para 30.
[17] CRPD-Com, 'General Comment No 7', para 28.
[18] ibid, para 3.
[19] CRPD-Com, 'General Comment No 4', para 40.
[20] The CRPD makes reference to CESCR, 'General Comment No 13' in CRPD-Com, 'General Comment No 4', paras 15, 20, 25, 10 (c).
[21] CRPD-Com, 'General Comment No 5', para 6.

Article 12 of the ICCPR and the right to an adequate standard of living under Article 11 of the ICESCR.[22]

Consequently, the Committee does not categorise the provision of Article 19 of the CRPD as a whole but rather differentiates between different parts of it, explaining that 'Article 19 entails civil and political as well as economic, social and cultural rights and is an example of the interrelation, interdependence and indivisibility of all human rights'.[23] The respective parts of the provision are then classified as follows:

> Article 19 (a), the right to choose one's residence and where, how and with whom to live, is immediately applicable as it is a civil and political right. Article 19 (b), the right to access individualized, assessed support services, is an economic, social and cultural right. Article 19 (c), the right to access service facilities, is an economic, social and cultural right, as many mainstream services, such as accessible information and communications technologies, websites, social media, cinemas, public parks, theatres and sports facilities, serve both social and cultural purposes.[24]

Regarding the right under Article 19 (a) of the CRPD, the CRPD-Com appears to base its categorisation on the parallels to Article 12 of the ICCPR. The Committee's statements on the normative content of the provision, however, call this conclusion into question. The CRPD-Com explains that the inability to choose one's place and mode of residence is often due to a lack of other choices outside of the own family or the institutionalised context, eg, due to the unavailability or inaccessibility of housing or support.[25] The Committee thereby implicitly recognises that the formal freedom of choice regarding one's residence remains without meaning when there are no real alternatives.[26] Consequently, Article 19 (a) of the CRPD is interpreted to require States parties not only to refrain from actively institutionalising persons with disabilities but also to provide alternative housing.[27] Such measures would traditionally be considered to fall into the category of socio-economic rights, as the right to housing can be found in the ICESCR.[28] It appears arbitrary to establish a set of obligations which have their roots in both Covenants but then focus in on only one of the obligations when it comes to categorising the right in question.

Article 19 (b) of the CRPD is categorised as a socio-economic right without any further elaboration. This can only be surmised to be based on the parallels to the right to social security in Article 9 of the ICESCR. The categorisation of the right under Article 19 (c) of the CRPD as socio-economic stands out. Instead

[22] ibid, para 9.
[23] ibid, para 7.
[24] ibid, para 39.
[25] ibid, para 25.
[26] *cf* 1.3.1.1. regarding the concept of positive freedom.
[27] This was also recognised by Ilias Bantekas, Michael A Stein and Dimitris Anastasiou (eds), *The UN Convention on the Rights of Persons with Disabilities: A Commentary* (Oxford University Press, 2018) 550.
[28] *cf* Article 11 of the ICESCR.

of referring to the resemblance with rights in the ICESCR, the Committee considers it to be decisive that the services covered by this provision 'serve both social and cultural purposes'.[29] However, the wording of the relevant section already shows that Article 19 (c) of the CRPD does not only pertain to the socio-economic sphere of rights-holders' lives. Although 'many' of the public services and facilities may traditionally belong into the social, cultural or economic sphere, such as 'employment, education and health care',[30] others clearly do not. There is no reason to assume that Article 19 (c) of the CRPD does not extend to the accessibility of infrastructure and services which are necessary to participate in public life, such as administrative facilities.

This 'purposes-approach' thus leads to arbitrary results. It makes no sense to categorise an obligation as socio-economic on the grounds that it enables the realisation of socio-economic rights if the obligation, at the same time, is found to enable the realisation of civil and political rights. If all rights are interdependent across categories, then this kind of relationship cannot serve to separate the two. The 'purposes-approach' also fails if applied to Article 19 (b) of the CRPD. This right, according to the CRPD-Com, serves both socio-economic and civil and political purposes. The Committee explicitly states that the individualised services envisioned by this provision need to extend to the 'participation in political and cultural life'.[31] Clearly, the measures to be undertaken pursuant to Article 19 (b) of the CRPD are interpreted as connected to the exercise of civil and political rights. In that respect, when laying out the relationship between Article 19 of the CRPD and the right to participation in political and public life under Article 29 of the CRPD, the Committee states that '[a]ppropriate support can provide valuable assistance to persons with disabilities in exercising their right to vote, to take part in political life and to conduct public affairs'.[32]

Also in relation to other rights, the 'purposes-approach' fails to provide consistent guidelines. Concerning Article 12 of the CRPD, the Committee recalls that equal recognition before the law is generally 'indispensable for the exercise of civil, political, economic, social and cultural rights'[33] as it is 'inextricably linked to the enjoyment of many other human rights'.[34] Legal capacity, according to the CRPD-Com, acquires special significance when persons want to decide on issues regarding their health, education and work but also in the context of voting, marrying, founding a family and the right to liberty.[35] The purposes served by the right under Article 12 of the CRPD fall into areas traditionally covered by both categories of rights. This again illustrates that the

[29] CRPD-Com, 'General Comment No 5', para 39.
[30] ibid, para 33.
[31] ibid, para 29.
[32] ibid, para 93.
[33] CRPD-Com, 'General Comment No 1', para 8.
[34] ibid, para 31.
[35] ibid, para 8.

'purposes-approach' adopted by the Committee in relation to Article 19 (c) of the CRPD cannot provide consistent guidance for categorisation.

The CRC-Com approaches the subject of categorising rights with even more hesitance, as its General Comment No 5 on General Measures of Implementation shows. While the Committee acknowledges that 'Article 4 … suggests a distinction between civil and political rights and economic, social and cultural rights',[36] the experts also state that '[t]here is no simple or authoritative division of human rights in general or of Convention rights into the two categories'.[37] In General Comment No 19 on Public Budgeting, the CRC-Com furthermore declares that 'caution should be exercised in differentiating between economic, social and cultural rights on the one hand, and civil and political rights on the other'.[38] Such an explicit recognition of the difficulties in separating the categories is remarkable in light of the legal relevance this differentiation carries according to the statements of the Committee, and it remains unique in the jurisprudence of the UN Committees.

However, the experts apparently were aware that some sort of statement regarding the categorisation of rights was required. Attempting to provide some guidance, the CRC-Com refers to its reporting guidelines, stating that this document groups 'articles 7, 8, 13-17 and 37 (a) under the heading "Civil rights and freedoms"'.[39] At the same time, the guidelines, according to the Committee,

> indicate by the context that these are not the only civil and political rights in the Convention. Indeed, it is clear that many other articles, including articles 2, 3, 6 and 12 of the Convention, contain elements which constitute civil/political rights, thus reflecting the interdependence and indivisibility of all human rights. Enjoyment of economic, social and cultural rights is inextricably intertwined with enjoyment of civil and political rights.[40]

Here, the CRC-Com recognises explicitly what the CRPD-Com struggled with implicitly: the difficulties inherent in categorising mixed provisions in the Convention. In the Committee's reporting guidelines, many rights are not clearly put into categories but under headings referring to different life situations, for example 'family environment and alternative care'.[41] However, there is no guidance as to how these 'elements' of mixed rights can be allocated to the respective categories. There is no further engagement in the jurisprudence of the Committee with the question which factors determine the allocation to either group. The experts do not explain what makes a right or an 'element' socio-economic or civil and political.[42] Since no substantive features for differentiation

[36] CRC-Com, 'General Comment No 5', para 6.
[37] ibid.
[38] CRC-Com, 'General Comment No 19', para 30.
[39] CRC-Com, 'General Comment No 5', para 6.
[40] ibid.
[41] See Rishmawi, *Article 4*, 16–17.
[42] This was also recognised by Tobin, 'Article 4', 129.

are provided, it can only be assumed that the experts are relying on the traditional categorisation of rights, ie their resemblance to rights in either the ICCPR or ICESCR.[43]

3.2.3. Failure to Clarify the Standard of Realisation for Obligations

The previous examples have shown that the CRPD-Com's and CRC-Com's delimitation of the categories is fragmented and inconsistent. But the uncertainty increases even more on the level of obligations. In most cases, the Committees fail to ascribe certain obligations to certain rights and also do not take a stance on the immediacy or progressiveness of obligations themselves. Thus, even in those rare cases where the category of a right has been discussed by the Committees, States parties will be unable to determine which of the obligations set out by the Committee belongs to which right, making it impossible to know the legally required timeframe of realisation.

The CRPD-Com, in General Comment No 5 on Living Independently and being Included in the Community under Article 19 of the CRPD, engages in detail with the duties to respect, protect and fulfil without allocating them to any of the sections of the provision.[44] But the Committee, in the same document, declares that the different subsections of Article 19 of the CRPD contain both immediately realisable civil and political and progressively realisable socio-economic rights.[45] According to the Committee's systematisation, it would be crucial to know which specific duty belongs to which subsection of the provision. However, the Committee discusses the duties listed in this section of the General Comment without any reference to the subsections. Similarly, the section regarding implementation at the national level does not clarify which of the listed duties relates to which subsection of Article 19 of the ICRPD and also takes no stance on the applicability of Article 4 (2) of the CRPD.[46] On the basis of this document, States parties have no way of ascertaining which obligation must be realised immediately and which progressively.

General Comment No 8 on the Right of Persons with Disabilities to Work and Employment under Article 27 of the CRPD sets out that this right has roots both in the ICESCR and the ICCPR. Namely, the right to be free from slavery, servitude, and compulsory labour under Article 8 (1), (2), (3) (a) of the ICCPR is held to be part of the right to work.[47] The Committee considers this aspect to be reflected in Article 27 (2) of the CRPD which sets out that 'States Parties

[43] See also Rishmawi, *Article 4*, 16 and Tobin, 'Article 4', 130.

[44] CRPD-Com, 'General Comment No 5', paras 47–68.

[45] ibid, para 39.

[46] ibid, para 97 (a)–(n).

[47] CRPD-Com, 'General Comment No 8 on the Right of Persons with Disabilities to Work and Employment' (2022) CRPD/C/GC/8, para 9.

shall ensure that persons with disabilities are not held in slavery or in servitude, and are protected, on an equal basis with others, from forced or compulsory labour'.[48]

However, when setting out States parties' obligations, the CRPD-Com only mentions that Article 4 (2) of the CRPD requires progressive realisation and the immediate guarantee of non-discrimination. No distinction is made between the different paragraphs of Article 27 of the CRPD.[49] The Committee then continues to lay out the obligations to respect, protect, and fulfil, again referencing the right of all persons with disabilities to work without differentiating between socio-economic and civil and political components.[50] This section of the General Comment suggests that all rights are progressively realisable. At least there is no information as to which parts are and which parts are not. The same issue arises when the CRPD-Com sets out measures for implementation at the national level. In this section, the CRPD-Com speaks of data collecting, strategies and plans of action, indicators and benchmarks, awareness-raising campaigns, reporting mechanisms, and other measures which indicate a progressive understanding of realisation.[51] Again, no line is drawn between socio-economic and civil and political aspects of the right in question.

An even more obscure picture emerges in the jurisprudence of the CRC-Com. The Committee's General Comments are structured around certain situations in the life of children instead of one particular right. Usually, those Comments concern a broad number of rights from the Convention, both traditionally civil and political and socio-economic rights. Even though Article 4 of the CRC, according to the Committee's interpretation, should be central in determining the scope of States parties' duties, many of the General Comments do not clarify which obligation belongs to which right and which right falls into which category.

One example is General Comment No 4 on Adolescent Health and Development. This document refers to 'civil rights and freedoms' as well as traditionally socio-economic rights such as the right to health.[52] In the General Comment's section on the nature of States' obligations, the Committee sets out a range of positive obligations to be fulfilled by States parties. This section neither connects those duties to certain rights in the Convention, nor does it take any position regarding the immediate or progressive realisability of the obligations. The whole section contains no reference to categories of rights or Article 4 of the CRC.[53]

[48] ibid, para 51.
[49] ibid, para 54.
[50] ibid, paras 55–62.
[51] ibid, para 82 (a)–(p).
[52] CRC-Com, 'General Comment No 4: Adolescent Health and Development in the Context of the Convention on the Rights of the Child' (2003) CRC/GC/2003/4 paras 10, 11, 29.
[53] See ibid, paras 39–43.

General Comment No 6 on the Treatment of Unaccompanied and Separated Children outside their Country of Origin is another example. The Comment sets out to 'outline the multifaceted challenges faced by States and other actors in ensuring that such children are able to access and enjoy their rights'.[54] In the following paragraphs, the experts refer to a range of rights, eg the rights to education and health,[55] but also procedural and legal safeguards in the context of asylum.[56] However, in its section on legal obligations of States parties and measures for their implementation, the Comment does not differentiate between the categories of rights.[57] The section stresses that States are under 'both negative and positive' obligations.[58] No attempt is made to determine which of the positive obligations are to be fulfilled immediately and which progressively.

This pattern repeats itself in General Comment No 9 on the Rights of Children with Disabilities. Again, this instrument restates all kinds of rights from the perspective of persons with disabilities, in this case, children with disabilities. According to the experts, the Comment 'is meant to provide guidance and assistance to States parties in their efforts to implement the rights of children with disabilities, in a comprehensive manner which covers all the provisions of the Convention'.[59] Accordingly, the Comment contains sections on 'Civil rights and freedoms',[60] as well as (among others) the rights to health and education.[61] In the section on 'General measures of implementation', however, the Committee again does not draw the line between immediate and progressive realisation of rights.[62] General Comment No 7 on Implementing Child Rights in Early Childhood likewise concerns rights which the Committee elsewhere declared to be civil and political in addition to socio-economic rights.[63] Although the Comment contains extensive remarks on States' obligations, there is no differentiation between immediate and progressively realisable ones.[64]

The trend continues in the CRC-Com's newer General Comments, namely No 23 on State Obligations regarding the Human Rights of Children in the

[54] CRC-Com, 'General Comment No 6', para 1.

[55] ibid, paras 41–43 and paras 46–49.

[56] ibid, paras 64–78.

[57] ibid, paras 12–17; this General Comment does refer to Article 4 of the CRC, but does not utilise it to differentiate between immediately and progressively realisable duties.

[58] CRC-Com, 'General Comment No 6', para 13.

[59] CRC-Com, 'General Comment No 9: The Rights of Children with Disabilities' (2007) CRC/C/GC/9, para 6.

[60] ibid, paras 34–40.

[61] ibid, paras 51–52, 62–69.

[62] ibid, paras 17–27; Article 4 of the CRC is mentioned, but no differentiation between the two categories of rights takes place.

[63] Namely the right to freedom of thought, conscience, and religion (Article 14 CRC) and the right to participation (Article 12 CRC), see CRC-Com, 'General Comment No 7: Implementing Child Rights in Early Childhood' (2006) CRC/C/GC/7/Rev.1, para 17.

[64] See ibid, paras 15–43.

Context of International Migration, and No 25 on Children's Rights in relation to the Digital Environment. Both texts, again, are oriented towards certain life situations and concern a mixture of both categories of rights.[65] The Comments provide no guidance regarding the categorisation of rights or the (non-) applicability of sentence two of Article 4 of the CRC. There are no discernible differences in the way the obligations are presented in the sections about socio-economic and civil and political rights respectively.[66] The same is true for the CRC-Com's most recent General Comment No 26 on Children's Rights and the Environment with a Special Focus on Climate Change. This General Comment covers both categories of rights but does not discriminate between immediate and progressive obligations.[67]

3.3. THE CEDAW-COM AND CERD

The CEDAW and ICERD do not contain any provision calling for the progressive realisation of socio-economic rights. Instead, the treaties concern non-discrimination regarding both categories of rights without any differentiation.[68] According to the CERD and CEDAW-Com, both treaties restate the whole range of human rights spanning the categories of socio-economic and civil and political rights.[69] For example, the CERD states that the scope of the principle of non-discrimination in the ICERD 'extends to any field of human rights regulated by the public authorities in the State party'.[70] It remains unclear whether the CEDAW-Com and CERD read the treaties to establish one uniform civil and political right of non-discrimination or whether the categorisation depends upon the nature of the right in relation to which equal treatment is sought.

[65] 'Civil rights and freedoms': CRC-Com, 'General Comment No 23 on State Obligations Regarding the Human Rights of Children in the Context of International Migration in Countries of Origin, Transit, Destination and Return' (2017) CRC/C/GC/23, paras 5–13 (right to liberty), paras 14–19 (due process), paras 20–26 (right to name, identity, and nationality under Articles 7 and 8 CRC); CRC-Com, 'General Comment No 25 on Children's Rights in Relation to the Digital Environment' (2021) CRC/C/GC/25, paras 50–79 ('Civil rights and freedoms'); traditional socio-economic rights: CRC-Com, 'General Comment No 23', paras 49–53 (right to an adequate standard of living under Article 27 CRC), paras 54–58 (right to health under Articles 23, 24, and 39 CRC), paras 59–63 (right to education and professional training under Articles 28, 29, 29, 30, and 31 CRC); CRC-Com, 'General Comment No 25', paras 93–98 (health and welfare), paras 99–111 (education, leisure and cultural activities).

[66] The same is true for CRC-Com, 'General Comment No 24 on Children's Rights in the Justice System' (2019) CRC/C/GC/24. It could be argued, however, that this Comment is only about civil and political rights and thus can do without reference to Article 4 of the CRC as the inapplicability of sentence two is implicit.

[67] CRC-Com, 'General Comment No 26 on Children's Rights and the Environment with a Special Focus on Climate Change' (2023) CRC/C/GC/26.

[68] See further 1.2.2.

[69] See, eg, CERD, 'General Recommendation No 20 on Article 5 of the Convention' (1996) A/51/18, para 1.

[70] CERD, 'General Recommendation No 32', para 9.

Instead, the Committees regularly speak of inequalities regarding a person's 'civil, political, economic, social and cultural rights'.[71]

The CERD sometimes refers to the terms 'economic, social and cultural rights' and 'civil and political rights' separately. However, the jurisprudence of the Committee does not follow the traditional differentiation between the two categories. One example of this is the CERD's General Recommendation No 29 on the concept of descent pursuant to Article 1 (1) of the ICERD. This document is divided into several sections, some of which are titled 'Administration of justice', 'Civil and political rights', 'Economic and social rights', and 'Right to education'. The categories of civil and political and socio-economic rights are clearly not constructed in the traditional sense, as they exclude the right to equal access to justice and education respectively.[72] In the General Recommendations of the CEDAW-Com, references to those categories are rare, and where they occur, there is no attempt to introduce a conclusive categorisation for the purposes of the Convention.[73]

The division into socio-economic and civil and political rights also does not play a role in the way in which the Committees structure their General Recommendations more generally. Both the CEDAW-Com and the CERD regularly adopt Recommendations not centred around one right but rather focused on certain groups of persons, such as refugees, migrants, Roma, indigenous peoples, people of African descent, older and rural women, or certain life situations or areas of particular concern such as contact with law enforcement or the justice system, human trafficking, violence against women, or climate change, to name just a few.[74] When the Committees set out the normative content of equality rights in these Recommendations, they do not conduct a categorisation along the lines of discrimination in the socio-economic or civil and political field.

Regarding the pace of realisation, the CERD does not provide any statements. The CEDAW-Com, however, finds that Article 2 of the CEDAW prescribes the immediate realisation of all rights in the Convention: 'The words "without delay" make it clear that the obligation of States parties to pursue their policy, by all appropriate means, is of an immediate nature.' The Committee further holds that the language in the provision is 'unqualified' and that, therefore, there cannot be any 'delayed or purposely chosen incremental implementation' of the

[71] See, eg, CEDAW-Com, 'General Recommendation No 35 on Gender-based Violence against Women, Updating General Recommendation No 19' (2017) CEDAW/C/GC/35, para 30 (a); similarly CERD, 'General Recommendation No 25 on Gender-related Dimensions of Racial Discrimination' (2000) A/55/18, para 3.

[72] CERD, 'General Recommendation No 29 on Article 1, Paragraph 1, of the Convention (Descent)' (2002) HRI/GEN/1/Rev.7, 226.

[73] See, eg, CEDAW-Com, 'General Recommendation No 32 on the Gender-related Dimensions of Refugee Status, Asylum, Nationality and Statelessness of Women' (2014) CEDAW/C/GC/32, para 21; CEDAW-Com, 'General Recommendation No 30 on Women in Conflict Prevention, Conflict and Post-conflict Situations' (2013) CEDAW/C/GC/30, para 76.

[74] The CRC follows a similar approach, see 3.2.3.

obligations under the CEDAW on grounds of resource or any other constraints.[75] This approach, at least on the surface, appears to be similar to the 'immediate and unqualified' nature other Committees ascribe to civil and political rights. A second look later on at this analysis will reveal, however, that there are considerable parallels to progressive realisation.[76]

3.4. THE HRC

The ICCPR, according the HRC's interpretation, concerns only civil and political rights.[77] Accordingly, the HRC adheres to the traditional interpretation of civil and political rights as immediate and unconditional, regardless of whether the positive or negative dimension is concerned:

> The article 2, paragraph 1, obligation to respect and ensure the rights recognized by the Covenant has immediate effect for all States parties. ... The requirement under article 2, paragraph 2, to take steps to give effect to the Covenant rights is unqualified and of immediate effect. A failure to comply with this obligation cannot be justified by reference to political, social, cultural or economic considerations within the State.[78]

While this approach appears doctrinally sound, issues arise in the context of the right to non-discrimination under Article 26 of the ICCPR. According to the HRC's interpretation, this provision 'prohibits discrimination in law or in fact in any field regulated and protected by public authorities'.[79] Accordingly, the HRC acknowledges that the prohibition of discrimination as laid down in the ICCPR also extends to, for example, the right to social security laid down in Article 9 of the ICESCR.[80] In the individual concurring opinion in the case of *Oulajin and Kaiss v the Netherlands*, the experts appropriately speak of 'the application of article 26 of the Covenant in the field of economic and social rights'.[81] This comprehensive scope of non-discrimination entails issues regarding the

[75] CEDAW-Com, 'General Recommendation No 28 on the Core Obligations of States Parties under Article 2 of the Convention on the Elimination of All Forms of Discrimination against Women' (2010) CEDAW/C/GC/28, para 29; see also CEDAW-Com, 'General Recommendation No 35', para 21.

[76] See 4.4.

[77] See HRC, 'General Comment No 24 on Issues Relating to Reservations Made upon Ratification or Accession to the Covenant or the Optional Protocols thereto, or in Relation to Declarations under Article 41 of the Covenant' (1994) CCPR/C/21/Rev.1/Add.6, para 7; HRC, 'General Comment No 28: Article 3 (The Equality of Rights Between Men and Women)' (2000) HRI/GEN/1/Rev.9, para 9.

[78] HRC, 'General Comment No 31', paras 5, para 14.

[79] HRC, 'General Comment No 18: Non-discrimination' (1989) HRI/GEN/1/Rev.1, para 12.

[80] See, eg, HRC, *Broeks v the Netherlands* [Adoption of Views] (9 April 1987) CCPR/C/OP/2 at 196, paras 12.2–12.3.

[81] HRC, *Oulajin and Kaiss v the Netherlands* [Adoption of Views] (23 October 1992) CCPR/C/46/D/406/1990, individual concurring opinion by Kurt Herndl, Rein Müllerson, Birame N'Diaye and Waleed Sadi.

categorisation of the right to non-discrimination itself. Does it remain a civil and political right in every context, or does its category change according to the area of application? The Committee's General Comments provide no answer to this question. There are, however, a number of individual opinions in the Committee's jurisprudence arguing that Article 26 of the ICCPR should be progressively realisable where non-discrimination regarding socio-economic rights is concerned.[82] It appears that the Committee is not clear on the standard of realisation applicable, even though it claims that all rights under the ICCPR are immediately realisable.

3.5. PERMEABILITY AND INDISTINGUISHABILITY

Another phenomenon further dissolves the boundaries between the two categories in the jurisprudence of the CRPD-Com, CRC-Com and HRC. The Committees' jurisprudence assumes a relationship between socio-economic and civil and political rights which goes beyond the often-invoked concept of interdependence and indivisibility. In a classical interpretation, this concept is taken to mean that the realisation of one right is conducive or even necessary for the realisation of another right.[83] However, the Committees' approach blurs the lines between categories by declaring that obligations – not rights – from one category are relevant for the realisation of rights from the other category. For example, the right to life under Article 6 of the ICCPR is interpreted by the HRC to create the obligation to provide basic healthcare services.[84] This obligation, at the same time, flows from the right to the highest attainable standard of health under Article 12 of the ICESCR.

This phenomenon has been described by Craig Scott as the permeability of human rights norms, based on a term coined by Rosalyn Higgins.[85] According to Scott's conception, permeability describes the capacity of human rights provisions in one treaty to serve as the vehicle for the direct or indirect protection of rights from another treaty which protects a different category of human rights.[86] He argues that the permeability of the ICCPR regarding rights from the ICESCR would entail a 'partial fusion' of both Covenants.[87] Scott made this argument in 1989 and declared that such an approach would permit individuals to claim violations of their rights under the ICESCR before the HRC because an individual claims procedure had not yet been adopted for the ICESCR regime.[88]

[82] See further 4.5.4.
[83] See, eg, UNGA, 'Draft International Covenants on Human Rights', ch II, paras 7–9.
[84] See, eg, HRC, *Toussaint v Canada* [Adoption of Views] (24 July 2018) CCPR/C/123/D/2348/2014, para 11.3.
[85] See Scott, 'Interdependence and Permeability'.
[86] ibid, 771.
[87] ibid, 811 (fn).
[88] ibid, 771.

This approach leads to considerable uncertainty regarding the categorisation of human rights. The question arises whether an obligation is to be fulfilled immediately or progressively if it can be attributed to both a socio-economic and civil and political right. This clear attribution of duties to one or the other category would be necessary in order to comply with the dichotomous understanding of rights. Accordingly, a conception of converging rights emerges which can be described with the term indistinguishability. As Scott noted, not only are the Covenants dependent on each other, they are partially fused in a way which allows no clear separation. Scott Leckie agrees that the permeability of human rights norms from the ICCPR and ICESCR 'should have long ago laid to rest' the strict differentiation between the categories of socio-economic and civil and political rights.[89] According to his understanding, this relationship between rights means that the categorisation cannot serve as a useful tool in interpreting and understanding human rights law in general and violations of human rights norms in particular.[90]

A very illustrative example of this relationship can be found in the HRC's jurisprudence regarding the rights of children under Article 24 of the ICCPR. In General Comment No 17 on this provision, the Committee states that 'measures, although intended primarily to ensure that children fully enjoy the other rights enunciated in the Covenant, may also be economic, social and cultural'.[91] The Committee continues to hold that economic and social measures should be taken to combat violence against and the exploitation of children. Furthermore, educational measures should be taken to enable children 'to enjoy the rights recognized in the Covenant, particularly the right to freedom of opinion and expression'.[92] The obligations or 'measures' are described as socio-economic clearly because they relate to rights in the ICESCR. This stands in contrast to the Committee's conception that all the rights in the ICCPR are civil and political.[93] The Committee's General Comment No 36 on the Right to Life similarly mentions several measures in areas which traditionally would be considered socio-economic, such as education, poverty, homelessness, healthcare, etc, which are required in order to realise the civil and political right to life.[94] The HRC herewith recognises that obligations flowing from socio-economic rights are at the same time obligations pursuant to civil and political rights.

A similar approach is taken by the CRPD-Com in its General Comment on Living Independently and being Included in the Community under Article 19 of the CRPD. As has been set out above, in the eyes of the CRPD-Com, Article 19 (a) of the CRPD reiterates the civil and political right to choose one's place of

[89] Leckie, 'Another Step Towards Indivisibility', 104.
[90] ibid, 104–05.
[91] HRC, 'General Comment No 17: Article 24 (Rights of the Child)' (1989) HRI/GEN/1/Rev.1, para 3.
[92] ibid.
[93] See HRC, 'General Comment No 24', para 7; HRC, 'General Comment No 28', para 9.
[94] See HRC, 'General Comment No 36: Article 6: Right to Life' (2019) CCPR/C/GC/36, paras 8, 26.

residence which also requires the State party to provide real alternatives to exercise this freedom of choice.[95] The duty of providing alternative housing options, however, would traditionally be ascribed to the socio-economic right to housing under, for example, Article 11 of the ICESCR or Article 28 of the CRPD. To be clear, the point made here by the CRPD-Com is not that fulfilling the (socio-economic) right to housing is conducive or necessary to realise the civil and political component of the right to independent living in the sense that both rights are interdependent and indivisible. Rather, the Committee's statements suggest that Article 19 (a) of the CRPD itself directly entails the obligation to provide alternative housing which then leads to considerable uncertainty as to whether this duty is progressively realisable or immediately realisable if a dichotomous understanding is applied.

The CRC-Com generally appears to be more aware of or at least more vocal about these uncertainties:

> The Committee underlines the fact that children's rights are interdependent and indivisible and that caution should be exercised in differentiating between economic, social and cultural rights on the one hand, and civil and political rights on the other. The realization of economic, social and cultural rights will frequently affect children's ability to fully exercise their political and civil rights, and vice versa.[96]

At a first glance, the second sentence of this remark appears like just another reference to the catchphrase 'interdependent and indivisible'. However, the affirmation that the realisation of one category of rights depends on the realisation of the other category as such does not explain why caution should be exercised regarding the establishment of those categories. The interrelationship could also (maybe even more easily) be factored in after delimiting two clear categories. The only sensible reason to call for caution here is the legal consequence of belonging to either group pursuant to Article 4 of the CRC and the uncertainties in differentiating between the two categories: Because there is no reliable way to differentiate between rights, the legally relevant (non-)application of Article 4 of the CRC will amount to an arbitrary decision. In other words, the categories of rights are not only influencing each other but they are also overlapping in the sense that one obligation can be ascribed both to a socio-economic and civil and political right.

An even clearer example of this kind of indistinguishability appears in the jurisprudence of the CESCR. The experts declare that the right to education under Articles 13 and 14 of the ICESCR

> is also, in many ways, a civil right and a political right, since it is central to the full and effective realization of those rights as well. In this respect, the right to education epitomizes the indivisibility and interdependence of all human rights.[97]

[95] See further 3.2.2.
[96] CRC-Com, 'General Comment No 19', para 30.
[97] CESCR, 'General Comment No 11', para 2.

Not only do the experts declare the right to education to be essential for the realisation of civil and political rights, but they hold that its relevance for these aspects makes this right in itself civil and political. The experts thus declare that a right belongs at the same time to both categories, which makes the categories indistinguishable.

3.6. CONCLUSION

Even though the Committees often explicitly insist upon the traditional divide between immediate and progressive realisation, they rarely undertake to categorise rights. In fact, no Committee provides a conclusive categorisation of all rights in their respective treaty, except for the HRC which considers all rights in the ICCPR to be civil and political. In the rare instances in which the Committees apply criteria to categorise rights, they rely on the resemblance to either the ICESCR or ICCPR which does not produce consistent results. Furthermore, more often than not, the Committees set out the obligations of States parties without clarifying whether these obligations must be fulfilled immediately or progressively. Thus, States parties have no clear way of knowing which standard of realisation applies to which right. These difficulties are compounded by the tendency of the experts to attribute one singular State obligation to both socio-economic and civil and political rights. This leads to considerable uncertainties, particularly in the context of mixed provisions in the CRPD and CRC and equality rights under the CEDAW, ICERD and ICCPR. Overall, it can be said that the categories of socio-economic and civil and political rights have become not only interdependent and indivisible but indistinguishable from each other.

This result alone calls into question the dichotomy between immediate and progressive categories of rights. After all, attaching legal consequences to an uncertain differentiation leads to legal uncertainty.[98] It also suggests that, at least subconsciously, the experts of the Committees might not be as committed to the differentiation between immediate and progressive realisation as they sometimes claim to be. Indeed, the next three chapters of this part will reveal that the rhetorical insistence upon the immediate/progressive rights divide is not backed by the remaining jurisprudence of the Committees.

[98] See also further 8.2.1.

4

Civil and Political Rights as Progressively Realisable

4.1. INTRODUCTION

EVEN THOUGH THE Committees frequently claim that civil and political rights must be considered to be immediate and unconditional, they are faced with the same difficulties as they are in the context of socio-economic rights when setting out positive civil and political rights obligations. Positive obligations require resources and societal transformation which, to some extent, render full immediate realisation factually impossible. This logical conclusion creates the suspicion that the Committees might not follow through with their claims of immediacy when faced with the realities of implementation. Accordingly, the hypothesis of convergence suggests that civil and political rights are most likely also interpreted to create obligations which are progressive in the narrow sense. The following chapters reveal what really lies behind the terminology of immediate realisation by inspecting the Committees' concrete description of States parties' positive obligations in the context of civil and political rights.

This chapter directly homes in on the temporal aspect of realisation and analyses instances where the experts implicitly or explicitly recognise that States parties are legally allowed a certain timeframe of realisation instead of demanding immediate fulfilment in the strict sense of the word. The Committees' approach to positive civil and political rights obligations will be at the centre of this inquiry. What complicates the analysis is the fact that the Committees, as noted in the previous chapter, rarely state which right belongs in which category. But in order to determine the standard applied to civil and political rights, it is necessary to know which rights the Committees consider as belonging in this category. This is why the examination of the standard of realisation will focus on two kinds of pronouncements: firstly, statements regarding rights which the Committees explicitly categorise as being (at least partly) civil and political, and, secondly, statements which apply to all rights in the respective treaty and, therefore, also apply to civil and political rights in those treaties which are interpreted to contain this category.

The most conclusive evidence in this regard can be found in the jurisprudence of the CRPD-Com (4.2) and the CRC-Com (4.3) which apply a progressive understanding of realisation in a number of civil and political contexts. But the CEDAW-Com and CERD (4.4) also construct an understanding of obligations which recognises that substantive equality will take time for States parties to establish, no matter whether the equal enjoyment of socio-economic or civil and political rights is concerned. The HRC (4.5) takes a similar approach regarding the right to life, children's rights, and equality.

4.2. THE CRPD-COM

The jurisprudence of the CRPD-Com shows a vast number of examples which reveal a conception of States parties' obligations analogous to progressive realisation. One particularly illustrative example is the concept of 'gradual implementation' of accessibility under Article 9 of the CRPD which is a cross-cutting norm applicable in all areas of the Convention (4.2.1). The CRPD-Com furthermore acknowledges that structural and long-term changes are necessary to enable de facto equality (4.2.2), equal recognition before the law (4.2.3), and the right to live independently under Article 19 (a) of the CRPD (4.2.4), and that these changes will necessarily take time even though the correspondent rights are categorised as civil and political.

4.2.1. Accessibility under Article 9 of the CRPD

The right to accessibility under Article 9 of the CRPD requires States parties to 'ensure to persons with disabilities access … to the physical environment' in a range of spatial and societal contexts. Even though the Committee recognises that accessibility concerns the enjoyment of all rights under the Convention, including civil and political rights (4.2.1.1), the experts develop a standard of 'gradual implementation' for this right which is analogous to progressive realisation (4.2.1.2).

4.2.1.1. Accessibility and Civil and Political Rights

While the CRPD-Com takes no explicit stance on the categorisation of Article 9 of the CRPD and the applicability of Article 4 (2) of the CRPD, the Committee clearly considers accessibility to be part of all rights in the CRPD, regardless of their category. Firstly, the Committee declares that accessibility has roots in classical civil and political rights, for example the right to have access, on general terms of equality, to public service under Article 25 (c) of the ICCPR.[1] Also, from the statements examined in the following paragraphs, it becomes

[1] CRPD-Com, 'General Comment No 2: Article 9: Accessibility' (2014) CRPD/C/GC/2, para 14.

clear that the experts acknowledge that accessibility must be provided in all contexts of the CRPD, including those which are covered by civil and political rights. Accordingly, the standard of 'gradual implementation' explored in the next subsection applies to all aspects in the Convention, including the category of civil and political rights.[2]

The CRPD-Com considers the right to accessibility to be a component of rights in the CRPD which it explicitly categorises as civil and political. One such right is the right to participation of persons with disabilities under Articles 4 (3) and 33 (3) of the CRPD. In General Comment No 7 on the Participation of Persons with Disabilities, the CRPD-Com holds that the duty to 'closely consult and actively involve' persons with disabilities under Article 4 (3) of the CRPD includes the obligation to provide access to relevant information and spaces of public decision-making.[3] Similarly, Article 33 (3) of the CRPD is interpreted to require States parties to provide sufficient funding for organisations of persons with disabilities in order to meet accessibility requirements for their membership.[4] In this General Comment, the CRPD-Com even explicitly refers to the right to accessibility under Article 9 of the CRPD and the corresponding General Comment No 2 when setting out that participation requires measures concerning accessibility.[5] The CRPD-Com also defines the denial of accessibility as a form of discrimination.[6] The prohibition of discrimination is usually categorised as an immediately realisable civil and political right.

Lastly, the Committee's statements in General Comment No 2 imply that the experts at least do not consider Article 9 of the CRPD to entirely fall into the category of socio-economic rights, even though it might contain some traditionally socio-economic aspects. The Committee describes accessibility as unconditional,[7] which, according to the experts' interpretation of Article 4 (2) of the CRPD, is a feature of civil and political rights.[8] The Committee furthermore does not refer to Article 4 (2) of the CRPD in order to claim a standard of progressive realisation. Instead, the Committee chooses to establish 'gradual implementation' as a similar concept with a different name. In contrast, General Comment No 5 explicitly refers to the concept of progressive realisation and the jurisprudence of the CESCR when talking about a right that the experts consider to be socio-economic.[9] It appears that the CRPD-Com is aware of the contradiction between the professed immediacy of civil and political rights and

[2] The civil and political dimension of accessibility in the jurisprudence of the Committees is confirmed by the fact that the CRC talks about accessibility under the heading 'civil rights and freedoms', see CRC-Com, 'General Comment No 9', paras 39–40.

[3] CRPD-Com, 'General Comment No 7', paras 17, 22, 45, 77.

[4] ibid, para 39.

[5] ibid, para 77.

[6] CRPD-Com, 'General Comment No 2', para 13; similarly ibid, para 23.

[7] ibid, para 25.

[8] See further 3.2.1.

[9] CRPD-Com, 'General Comment No 5', para 41.

the gradual nature of realisation proposed for accessibility under Article 9 of the CRPD and thus chooses to use a different terminology.

4.2.1.2. Gradual Implementation and Progressive Realisation

In its second General Comment, the CRPD-Com engages in detail with the right to accessibility under Article 9 of the CRPD and establishes a standard of 'gradual implementation' of this right. This concept shows considerable parallels to progressive realisation.[10] The Committee's jurisprudence reveals that gradual implementation, too, requires States parties to immediately undertake steps in order to embark upon the process of providing full accessibility in the future. This approach resembles the differentiation between immediate obligations of conduct and progressive obligations of result laid out above.[11] However, the CRPD-Com seemingly prefers to develop a congruent standard with slightly different terminology. One reason for this rather awkward detour might be that the experts describe certain elements of accessibility as civil and political while also being confronted with the fact that a gradual standard of realisation is needed because of the positive duties pursuant to Article 9 of the ICRPD.

The Committee, on the one hand, sets out an immediate component of the right to accessibility by declaring that '[p]ersons with disabilities should have equal access to all goods, products and services that are open or provided to the public …; denial of access should be considered to constitute a discriminatory act'.[12] The Committee furthermore holds that '[t]he obligation to implement accessibility is *unconditional*, ie, the entity obliged to provide accessibility may not excuse the omission to do so by referring to the burden of providing access for persons with disabilities' (emphasis added).[13] These statements, in their absoluteness, imply that every lack of accessibility must be considered to be in breach of Article 9 of the CRPD and that considerations of limited resources may not justify the interpretation of this right as containing progressively realisable duties. This would not leave any leeway for removing barriers to accessibility over time.[14]

On the other hand, General Comment No 2 contains several references to the 'gradual' implementation of Article 9 of the CRPD, for example the following: 'Barriers to access to existing objects, facilities, goods and services aimed at or open to the public shall be removed gradually in a systematic and, more

[10] This has also been noted by Anna Lawson in A Lawson, 'Article 9: Accessibility' in I Bantekas, MA Stein and D Anastasiou (eds), *The UN Convention on the Rights of Persons with Disabilities: A Commentary* (Oxford, Oxford University Press, 2018) 271 and A Lawson, 'Accessibility Obligations in the UN Convention on the Rights of Persons with Disabilities: Nyusti & Takács v. Hungary' (2014) 30 *South African Journal on Human Rights* 380, 387.

[11] See further 2.2.3.

[12] CRPD-Com, 'General Comment No 2', para 13; similarly ibid, para 23.

[13] ibid, para 25.

[14] See Lawson, 'Article 9', 271.

importantly, continuously monitored manner, with the aim of achieving full accessibility.'[15] Furthermore, States parties are described as struggling with the training of stakeholders and the involvement of persons with disabilities and their representative organisations 'in *the process of ensuring access* to the physical environment, transport and communication' (emphasis added).[16]

Thus, General Comment No 2 leaves the reader puzzled as to how it is possible to reconcile the statements of 'unconditionality' and 'failure to provide accessibility equals discrimination' with the gradual nature of duties.[17] Only a closer look at the larger context of the Comment reveals that the Committee considers as immediate only the obligation to take steps, while the overall full realisation of accessibility is seen as gradual. The first step in resolving the apparent contradiction in the CRPD-Com's approach lies in understanding the Committee's differentiation between newly created and already existing objects and their accessibility. According to the Committee,

> [a] clear distinction should be drawn between the obligation to ensure access to all *newly designed, built or produced* objects, infrastructure, goods, products and services and the obligation to remove barriers and ensure access to the *existing* physical environment and *existing* transportation, information and communication, and services open to the general public. (emphases added)[18]

On the one hand, there is a strict duty to ensure full access to new goods, products, etc, by strictly applying universal design.[19] On the other hand, the Committee recognises that the duty to adapt existing things to meet the standard of accessibility must be interpreted to be a gradual duty. Accordingly, the CRPD-Com declares that 'States parties are obliged to ensure that persons with disabilities have access to the *existing* physical environment, transportation, information and communication and services open to the general public. However, … this obligation is to be implemented *gradually*' (emphasis added).[20]

Quite intuitively, the reason for this differentiation lies (at least partially) in the cost of the measures needed to ensure accessibility in both situations respectively. A vivid example is provided by the Committee in General Comment No 2 which can be used to illustrate the underlying rationale:

> Making a building accessible from the outset might not increase the total cost of construction at all in many cases, or only minimally in some cases. On the other hand, the cost of subsequent adaptations in order to make a building accessible may be considerable in some cases, especially with regard to certain historical buildings.[21]

[15] CRPD-Com, 'General Comment No 2', para 14; see also ibid, paras 24, 25, 27, 30.
[16] ibid, para 10.
[17] This has also been recognised by Uerpmann-Wittzack, 'Die UN-Behindertenrechtskonvention', 200.
[18] CRPD-Com, 'General Comment No 2', para 24.
[19] ibid; see also ibid, para 15.
[20] ibid, para 24; see also ibid, para 14.
[21] ibid, para 15; see also ibid, para 11.

The same argument is extended regarding information and communications technology (ICT).[22] Hence, the Committee recognises that the cost connected to adapting the physical environment, information systems, and the legal system to the needs of persons with disabilities is a relevant factor for the normative content of Article 9 of the CRPD. This is further confirmed when the Committee notes that States must adopt an action plan to 'provide both the human and material resources necessary to remove the barriers' and later 'continue providing sufficient funds to remove barriers to accessibility'.[23] Therefore, the distinction between new and existing objects and services can be understood as an approximation for the distinction between costly and free or cheap duties. Even though retrofitting might not always be significantly more expensive than planning accessibility from the outset, the Committee's argument shows that cost is the decisive factor for the determination of the immediacy or progressiveness of obligations. The full provision of accessibility may only be delayed by States parties if a lack of available resources provides sufficient grounds for it. This is the same argument which constituted the basis for accepting a standard of progressive realisation in the context of socio-economic rights.[24]

The second step in clarifying the Committee's position requires exploring the meaning of 'unconditional'. The relevant statement must be seen in the context of the whole paragraph, which sets out a comparison to reasonable accommodation. After describing Article 9 of the CRPD as unconditional, the Committee goes on to state that '[t]he duty of reasonable accommodation, contrarily, exists only if implementation constitutes no undue burden on the entity'.[25] What matters here is the focus on the existence of a duty as a whole. Hence, describing the right of accessibility as unconditional must be understood to pre-empt a complete refusal of the State to take *any steps* toward making an object or service accessible by referencing the costs. In other words, States parties cannot refer to the cost of establishing accessibility to justify not taking any steps, ie completely refusing to work towards the realisation of accessibility.[26]

However, since removing barriers is a gradual duty, the State party can argue that it is not yet under a duty to provide complete accessibility. Thus, not every instance where accessibility has not been achieved completely constitutes a case of disability-based discrimination.[27] After this adjustment, it becomes clear that, when the Committee refers to a 'denial of access' as being discriminatory,[28] this phrase must be read as a 'denial of access to newly created objects, services, etc' or as a 'denial of taking any/sufficient steps towards the gradual

[22] ibid, para 15.
[23] ibid, para 33.
[24] See further 1.2.3.
[25] CRPD-Com, 'General Comment No 2', para 25.
[26] This aspect is further explored below, see 8.3.2.1.
[27] The same conclusion is drawn by Lawson, 'Accessibility Obligations in the ICRPD', 390.
[28] CRPD-Com, 'General Comment No 2', para 13; similarly ibid, para 23.

implementation of accessibility'. Furthermore, the Committee clarifies that denying accessibility by actively and purposefully creating or maintaining barriers for disabled persons (eg, by prohibiting guide dogs in public buildings) will always be discriminatory.[29]

This result is confirmed when the Committee states that 'the potential cost of subsequent removal of barriers may not be used as an excuse to avoid the obligation to remove barriers to accessibility *gradually*' (emphasis added).[30] Here it becomes clear that there is no contradiction between unconditionality and gradual implementation, ie, that the duty to remove barriers to accessibility is both gradual and unconditional. The Committee explicitly relates the irrelevance of limited resources to the duty to remove barriers gradually, or, in other words, to take steps *in general*. This, however, does not mean that the pace of realisation is not influenced by the cost and available resources. In essence, the Committee insists that resource limitations cannot justify complete inaction; there are always some steps States parties can and must take immediately.

The CRPD-Com engages in detail with the immediate obligation to take steps flowing from gradual implementation, speaking of policies, strategies, and timelines, as the CESCR does too.[31] The experts declare that '[a]n analysis of the situation to identify the obstacles and barriers that need to be removed can be carried out in an efficient manner and within a short- to mid-term framework'.[32] Also, action plans, timelines and deadlines are mentioned as necessary elements.[33] The CRPD-Com also determines that '[i]f no relevant legislation is in place, adopting a suitable legal framework is the first step'.[34] The CRPD-Com further holds that '[b]arriers should be removed in a continuous and systematic way, gradually yet steadily',[35] which is reminiscent of the CESCR's standard of 'deliberate, concrete and targeted steps'.[36]

4.2.2. Equality and Non-discrimination under Article 5 CRPD

The CRPD-Com implicitly acknowledges that the creation of de facto or substantive equality is not an immediate obligation. The experts recognise that Article 5 of the CRPD 'prohibits de jure or de facto discrimination in any field regulated and protected by public authority'.[37] This means that the obligation

[29] ibid, para 29.
[30] ibid, para 15.
[31] *cf* 2.3.1.
[32] CRPD-Com, 'General Comment No 2', para 27.
[33] ibid, para 33.
[34] ibid, para 28.
[35] ibid, para 27.
[36] *cf* 2.4.1.
[37] CRPD-Com, 'General Comment No 6 on Equality and Non-discrimination' (2018) CRPD/C/GC/6, para 13.

of non-discrimination under the CRPD extends to all fields in the Convention, no matter the category of the correspondent rights. This reflects the definition of discrimination provided in Article 2 of the CRPD which speaks of inequalities in the enjoyment of 'all human rights and fundamental freedoms in the political, economic, social, cultural, civil or any other field'.

The CRPD's definition of discrimination builds upon the definitions contained in Article 1 of the ICERD and Article 1 of the CEDAW but adds two new aspects: the phrase 'on an equal basis with others' and the inclusion of a denial of reasonable accommodation as a form of discrimination. These new features, according to the CRPD-Com, represent the inclusion of de facto or substantive equality as a principle of the Convention.[38] Substantive equality or the 'equalization of opportunities', according to the CRPD-Com, seeks to 'address structural and indirect discrimination and takes into account power relations'.[39]

It becomes clear that the experts consider this substantive dimension of equality to be a long-term goal instead of an immediate obligation of result. The experts start out with the common assertion that non-discrimination is an immediate obligation, stating that '[p]romoting equality and tackling discrimination are cross-cutting obligations of immediate realization. They are not subject to progressive realization.'[40] The wording of this statement, however, does not indicate that the complete creation of substantive equality is an immediate obligation, but rather relates to the 'promoting' and 'tackling' of this goal. Consequently, while States parties must immediately embark upon the path towards substantive equality by taking steps, this can only be understood as an immediate obligation of conduct rather than result. The Committee thus only rejects the narrow meaning of progressive realisation by holding that action must be taken immediately. What it does not reject but implicitly endorses is the umbrella meaning of progressive realisation, as the following examples will illustrate.

The language of later sections of General Comment No 6 on Equality and Non-discrimination further supports this conclusion. The experts see societal transformation over time as a necessary precondition for the creation of substantive equality when they hold that the model of equality under the Convention requires States parties 'to combat stigma, stereotyping, prejudice and violence'.[41] According to the CRPD-Com, '[d]iscrimination cannot be combated without awareness-raising among all sectors of government and society', and, consequently, States parties must take 'adequate awareness-raising measures and measures to change or abolish compounded pejorative disability stereotypes and

[38] ibid, para 17.
[39] ibid, para 10.
[40] ibid, para 12.
[41] ibid, para 11.

negative attitudes'.[42] Accordingly, for cases '[w]here the discrimination is of a systemic nature', the remedy scheme of States parties must include 'forward-looking, non-pecuniary remedies'.[43]

The CRPD-Com also describes the right to accessibility under Article 9 of the CRPD as 'a precondition and a means to achieve de facto equality for all persons with disabilities'.[44] As has been seen in the previous subsection, the 'gradual implementation' of accessibility is analogous to progressive realisation.[45] If a progressively realisable right is a means of achieving de facto equality, then the realisation of de facto equality in itself is also necessarily progressive in nature. In other words, if States parties are allowed to realise a necessary precondition of equality over time, it would be contradictory to immediately demand the result of this measure in the context of a different right.

Another hint at the progressiveness of the obligation to create substantive equality is the regime of specific measures under Article 5 (4) of the CRPD. According to the treaty text itself, specific measures can be necessary to 'accelerate or achieve de facto equality of persons with disabilities'. Such 'positive or affirmative measures', for example, 'outreach and support programmes, allocation and/or reallocation of resources, targeted recruitment, hiring and promotion, quota systems' are not to be considered discriminatory, even though they prioritise the disadvantaged group.[46] The notion of 'acceleration' necessarily presupposes a process over time instead of a one-off immediate obligation to create de facto equality.[47] Accordingly, the experts hold that specific measures must be adopted 'with a view to achieving inclusive equality'.[48] The progressive nature of de facto equality is further illustrated by the fact that specific measures under Article 5 (4) of the CRPD are 'usually temporary in nature',[49] meaning that they should be discontinued when they have reached their purpose in accelerating the progress towards substantive equality.

Lastly, the CRPD-Com declares that 'in close consultation' with persons with disabilities and their organisations, 'an equality policy and strategy' must be developed by States parties.[50] The experts of the CRPD-Com state that States parties 'must collect and analyse appropriate data and research information in order to identify inequalities, discriminatory practices and patterns of disadvantage, and analyse the effectiveness of measures promoting equality'.[51] This data

[42] ibid, para 39.
[43] ibid, para 22.
[44] ibid, para 40.
[45] See 4.2.1.2.
[46] CRPD-Com, 'General Comment No 6', para 28.
[47] The same is true for the regime of special measures under the CEDAW and ICERD, see further 4.4.2.
[48] CRPD-Com, 'General Comment No 6', para 73 (o).
[49] ibid, para 28.
[50] ibid, para 73 (j).
[51] ibid, para 34.

should also include 'indicators to assess the implementation and monitor the *progress* and effectiveness of new or ongoing initiatives and policies' (emphasis added).[52]

4.2.3. Equal Recognition before the Law under Article 12 CRPD

Regarding the right to equal recognition before the law under Article 12 of the CRPD, the CRPD-Com's General Comment No 1 stresses the immediate and unconditional nature of duties flowing from this right, insisting that '"[p]rogressive realization" (art. 4, para. 2) does not apply'.[53] However, the following statement clarifies that the experts only reject the application of progressive realisation in the narrow sense while embracing a concept analogous to the umbrella sense of the term:

> Upon ratifying the Convention, States parties must immediately *begin taking steps towards the realization* of the rights provided for in article 12. Those steps must be deliberate, well-planned and include consultation with and meaningful participation of people with disabilities and their organizations. (emphasis added)[54]

While the Committee used the phrase 'take steps to immediately realize' a few sentences before,[55] it now refers to an obligation to 'immediately begin taking steps towards the realization of the rights'. This language points to an obligation of conduct rather than an obligation of result. Steps towards the realisation of equality before the law are not equal to the full realisation of the right. Furthermore, the Committee declares that those steps must be 'deliberate, well-planned and include consultation with and meaningful participation of people with disabilities and their organizations',[56] which is in line with what is required of progressive realisation in the context of the ICESCR.

It appears that the experts are subject to the misconception that progressive realisation pursuant to Article 4 (2) of the CRPD does not encompass immediate obligations but instead only progressive obligations in the narrow sense of the word and thus reject the application of this concept while setting out a standard analogous to progressive realisation in the following paragraphs.

4.2.4. Independent Living under Article 19 of the CRPD

A gradual notion of realisation also appears in the CRPD-Com's interpretation of the right to independent living under Article 19 of the CRPD. The experts of

[52] ibid, para 71.
[53] CRPD-Com, 'General Comment No 1', para 30.
[54] ibid.
[55] ibid.
[56] ibid.

the CRPD-Com consider Article 19 (a) of the CRPD to establish the civil and political right to choose one's residence, while Article 19 (b) and (c) of the CRPD set out socio-economic rights.[57] As mentioned above, the experts also insist that the civil and political rights under Article 19 CRPD are 'absolute and immediately applicable' while socio-economic rights are 'progressively applicable'.[58] It becomes clear over the course of this Comment, however, that the experts set out a standard of realisation analogous to the umbrella meaning of progressive realisation when talking about the civil and political aspects of Article 19 of the CRPD. The experts implicitly construct immediate obligations of conduct while accepting that the long-term goals in this context are progressive in the narrow sense of the word. Again, confusion appears to arise from the ambiguity of the term progressive realisation.

Regarding Article 19 (a) of the CRPD, the experts recognise that the formal freedom to choose one's residence is meaningless without real alternatives to choose from, ie, without housing options provided by the State party.[59] General Comment No 5 on Article 19 of the CRPD accordingly sets out that '[d]einstitutionalization also requires a systemic transformation'[60] which includes removing barriers to the right to live independently and be included in the community, eg, by making inaccessible housing options accessible for persons with disabilities.[61] It must be noted that these statements are made under the heading 'Obligation to fulfil' which does not differentiate between the socio-economic and civil and political elements contained within Article 19 of the CRPD. Thus, this transformative (and therefore necessarily progressive) approach must be understood to also refer to the right under Article 19 (a) of the CRPD which was declared to be civil and political.

This result is explicitly confirmed when the CRPD-Com states that the '[f]ull realization also requires structural changes that may need to be taken in stages, whether civil and political or social, economic and cultural rights are at stake'.[62] The Committee seemingly was aware of the fact that realising rights in stages equals progressive realisation and therefore saw fit to clarify that this standard applies to both categories of rights which would otherwise not be self-evident according to the dichotomous understanding. The experts also repeatedly stress that monitoring and follow-up procedures are critical in the process of realising the right to independent living.[63]

The CRPD-Com also determines that Article 19 (a) of the CRPD requires States parties to '[a]dopt clear and targeted strategies for deinstitutionalization, with specific time frames and adequate budgets, in order to eliminate all forms

[57] CRPD-Com, 'General Comment No 5', para 39.
[58] ibid.
[59] ibid, para 25.
[60] ibid, para 58; see also ibid, para 41.
[61] ibid, para 54.
[62] ibid, para 7.
[63] ibid, paras 70, 15 (i), 97 (n).

of isolation, segregation and institutionalization of persons with disabilities'.[64] This further clarifies that deinstitutionalisation as a part of the civil and political right under Article 19 (a) of the CRPD is a process of realisation which demands long-term planning and 'structural reforms' from States parties.[65] The experts signal that, while the adoption of strategies, plans of action, and timelines is to be tackled immediately, the aim of these measures – structural reform – is a long-term goal. This coincides with the CESCR's conception of progressive realisation which determines that planning and strategising are obligations which can and therefore must be undertaken immediately.[66] Another parallel to the approach of the CESCR is the requirement of consulting and actively involving persons with disabilities and their organisations in the process of drafting these policies.[67]

An additional implicit reference to progressive realisation is the CRPD-Com's recognition that retrogressive measures require particular justification. Using the term retrogressive implies that the opposite of it, namely progress, must be the rule when realising the right in question. The Committee states that '[w]hen a State party seeks to introduce retrogressive measures with respect to article 19, … the State is obliged to demonstrate that such measures are temporary, necessary and non-discriminatory and that they respect its core obligations'.[68] Again, this statement can only be understood to refer to Article 19 of the CRPD as a whole as it is made under the heading 'Obligations of States parties' which does not differentiate between different parts of this provision. Furthermore, the following paragraph states that '[t]he duty of progressive realization *also* entails a presumption against retrogressive measures in the enjoyment of economic, social and cultural rights' (emphasis added),[69] indicating that the previous paragraph is not limited to socio-economic rights.

4.3. THE CRC-COM

The CRC-Com's jurisprudence shows several instances where the realisation of civil and political rights is described as contingent on transforming the attitude of society. This conception of obligations necessarily sets a long-term goal which must be realised progressively by the States parties, as becomes clear in the following analysis. The Committee's jurisprudence regarding the general measures of implementation required by the CRC illustrates that the experts envision an immediate obligation of conduct, namely devising a children's rights strategy, aimed at a progressive improvement of the enjoyment of rights under

[64] ibid, para 97 (g).
[65] ibid, para 57.
[66] *cf* 2.3.1.
[67] See CRPD-Com, 'General Comment No 5', para 56.
[68] ibid, para 43.
[69] ibid, para 44.

the Convention (4.3.1). This approach is mirrored in the CRC-Com's General Comments on the right to be heard under Article 12 of the CRC (4.3.2), the right to be free from all forms of violence under Article 19 of the CRC (4.3.3), and children's rights in the criminal justice system under Article 40 of the CRC (4.3.4).

4.3.1. General Measures of Implementation

When the CRC-Com talks about general measures of implementation, it frequently does not draw a line between socio-economic and civil and political rights. Nevertheless, many of the measures set out in this context indicate a progressive notion of realisation. The language of the CRC-Com's General Comment No 5 on General Measures of Implementation gives a first impression of this approach. When elaborating upon the requirements for a children's rights strategy, the CRC-Com holds that

> it must include a description of a sustainable *process* for realizing the rights of children throughout the State; it must go beyond statements of policy and principle, to set real and achievable targets in relation to the *full range* of economic, social and cultural and civil and political rights for all children. (emphases added)[70]

The experts thus recognise that the 'full range' of all rights requires a 'process' of realisation which is best fostered by establishing certain targets on the way to the full realisation of rights. Later on in the Comment, the experts also speak of a 'process of implementation'.[71] Furthermore, the CRC-Com's acknowledgment that prioritisation is inevitable, and that targets must be achievable, points at the recognition of factors limiting the pace of realisation of rights.[72] It can reasonably be assumed that one important factor is the availability of (financial) resources.[73]

The CRC-Com's General Comment No 5 also contains a lengthy section on the implementation of children's rights through 'administrative and other measures' which does not differentiate between the two categories of rights. In the first subsection of this part, the experts lay out the requirements for a 'comprehensive national strategy rooted in the Convention'.[74] Already the focus on a strategy and a 'national plan of action'[75] as such implies the gradual progress towards a goal over time. Furthermore, the CRC-Com declares that '[p]articular attention will need to be given to identifying and giving priority to marginalized

[70] CRC-Com, 'General Comment No 5', para 32.
[71] ibid, para 58.
[72] See ibid, para 32.
[73] For more detail on the issue of resource dependency, see 5.3.
[74] CRC-Com, 'General Comment No 5', paras 28–36.
[75] ibid, paras 29, 32.

and disadvantaged groups of children'.[76] This focus on vulnerable groups – and prioritisation in general – is a classic feature of progressive realisation. '[M]eaningful consultation' with children is also set out as a requirement of policy-making in this context.[77]

Monitoring as a measure specifically aimed at ensuring progress in rights realisation is frequently mentioned in the CRC-Com's jurisprudence regarding civil and political rights. In General Comment No 5, the CRC-Com declares that measures of 'continuous review', 'regular updating' and 'periodic reports to parliament and to the public' are necessary to realise the rights under the Convention.[78] In this context, the experts also talk about the 'independent monitoring of progress towards implementation'.[79] Furthermore, the Committee recommends the establishment of nationally applicable indicators which can be used to 'build up a complete picture of progress towards implementation'.[80]

Lastly, in General Comment No 19 on Public Budgeting, the Committee regularly speaks of the 'advancing' of children's rights as a whole, eg, when setting out that 'all government branches, levels and structures are responsible for *advancing* the rights of the child' or that Article 44 of the CRC obligates States parties to report their '*progress in advancing* the rights of children' (emphases added).[81] In General Comment No 2 on the Role of Independent National Human Rights Institutions (NHRIs) in the Promotion and Protection of the Rights of the Child, the experts hold that '[t]he role of NHRIs is to monitor independently the State's compliance and *progress towards implementation* and to do all it can to ensure full respect for children's rights' (emphasis added).[82]

4.3.2. The Right to be Heard under Article 12 of the CRC

According to General Comment No 5, the right to be heard under Article 12 of the CRC is one of the provisions in the Convention that 'contain elements which constitute civil/political rights'.[83] But in this document, the Committee does not further clarify which elements belong to which category. The CRC-Com's General Comment No 12 on this right also does not address this question. The Comment's section on State parties' duties does not differentiate between

[76] ibid, para 30; see also CRC-Com, 'General Comment No 13', para 72 (g).
[77] CRC-Com, 'General Comment No 5', para 29.
[78] ibid, para 33.
[79] ibid, para 46.
[80] ibid, para 48.
[81] CRC-Com, 'General Comment No 19', paras 23, 32; see also ibid, paras 22, 95, 97.
[82] CRC-Com, 'General Comment No 2: The Role of Independent National Human Rights Institutions in the Promotion and Protection of the Rights of the Child' (2002) CRC/GC/2002/2, para 25.
[83] CRC-Com, 'General Comment No 5', para 6.

immediately and progressively realisable obligations.[84] Only in its very last section, the Comment sets out that

> [i]nvestment in the realization of the child's right to be heard in all matters of concern to her or him and for her or his views to be given due consideration, is a clear and immediate legal obligation of States parties.[85]

This statement implies that the immediacy of obligations is limited to obligations of conduct, namely to investment in the realisation instead of full realisation. This is in line with the standard of progressive realisation which requires States parties to immediately take steps. The remarks following the above statement confirm this interpretation. The Committee declares that realising Article 12 of the CRC will require 'dismantling … legal, political, economic, social and cultural barriers' and 'challeng[ing] assumptions about children's capacities' as well as a 'commitment to resources and training'.[86] With these statements, the experts recognise the role that resources and deeply rooted societal barriers play for the realisation of the right. The last paragraph of the Comment goes on to recognise the effect these limiting factors will have on the pace of realisation: 'Fulfilling these obligations will present a challenge for States parties. But it is an attainable goal if the strategies outlined in this General Comment are systematically implemented and a culture of respect for children and their views is built.'[87]

While the full realisation of the right is the ultimate goal for States parties, the experts acknowledge that, due to the factors mentioned above, this goal will only be realised over time by progressively fostering social change.

4.3.3. The Right to be Free from All Forms of Violence under Article 19 of the CRC

Similar tendencies are discernible in the context of the right to be free from all forms of violence under Article 19 of the CRC. This right is categorised by the CRC-Com to be a 'a civil right and freedom' in General Comment No 13. Accordingly, the implementation of Article 19 of the CRC is held to be an 'immediate and unqualified obligation of States parties'.[88] However, it becomes clear in the following statements that the notion of immediacy is only

[84] CRC-Com, 'General Comment No 12: The Right of the Child to be Heard' (2009) CRC/C/GC/12, paras 48–67.
[85] ibid, para 135.
[86] ibid.
[87] ibid, para 136 (the original document misnumbers this paragraph as 134); see also CRC-Com, 'General Comment No 14 on the Right of the Child to have his or her Best Interests Taken as a Primary Consideration (art. 3, para. 1)' (2013) CRC/C/GC/14, para 15 (h): Here, the CRC-Com stresses that States parties must combat 'all negative attitudes and perceptions which impede the full realization of the right of the child to have his or her best interests assessed and taken as a primary consideration'.
[88] CRC-Com, 'General Comment No 13', para 65.

meant to refer to the obligation to take steps and not to the result of full realisation. Thus, immediate realisation only contrasts progressive realisation in the narrow sense of the word and is not in contradiction to the umbrella concept. For example, directly after insisting upon the immediacy and absoluteness of the right, the experts go on to state the following:

> In the light of article 4, whatever their economic circumstances, States are required to undertake all possible measures towards the realization of the rights of the child, paying special attention to the most disadvantaged groups (see the Committee's general comment No. 5, para. 8). The article stresses that available resources must be utilized to the maximum extent.[89]

It appears that the CRC-Com is referring to the second sentence of Article 4 of the CRC, which sets out the relevance of limited resources (and, implicitly, progressive realisation)[90] for socio-economic rights. This statement is in direct contrast to the classification of Article 19 of the CRC as an 'immediate and unqualified' civil and political right and one of many examples where the CRC-Com applies Article 4 of the CRC as a whole to civil and political rights.[91] A progressive notion of realisation is also reflected in the wording 'undertake all possible measures towards'.

Additionally, this section of the text cites the CRC-Com's own General Comment No 5 concerning General Measures of Implementation. The cited paragraph elaborates further on what the second sentence of Article 4 of the CRC means, stating that it is similar to what the ICESCR sets out. Furthermore, General Comment No 5 in turn refers to the ICESCR's General Comment No 3 on the Nature of States Parties' Obligations by citing the following statement: '[E]ven where the available resources are demonstrably inadequate, the obligation remains for a State party to strive to ensure the widest possible enjoyment of the relevant rights under the prevailing circumstances.'[92] Thus, the notion that 'resource limitations cannot justify inaction' is clearly being incorporated into the CRC-Com's interpretation of the civil and political right to freedom from all forms of violence under Article 19 of the CRC.

This is confirmed when the CRC-Com states that 'resource constraints cannot provide a justification for a State party's failure to take *any, or enough, of the measures* that are required for child protection' (emphasis added).[93] Like the CRPD-Com, the CRC-Com holds that resource limitations are no excuse for complete inaction or for inadequate steps towards the goal of realisation. Implied in this statement is the finding that, in contrast to the obligation to take steps, complete realisation is subject to the availability of resources.

[89] ibid.

[90] *cf* 1.2.2.

[91] This frequently occurs in the jurisprudence of the CRC, see further 5.3.1.

[92] CRC-Com, 'General Comment No 5', para 8, referencing CESCR, 'General Comment No 3', paras 11, 16.

[93] CRC-Com, 'General Comment No 13', para 73.

Interestingly, the statement that limited resources cannot justify the failure to take 'any, or enough,' of the required measures appears almost word for word in the CRC-Com's General Comment on the Aims of Education (a traditional socio-economic right) in the context of the second sentence of Article 4 of the CRC.[94]

The Committee furthermore repeatedly engages with societal transformation as a necessary part of realising the right under Article 19 of the CRC. The experts declare that

> [w]idespread social and cultural attitudes and practices condone violence. The impact of measures taken is limited by a lack of knowledge, data and understanding of violence against children and its root causes [and] by reactive efforts focusing on symptoms and consequences rather than causes.[95]

In order to address these root causes, States parties should take measures to challenge 'attitudes which perpetuate the tolerance and condoning of violence in all its forms'.[96] For example, '[e]ducational measures should address attitudes, traditions, customs and behavioural practices which condone and promote violence against children'.[97] The experts focus on social transformation instead of a certain standard of protection as an immediate result, thereby implicitly recognising that the full implementation of the right will take time.

Other General Comments which touch on the right to be free from all forms of violence likewise present a progressive notion of eliminating the structural causes of violence against children. In its General Comment No 8 on the Right to be Protected from Corporal Punishment, the Committee recognises that a 'change in attitudes and practice' will be necessary to counteract this specific form of violence and to fully realise the right under Article 19 of the CRC.[98] Accordingly, the CRC-Com repeatedly speaks of the '*progress* towards achieving full respect for children's rights to protection from all forms of violence' (emphasis added).[99] The CRC-Com's and CEDAW-Com's joint General Comment No 18 on Harmful Practices concerns, among other rights, the right to freedom from all forms of violence under Article 19 of the CRC.[100] In this text, the Committees acknowledge that the elimination of harmful practices is dependent upon a process of transforming attitudes and addressing the underlying systemic

[94] CRC-Com, 'General Comment No 1: Article 29 (1): The Aims of Education' (2001) CRC/GC/2001/1, para 28; see also, in the context of HIV and health care, CRC-Com, 'General Comment No 3: HIV/AIDS and the Rights of the Child' (2003) CRC/GC/2003/3, para 14.

[95] CRC-Com, 'General Comment No 13', para 12.

[96] ibid, para 47 (a) (i).

[97] ibid, para 44.

[98] CRC-Com, 'General Comment No 8', para 45.

[99] ibid, para 53, see also ibid, para 51.

[100] CRC-Com, 'General Comment No 18 on Harmful Practices' (2019) CRC/C/GC/18/Rev.1, para 14 (fn).

and structural causes.[101] The experts regularly speak of 'progress' in protecting women and children or eliminating harmful practices towards these groups.[102]

In General Comment No 13, the CRC-Com also clarifies that States parties must provide information regarding the 'prevalence of all forms of violence and progress towards their elimination'[103] and recommends that 'States parties publish an annual report on *progress* made with regard to the prohibition, prevention and elimination of violence' (emphasis added).[104] Furthermore, the Comment envisions 'comprehensive, strategic and time-bound coordinating frameworks for child caregiving and protection'[105] and speaks of the 'process of developing a national coordinating framework'.[106] Later on, the Committee determines that the realisation of children's rights requires a child rights approach which '*furthers the realization* of the rights of all children as set out in the Convention by developing the capacity of duty bearers to meet their obligations to respect, protect and fulfil rights (art. 4)' (emphasis added).[107] All these examples further illustrate the conclusion that the CRC-Com envisions that States parties must immediately start a sustainable and effective process of actively eliminating violence against children aimed at reaching this goal as quickly as possible.

4.3.4. Rights in Criminal Law and Criminal Proceedings under Article 40 of the CRC

The experts of the CRC-Com also set out the realisation of children's rights in the justice system as a gradual process. In general, 'States parties should immediately embark on a process to reduce reliance on detention to a minimum'.[108] Clearly, the Committee acknowledges that reducing the number of children and juveniles behind bars to a minimum, while being a central aim of the Convention, cannot be achieved immediately. This further becomes clear when inspecting the CRC-Com's promotion of diversion measures for children accused of criminal offences. Here, the experts hold that diversion avoids 'stigmatization and criminal records' and 'yields good results for children'.[109] Therefore, '[d]iversion should be the preferred manner of dealing with children in the majority of cases' and 'States parties should *continually extend* the range of offences for which diversion is possible', ultimately making diversion 'an integral part of the

[101] ibid, para 17.
[102] ibid, paras 35, 37.
[103] CRC-Com, 'General Comment No 13', para 10.
[104] ibid, para 72 (j).
[105] ibid, para 73.
[106] ibid, para 71.
[107] ibid, para 59.
[108] CRC-Com, 'General Comment No 24', para 83.
[109] ibid, para 15.

child justice system' (emphasis added).[110] The Committee declares that diversion should be used as a tool to gradually reduce the number of children behind bars but does not demand that this measure immediately replaces incarceration completely.

4.4. THE CEDAW-COM AND CERD

The jurisprudence of the CEDAW-Com and CERD shows the focus on a process of societal transformation even more clearly than the jurisprudence of the CRPD-Com and CRC-Com. Both the CEDAW-Com and the CERD apply a standard analogous to progressive realisation concerning the pursuit of de facto equality in the enjoyment of all rights.[111] The experts' conception of the general obligation of non-discrimination shows that they acknowledge that the creation of de facto equality requires time due to entrenched attitudes and traditions, while de jure non-discrimination cannot be postponed (4.4.1). The Committees' progressive understanding of realisation is confirmed by their take on the regime of special measures under the CEDAW and ICERD (4.4.2).

4.4.1. General Obligation of Non-discrimination

The CEDAW-Com and CERD centre their approach to non-discrimination around the acknowledgment that eliminating discrimination based on gender or race not only requires the creation of formal or de jure equality in the form of non-discrimination in legislation but also the pursuit of substantive or de facto equality.[112] Barriers to substantive equality, according to the Committees, mainly

[110] ibid, para 16.

[111] This trend is more obvious and pronounced in the jurisprudence of the CEDAW. The CERD appears to somewhat lag behind in this context. For example, the first reference to substantive or de facto equality in a General Recommendation appeared several decades later in the jurisprudence of the CERD compared to the jurisprudence of the CEDAW-Com, see CEDAW-Com, 'General Recommendation No 5: Temporary Special Measures' (1988) A/43/38, preamble 1 and CERD, 'General Recommendation No 32', para 6.

[112] See, eg, CEDAW-Com, 'General Recommendation No 13: Equal Remuneration for Work of Equal Value' (1989) A/44/38, preamble 3: '[A]lthough reports of States parties indicate that, even though the principle of equal remuneration for work of equal value has been accepted in the legislation of many countries, more remains to be done to ensure the application of that principle in practice, in order to overcome the gender-segregation in the labour market'; see also CEDAW-Com, 'General Recommendation No 23: Political and Public Life' (1997) A/52/38, para 16; CEDAW-Com, 'General Recommendation No 25: Article 4, Paragraph 1, of the Convention (Temporary Special Measures)' (2004) HRI/GEN/1/Rev.7, para 8; CEDAW-Com, 'General Recommendation No 29 on Article 16 of the Convention on the Elimination of All Forms of Discrimination against Women (Economic Consequences of Marriage, Family Relations and their Dissolution)' (2013) CEDAW/C/GC/29, para 8; CERD, 'General Recommendation No 32', para 6: 'The principle of equality underpinned by the Convention combines formal equality before the law with equal protection of the law,

are historical, structural, and societal circumstances.[113] Realising the aims of the Conventions thus requires a transformation of societal attitudes and the active engagement with existing prejudices.[114] In the words of the CEDAW-Com:

> The position of women will not be improved as long as the underlying causes of discrimination against women, and of their inequality, are not effectively addressed. The lives of women and men must be considered in a contextual way, and *measures adopted towards a real transformation* of opportunities, institutions and systems so that they are no longer grounded in historically determined male paradigms of power and life patterns. (emphasis added)[115]

In order to achieve this goal, States parties must, among other measures, establish educational and information programmes to combat prejudice.[116] The concept of societal transformation envisioned in this context as such already hints at a progressive conception of realisation; social change takes time.[117] The CERD fittingly talks about a constant 'struggle against racial discrimination' instead of the instant abolition of discrimination.[118]

The CEDAW-Com engages in detail with the nature of obligations in the context of promoting substantive equality. Upon closer examination, it becomes clear that the CEDAW-Com envisions a combination of immediate obligations of conduct and progressive obligations of result, which coincides with progressive realisation. As mentioned above, the CEDAW-Com insists that '[t]he words "without delay" make it clear that the obligation of States parties to pursue their policy, by all appropriate means, is of an immediate nature'.[119] The Committee further holds that the this provision is 'unqualified' and that States parties may not embark upon 'delayed or purposely chosen incremental implementation' of the obligations under the CEDAW on grounds of resource or any

with substantive or de facto equality in the enjoyment and exercise of human rights as the aim to be achieved by the faithful implementation of its principles.'

[113] See CEDAW-Com, 'General Recommendation No 23', para 10; CERD, 'General Recommendation No 32', para 22.

[114] CEDAW-Com, 'General Recommendation No 14: Female Circumcision' (1990) HRI/GEN/1/Rev.7, preamble 7; CEDAW-Com, 'General Recommendation No 23', para 28; CEDAW-Com, 'General Recommendation No 25', para 7; CEDAW-Com, 'General Recommendation No 31 on Harmful Practices' (2014) CEDAW/C/GC/31, para 17; CERD, 'General Recommendation No 30 on Discrimination Against Non-citizens (2005) A/59/18 para 11; CERD, 'General Recommendation No 31 on the Prevention of Racial Discrimination in the Administration and Functioning of the Criminal Justice System' (2005) A/60/18, para 5 (c).

[115] CEDAW-Com, 'General Recommendation No 25', para 10.

[116] CEDAW-Com, 'General Recommendation No 3: Education and Public Information Campaigns' (1987) HRI/GEN/1/Rev.7; CEDAW-Com, 'General Recommendation No 19', para 24 (f); CEDAW-Com, 'General Recommendation No 33 on Women's Access to Justice' (2015) CEDAW/C/GC/33, paras 30–31; CERD, 'General Recommendation No 29 on Article 1, Paragraph 1, of the Convention (Descent)' (2002) HRI/GEN/1/Rev.7, para (y).

[117] See also Brems, 'Minimum and Maximum Perspectives', 367.

[118] CERD, 'General Recommendation No 15 on Article 4 of the Convention' (1993) HRI/GEN/1/Rev.7, para 1.

[119] CEDAW-Com, 'General Recommendation No 28', para 29; see also CEDAW-Com, 'General Recommendation No 35', para 21.

other constraints.[120] Notably, the CEDAW-Com's declaration of immediacy only refers to the duty of States to 'pursue their policy', not to the complete realisation of equality between women and men.[121] Accordingly, the statement that there may be no delay or purposeful incremental realisation must be understood to refer to the pursuit of a policy gradually moving towards the full realisation of the goal of the CEDAW.

In the same General Recommendation, the CEDAW-Com uses the language of obligations of conduct and result when setting out the tripartite structure of obligations underlying Article 2 of the CEDAW. According to the experts, '[t]he obligation to fulfil requires that States parties take a wide variety of steps to ensure that women and men enjoy equal rights de jure and de facto ... This entails obligations of means or conduct and obligations of results'.[122] A later statement by the CEDAW-Com clarifies that the obligation to 'pursue by all appropriate means' a policy of eliminating discrimination against women is an 'obligation to use means or a certain way of conduct'.[123] This obligation of conduct is then held to be of immediate effect. States parties need to

> *immediately* assess the de jure and de facto situation of women and *take concrete steps* to formulate and implement a policy that is targeted as clearly as possible towards the goal of fully eliminating all forms of discrimination against women and achieving women's substantive equality with men. (emphasis added)[124]

This corresponds with the immediate obligation to take steps in the jurisprudence of the CESCR. The notion of a policy 'targeted as clearly as possible' towards substantive equality coincides with the CESCR's repeated insistence on immediate steps which are 'deliberate, concrete and targeted as clearly as possible towards meeting the obligations recognized in the Covenant'.[125] Another parallel is the requirement of focusing the policy on those groups most marginalised.[126]

The experts of both Committees often employ other terminology reminiscent of progressive realisation. The CEDAW-Com's General Recommendations regularly make reference to the duty to adopt policies and programmes 'aimed at' achieving substantive equality.[127] In the context of the right to access to justice, the CEDAW-Com holds that States parties are under an obligation to '[t]ake steps to promote a culture and a social environment in which justice-seeking

[120] CEDAW-Com, 'General Recommendation No 28', para 29; see also CEDAW-Com, 'General Recommendation No 35', para 21.
[121] This is also indicated by the wording of the CEDAW and ICERD, see further 7.3.3.
[122] CEDAW-Com, 'General Recommendation No 28', para 9.
[123] ibid, para 23.
[124] ibid, para 24.
[125] CESCR, 'General Comment No 3', para 2; see also CESCR, 'Evaluation of the Obligation to Take Steps to the Maximum of Available Resources', para 3, 8 (a); CESCR, 'General Comment No 15', para 17; CESCR, 'General Comment No 13', para 43; CESCR, 'General Comment No 14', para 30.
[126] See CEDAW-Com, 'General Recommendation No 28', para 26.
[127] ibid, paras 10, 20; CEDAW-Com, 'General Recommendation No 25', para 8.

by women is viewed as both legitimate and acceptable'.[128] Regarding political participation, the CEDAW-Com states that '[m]easures that should be identified, implemented and monitored for effectiveness include … those *designed to* … [e]nsure that barriers to equality are overcome' (emphasis added).[129] This language clearly supports the idea that States parties must work towards the goal of substantive equality, taking measures which are aimed at and designed to bring about complete equality as soon as possible without demanding this result at once.

This is confirmed by the CEDAW-Com's insistence that '[t]he emphasis is on movement forward' and that States parties should begin with an 'evaluation of the situation to the formulation and initial adoption of a comprehensive range of measures'.[130] States parties thus must initially collect information in order to evaluate the current level of progress towards substantive equality and then continue with formulating and implementing initial measures. This policy aimed at the promotion of substantive equality, according to the CEDAW-Com, requires the development of 'concrete goals', 'targets' and 'timetables',[131] 'clear objectives' and 'timelines',[132] as well as action plans and strategies (eg, 'long term strategies' which must be 'aimed at eliminating harmful practices').[133] The CERD likewise sets out the requirement of national strategies and programmes of action, eg, 'with a view to improving the situation of Roma and their protection against discrimination'[134] or concerning the struggle against racial discrimination in the justice system.[135]

In order to ensure sufficient supervision of this process in the States parties, the CEDAW-Com sets out the need for '[d]eveloping and establishing valid indicators of the status of and progress in the realisation of human rights of women'[136] and 'recommends that States parties provide statistical data

[128] CEDAW-Com, 'General Recommendation No 33', para 35 (d).

[129] CEDAW-Com, 'General Recommendation No 23', para 45 (c).

[130] CEDAW-Com, 'General Recommendation No 28', para 24.

[131] CEDAW-Com, 'General Recommendation No 25', para 36.

[132] CEDAW-Com, 'General Recommendation No 34 on the Rights of Rural Women' (2016) CEDAW/C/GC/34, para 54 (a).

[133] CEDAW-Com, 'General Recommendation No 31', paras 36, 74; see also CEDAW-Com, 'General Recommendation No 6: Effective National Machinery and Publicity' (1982) HRI/GEN/1/Rev.7, para 1 (c); CEDAW-Com, 'General Recommendation No 28', para 38 (a).

[134] CERD, 'General Recommendation No 27 on Discrimination Against Roma' (2000) HRI/GEN/1/Rev.7, para 2; similarly regarding the elimination of discrimination based on descent, see CERD, 'General Recommendation No 29', para (e); similarly regarding the elimination of discrimination against people of African descent specifically, see CERD, 'General Recommendation No 34: Racial Discrimination Against People of African Descent' (2011) CERD/C/GC/34, para 11.

[135] CERD, 'General Recommendation No 31', paras 5 (a)–(j); see also CERD, 'General Recommendation No 35: Combating Racist Hate Speech' (26 September 2013) CERD/C/GC/35, para 47.

[136] CEDAW-Com, 'General Recommendation No 28', para 38 (f); see also ibid, para 28; CEDAW-Com, 'General Recommendation No 33', para 18 (b); in the context of access to justice, the experts reference the progress indicators for measuring the implementation of the Inter-American Convention on the Prevention, Punishment and Eradication of Violence against Women (Convention of Belém do Pará), adopted on 21 May 2013, see CEDAW-Com, 'General Recommendation No 33', para 18 (b) (fn). About the progressive nature of this Convention, see 8.2.2.

disaggregated by sex in order to measure the achievement of progress towards women's de facto or substantive equality'.[137] Similarly, the CERD requires States parties to develop 'indicators against which progress can be measured'.[138] Lastly, the experts of the CEDAW-Com declare that independent monitoring should be implemented in order 'to track progress', for example by establishing 'an independent national rapporteur on trafficking in persons to track and report on the progress of transformative anti-trafficking strategies, promoting gender equality and the empowerment of women'.[139] All of these statements explicitly refer to the measurement of progress and not to the determination of a final level of implementation which must be reached at once.

4.4.2. Special Measures

Further confirmation of this result can be found in the Committees' approach to the regime of special measures. Both the CEDAW and ICERD contain provisions setting out the duty and admissibility of undertaking 'temporary', 'special', and 'concrete' measures aimed at 'accelerating de facto equality' or ensuring 'adequate development' of certain racial groups or women.[140] The treaties provide that, as long as these measures do not lead to the 'maintenance of unequal or separate' rights or standards, they are not to be considered discriminatory, even though they privilege a certain group. These provisions in themselves indicate a progressive notion of realisation.[141] The Committees' interpretation of the special measures regime implicitly recognises this.

[137] CEDAW-Com, 'General Recommendation No 25', para 35; see also CEDAW-Com, 'General Recommendation No 9: Statistical Data Concerning the Situation of Women' (1989) HRI/GEN/1/Rev.7; CEDAW-Com, 'General Recommendation No 17: Measurement and Quantification of the Unremunerated Domestic Activities of Women and their Recognition in the Gross National Product' (1991) HRI/GEN/1/Rev.7; CEDAW-Com, 'General Recommendation No 19', para 24 (c); CEDAW-Com, 'General Recommendation No 23', para 48 (d); CEDAW-Com, 'General Recommendation No 31', para 37; CEDAW-Com, 'General Recommendation No 28', para 38 (f).

[138] CERD, 'General Recommendation No 31', para 5 (i); see also CERD, 'General Recommendation No 34', para 16; CERD, 'General Recommendation No 35', para 47.

[139] CEDAW-Com, 'General Recommendation No 38 on Trafficking in Women and Girls in the Context of Global Migration' (2020) CEDAW/C/GC/38, para 115; see also CEDAW-Com, 'General Recommendation No 31', para 35.

[140] Article 4 (1) of the CEDAW: 'Adoption by States Parties of temporary special measures aimed at accelerating de facto equality between men and women shall not be considered discrimination as defined in the present Convention, but shall in no way entail as a consequence the maintenance of unequal or separate standards; these measures shall be discontinued when the objectives of equality of opportunity and treatment have been achieved.'

Article 2 (2) of the CERD: 'States Parties shall, when the circumstances so warrant, take, in the social, economic, cultural and other fields, special and concrete measures to ensure the adequate development and protection of certain racial groups or individuals belonging to them, for the purpose of guaranteeing them the full and equal enjoyment of human rights and fundamental freedoms.' See also Article 1 (4) of the CERD.

[141] See further 7.4.3.

As the Committees explain, the term special measures (also sometimes called positive discrimination or affirmative action) describes a concept which refers to measures taken by States parties which temporarily privilege a certain group in order to compensate structural discrimination of that group in the long term.[142] Both Committees stress that this obligation to adopt special measures where necessary applies to the whole range of rights under the Conventions.[143] According to the CEDAW-Com, special measures are 'part of a necessary strategy by States parties directed towards the achievement of de facto or substantive equality'.[144] In the words of the CERD, special measures are part of an effort to produce 'adequate advancement' as envisioned by Article 2 (2) of the CERD, which 'implies goal-directed programmes which have the objective of alleviating and remedying disparities in the enjoyment of human rights and fundamental freedoms affecting particular groups and individuals'.[145] Both these statements illustrate how States must develop a strategy including special measures aimed at progressively creating de facto equality.

The CEDAW-Com is particularly clear in its conception of special measures as a means of 'accelerating' a process of realisation. As the CEDAW-Com states again and again, temporary special measures are meant to 'accelerate the improvement of the position of women to achieve their de facto or substantive equality with men'[146] or 'should aim to accelerate the equal participation of women in the political, economic, social, cultural, civil or any other field'.[147] The concept of acceleration is only compatible with a progressive model of realisation; an immediate obligation of complete fulfilment would not entail any period of gradual improvement which could be expedited. Accordingly, the CEDAW-Com considers special measures to be separate and in addition to 'other general social policies adopted and implemented in order to improve the situation of women'.[148]

The conception of special measures as part of a progressive mode of realisation is further confirmed by their necessarily temporary nature. Special measures, according to Article 1 (4) of the CERD and Article 4 (1) of the CEDAW, shall not be continued after the objectives for which they were taken have been achieved. Accordingly, the CERD describes special measures as 'functional and goal related' and declares that they shall end when equality goals are sustainably reached.[149] The timeframe of these measures is held to depend

[142] CERD, 'General Recommendation No 32', para 12; CEDAW-Com, 'General Recommendation No 25', para 17.

[143] CEDAW-Com, 'General Recommendation No 25', para 18; CERD, 'General Recommendation No 32', para 33; see also Article 2 (2) of the CERD.

[144] CEDAW-Com, 'General Recommendation No 25', para 18.

[145] CERD, 'General Recommendation No 32', para 22.

[146] CEDAW-Com, 'General Recommendation No 25', para 15.

[147] ibid, para 18; see also ibid, paras 14, 38, 39; CEDAW-Com, 'General Recommendation No 5'.

[148] CEDAW-Com, 'General Recommendation No 25', para 26.

[149] CERD, 'General Recommendation No 32', para 27; interestingly, the CERD references a General Comment by the CESCR in this context which explicitly refers to the requirement of special

on their objectives, means, and results.[150] Similarly, the CEDAW-Com states that '[t]he duration of a temporary special measure should be determined by its functional result in response to a concrete problem and not by a predetermined passage of time'.[151] Consequently, the effects of special measures must be continuously monitored.[152] According to the CEDAW-Com, this requires States parties to 'provide statistical data disaggregated by sex in order to measure the achievement of *progress* towards women's de facto or substantive equality and the effectiveness of temporary special measures' (emphasis added).[153] It becomes clear that special measures are a temporary companion on the route to the complete realisation of full equality, serving to expedite the passage of a certain stretch of the way.

4.5. THE HRC

A number of statements made by the HRC point towards a progressive understanding of obligations under the ICCPR. In contrast to the jurisprudence of the other Committees, particularly compared to the CRPD-Com and CRC-Com, these examples are more rare. The HRC is still more hesitant to engage with positive obligations under civil and political rights and, thus, has not been confronted with the contradiction between immediacy/unconditionality and positivity in as many cases. But in the HRC's jurisprudence regarding the general obligations provision of Article 2 of the ICCPR, a closer look reveals that the claim of 'immediacy' refers to obligations of conduct (4.5.1). This understanding is also reflected in the context of right to life under Article 6 of the ICCPR, which is one of the few areas in which the HRC has begun to set out extensive positive obligations (4.5.2). Further examples will be presented from the Committee's jurisprudence on children's rights (4.5.3) and equality rights (4.5.4).

4.5.1. General Obligations under Article 2 of the ICCPR

In its General Comment No 31 on the Nature of the General Legal Obligation Imposed on States Parties to the Covenant, the HRC declares that

> [t]he requirement under article 2, paragraph 2, to take steps to give effect to the Covenant rights is unqualified and of immediate effect. A failure to comply with this

measures being a 'reasonable, objective and proportional means to redress de facto discrimination', thereby introducing the concept of reasonableness; see also CESCR, 'General Comment No 20', para 9.

[150] CERD, 'General Recommendation No 32', para 27.

[151] CEDAW-Com, 'General Recommendation No 25', para 20.

[152] CERD, 'General Recommendation No 32', para 35; CEDAW-Com, 'General Recommendation No 25', para 34.

[153] CEDAW-Com, 'General Recommendation No 25', para 35.

obligation cannot be justified by reference to political, social, cultural or economic considerations within the State.[154]

It must be noted that this statement by the HRC relates the immediacy of obligations to the requirement 'to take steps'. These words indicate not that the complete fulfilment of all rights is an immediate obligation, but instead that the obligation is to take steps to initiate progress towards that goal.[155] Thus, the HRC, too, proceeds from a notion of immediacy which is not in contradiction to the umbrella meaning of progressive realisation.

4.5.2. The Right to Life under Article 6 of the ICCPR

Article 6 (1) of the ICCPR sets out the right to life as follows: 'Every human being has the inherent right to life. This right shall be protected by law. No one shall be arbitrarily deprived of his life.' Paragraphs (2)–(6) of the provision are concerned with specific safeguards in connection to the death penalty.[156] The HRC has adopted a wide interpretation regarding the scope of the right to life under Article 6 (1) of the ICCPR from early on.[157] According to General Comment No 36 on the Right to Life, Article 6 of the ICCPR 'should not be interpreted narrowly'.[158] The same assertion can also be found in the Committee's earlier General Comment No 6 on the same matter, which further states that 'it would be desirable for States parties to take all possible measures to reduce infant mortality and to increase life expectancy, especially in adopting measures to eliminate malnutrition and epidemics'.[159] In General Comment No 36, the HRC extends the scope of the right to life even further by holding that it not only 'concerns the entitlement of individuals to be free from acts and omissions that are intended or may be expected to cause their unnatural or premature death' but also entails the duty for State parties to ensure that rights holders 'enjoy a life with dignity'.[160]

The Committee derives wide-ranging positive obligations from the right to life in order to ensure this extensive scope. States parties are under the duty to provide, inter alia, sexual education and contraceptive methods, pre- and postnatal health care,[161] and to take adequate measures to prevent suicide.[162]

[154] HRC, 'General Comment No 31', para 14.
[155] See also 7.3.1.
[156] See HRC, 'General Comment No 36', para 5.
[157] The most recent General Comment No 36 on the Right to Life was adopted in 2019. It officially replaces two previous General Comments concerning the right to life, namely General Comments No 6 of 1982 and No 14 of 1984, see HRC, 'General Comment No 36', para 1.
[158] HRC, 'General Comment No 36', para 3.
[159] HRC, 'General Comment No 6: Article 6 (Right to Life)' (1982) HRI/GEN/1/Rev.7, para 5.
[160] HRC, 'General Comment No 36', para 3.
[161] ibid, para 8.
[162] ibid, para 9.

Furthermore, States parties must 'take appropriate measures to address the general conditions in society that may give rise to direct threats to life or prevent individuals from enjoying their right to life with dignity'.[163] This includes the obligation to take action against, inter alia, preventable accidents, environmental degradation, life-threatening diseases, substance abuse, malnutrition, poverty, and homelessness.[164] This extensive interpretation of the right to life was not without its critics during the drafting and feedback process of General Comment No 36.[165]

Obligations relating to ensuring a life with dignity and to preventing untimely death inherently require substantive State action and resources which suggests a progressive mode of implementation.[166] The HRC implicitly acknowledges this when stating that States parties must develop and implement 'strategic plans for *advancing* the enjoyment of the right to life', including 'detailed plans to *promote* education for non-violence', 'campaigns for *raising awareness* of gender-based violence', 'measures to fight stigmatization', and measures aimed at '*improving* access to medical examinations and treatments *designed to reduce* maternal and infant mortality' (emphases added).[167]

The experts further determine that, generally, 'States parties should … develop strategic plans for advancing the enjoyment of the right to life'.[168] In particular, 'detailed plans to promote education for non-violence; and campaigns for raising awareness of gender-based violence and harmful practices, and for improving access to medical examinations and treatments designed to reduce maternal and infant mortality' are described as necessary.[169] The obligation to develop plans aimed at advancing the protection of the right to life would be superfluous if States parties were under the obligation to fulfil all aspects of the right at once. It will also be seen later on that the HRC considers the extensive obligations connected to the right to life to be subject to the availability of resources, which also is a staple of progressive realisation.[170]

An earlier draft of HRC General Comment No 36 even contained an explicit reference to progressive realisation: '[G]iven their wide ranging implications some of the obligations relating to the general conditions necessary for full enjoyment of the right to life can only be realised progressively.'[171] While the fact that this phrase was deleted from the draft could be taken to mean that the

[163] ibid, para 26.
[164] ibid.
[165] See further 8.4.3.1.
[166] See also McGoldrick, *The Human Rights Committee*, 346–47.
[167] HRC, 'General Comment No 36', para 26.
[168] ibid.
[169] ibid (fns omitted).
[170] See 5.5.1.
[171] As cited in J Tobin and N Peleg, 'Article 6: The Rights to Life, Survival, and Development' in J Tobin (ed), *The UN Convention on the Rights of the Child: A Commentary* (Oxford, Oxford University Press, 2019) 203 (fn).

experts decided against the application of such a standard, on the other hand, the mere consideration of this concept in the context of a traditional civil and political right shows that the HRC was at least aware of the dilemma created by extensive positive duties and a strict standard of 'immediate' realisation. Furthermore, the rejection of the notion of progressive realisation, as will be argued later on, is usually based on an interpretation of this concept which does not coincide with the modern understanding.[172]

Lastly, it is interesting to note that an approach of progressive development is also taken in the context of abolishing the death penalty under Article 6 (2)–(6) of the ICCPR. The reason for the progressiveness in this case can be surmised to lie in the necessarily gradual nature of overcoming legal beliefs regarding the death penalty in the respective States parties.[173] The Committee considers the eradication of the death penalty to be part of the 'progressive development of human rights' and that Article 6 (6) of the ICCPR 'reaffirms the position that States parties that are not yet totally abolitionist should be on an irrevocable path towards complete eradication of the death penalty'.[174] Even though Article 6 (6) of the ICCPR does not explicitly set out an obligation to abolish the death penalty, the HRC considers it to be 'contrary to the object and purpose of article 6 for States parties to take steps to increase' use of the death penalty.[175] The Committee thus invokes a notion similar to the prohibition of retrogressive steps as commonly applied in the context of progressive realisation.[176]

4.5.3. Children's Rights under Article 24 of the ICCPR

In the context of children's rights under Article 24 of the ICCPR, the Committee proposes similarly extensive positive obligations in order to ensure the fulfilment of rights under the ICCPR for children. General Comment No 17 on the Rights of Children sets out that 'every possible economic and social measure should be taken to reduce infant mortality and to eradicate malnutrition among children' and that

> [i]n the cultural field, every possible measure should be taken to foster the development of their personality and to provide them with a level of education that will enable them to enjoy the rights recognized in the Covenant, particularly the right to freedom of opinion and expression.[177]

Maybe even more obviously than in the previous statements of the HRC, the experts set out a process of continuous 'development' necessary for the effective

[172] See, eg, 7.4.2.
[173] See also Brems, 'Minimum and Maximum Perspectives', 366.
[174] HRC, 'General Comment No 36', para 50.
[175] ibid.
[176] *cf* 2.4.3.
[177] HRC, 'General Comment No 17', para 3.

enjoyment of central civil and political rights. This statement also illustrates the indistinguishability explained in chapter 3.[178] Education is perceived by the experts not as a separate right facilitating the realisation of children's civil and political rights, but as a duty under the rights to freedom of opinion and expression. Thus, this particular obligation cannot be ascribed to one of the two categories, as it flows simultaneously from both.

4.5.4. Equality under Articles 3, 23 (4) and 26 of the ICCPR

As indicated above, applying the right to non-discrimination under Article 26 of the ICCPR to socio-economic rights leads to uncertainties about the applicable standard of realisation.[179] Several examples from the jurisprudence of the HRC show that Article 26 of the ICCPR is understood, by some experts, to be subject to limited resources and progressive realisation. This becomes particularly clear in a number of individual opinions in cases concerning the Dutch social security system. Although this understanding has not yet taken hold in the majority opinions of the HRC, there appears to be an emerging tendency towards understanding the obligation to create substantive equality as progressive, similarly to the approach identified in the jurisprudence of the CEDAW-Com and CERD.

Nisuke Ando states in his individual dissenting opinion in *Derksen v the Netherlands* that the Committee should be 'especially prudent' in the determination of a violation of Article 26 of the ICCPR if this provision is applied to socio-economic rights, thus disagreeing that there had been a violation in the present case. The reasons given include the argument that socio-economic rights under the ICESCR (such as the right to social security concerned in this case) are only progressively realisable. The expert closes his individual opinion by making the following analogy:

> To tell the State party that it is violating article 26 unless it treats all married couples and unmarried partners *exactly on the same footing at once* sounds like telling the State party not to start putting water in an empty cup it if cannot fill the cup *all at once*! (emphases added)[180]

Although Ando does not state that non-discrimination in the context of social security is a socio-economic right, he clearly considers a standard of progressive realisation to be appropriate in this context. This becomes even more clear in an earlier individual opinion. This time concurring in the majority's finding, Nisuke Ando, together with his colleagues Kurt Herndl and Birame N'Diaye, found that the implementation of Article 26 of the ICCPR 'may take different

[178] See 3.5.
[179] See 3.4.
[180] HRC, *Derksen v the Netherlands* [Adoption of Views] (1 April 2004) CCPR/C/80/D/976/2001, individual dissenting opinion by Nisuke Ando.

forms, depending on the nature of the right to which the principle of non-discrimination is applied'. According to the experts, the ever-changing nature of 'socio-economic and cultural needs of society' often leads to legislation lagging behind those developments. Therefore, 'article 26 of the Covenant should not be interpreted as requiring absolute equality or non-discrimination in that field at all times'. Instead, the experts propose differentiating between the immediate obligation to provide civil and political rights without discrimination, while socio-economic rights and non-discrimination in that context are described as progressively realisable. A final point used to underpin the progressive nature of Article 26 of the ICCPR in this case is that 'legislative review is a complex process entailing consideration of many factors, including limited financial resources, and the potential effects of amendments on other existing legislation'.[181]

Later in the same year, in the case *Oulajin and Kaiss v the Netherlands*, a similar individual concurring opinion was given by Kurt Herndl, Rein Müllerson, Birame N'Diaye and Waleed Sadi. After referencing and reiterating parts of the individual opinion in *Sprenger v the Netherlands*, the experts add that

> social security legislation … necessarily must make distinctions. It is for the legislature of each country, which best knows the socio-economic needs of the society concerned, to try to achieve social justice in the concrete context. Unless the distinctions made are manifestly discriminatory or arbitrary, it is not for the Committee to re-evaluate the complex socio-economic data and substitute its judgement for that of the legislatures of States parties.[182]

In relation to the concrete claims by the applicant, the concurring members held that they 'appear to run counter to a general sense of proportion, and their denial by the government concerned cannot be considered unreasonable in view of the budget limitations'.[183] This individual opinion not only accepts that non-discrimination must be understood as a progressive obligation, but also introduces aspects of reasonableness, such as proportionality and budget limitations.[184]

The HRC's jurisprudence on equality in social security matters includes one majority decision which can be considered to show tendencies of progressiveness. In *JHW v the Netherlands*, the Committee found that the issue raised by the applicant was 'moot' and the communication inadmissible because the government had since established the pertinent legislation. The experts based this finding on the claim that 'social security legislation and its application

[181] HRC, *Sprenger v the Netherlands* [Adoption of Views] (31 March 1992) CCPR/C/44/D/395/1990, individual concurring opinion by Nisuke Ando, Kurt Herndl and Birame N'Diaye.

[182] HRC, *Oulajin and Kaiss v the Netherlands*, individual concurring opinion by Kurt Herndl, Rein Müllerson, Birame N'Diaye and Waleed Sadi.

[183] ibid.

[184] See also Y Tyagi, *The UN Human Rights Committee: Practice and Procedure* (Cambridge, Cambridge University Press, 2011) 676.

usually lag behind socio-economic developments in society'.[185] It thus appears that, at least where non-discrimination in the traditionally socio-economic area of social security is concerned, the HRC considers Article 26 of the ICCPR to be progressively realisable. Even though this approach is somewhat related to the traditional understanding of the dichotomy between socio-economic and civil and political rights, it also leads to a dissolution of the boundaries between the categories. Because if any rights can be categorised as civil and political with some amount of certainty, it is those which are contained in the ICCPR. Thus, the right under Article 26 of the ICCPR is a traditional civil and political right which is at least partly subject to resource limitations and progressive realisation.

Furthermore, it cannot be said that the notion of progressive realisation is limited to socio-economic aspects of non-discrimination in the HRC's jurisprudence. The HRC's approach to equality rights in general clearly envisions the progressive achievement of substantive equality, comparable to the approaches of the CERD and the CEDAW-Com, as the following examples show. General Comment No 28 on the Equality of Rights Between Men and Women under Article 3 of the ICCPR recognises that States parties must actively remove obstacles to the equal enjoyment of the civil and political rights under the Covenant by women and men, inter alia by undertaking education measures. States parties must work towards substantive equality by taking 'positive measures in all areas so as to achieve the effective and equal empowerment of women'.[186] In connection with this, States parties are required to provide information about the 'actual role of women in society' in order to enable the Committee to determine what 'progress' has been made and what steps must further be taken.[187] Regarding the topic of non-discrimination in the context of children's rights, the Committee held that '[r]eports by States parties should indicate how legislation and practice ensure that measures of protection are *aimed at removing all discrimination* in every field' (emphasis added).[188]

The Committee also adopts a standard of progressive realisation regarding spousal equality under Article 23 (4) of the ICCPR. In *Hendriks v the Netherlands*, the HRC recognises that the applicant's right to spousal equality was not respected but did not find a violation of Article 23 (4) of the ICCPR due to the fact that the Dutch government was on the way to creating the necessary legislative reforms to address this issue.[189] This arguably shows that the experts assume a progressive mode of implementation for Article 23 (4) ICCPR.[190]

[185] HRC, *JHW v the Netherlands* [Inadmissibility Decision] (5 May 1992) CCPR/C/48/D/501/1992, para 5.2.

[186] HRC, 'General Comment No 28', para 3.

[187] ibid.

[188] HRC, 'General Comment No 17', para 5.

[189] HRC, *Hendriks v the Netherlands* [Adoption of Views] (27 July 1988) CCPR/C/33/D/201/1985, paras 10.4, 11.

[190] See also A Conte and R Burchill, *Defining Civil and Political Rights: The Jurisprudence of the United Nations Human Rights Committee*, 2nd edn (London, Routledge, 2016) 238.

4.6. CONCLUSION

As suspected, the Committees implicitly accept that certain aspects of the positive dimension of civil and political rights must be gradual or progressive. It becomes apparent that the Committees' claim of immediacy mostly refers to formal equality and obligations of conduct, analogous to the obligation 'to take steps' in the context of socio-economic rights. Accordingly, the Committees' claim that civil and political rights are immediately *applicable* is true, while the concept of immediate (full) *realisation* is a myth. Regarding the full positive realisation of rights and de facto equality, the Committees acknowledge that some time is required, not only because of limited resources but also because changing attitudes in a society will take time, no matter how much effort the State party puts in.

The gradual nature of full realisation is confirmed by the frequent references to monitoring, benchmarks, indicators, and data collecting which are explicitly connected to ensuring progress in the realisation of rights. Clearly, the adherence to the differentiation between immediate and progressive realisation is based on a misunderstanding about the umbrella meaning of the latter term. When saying that progressive realisation cannot apply to civil and political rights, the experts want to stress that States parties must not wait until taking action, thus rejecting the narrow reading of the concept. However, implicitly they apply the umbrella meaning of the term by accepting that immediate action is required while full realisation may take time. The same misunderstanding is present in many literary accounts, as part III of this book will show.

5

Civil and Political Rights as Subject to Resource Availability

5.1. INTRODUCTION

THIS CHAPTER WILL inspect the standard applied to civil and political rights with regard to a second parallel to progressive realisation: the dependence of realisation on the resources available to the State party. Article 2 (1) of the ICESCR reflects the connection between this aspect and the concept of progressive realisation. According to this provision, each State party must take steps 'to the maximum of its available resources, with a view to achieving progressively the full realization'. The acknowledgment that certain obligations demand such a large amount of resources that they cannot be realised immediately is an integral part of – and one of the underlying reasons for – progressive realisation.[1]

Chapter 3 has shown that the Committees repeatedly reject the applicability of this provision entirely, also arguing that civil and political rights are 'absolute', ie, not subject to the availability of resources. However, the suspicion arises that the Committees, when faced with positive and costly civil and political rights obligations, might implicitly or explicitly accept that those obligations can only be fulfilled to the maximum of available resources. It is this kind of evidence which will be inspected in this chapter. Each of the Committees has developed a different way of incorporating resource considerations into its system of States parties' obligations. This chapter will again inspect the jurisprudence of the CRPD-Com (5.2), the CRC-Com (5.3), the CEDAW-Com and CERD (5.4) and the HRC (5.5).

5.2. THE CRPD-COM

In the CRPD-Com's jurisprudence, resource considerations are introduced to all Convention rights through the concept of reasonable accommodation. According to Article 5 (3) of the CRPD, the denial of reasonable accommodation is to be

[1] See further 1.2.3.

considered impermissible discrimination. The term reasonable accommodation, according to the definition in Article 2 of the CRPD, refers to 'necessary and appropriate modification and adjustments not imposing a disproportionate or undue burden, where needed in a particular case', to ensure the equal enjoyment of all rights by persons with disabilities. The treaty itself, by including the concept of the 'disproportionate or undue burden', introduces resource considerations as a limit to what a State party must provide. Because reasonable accommodation is required across all aspects of the treaty, this notion of resource limitation extends to both categories of rights, which is also reflected in the jurisprudence of the CRPD-Com.

This section will first show that the CRPD-Com's interpretation of reasonable accommodation and the disproportionate and undue burden introduces resource considerations which are analogous to the 'available resources' concept in the context of progressive realisation (5.2.1). Secondly, this section will present examples where civil and political rights are interpreted by the CRPD-Com to be limited by available resources by way of testing for a 'disproportionate or undue burden' (5.2.2). Thirdly, it will be shown that this notion of limited resources is gradually detached from the concept of reasonable accommodation which introduces resource limitations as a general principle of the CRPD (5.2.3). Lastly, this section will present positive duties which are factually treated as absolute, ie, where a disproportionate burden is not considered, comparing this to the concept of the minimum core in socio-economic rights jurisprudence (5.2.4).

5.2.1. Reasonable Accommodation and Progressive Realisation

Reasonable accommodation is analogous to the individual-oriented aspect of progressive realisation. As explained above, progressive realisation requires States parties to do as much as possible at any point in time. In an individual case, this means that a State party can only deny positive measures requested by a rights holder if these measures would be disproportionate in light of available resources.[2] The same principle is introduced into the jurisprudence of the CRPD-Com by way of the concept of reasonable accommodation and disproportionate burdens under Articles 5 (3) and 2 of the CRPD. In individual cases, a State party to the CRPD is obliged to provide appropriate modification and adjustment required to enable the enjoyment of rights unless these measures would constitute a disproportionate or undue burden.

The CRPD-Com's differentiation between reasonable accommodation under Article 5 (3) of the CRPD and accessibility under Article 9 of the CRPD illustrates that the former proceeds from the same assumptions as progressive realisation. Although both Article 9 and Article 5 (3) of the CRPD are

[2] See further 2.3.3.

described as being aimed at guaranteeing accessibility,[3] the Committee strictly delimits their scopes. The duty to provide reasonable accommodation is determined to apply *ex nunc* when a certain person requests access to inaccessible objects, infrastructure or services or when the duty bearer should have known that accommodation is necessary to overcome barriers to exercising rights.[4] Accessibility duties, on the other hand, are described as arising *ex ante*. They are not triggered by the request of accessibility in a certain situation. This means that States parties must always work towards providing accessibility for groups without focusing on the needs of a particular person.[5] The Committee sums up the differences in the following way: 'Accessibility duties relate to groups and must be implemented gradually but unconditionally, … [r]easonable accommodation duties, on the other hand, are individualized, apply immediately to all rights and may be limited by disproportionality.'[6]

This delimitation shows how the limited resources argument becomes relevant in both the duties under Articles 5 (3) and 9 of the CRPD. As discussed above, 'unconditional', in the context of accessibility, must be interpreted to mean that states cannot reject taking any steps at all. But the right to accessibility is progressively realisable (or 'gradually implementable') precisely because it is limited by the availability of resources.[7] Reasonable accommodation, on the other hand, takes into view a certain person at a precise point in time. In this context, the limitations caused by resources must be factored in by asking the question whether, at this point in time and under the precise circumstances of the case, denying accessibility is reasonable and proportionate. Reasonable accommodation thus asks the question whether the duty of progressive realisation (or gradual implementation) as an obligation of conduct turns into an immediate obligation of result in an individual case. Disproportionality in the individual case and progressive implementation over time are just two ways of recognising the relevance of limited resources in shaping the contours of States parties' obligations.

The interrelationship between progressive realisation and reasonable accommodation is confirmed by the fact that progressive realisation must be considered when evaluating which accommodations constitute an undue burden. The CRPD-Com held that an accommodation is an undue burden in the sense of Article 2 of the CRPD if the provision of accessibility to a single person would considerably delay the overall progress towards the general realisation of

[3] CRPD-Com, 'General Comment No 6', para 24.

[4] ibid, para 24 (b).

[5] ibid, para 24 (a).

[6] ibid, paras 41 (a), (b); the right to accessibility thus relates to systemic and not individual progress towards an inclusive society, see A Nilsson, 'Article 2: Definitions' in I Bantekas, MA Stein and D Anastasiou (eds), *The UN Convention on the Rights of Persons with Disabilities: A Commentary* (Oxford, Oxford University Press, 2018) 79.

[7] See further 4.2.1.

accessibility, for example due to consuming excessive resources.[8] The CESCR took the same approach, arguing that the reasonableness of an individual measure depends on the question whether the required resources are already earmarked for general policies targeted at progressively realising the right:

> The State party did not explain that denying the authors social housing was necessary because it was putting its resources towards a general policy or an emergency plan to be implemented by the authorities with a view to progressively realizing the right to housing, especially for persons in a particularly vulnerable situation.[9]

Conversely, the potentially positive effects of individual accommodation measures on the overall realisation of a right for groups are also treated as factors in the evaluation of the proportionality and reasonableness of accommodation measures.[10] For example, in the CRPD-Com's case of *Sahlin v Sweden*, the author claimed an 'erroneous proportionality assessment' and therefore a violation of the duty to provide reasonable accommodation.[11] The assessment was described as insufficient in part because the State party's courts did not factor in the positive effects that the individual measure could have on the overall progressive realisation of the right. The Committee held that the reasoning of the courts 'focused on the specific measure taken for the author, but failed to take into account the negative impact of the Court's assessment in more general terms'[12] and, therefore, 'that the decisions and interventions of the authorities of the State party limited the possibility for persons with disabilities of being selected for positions requiring the adaptation of the working environment to their needs'.[13] Also, in another decision, the CRPD-Com interpreted progressive realisation to include the duty to 'take all necessary preventive measures to enable public authorities' to provide reasonable accommodation.[14]

5.2.2. Available Resources Limiting Civil and Political Rights

Reasonable accommodation and, therefore, resource considerations in the form of the 'disproportionate or undue burden' limit are applied by the CRPD-Com

[8] See, eg, CRPD-Com, 'General Comment No 4', para 28: 'The extent to which reasonable accommodation is provided must be considered in the light of the overall obligation to develop an inclusive education system, maximizing the use of existing resources and developing new ones.'

[9] CESCR, *Djazia and Bellili v Spain*, para 17.5; see also CESCR, *Goumari and Tidli v Spain* [Adoption of Views] (18 February 2021) E/C.12/69/D/85/2018; CESCR, *López Albán v Spain* [Adoption of Views] (11 October 2019) E/C.12/66/D/37/2018.

[10] CRPD-Com, 'General Comment No 6', paras 24 (b), 26 (e); the Committee seems to have accepted this argument after it was introduced by a dissenting minority in the decision in *Jungelin v Sweden*.

[11] CRPD-Com, *Sahlin v Sweden* [Adoption of Views] (21 August 2020) CRPD/C/23/D/45/2018, para 8.3.

[12] ibid, para 8.10.

[13] ibid, para 8.11.

[14] CRPD-Com, *JM v Spain* [Adoption of Views] (21 August 2020) CRPD/C/23/D/37/2016, para 9.6.

in the context of civil and political rights. Firstly, the failure to provide reasonable accommodation is set out as discrimination in Article 5 (3) of the CRPD. The right to non-discrimination itself is traditionally perceived as belonging in the category of civil and political rights. Accordingly, the experts of the CRPD-Com consider the rights under Article 5 of the CRPD to be of immediate effect and not subject to progressive realisation under Article 4 (2) of the CRPD.[15] At the same time, however, the limit of disproportionate and undue burdens under Article 5 (3) of the CRPD reintroduces resource considerations and therefore progressive realisation to the non-discrimination regime in the CRPD.

Secondly, the duty to provide reasonable accommodation is applied across the whole Convention and all rights, be they civil and political rights or socio-economic rights.[16] One example of this appears in the CRPD-Com's General Comment No 7 on the Participation of Persons with Disabilities in the Implementation and Monitoring of the Convention. The Committee determines that the right to participate under Articles 4 (3) and 33 (3) of the CRPD is an immediately realisable civil and political right 'not subject to any form of budgetary restriction'.[17] However, according to the General Comment, Article 4 (3) of the CRPD also mandates the provision of reasonable accommodation where required.[18] If reasonable accommodation is part of the duties under Article 4 (3) of the CRPD, then the provision cannot generally be considered 'absolute', because the duty to provide reasonable accommodation is limited by disproportionality.

The most compelling evidence for this argument against the absoluteness of civil and political rights can be found in the CRPD-Com's views on Individual Communications regarding jury duty in Australia: *Beasley v Australia, Lockrey v Australia*, and *JH v Australia*.[19] This group of cases concerns reasonable accommodation and accessibility in the context of a number of classical civil and political rights: freedom of expression under Article 21 of the CRPD, the right to participation in political and public life under Article 29 of the CRPD, and the right to access to justice under Article 13 of the CRPD.[20] All three cases were brought before the Committee by Australian applicants with hearing impairments. The applicants were summoned to be jurors but did not receive

[15] CRPD-Com, 'General Comment No 6', para 12.

[16] See CRPD-Com, 'General Comment No 6', para 12, where the Committee declares that equality and non-discrimination under Articles 3 and 5 of the CRPD are 'an interpretative tool for all the other principles and rights enshrined in the Convention'; see also Ringel, 'Non-discrimination', 119.

[17] CRPD-Com, 'General Comment No 7', para 28.

[18] ibid, paras 22, 39, 71.

[19] CRPD-Com, *Beasley v Australia* [Adoption of Views] (1 April 2016) CRPD/C/15/D/11/2013; CRPD-Com, *Lockrey v Australia* [Adoption of Views] (1 April 2016) CRPD/C/15/D/13/2013; CRPD-Com, *JH v Australia* [Adoption of Views] (31 August 2018) CRPD/C/20/D/35/2016.

[20] In *Beasley* and *Lockrey*, admissibility was affirmed regarding the claims under Articles 5, 9, 13, 21, and 29 of the CRPD, see CRPD-Com, *Beasley v Australia*, para 7.7 and CRPD-Com, *Lockrey v Australia*, para 7.7; in *JH*, the Committee declared the author's claims under Articles 5 and 21 of the CRPD to be admissible, see CRPD-Com, *JH v Australia*, para 6.4.

the necessary technical or personal support needed to enable their participation in the proceedings.[21]

Australia claimed in all three cases that rejecting the accommodation measures was permissible as they would have 'an impact on the complexity, cost and duration of trials and therefore ... consequences for resources'.[22] The experts of the CRPD-Com considered this line of argument to relate to the notion of 'disproportionate or undue burden' under Article 2 of the CRPD.[23] However, the threshold of establishing such a disproportionate burden was not considered to be reached as the State party did 'not provide any data or analysis to demonstrate that it would constitute a disproportionate or undue burden'.[24] The Committee thus considers that the State has not taken the necessary steps to ensure reasonable accommodation and concludes that the refusal of the requested accommodation measures 'without thoroughly assessing whether that would constitute a disproportionate or undue burden, amounts to disability-based discrimination'.[25] In the latest case of *JH v Australia*, the State party supplemented its arguments by providing the Committee with an estimate of the costs necessary for accommodation.[26] Australia's argument regarding cost and complexity was still declared to be insufficient to establish the existence of a disproportionate or undue burden because it did not lay out the cost of accommodation in the individual case of the author.[27]

It becomes clear that, while Australia's arguments were not sufficient in these cases, resource limitations enter the Committee's considerations through the concept of the disproportionate or undue burden in the context of reasonable accommodation. The CRPD-Com shows a general willingness to engage with resource-oriented arguments regarding the proportionality of accommodation measures in the context of political participation, freedom of expression, and access to justice. This alone proves that the positive aspects of the rights under Articles 13, 21 and 29 of the CRPD are not interpreted as absolute by the Committee.

Another interesting point in these jury duty cases concerns the right to freedom of expression under Article 21 of the CRPD read alone, meaning read without reference to the duty to provide reasonable accommodation under Article 5 (3) of the CRPD. Australia notably claims in its arguments that this right is subject to available resources and thus progressively realisable and that

[21] CRPD-Com, *Beasley v Australia*, paras 2.1, 2.4; CRPD-Com, *Lockrey v Australia*, paras 2.1., 2.4; CRPD-Com, CRPD-Com, *JH v Australia*, paras 2.1, 2.4.

[22] CRPD-Com, *Beasley v Australia*, para 6.2; CRPD-Com, *Lockrey v Australia*, para 6.2; similarly CRPD-Com, *JH v Australia*, para 7.5.

[23] CRPD-Com, *Beasley v Australia*, para 8.5; CRPD-Com, *Lockrey v Australia*, para 8.5.

[24] CRPD-Com, *Beasley v Australia*, para 8.5; CRPD-Com, *Lockrey v Australia*, para 8.5.

[25] CRPD-Com, *Beasley v Australia*, para 8.5; similarly, CRPD-Com, *Lockrey v Australia*, para 8.5.

[26] According to the then preliminary findings of the study 'Participation in the administration of justice: deaf citizens as jurors', approximately US$ 300,000 would have to be allocated for that purpose.

[27] CRPD-Com, *JH v Australia*, para 7.5.

its measures sufficed in fulfilling this standard.[28] The authors reject this notion and state that Article 21 of the CRPD is not subject to available resources and progressive realisation.[29] In its decision on the merits, the experts recognise these divergent opinions but do not state whether progressive realisation under Article 4 (2) of the CRPD is applicable,[30] even though the right to freedom of expression historically belongs in the category of allegedly immediate civil and political rights.[31] Instead of engaging with this question, the CRPD-Com argues that the cases concerned here fall under the material scope of Article 21 of the CRPD and that the refusal to provide the requested measures violates this right.[32]

It can only be suspected that the individual perspective of reasonable accommodation ('was it legal to deny a positive measure under these precise circumstances?') can be and is being applied in the context of the rights under Article 21 of the CRPD as well. And because the Committee found (in the context of reasonable accommodation) that there are no sufficient grounds for assuming a disproportionate burden, there is no reason to argue about resources regarding those other rights. Otherwise, if Article 21 CRPD was really treated as absolute, this would mean that the refusal to provide necessary measures could, on the one hand, be justified by limited resources in the context of Article 5 (3) of the CRPD and, on the other hand, not be justified under any circumstances when applying Article 21 of the CRPD. This point is corroborated by the fact that the Committee finds violations of Articles 9, 13 (1), 21, and 29 (b) of the CRPD, each 'read alone and in conjunction with' (among other provisions) Article 5 (3) of the CRPD.[33]

5.2.3. Proportionality Assessments Separated from Reasonable Accommodation

The CRPD-Com's views regarding Individual Communications show an increasing tendency to detach the concept of disproportionality from the concept of reasonable accommodation, thereby incorporating the notion of resource dependency into civil and political rights themselves directly.[34] Thus, the concept of proportionality – which necessarily entails a progressive mode of implementation – is extended beyond reasonable accommodation and acts as a general principle in the CRPD-Com's jurisprudence.

[28] CRPD-Com, *Beasley v Australia*, para 4.7; CRPD-Com, *Lockrey v Australia*, para 4.7.
[29] CRPD-Com, *Beasley v Australia*, para 8.7; CRPD-Com, *Lockrey v Australia*, para 8.7.
[30] CRPD-Com, *Beasley v Australia*, para 8.7; CRPD-Com, *Lockrey v Australia*, para 8.7.
[31] See Article 19 of the ICCPR.
[32] CRPD-Com, *Beasley v Australia*, para 8.8; CRPD-Com, *Lockrey v Australia*, para 8.8.
[33] CRPD-Com, *Beasley v Australia*, paras 8.6, 8.8, 8.9; CRPD-Com, *Lockrey v Australia*, paras 8.6, 8.8, 8.9.
[34] This tendency arguably emerged already in the previous section where, presumably, the CRPD transferred the rejection of the disproportionate burden to Article 21 CRPD.

There are many instances of this approach in the Committee's jurisprudence regarding accessibility under Article 9 of the CRPD. Although accessibility has been set out in the Committee's General Comment No 6 as a group-oriented measure distinct from the individual viewpoint of reasonable accommodation,[35] many Individual Communications incorporate the proportionality assessment of reasonable accommodation into the determination of violations of Article 9 of the CRPD without mentioning Article 5 (3) of the CRPD. This not only shows how reasonable accommodation – or the evaluation of proportionality in the individual case – represents the individual-oriented flipside of progressive realisation (or gradual implementation),[36] but also proves that resource considerations permeate the CRPD-Com's jurisprudence as a whole.

A first example of this tendency is the case of *X v Argentina* which concerns issues of accessibility in the context of imprisonment. According to the Committee's interpretation of Article 9 of the CRPD, this case should concern the gradual removal of barriers to accessibility concerning existing objects.[37] The Committee accordingly declares that States parties are generally obligated to 'take all relevant measures, including the identification and removal of obstacles and barriers to access' in order to enable detained persons with disabilities to independently partake in all aspects of daily life.[38] After acknowledging the State party's efforts, the Committee finds that 'the State party has not asserted that there are any *obstacles* that would prevent it from taking the necessary measures to facilitate the author's mobility or denied the author's allegations that architectural barriers to accessibility persist' (emphasis added).[39] This language seems to point at the failure of the State party to establish an undue or disproportionate burden under Article 2 of the CRPD. In conclusion, the experts hold that, '[c]onsequently, … in the absence of sufficient explanations', the State party violated its obligations not only under Article 14 (2), but also Article 9 (1) (a) and (b) of the CRPD.[40] The absence of accessibility in the particular case of the author is seen as the reason for a violation of the duties under Article 9 of the CRPD. The experts do not, however, apply an absolute understanding of State duties but rather consider the possibility of 'sufficient explanations' for the lack of accessibility. This introduces a concept analogous to the disproportionate burden into the Committee's approach to accessibility even though reasonable accommodation and the provisions establishing this concept are not mentioned.

Another instance of this approach to accessibility can be observed in the CRPD-Com's decision in *F v Austria*, where a visually impaired Austrian citizen

[35] CRPD-Com, 'General Comment No 6', paras 24 (a), (b).

[36] See further 5.2.1.

[37] *cf* 4.2.1.2.

[38] CRPD-Com, *X v Argentina* [Adoption of Views] (11 April 2014) CRPD/C/11/D/8/2012, para 8.5.

[39] ibid.

[40] ibid.

claimed a violation of his Convention rights due to the State's omission to install live audio information at new tram stops in Linz. While the CRPD-Com apparently considers this case to belong in the category of accessibility to new objects, services and infrastructure,[41] the Committee conducts a resource-oriented proportionality assessment asking 'whether the State party has taken sufficient measures' to ensure equal access to information for persons with disabilities.[42] The Committee argues that the technology for digital audio systems was already known to the service provider, could have been installed at a limited cost and would have been crucial for providing the author and other visually impaired persons with equal access to the relevant information.[43]

This standard of review is reminiscent of the test developed in the context of reasonable accommodation as the sufficiency of measures taken by the State party is evaluated by weighing opposing interests. However, the Committee does not find a violation of the duty to provide reasonable accommodation; Article 5 (3) of the CRPD is not cited as a norm violated by the State party.[44] Consequently, the duty to ensure accessibility to new objects, services and infrastructure is not treated as an absolute duty, but limited resources are found to play a role in its interpretation. This is in line with the above finding that the differentiation between accessibility of new and existing objects acts only as an approximation for an approach to positive obligations which introduces into the equation available resources and, implicitly, progressive realisation.[45]

A similar example of this integration of a disproportionate and undue burden assessment into accessibility occurs in *Bacher v Austria*. Even though the CRPD-Com only admitted the author's claims regarding accessibility under Article 9 of the CRPD,[46] the experts continue to reiterate the content of reasonable accommodation as it is defined in Article 2 of the CRPD without making reference to this provision.[47] The legal question at hand is then determined to be whether 'the decisions adopted by the courts of the State party have enabled the respect of the rights of Mr. Bacher under article 9'.[48] Again, the Committee applies an individual-oriented and proportionality-dependent perspective analogous to reasonable accommodation even though no claim regarding Article 5 (3)

[41] See CRPD-Com, *F v Austria* [Adoption of Views] (21 August 2015) CRPD/C/14/D/21/2014, para 8.5: 'New investments, research and production should contribute to eliminating inequality, not creating new barriers.'

[42] ibid, para 8.6.

[43] ibid, para 8.7. The author likewise centres his argumentation around the proportionality of expenses, stating that the instalment of an audio system would have been within the budget and therefore 'reasonable in economic terms' instead of treating the obligation to provide accessibility in new infrastructure as absolute, see ibid, para 2.4.

[44] ibid, para 8.7.

[45] See further 4.2.1.2.

[46] CRPD-Com, *Bacher v Austria* [Adoption of Views] (16 February 2014) CRPD/C/19/D/26/2014, paras 8.10, 8.12.

[47] ibid, para 9.5.

[48] ibid, para 9.7.

of the CRPD is admitted. Article 9 of the CRPD is thus read to be subject to available resources because Article 2 of the CRPD by itself does not create a free-standing right to reasonable accommodation.[49]

The case of *Given v Australia* shall act as a last particularly striking illustration as it concerns not only Article 9 of the CRPD and accessibility but also the classical civil and political right to take part in political and public life under Article 29 of the CRPD. The author in this case suffered from cerebral palsy and complained to the Committee due to a lack of sufficient technological assistance which would enable her to cast a secret ballot in the Australian federal elections. It is interesting to note that the parties to this dispute disagree about the immediate or progressive nature of the rights under Article 29 of the CRPD. The author argues that these rights derive from Article 25 of the ICCPR and are therefore 'immediately realizable at and from the entry into force of the Convention in the State party'.[50] The State party, however, clearly envisions a progressive mode of realisation. For one, Australia lays out its general legislative and administrative measures to provide accessible voting facilities and sets out the ways in which the author could have benefited from this system, arguing that 'although the author was not able to vote in her preferred way, this situation does not constitute a breach of the State party's obligations under article 29 (a) (i) of the Convention'.[51] The State party thus clearly interprets Article 29 of the CRPD to create a duty of conduct with a view to progressive realisation instead of an absolute obligation of result.

Furthermore, Australia argues that Article 29 (a) (ii) of the CRPD entails only 'a general or aspirational obligation required of States parties, which need only to be met where appropriate'. Australia considers that there is no duty to 'provide assistive and new technologies to each and every voter who cannot vote without assistance' since this would not be possible from a practical point of view in light of the differing needs.[52] Australia further argues that 'it falls within its broad discretion to decide how to allocate limited resources, and that it is justifiable that, at this stage, only voters with visual impairments are provided with the option of using assistive technologies when voting'.[53]

The Committee finds a violation of Article 29 (a) (i) and (ii), read alone and in conjunction with Articles 5 (2), 4 (1) (a), (b), (d), (e) and (g) and 9 (1) and (2) (g) of the CRPD.[54] Notably, Article 5 (3) of the CRPD is not mentioned by the CRPD-Com. The Committee's statements establishing these violations are made without linking the arguments to Article 9 or 29 of the CRPD specifically.

[49] See CRPD-Com, *Y v Tanzania* [Adoption of Views] (31 August 2018) CRPD/C/20/D/23/2014, para 7.6.

[50] CRPD-Com, *Given v Australia* [Adoption of Views] (16 February 2018) CRPD/C/19/D/19/2014, para 3.2.

[51] ibid, para 4.9.

[52] ibid, para 4.11.

[53] ibid.

[54] ibid, para 8.10.

The State party's argument regarding gradual implementation and limited resources is rejected by the CRPD-Com by recalling its General Comment No 6 which establishes that 'the obligation to implement accessibility is unconditional' and that, thus, the omission to provide accessibility cannot be justified by 'referring to the burden of providing access for persons with disabilities'.[55] Ironically, the Committee then goes on to refer to the inability of the State party to establish such an undue burden, finding that

> the State party has not provided any information that could justify the claim that the use of such an electronic voting option would have constituted a disproportionate burden, so as to prevent its use in the 2013 federal election *for the author and for all persons requiring such accommodation.* (emphasis added)[56]

It appears that the experts generally find the concept of a disproportionate or undue burden to apply in this context, even though Article 5 (3) of the CRPD is not considered. The absence of a disproportionate burden is, moreover, noted in relation to the author and 'all persons requiring such accommodation'. It becomes clear that the Committee considers the general use of electronic voting options, irrespective of the author's specific case, not to be too much to ask. In other words, the State party did not provide sufficient grounds which would enable the Committee to find that Australia took steps to the maximum of its available resources towards the progressive realisation of Articles 29 and 9 of the CRPD in general. Consequently, the assessment of proportionality regarding positive measures in the context of Articles 9 and 29 of the CRPD introduces resource considerations and, therefore, the idea of progressive realisation to those rights.

5.2.4. Minimum Core

Another feature of progressive realisation is the concept of minimum core obligations which are not subject to available resources and thus must be realised immediately.[57] The CRPD-Com recognises this concept not only explicitly in relation to socio-economic rights,[58] but also implicitly regarding civil and political rights. In these cases, the CRPD-Com argues that a 'disproportionate or undue burden' is irrelevant for certain aspects of a right. This implies that these rights are generally perceived as progressively realisable. It only makes sense to emphasise the fact that a certain aspect must be fulfilled irrespective of available resources if other aspects of the same right are dependent on resource availability (and, therefore, progressively realisable).

[55] ibid, para 8.8.
[56] ibid, para 8.9.
[57] See further 2.5.3.
[58] See, eg, CRPD-Com, 'General Comment No 4', para 41.

A first example of this parallel can be seen in the CRPD-Com's General Comment No 5 on Living Independently and being Included in the Community under Article 19 of the CRPD. As laid out in the previous chapter, this right is treated as progressively realisable by the Committee even though the experts consider Article 19 (a) of the CRPD to be a civil and political right.[59] The Committee lays out the 'core elements' of the right, which are necessary to 'ensure that the realization of a standardized minimum support level ... is carried out by every State party' and which must always be respected, 'particularly in times of financial or economic crisis'.[60] This implies that, generally, financial or economic crises can have an influence on the level of realisation of rights (just not regarding their core elements) and that those rights are consequently subject to available resources. However, the experts do not limit the applicability of this section about core elements to the socio-economic aspects of Article 19 (b) and (c) of the CRPD. This clearly contradicts the Committee's interpretation of Article 4 (2) of the CRPD as establishing the immediate realisation of all civil and political rights. The identification of core elements would be superfluous if Article 19 (a) of the CRPD would have to be realised in its entirety without delay.

Another group of duties which are treated like minimum core obligations are what the CRPD-Com calls procedural accommodations. The Committee clarifies that procedural accommodations in the context of access to justice under Article 13 (1) of the CRPD and support measures for disabled persons in exercising their legal capacity under Article 12 (3) of the CRPD are not limited by the concept of disproportionality.[61] Similarly, in General Comment No 1, the duty to provide reasonable accommodation is described as 'separate from, and complementary to' the obligation under Article 12 (3) of the CRPD to provide the required support for disabled people in exercising their legal capacity.[62] The CRPD-Com describes the latter to be an 'unconditional' duty; 'the fact that support to exercise capacity may impose a disproportionate or undue burden does not limit the requirement to provide it'.[63] This means that, while reasonable accommodation measures in general are subject to the availability of resources pursuant to the concept of disproportionate or undue burdens, the specific subject area of procedural accommodations is described as not limited in this way.

This is reflected in the Committee's Individual Communications. In *Al Adam v Saudi Arabia*, the CRPD-Com explains that procedural accommodations

> are distinguishable from reasonable accommodation in that procedural accommodations are not limited by disproportionality. In the case of the author, the State

[59] See further 4.2.4.

[60] CRPD-Com, 'General Comment No 5', paras 38 (a)–(h).

[61] CRPD-Com, 'General Comment No 6', para 25 (d).

[62] CRPD-Com, 'General Comment No 1', para 34.

[63] CRPD-Com, 'General Comment No 6', para 48; see also CRPD-Com, 'General Comment No 1', para 34.

> party is therefore under the obligation to take all procedural accommodation that is necessary to enable his effective participation in the process, taking into account his hearing impairment.[64]

This wording implies an absolute understanding of Articles 12 (3) and 13 (1) of the CRPD in line with the Committee's conception of procedural accommodation.[65] In *Makarova v Lithuania*, the Committee finds a violation of the Convention due to the State party's failure to provide the author with legal representation and sufficient support to attend the hearings:

> Considering that the State party did not provide any form of 'reasonable accommodation' for Ms. Makarova to take part in the court hearings and subsequent appeal procedure related to her case, the Committee considers that the State party violated her rights under articles 12 (3) and 13 (1) of the Convention.[66]

It is surprising that the Committee refers to a failure to provide reasonable accommodation and then references Articles 12 (3) and 13 (1) instead of Article 5 (3) of the CRPD, even though the pursuant duties are described as 'separate'.[67] This approach suggests that procedural accommodations are a specific part of reasonable accommodation. Particularly, procedural accommodations are those aspects where the importance of the rights holder's interests will regularly outweigh the costs for necessary measures by the state, save for exceptional circumstances.

Another group of minimum core cases concerns the duty to expeditiously and effectively adjudicate violations of the prohibition of torture and inhuman and degrading treatment by State and non-State actors. This duty plays a central role in the cases of *X v Tanzania, Y v Tanzania, and Z v Tanzania.*[68] Those cases concern the claims of Tanzanian citizens who became victims of serious physical violence targeted at persons with albinism.[69] The Committee finds violations of the authors' rights under Articles 15 and 17 of the CRPD due to the authorities' failure to effectively prosecute the persons responsible.[70] There is no reference to

[64] CRPD-Com, *Al Adam v Saudi Arabia* [Adoption of Views] (20 September 2018) CRPD/C/20/D/38/2016, para 11.5.

[65] See also CRPD-Com, *Vela v Mexico* [Adoption of Views] (6 September 2019) CRPD/C/22/D/32/2015, para 10.7.

[66] CRPD-Com, *Makarova v Lithuania* [Adoption of Views] (18 August 2017) CRPD/C/18/D/30/2015, para 7.6 (fn omitted).

[67] CRPD-Com, 'General Comment No 1', para 34.

[68] CRPD-Com, *X v Tanzania* [Adoption of Views] (18 August 2017) CRPD/C/18/D/22/2014; CRPD-Com, *Y v Tanzania*; CRPD-Com, *Z v Tanzania* [Adoption of Views] (19 September 2019) CRPD/C/22/D/24/2014.

[69] CRPD-Com, *X v Tanzania*, paras 1–2.7; CRPD-Com, *Y v Tanzania*, paras 1.1–2.8; CRPD-Com, *Z v Tanzania*, paras 2.1–2.7.

[70] CRPD-Com, *X v Tanzania*, paras 8.1–8.7; CRPD-Com, *Y v Tanzania*, paras 8.1–8.10; CRPD-Com, *Z v Tanzania*, paras 8.1–8.10. It must be noted, however, that the State party took very little measures in these cases and did not try to justify this inaction in any way. Therefore, the lack of an engagement with disproportionality or available resources could also be due to the absence of State arguments in this regard.

a limit of disproportionality regarding this obligation. Similarly, the right to an effective remedy in the case of violations of rights has been described as part of States parties' minimum core obligations by the CESCR.[71]

5.3. THE CRC-COM

The CRC-Com's jurisprudence also shows evidence of the application of a limited resources approach across the Convention, including civil and political rights. Firstly, the experts regularly apply the general obligations provision under Article 4 of the CRC to all rights in the Convention regardless of their category even though the second sentence of this provision contains the phrase 'to the maximum extent of their available resources' (5.3.1). Secondly, Article 4 of the CRC is read by the Committee to establish extensive budgeting and prioritisation obligations regarding all rights under the Convention which likewise points at resource dependency and progressive realisation (5.3.2). Thirdly, the right to life, survival, and development under Article 6 of the CRC is interpreted as one singular right to life, incorporating the notion of ensuring rights 'to the maximum extent possible' in to this traditionally civil and political right (5.3.3). Fourthly, the CRC-Com's jurisprudence also shows parallels to the concept of the minimum core (5.3.4).

5.3.1. The Application of the Second Sentence of Article 4 of the CRC to Civil and Political Rights

The CRC-Com applies the general obligations provision of Article 4 of the CRC in a way which introduces resource considerations to all rights in the Convention. This provision sets out the general obligations of States parties as follows:

> States Parties shall undertake all appropriate legislative, administrative, and other measures for the implementation of the rights recognized in the present Convention. With regard to economic, social and cultural rights, States Parties shall undertake such measures to the maximum extent of their available resources and, where needed, within the framework of international co-operation.

The CRC-Com reads this wording to establish a differentiation between immediately realisable civil and political and progressively realisable socio-economic rights. Civil and political rights are held to be 'immediate and unqualified',[72]

[71] See CESCR, 'General Comment No 22', para 49 (h).

[72] Regarding the right of the child to freedom from all forms of violence, see CRC-Com, 'General Comment No 13', para 65; see also, regarding the right of the child to protection from corporal punishment and other cruel or degrading forms of punishment, CRC-Com, 'General Comment No 8', para 22.

while socio-economic rights must be realised 'to the maximum extent of … available resources' and thus progressively.[73]

However, the Committee's further jurisprudence does not comply with this strict differentiation. Not only does the Committee set out States' duties without a statement as to their immediacy or progressiveness,[74] the experts also implicitly or explicitly apply the recognition of resource limitations as contained in the second sentence of Article 4 of the CRC to civil and political rights. Several General Comments contain sections about resource and budget allocation which are not tied to specific rights in the Convention. More often than not, these sections reference the second sentence of Article 4 CRC indiscriminately, ie, without declaring that it only applies to socio-economic rights. Effectively, the CRC-Com applies Article 4 of the CRC as a whole to civil and political rights.

A first example for this can be found in General Comment No 6 on the Treatment of Unaccompanied and Separated Children Outside their Country of Origin which concerns a number of rights across both categories.[75] The only engagement with Article 4 of the CRC occurs when the Committee rejects the applicability of Article 2 (3) of the ICESCR, declaring that Article 4 of the CRC requires 'making the assignment of available resources to such [unaccompanied or separated] children a priority', where necessary by accepting and facilitating international help.[76] The Committee evidently refers to the second sentence of Article 4 of the CRC and the familiar theme of prioritisation in resource allocation.[77] There is no sign in the text implying that the experts intended to reduce the scope of this section to socio-economic rights. Rather, the CRC-Com is applying the second sentence of Article 4 of the CRC to all rights without distinction between the categories.

An even more obvious example of this can be observed in General Comment No 9 on the rights of children with disabilities which also concerns all rights under the CRC-Com, including 'civil rights and freedoms'.[78] When talking about budgets under the heading 'General measures of implementation (arts. 4, 42 and 44 (6))', the Committee explicitly refers to the second sentence of Article 4 of the CRC and the duty to take measures to the maximum of available resources when declaring that 'children should be a priority'.[79] The Committee directly cites the

[73] CRC-Com, 'General Comment No 19', para 25.

[74] See further 3.2.3.

[75] General Comment No 6, according to the Committee, is meant 'to provide guidance on the protection, care and proper treatment of unaccompanied and separated children based on the *entire legal framework* provided by the Convention on the Rights of the Child' (emphasis added), CRC-Com, 'General Comment No 6', para 1. For example, the right of the child to express their views freely under Article 12 of the CRC is seen as relevant in this context, see ibid, para 25. This right, according to the experts, belongs in a group of rights which 'contain elements which constitute civil/political rights', CRC-Com, 'General Comment No 5', para 6.

[76] CRC-Com, 'General Comment No 6', para 16.

[77] *cf* 2.3.1.

[78] CRC-Com, 'General Comment No 9', para 34.

[79] ibid, para 20.

second sentence without limiting its relevance only to socio-economic rights. From earlier sections of the Comment, it becomes clear that the Committee acknowledges the relevance of resources not only for socio-economic rights but for the national human rights policy in general.[80] Interestingly, the duty to utilise the maximum extent of available resources is also restated in the context of eliminating disability discrimination,[81] even though the prohibition of discrimination is generally accepted to be an immediately realisable civil and political right.

Another example of this approach to Article 4 CRC appears in General Comment No 7 on implementing child rights in early childhood. Again, this General Comment concerns all rights in the Convention.[82] The only reference to Article 4 of the CRC is located in a section about resource allocation. The experts urge States parties to 'adopt comprehensive, strategic and time-bound plans' which 'requires an increase in human and financial resource allocations for early childhood services and programmes (art. 4)'.[83] Without restricting this to socio-economic rights, the Committee recalls the limited resources aspect from sentence two of Article 4 CRC. The general applicability of these statements becomes even more clear when the CRC-Com continues to acknowledge that

> States parties implementing child rights in early childhood do so from very different starting points, in terms of existing infrastructures for early childhood policies, services and professional training, as well as levels of resources potentially available to allocate to early childhood.[84]

In a similar vein, in General Comment No 2 on NHRIs, the Committee holds that, while allocating resources to NHRIs

> is a very sensitive issue and that State parties function with varying levels of economic resources, the Committee believes that it is the duty of States to make reasonable financial provision for the operation of national human rights institutions in light of article 4 of the Convention.[85]

Again, this statement is placed in a general section about resource allocation and can only be understood to refer to all relevant rights. This is confirmed when the Committee holds that, '[w]here resources are limited, consideration must be given to ensuring that the available resources are used most effectively for the promotion and protection of everyone's human rights'.[86]

[80] See, eg, ibid, para 18.
[81] ibid, para 14 (a).
[82] CRC-Com, 'General Comment No 7', para 1: 'Through this general comment, the Committee wishes to encourage recognition that young children are holders of all rights enshrined in the Convention and that early childhood is a critical period for the realization of these rights.'
[83] ibid, para 38.
[84] ibid.
[85] CRC-Com, 'General Comment No 2', para 11.
[86] ibid, para 6.

Another example of this approach is the Committee's interpretation of Article 4 of the CRC in the context of the right to freedom from all forms of violence under Article 19 (1) of the CRC. In its General Comment No 13, the Committee declares that this right establishes an immediately realisable and 'unqualified' civil and political right.[87] Following this statement, however, the experts hold that,

> in the light of article 4, whatever their economic circumstances, States are required to undertake all possible measures towards the realization of the rights of the child, paying special attention to the most disadvantaged groups (see the Committee's general comment No. 5, para. 8). The article stresses that available resources must be utilized to the maximum extent.[88]

Again, the Committee refers to the second sentence of Article 4 of the CRC, using terminology analogous to progressive realisation. Also very striking is the fact that the Committee took large portions of this statement word for word from a passage in General Comment No 5 which explicitly engages with the concept of progressive realisation flowing from the second sentence of Article 4 of the CRC in the context of socio-economic rights.[89] This fact deserves special emphasis: the CRC-Com is referring to a passage concerning the progressive realisation of socio-economic rights to explain the implementation of Article 19 of the CRC which before has been placed explicitly in the 'immediate and unqualified' category of civil and political rights.

The requirement of taking steps to the maximum of available resources also appears later in the Comment's section on 'Resource allocation': 'Human, financial and technical resources needed across different sectors must be allocated to the maximum extent of available resources.'[90] Clearly, sentence two of Article 4 of the CRC is being applied to Article 19 of the CRC. In light of this, the passage 'whatever their economic circumstances' then must be read to mean that, while resource-related restrictions are irrelevant to taking steps in general, they do in fact influence the pace of overall realisation of the right. In substance, this interpretation is in line with a strict reading of progressive realisation in the context of socio-economic rights, which requires States parties to make the most of their resources available at any time.[91]

Limited resources are also acknowledged later on in this Comment when the Committee recognises the 'different starting points of States parties regarding

[87] CRC-Com, 'General Comment No 13', para 65; see also CRC-Com, 'General Comment No 8', para 22 regarding the right to be free from corporal punishment.

[88] CRC-Com, 'General Comment No 13', para 65.

[89] See CRC-Com, 'General Comment No 5', para 8.

[90] CRC-Com, 'General Comment No 13', para 72 (h). John Tobin and Judy Cashmore also consider this formulation to hint at resource dependency and progressive realisation, see J Tobin and J Cashmore, 'Article 19: The Right to Protection against All Forms of Violence' in J Tobin (ed), *The UN Convention on the Rights of the Child: A Commentary* (Oxford, Oxford University Press, 2019) 692.

[91] See also Tobin and Cashmore, 'Article 19', 705.

the implementation of the required measures from the legal, institutional, cultural, and financial point of view'.[92] If resources were really irrelevant because Article 19 of the CRC is 'unqualified', these different starting points regarding resources would not be relevant. The recognition of this aspect, however, points at the acceptance of available resources as a determinant of the pace of realisation.

A last point to mention here relates to the requirement of utilising the framework of international cooperation in the context of undertaking measures to the maximum of available resources as set out by sentence two of Article 4 of the CRC. This aspect, too, is often indiscriminately applied to all rights in the Convention.[93]

5.3.2. Budgeting and Prioritisation

In general, the CRC-Com reads extensive obligations regarding budgeting into Article 4 of the CRC and devotes a lengthy General Comment to this topic. General Comment No 19 on Public Budgeting is intended by the experts to 'assist States parties in the implementation of article 4 in relation to public budgets'.[94] The Comment provides detailed guidance regarding the utilisation of budgeting strategies to realise the whole range of rights in the Convention.

This General Comment, on the surface, adheres to a traditional strict reading of Article 4 of the CRC, differentiating between immediately realisable civil and political rights and progressively realisable socio-economic rights.[95] Besides this one restatement of the traditional division, however, the Comment does not draw a line between the two categories of rights. The experts, without distinction, declare that 'children's rights shall be given serious consideration in decisions regarding the allocation of resources that become available'.[96] This means that the Committee's guidance on budgeting must be understood to also apply to civil and political rights, even though the idea of developing a budgeting approach informed by children's rights can only be understood as reflecting the requirement of granting children the maximum possible room in public budgets, ie, making the most of – necessarily limited – resources. Thus, setting out budgeting rules is a reflection of the normative relevance of resource limitations and, thus, the concept of progressive realisation.[97]

The idea of prioritisation also extends to particularly vulnerable persons within the group of children; the CRC-Com aims to provide 'recommendations

[92] CRC-Com, 'General Comment No 13', para 70.

[93] See CRC-Com, 'General Comment No 19', paras 64, 75; CRC-Com, 'General Comment No 6', para 16; CRC-Com, 'General Comment No 23', paras 64, 65.

[94] CRC-Com, 'General Comment No 19', para 1.

[95] ibid, para 25.

[96] ibid, para 79.

[97] See also Tobin, 'Article 4', 141.

on how to realize all the rights under the Convention, especially those of children in vulnerable situations' through public budget decision-making.[98] This focus on providing relief to particularly vulnerable children appears again and again in the jurisprudence of the CRC-Com. In General Comment No 5, the Committee holds that 'the strategy will inevitably set priorities' and that '[p]articular attention will need to be given to identifying and giving priority to marginalized and disadvantaged groups of children'.[99] The theme of 'vulnerable groups first' is also present in the socio-economic rights context as an essential requirement for progressive realisation.[100] The priority of vulnerable groups would not make any sense if the State party was under an unconditional and immediate obligation to realise all rights and instead points at a progressive implementation of the CRC-Com, regardless of the right concerned.

5.3.3. The Right to Life, Survival and Development under Article 6 of the CRC

Article 6 of the CRC contains a formulation of the right to life which is unique in the UN human rights treaty system: '1. States Parties recognize that every child has the inherent right to life. 2. States Parties shall ensure to the maximum extent possible the survival and development of the child.' The wording 'maximum extent possible' is reminiscent of the obligation under Article 4 of the CRC (and also Article 2 of the ICESCR) to employ the maximum of available resources for the realisation of socio-economic rights and thus hints at progressive realisation.

Traditionally, the right to life is a civil and political right stemming from Article 6 of the ICCPR. In the CRC-Com's reporting guidelines, the right to life is located under the heading 'General Principles' and not the heading 'Civil rights and freedoms'.[101] But the Committee also noted that 'many other articles, including articles 2, 3, 6 and 12 of the Convention, contain elements which constitute civil/political rights'.[102] The question remains which parts of the provision are considered to constitute civil and political rights, particularly with regards to the rights to survival and development in the second paragraph. One way to conform with the traditional divide between rights would be to differentiate between the first and second paragraph, declaring the rights to survival and development to fall into the category of socio-economic rights which would explain the phrase 'to the maximum extent possible' in paragraph two.

[98] CRC-Com, 'General Comment No 19', para 1.
[99] CRC-Com, 'General Comment No 5', paras 30, 32.
[100] See further 2.3.1.
[101] CRC-Com, 'Treaty-specific Guidelines Regarding the Form and Content of Periodic Reports to be Submitted by States Parties under Article 44, Paragraph 1 (b), of the Convention on the Rights of the Child' (3 March 2015) CRC/C/58/Rev.3, paras 23–27, 28–29.
[102] CRC-Com, 'General Comment No 5', para 6.

However, the Committee's jurisprudence does not establish such a clear differentiation. The Committee's interpretation of the right to life, survival and development under Article 6 of the CRC instead exhibits a lack of clear delimitation between the two paragraphs.[103] If a separation between paragraphs 1 and 2 of Article 6 of the CRC is not conducted by the Committee, the right to life in general must be read in light of the phrase 'to the maximum extent possible' as set out in the second paragraph.[104] This would then necessarily extend to those aspects of the right which the CRC-Com considers to fall into the category of civil and political rights.

In its General Comment No 11 on indigenous children, the Committee addresses Article 6 of the CRC under the heading 'The right to life, survival and development'.[105] It must be noted that, here, the CRC-Com uses the singular version of 'right' instead of splitting up Article 6 of the CRC into several rights.[106] In the following paragraph, however, the experts state that 'Articles 6 and 27 provide the right of children to survival and development as well as an adequate standard of living' after voicing their concerns about high child and infant mortality, malnutrition and disease. With reference to Article 4 of the CRC, this right is then declared to be realisable to the maximum of available resources.[107] This could be taken to establish a differentiation between, on the one hand, the civil and political right to life under Article 6 (1) of the CRC and, on the other hand, the socio-economic right to survival and development under Article 6 (2) CRC.

But this division is not upheld in the following sections of the General Comment. The experts mention the duty of 'ensuring the children's right to life, survival and development to the maximum extent possible',[108] again speaking about a singular right consisting of a mixture of both paragraphs. This statement connects the phrase 'maximum extent possible' directly to the right to life. Similar wording is contained in the joint General Comment of the CRC-Com and the Committee on the Protection of the Rights of All Migrant Workers

[103] See also Tobin and Peleg, 'Article 6', 190, 220–22. Tobin and Peleg also note this trend in Concluding Observations, see ibid, 229; see also S Schmahl, *Convention on the Rights of the Child: Article-by-Article Commentary* (Baden-Baden, Nomos, 2021) 127, where Schmahl considers this approach to be a departure from the traditional understanding of the right to life and questions whether this is within the mandate of the Committee.

[104] Accordingly, Tobin and Peleg consider the right to life to be subject to available resources, see Tobin and Peleg, 'Article 6', 203.

[105] CRC-Com, 'General Comment No 11: Indigenous Children and their Rights under the Convention' (2009) CRC/C/GC/11, para 34.

[106] This is also the terminology the Committee uses in several other places, see, eg, CRC-Com, 'General Comment No 14', para 42; CRC-Com, 'General Comment No 13', para 62; CRC-Com, 'General Comment No 15 on the Right of the Child to the Enjoyment of the Highest Attainable Standard of Health (art. 24)' (2013) CRC/C/GC/15, paras 16–18; CRC-Com, 'General Comment No 16', paras 18–20; CRC-Com, 'General Comment No 19', paras 48–51; CRC-Com, 'General Comment No 25', paras 14–15.

[107] CRC-Com, 'General Comment No 11', para 34.

[108] ibid, para 35.

and Members of their Families (CMW) on the general principles regarding the human rights of children in the context of international migration. The Committees identify the obligation of 'prevention and reduction – to the maximum extent possible – of migration-related risks faced by children, which may jeopardize a child's right to life, survival and development'.[109] This formulation implies that the right to life is a singular right and that its extent is determined by resource limitations.

In General Comment No 21 on Children in Street Situations, the CRC-Com separates its remarks into two subheadings: 'Right to life' and 'Right to survival and development'.[110] But again, no clear division between the two rights is discernible. Under the subheading 'Right to life', the Committee sets out the risks for children in street situations posed by, among other factors, accidents, substance abuse, unsafe sexual practices, and inadequate nutrition, health care and shelter.[111] This contradicts the statements in General Comment No 11, where malnutrition and disease are mentioned in connection to the right to survival and development. In a footnote to the same paragraph, the experts recognise that there cannot be a strict division: 'The preparatory work of the Convention indicate that the rights to life, survival and development under article 6 were understood as complementary and not mutually exclusive, and that the article poses positive obligations.'[112] The legislative history indeed suggests that the rights to survival and life overlap where the prevention of deaths from preventable causes, eg, infant mortality, is concerned.[113]

Later in General Comment No 21, the CRC-Com extends the reach of the right to life (still presented separately from the right to survival and development) even further by holding that it

> concerns individuals' entitlement to be free from acts and omissions intended or expected to cause their unnatural or premature death, and to enjoy a life with dignity. … This conception of the right to life extends not only to civil and political rights but also to economic, social and cultural rights.[114]

It remains unclear what the experts want to say with the second sentence of this quote, particularly with a view to Article 4 of the CRC. One would expect that

[109] CRC-Com, 'General Comment No 22 on the General Principles Regarding the Human Rights of Children in the Context of International Migration' (2017) CRC/C/GC/22, para 42; see also CRC-Com, 'General Comment No 6', para 23.

[110] CRC-Com, 'General Comment No 21', paras 29–31.

[111] ibid, para 29.

[112] CRC-Com, 'General Comment No 21', para 29 (fn).

[113] According to the Report of the Working Group on a draft of the CRC, '[t]he approach to the right to life in the Covenants was rather negative, while that of the convention should be positive and should take into account economic, social and cultural conditions', see UNCHR, 'Report of the Working Group on a Draft Convention on the Rights of the Child on its 10th Session' (6 April 1988) E/CN.4/1988/28, para 21. Notably, the argument was not that a positive right to development should be added but rather that the right to life should be extended to include positive aspects which, at least at the time, were considered to be socio-economic in nature.

[114] CRC-Com, 'General Comment No 21', para 29.

a differentiation between the right to life and the right to survival and development would lead to a location of traditionally socio-economic aspects in the scope of the latter, as has been suggested in General Comment No 11. However, the above formulation suggests a mix of both categories in the first paragraph of Article 6 of the CRC.

A look at the decision in *Villagrán Morales et al v Guatemala* by the Inter-American Court of Human Rights (IACtHR), which was cited by the CRC-Com in this context,[115] can provide some orientation. The joint concurring opinion of judges Cançado Trindade and Abreu-Burelli in this case argues that the inclusion of a life with dignity into the scope of the right to life leads to the following consequence: 'This outlook conceptualizes the right to life as belonging, at the same time, to the domain of civil and political rights, as well as economic, social and cultural rights, thus illustrating the interrelation and indivisibility of all human rights.'[116] The judges of the IACtHR thus consider the right to life itself to belong in both categories of rights instead of being composed of two discernible rights of either category. This is in line with the fact that the CRC-Com struggles to clearly delimit different rights with discernible categories under Article 6 CRC and again supports the conception of an extensive right to life including the aspects of survival and development (and thus including the resource considerations recognised in Article 6 (2) of the CRC).

As a last aspect regarding the right to life, the CRC-Com reiterates that 'growing up in conditions of absolute poverty threatens children's survival and their health and undermines their basic quality of life'.[117] Again, the strict demarcation of the right to life and the right to survival and development fails; the Committee refers to survival under the heading 'the right to life'. Furthermore, the footnote to this statement refers to a paragraph in the CRC-Com's General Comment No 7 which concerns the right to an adequate standard of living under Article 27 of the CRC. This section sets out that '[y]oung children are entitled to a standard of living adequate for their physical, mental, spiritual, moral and social development'.[118] The right to an adequate standard of living, however, traditionally belongs in the category of socio-economic rights.[119]

The evidence collected above suggests that the CRC-Com does not differentiate between a narrow and negative civil and political right to life under Article 6 (1) of the CRC and a positive socio-economic right to survival and development under Article 6 (2) of the CRC. Instead, one extensive right to life consisting of several aspects creating a range of positive duties is constructed.[120]

[115] ibid, para 29 (fn).

[116] IACtHR, *Villagrán Morales et al v Guatemala* (1999) Series C No 63, joint concurring opinion of judges Cançado Trindade and Abreu-Burelli, para 4.

[117] CRC-Com, 'General Comment No 21', para 30.

[118] CRC-Com, 'General Comment No 7', para 26.

[119] See Article 11 of the ICESCR.

[120] See also M Nowak, *Article 6: The Right to Life, Survival and Development*, A Commentary on the United Nations Convention on the Rights of the Child Series 6 (Leiden, Nijhoff, 2005) 18–49,

This is not surprising considering that the HRC early on interpreted the right to life under the ICCPR to include a number of positive aspects, explicitly setting out the duties to reduce infant mortality, malnutrition, and epidemics.[121] It is unlikely that the CRC-Com intends to reduce this well-established scope of the right to life in the context of children's rights. This approach of combining both paragraphs of Article 6 of the CRC not only establishes a traditionally civil and political right with extensive positive obligations but also necessarily entails the integration of the phrase 'maximum extent possible' into the right as a whole, therefore introducing the notion of resource limitations to civil and political rights.

After extending the scope of the right to life to include all the aspects mentioned above, it is not surprising that the subheading 'right to survival and development' in General Comment No 21 does not set out any additional substantive aspects of Article 6 of the CRC. The experts simply state, in a very general manner, that development must be understood 'as a holistic concept, embracing the child's physical, mental, spiritual, moral, psychological and social development'.[122] These aspects were already included in the Committee's remarks on the right to life under Article 6 (1) of the CRC by reference to General Comment No 7.

5.3.4. Minimum Core

As is the case in the jurisprudence of the CRPD-Com,[123] the CRC-Com declares that fair trial guarantees in the context of criminal proceedings under Article 40 (2) of the CRC are 'minimum standards'.[124] This would not make sense if Article 40 of the CRC were to be perceived as immediately realisable in all aspects. Rather, the CRC-Com highlights the most important aspects which must be realised immediately while progressive realisation of positive aspects remains the norm.

5.4. THE CEDAW-COM AND CERD

In the jurisprudence of the CEDAW-Com and CERD, references to the relevance of limited resources are much more scarce. According to the CERD,

who structures his commentary on Article 6 of the CRC by differentiating between the duties to respect, protect, and fulfil instead of separating the rights to life and survival and development.

[121] HRC, 'General Comment No 6', para 5; see also Nowak, *Article* 6, 36; the CRC has recognised before that General Comments of other Committees should be seen as complementary in the interpretation of the Convention, see CRC-Com, 'General Comment No 5', para 5.

[122] CRC-Com, 'General Comment No 21', para 31.

[123] See further 5.2.4.

[124] CRC-Com, 'General Comment No 24', para 38.

the requirement of 'immediate and positive measures' against incitement and discrimination in Article 4 of the ICERD, together with other provisions in the Convention, obligates States parties to 'dedicate the widest possible range of resources to the eradication of hate speech'.[125] The Committee herewith sets out an immediate duty of conduct which is limited by the availability of resources which coincides with the concept of the immediate obligation to undertake steps to the maximum of available resources.

In its General Recommendation No 24 on women and health, the CEDAW-Com holds that States parties must 'take appropriate legislative, judicial, administrative, budgetary, economic and other measures to the maximum extent of their available resources'.[126] Notably, the Committee does not speak of a singular 'right to health' in this General Recommendation but instead of 'rights relating to women's health'.[127] Reference is made frequently to aspects which (at least partly) lie outside the scope of a traditionally conceived right to health, such as family planning,[128] gender-based violence,[129] female genital mutilation,[130] and the prevention of maternal mortality.[131] The application of the phrase 'maximum extent of available resources' thus cannot be understood to be limited to the realisation of non-discrimination in the context of a classical socio-economic right. The CEDAW-Com also considers States parties to be under an obligation to 'work towards the mobilization of public resources' required to reduce the risk factors for human trafficking.[132] This statement clarifies that not all resources required to solve the problem are available at once but that the acquisition of these resources is a process that takes time which consequently influences the pace of realisation regarding the relevant human rights. Furthermore, the CEDAW-Com recognises the relevance of (financial) resources when declaring that States parties are under an obligation to seek international cooperation in order to overcome constraints in this area.[133]

5.5. THE HRC

While the recognition of positive duties has existed for a while in the jurisprudence of the HRC,[134] only recently has an extensive engagement with the 'fulfil'

[125] CERD, 'General Recommendation No 35', para 10.

[126] CEDAW-Com, 'General Recommendation No 24: Article 12 of the Convention (Women and Health)' (1999) HRI/GEN/1/Rev.7, para 17; see also ibid, para 27.

[127] ibid, para 15.

[128] ibid, paras 17, 23.

[129] ibid, para 15 (b).

[130] ibid, para 15 (d).

[131] ibid, para 17.

[132] CEDAW-Com, 'General Recommendation No 38', para 47.

[133] CEDAW-Com, 'General Recommendation No 28', para 29; see also see also CEDAW-Com, 'General Recommendation No 35', para 21.

[134] See, eg, HRC, 'General Comment No 31', para 6: 'The legal obligation under article 2, paragraph 1, is both negative and positive in nature'; see also HRC, 'General Comment No 37 on the

dimension of rights been undertaken by this Committee. Consequently, the HRC is now faced with the question how these extensive positive obligations and the proclaimed immediacy and unconditionality of rights under the ICCPR can be reconciled. As expected, the HRC also solves this dilemma by implicitly accepting that limited resources determine the scope of rights. This tendency is particularly clear in the Committee's jurisprudence regarding disproportionate burdens in the context of the right to life under Article 6 of the ICCPR and the right to peaceful assembly under Article 21 of the ICCPR (5.5.1). The HRC also establishes a minimum level of rights to be fulfilled which is similar to the concept of the minimum core (5.5.2).

5.5.1. Disproportionate Burdens

The HRC introduces resource considerations into its jurisprudence by accepting the relevance of 'disproportionate burdens'. The recognition that States parties must only take positive measures if those measures do not pose a disproportionate burden appears again and again in different contexts but particularly in the context of the right to life under Article 6 of the ICCPR. Such an implicit recognition of the relevance of available resources is discernible in General Comment No 36 on the Right to Life under Article 6 of the ICCPR when the Committee sets out the requirement of protective measures against the deprivation of life by non-state actors.[135] Regarding the duty to protect, eg, in the context of (organised) crime, militias or other armed groups, the HRC holds that

> States parties are thus under a due diligence obligation to take reasonable, positive measures that do not impose disproportionate burdens on them in response to reasonably foreseeable threats to life originating from private persons and entities whose conduct is not attributable to the State.[136]

This statement shows that the Committee does not consider States parties' positive duties to be unqualified. Rather, the reference to the 'disproportionate burden' limit displays an acceptance of available resources as a limiting factor.[137] This result is confirmed when taking into account the origin of this 'disproportionate burden' standard. In this context, the HRC refers to a decision

Right to Peaceful Assembly (Article 21)' (2020) CCPR/C/GC/37, para 23; HRC, 'General Comment No 12: Article 1 (Right to Self-determination)' (1984) HRI/GEN/1/Rev.7, para 6; HRC, 'General Comment No 18', para 5; HRC, 'General Comment No 23: Article 27 (Rights of Minorities)' (1994) HRI/GEN/1/Rev.7, para 6.2; HRC, 'General Comment No 25: Article 25 (Participation in Public Affairs and the Right to Vote)' (1996) HRI/GEN/1/Rev.7, para 12; HRC, 'General Comment No 28', paras 3, 29.

[135] HRC, 'General Comment No 36', paras 18–31.

[136] ibid, para 21.

[137] See also Tobin and Peleg, 'Article 6', 203 and Tobin, 'Article 4', 130.

of the IACtHR. In the relevant case, *Sawhoyamaxa Indigenous Community v Paraguay*, the IACtHR held that

> [i]t is clear for the Court that a State cannot be responsible for all situations in which the right to life is at risk. Taking into account the difficulties involved in the planning and adoption of public policies and the operative choices that have to be made in view of the priorities and the resources available, the positive obligations of the State must be interpreted so that an impossible or disproportionate burden is not imposed upon the authorities.[138]

The referenced paragraph explicitly bases the notion of disproportionality on the fact that States parties must make 'operative choices' in the distribution of available resources. Furthermore, the judges implicitly refer to the general principle that impossible obligations cannot exist in international law.[139]

The distribution aspect of the limited resources argument further emerges when the experts of the HRC stress that particular focus must lie on the protection of vulnerable groups.[140] This is found to include the provision of reasonable accommodation for persons with disabilities.[141]

The relatively recent Individual Communication in *Toussaint v Canada* illustrates that there is a new emergence of these aspects in line with General Comment No 36.[142] Recalling an earlier General Comment on the right to life, the experts state that 'the right to life concerns the entitlement of individuals to be free from acts and omissions that are intended or may be expected to cause their unnatural or premature death, as well as to enjoy a life with dignity' and that 'as a minimum' States parties must provide access to healthcare services when the denial of access would expose the rights holder to a 'reasonably foreseeable' risk of death.[143] According to the Committee, the fact that the author's treatment was not covered by Canada's Interim Federal Health Program (IFHP) entails a violation of Article 6 of the ICCPR because the author required long-term intensive medical management of her diabetes in order to prevent potentially fatal complications like blood clots, embolisms, and kidney failure.[144] This decision can be read to include an implicit proportionality analysis, tied to the obligation to take action where a 'reasonably foreseeable' risk for life can be determined. The Committee found the exclusion from the IFHP to entail such 'serious implications' that this omission could not be justified.[145]

[138] IACtHR, *Sawhoyamaxa Indigenous Community v Paraguay* (29 March 2006) Series C No 146, para 155.

[139] See further 8.2.2.

[140] HRC, 'General Comment No 36', paras 9, 23.

[141] ibid, para 24.

[142] Notably, the views in this case were adopted in 2018, ie, shortly before the adoption of the General Comment in 2019.

[143] HRC, *Toussaint v Canada*, para 11.3.

[144] ibid, paras 11.4–11.5, referring to the medical opinions cited in ibid, para 2.9.

[145] ibid, para 11.5.

The disproportionate burden limit also appears in right to life cases concerning the investigation of forced disappearances, particularly in Bosnia-Herzegovina. Regarding the obligation to investigate enforced and involuntary disappearances, the Committee acknowledges that positive duties are limited by what is possible and proportionate. A deeper engagement with the question of how to determine proportionality, however, has not yet taken place as most relevant cases concern at least one clearly inappropriate omission by the State party (eg, not informing the relatives of the disappeared person about the investigative progress). The Committee holds that

> the obligation to investigate allegations of enforced disappearances and to bring the culprits to justice is not an obligation of result, but of means, and that it must be interpreted in a way which does not impose an impossible or disproportionate burden on the authorities.[146]

The limit of disproportionate burdens also plays a role in the context of the right to peaceful assembly under Article 21 of the ICCPR. According to General Comment No 37 on this provision, 'States parties are obliged to take all reasonable measures that do not impose disproportionate burdens upon them to protect all participants and to allow such assemblies to take place in an uninterrupted manner'.[147] Additionally, the Committee refers to the obligation to pay special attention to vulnerable groups in this context.[148]

5.5.2. Minimum Core

When setting out States parties' obligations regarding the rights of persons deprived of their liberty under Article 10 of the ICCPR, the Committee focuses on inviolable minimum core requirements, indirectly accepting that there are obligations beyond this which are subject to available resources. According to General Comment No 21 regarding the Humane Treatment of Persons Deprived of their Liberty, '[t]reating all persons deprived of their liberty with humanity and with respect for their dignity is a fundamental and universally applicable rule [which,] as a minimum, cannot be dependent on the material resources available in the State party'.[149]

[146] HRC, *Prutina et al v Bosnia and Herzegovina* [Adoption of Views] (28 March 2013) CCPR/C/107/D/1917,1918,1925/2009&1953/2010, para 9.5; see also HRC, *Rizvanović v Bosnia and Herzegovina* [Adoption of Views] (21 March 2014) CCPR/C/110/D/1997/2010, para 9.5; HRC, *Kožljak v Bosnia and Herzegovina* [Adoption of Views] (28 October 2014) CCPR/C/112/D/1970/2010, para 9.5; HRC, *Hero v Bosnia and Herzegovina* [Adoption of Views] (28 October 2014) CCPR/C/112/D/1966/2010, para 9.5; *Selimović et al v Bosnia and Herzegovina* [Adoption of Views] (17 July 2014) CCPR/C/111/D/2003/2010, para 12.5.

[147] HRC, 'General Comment No 37', para 27.

[148] ibid, para 25.

[149] HRC, 'General Comment No 21: Article 10 (Humane Treatment of Persons Deprived of Their Liberty)' (1992) HRI/GEN/1/Rev.7, para 4; see also HRC, *Mukong v Cameroon* [Adoption of Views] (21 July 1994) CCPR/C/51/O/458/1991, para 9.3.

The previous General Comment No 9 on Article 10 of the ICCPR is even more clear in this respect. Here, the Committee holds that

> [t]he humane treatment and the respect for the dignity of all persons deprived of their liberty is a basic standard of universal application which cannot depend entirely on material resources. While the Committee is aware that in other respects the modalities and conditions of detention may vary with the available resources, they must always be applied without discrimination, as required by article 2 (1).[150]

Apparently, the Committee is of the opinion that Article 10 (1) of the ICCPR and the duty to treat prisoners with humanity and respect for their inherent dignity as well as the prohibition of discrimination in this context constitute an unconditional minimum level. Regarding other aspects of 'the modalities and conditions of detention', available resources do play a role.

5.6. CONCLUSION

There are many examples in the jurisprudence of the Committees showing that they consider civil and political rights to be subject to available resources which consequently supports the claim that these rights are interpreted to contain a progressive element. The Committees furthermore set out particularly important parts of civil and political rights which are exempt from this dependence on resources, thus adopting an approach similar to the minimum core developed in the context of socio-economic rights. Another parallel to the socio-economic rights regime is the occasional reference to international assistance as part of the concept of available resources.

The fact that some obligations are too costly to realise entirely at once is one central reason for the concept of progressive realisation. Thus, when the Committees hold that the realisation of a right is subject to the availability of resources, they necessarily also accept that the applicable standard of realisation entails obligations which are progressive in the narrow sense. Instances where the Committees acknowledge that States parties are only obliged to fulfil positive aspects of civil and political rights to the maximum of their available resources are thus equivalent to an implicit recognition that these rights are also progressively realisable. This constitutes further evidence of a convergence of both standards of realisation in the jurisprudence of the UN Committees.

[150] HRC, 'General Comment No 9: Article 10 (Humane Treatment of Persons Deprived of their Liberty)' (1982) HRI/GEN/1/Rev.7, para 1.

6

The Application of the Margin of Appreciation and the Reasonableness Standard to Civil and Political Rights

6.1. INTRODUCTION

ANOTHER WAY IN which the Committees implicitly condone a uniform standard of obligations is by granting States parties a margin of appreciation and applying a standard of review similar to the reasonableness standard when dealing with civil and political rights. As has been shown above, this leeway in implementation fenced in by reasonableness has been developed specifically for progressively realisable rights in the UN system and is indivisible from this concept.[1] This is illustrated by the decision to introduce reasonableness and the margin of appreciation into the regime of the ICESCR by means of Article 8 (4) of the ICESCR-OP which prescribes that the CESCR 'shall consider the reasonableness of the steps taken' by the State party while 'bear[ing] in mind that the State Party may adopt a range of possible policy measures for the implementation of the rights set forth in the Covenant'.

Requiring States parties to take reasonable action within a certain margin of appreciation means focusing on the efforts of these States parties instead of demanding a certain result which should be fulfilled immediately. In other words, applying reasonableness as a standard of review signifies the evaluation of obligations of conduct, not result. This coincides with the structure of obligations developed for socio-economic rights under the terminology of progressive realisation. Accordingly, the application of the margin of appreciation doctrine and reasonableness review means accepting a progressive mode of realisation.

In a first step, the following section will explore instances where the Committees implicitly or explicitly recognise a margin of appreciation or discretion for States parties (6.2). The second section will show that the Committees apply a standard of review reminiscent of the reasonableness standard (6.3).

[1] See further 2.6.

6.2. THE MARGIN OF APPRECIATION OR DISCRETION

The margin of appreciation reflects the acceptance that, in the judicial review of progressively realisable rights and consequent obligations of conduct, the Committees cannot replace policy decisions of the States parties with policies they consider superior. In the jurisprudence of all Committees, an implicit or explicit application of the margin of appreciation can be observed. While not all applications of the margin of appreciation can be understood as implying a progressive model of realisation,[2] there are instances where this doctrine clearly is applied in a similar way to that envisioned in Article 8 (4) of the ICESCR-OP and Article 10 (4) of the CRC-OP3. Those instances are relevant where the margin of appreciation is invoked to grant States parties leeway in exercising obligations of conduct. Such examples can be found in the jurisprudence of the CRPD-Com (6.2.1), the CRC-Com (6.2.2), the CEDAW-Com and CERD (6.2.3), and the HRC (6.2.4).

6.2.1. The CRPD-Com

The CRPD-Com regularly grants a margin of appreciation when inspecting the reasonableness and proportionality of accommodating measures pursuant to Articles 5 (3) and 2 of the CRPD even in cases where civil and political rights are concerned.[3] It has already been established above that the CRPD-Com applies the margin of appreciation doctrine in *Jungelin v Sweden*, which can be considered to concern socio-economic rights.[4] This doctrine is then transferred to all later Individual Communications concerning reasonable accommodation in the context of civil and political rights. All three of the CRPD-Com's jury duty cases cite the relevant paragraph in *Jungelin v Sweden*, establishing that States parties enjoy a margin of appreciation 'when assessing the reasonableness and proportionality of accommodation measures' in the context of the rights to political participation under Article 29 of the CRPD and access to justice under Article 13 of the CRPD.[5] The same reference is made in *Bacher v Austria* and *Sahlin v Sweden*.[6] Regarding procedural accommodations in the context of the rights to equal recognition before the law under Article 12 of the CRPD and access to justice under Article 13 of the CRPD, the Committee repeatedly

[2] The margin of appreciation does not indicate progressive realisation if, eg, it is granted to accommodate differences in moral perceptions in the States parties. In this case, the margin does not refer to the method of realising a right over time but rather to the content of the right itself. See HRC, *Hertzberg v Finland* [Adoption of Views] (2 April 1982) CCPR/C/15/D/61/1979.

[3] See also Uerpmann-Wittzack, 'Die UN-Behindertenrechtskonvention', 208, speaking of reasonable accommodation as a gateway for the margin of appreciation.

[4] See further 2.6.1.

[5] CRPD-Com, *Beasley v Australia*, para 8.4; CRPD-Com, *Lockrey v Australia*, para 8.4; CRPD-Com, *JH v Australia*, para 7.4.

[6] CRPD-Com, *Bacher v Austria*, para 9.7; CRPD-Com, *Sahlin v Sweden*, para 8.6.

stresses that 'States parties have a certain margin of appreciation to determine the procedural arrangements to enable persons with disabilities to exercise their legal capacity'.[7]

The CRPD-Com also emphasises that the margin of appreciation has its limits and cannot be interpreted to lead to an abdication of the role of the Committee as a supervisory body. In *Jungelin v Sweden*, an individual dissenting opinion by several Committee members stressed that it is still for the Committee to evaluate the reasonableness of measures taken by the State party.[8] This notion has been integrated into the majority decisions in the above-mentioned civil and political rights cases by adding to the assurance of the margin of appreciation the following statement:

> However, States parties must ensure that such an assessment is made in a thorough and objective manner, covering all the pertinent elements, before reaching a conclusion that the respective support and adaptation measures would constitute a disproportionate or undue burden for a State party.[9]

The CRPD-Com also sees itself as competent to evaluate these requirements. Thus, just like the CESCR, the CRPD-Com considers that it is ultimately the role of the Committee to determine the reasonableness of measures and therefore the violation of Convention rights.

6.2.2. The CRC-Com

A clear utilisation of a margin of appreciation in order to deal with the progressive realisation of rights appears in the CRC-Com's General Comment No 5 on General Measures of Application of the Convention under Articles 4, 42 and 44 (6) of the CRC. Here, the experts hold that 'implementation is the process whereby States parties take action to ensure the realisation of all rights in the Convention for all children in their jurisdiction' and then reference Article 4 of the CRC which demands that States parties take 'all appropriate legislative, administrative and other measures'.[10] This statement indicates the establishment of an obligation of conduct, namely the obligation to take appropriate steps to enable a process towards the full realisation of all rights under the Convention. The CRC-Com goes on to stress that 'it is the State which takes on obligations under the Convention',[11] implying that it is not the Committee prescribing in

[7] CRPD-Com, *Noble v Australia* [Adoption of Views] (2 September 2016) CRPD/C/16/D/7/2012, para 8.6; CRPD-Com, *Makarova v Lithuania*, para 7.6; CRPD-Com, *Leo v Australia* [Adoption of Views] (30 August 2019) CRPD/C/22/D/17/2013, para 8.7; CRPD-Com, *Doolan v Australia* [Adoption of Views] (30 August 2019) CRPD/C/22/D/18/2013, para 8.7.

[8] CRPD-Com, *Jungelin v Sweden*, Appendix paras 1–6.

[9] CRPD-Com, *Beasley v Australia*, para 8.6; CRPD-Com, *Lockrey v Australia*, para 8.6; see also CRPD-Com, *JH v Australia*, para 7.4.

[10] CRC-Com, 'General Comment No 5', para 1.

[11] ibid.

detail which policy to adopt which entails a margin of appreciation for States parties in this regard.[12]

However, in General Comment No 19 on Public Budgeting, the CRC-Com holds that the words 'shall undertake' in Article 4 of the CRC 'mean that States parties have no discretion as to whether or not to satisfy their obligation to undertake the appropriate legislative, administrative and other measures necessary to realize children's rights, which includes measures related to public budgets'.[13]

While, at first, this statement may appear to preclude any room for manoeuvre regarding the general obligations to be undertaken by the States parties under Article 4 of the CRC, a closer inspection reveals that this is not what the CRC-Com intended to say. The experts find that States have no discretion regarding whether or not they fulfil their obligation to undertake appropriate steps. This does not mean, however, that there is no margin of appreciation in determining what is appropriate for each State party. Rather, the denial of discretion is limited to the taking of steps overall, which coincides with the immediate obligation to take steps.

This result is confirmed when recalling a similar statement by the CRC-Com in the context of the socio-economic right to an adequate standard of living under Article 27 of the CRC. In General Comment No 21 on Children in Street Situations, the CRC-Com engages with the formulation 'shall take' in Article 27 (3) of the CRC, likewise taking it to mean that '[t]hose prescriptions leave no leeway for the discretion of States'.[14] However, the Committee continues to hold that the implementation of the measures required under Article 27 (3) of the CRC takes place 'in accordance with national conditions and within the means of States parties' and, pursuant to Article 4 of the CRC, 'to the maximum extent of States parties' available resources and, where needed, within the framework of international cooperation'.[15]

A similar kind of discretion is granted to States parties in the context of the rights of children in the criminal justice system. As has been argued above, the Committee's interpretation of the rights of children in the criminal justice system entails the progressive obligation of States parties to gradually increase the use of diversion measures and gradually reduce the reliance on incarceration.[16] Unsurprisingly, the experts of the CRC-Com find that '[i]t is left to the discretion of States parties to decide on the exact nature and content of measures of diversion, and to take the necessary legislative and other measures for their implementation'.[17]

The CRC-Com makes clear that this primary competence to decide on a policy of progressive realisation cannot go unchecked but must fulfil certain

[12] See also Schmahl, *CRC-Commentary*, 26.
[13] CRC-Com, 'General Comment No 19', para 18.
[14] CRC-Com, 'General Comment No 21', para 49.
[15] ibid.
[16] See further 4.3.4.
[17] CRC-Com, 'General Comment No 24', para 17.

requirements. The Committee repeatedly holds that States parties must take 'appropriate' measures in light of the circumstances.[18] It will be seen later on that the CRC-Com's interpretation of the requirement of appropriateness is very similar to what has been read into the requirement of reasonableness as set out by Article 8 (4) of the ICESCR-OP and Article 10 (4) of the CRC-OP3 for the review of socio-economic rights.[19]

6.2.3. The CEDAW-Com and CERD

The CEDAW-Com accepts a certain degree of leeway of States parties in devising policies for furthering substantive equality akin to the margin of appreciation. This becomes clear in the statements of the experts regarding States parties' obligation 'to pursue by all appropriate means and without delay a policy of eliminating discrimination against women' under Article 2 of the CEDAW. In General Recommendation No 28 on the Core Obligations of States Parties under Article 2 of the CEDAW, the experts determine that

> [t]his obligation to use means or a certain way of conduct gives a State party a great deal of flexibility for devising a policy that will be appropriate for its particular legal, political, economic, administrative and institutional framework and that can respond to the particular obstacles and resistance to the elimination of discrimination against women existing in that State party.[20]

This statement mirrors the argument made above: an obligation of conduct requires a certain flexibility for States parties in the adoption and implementation of policies which best suit their individual circumstances. However, the CEDAW-Com also stresses that 'ultimately, it is for the Committee to determine whether a State party has indeed adopted all necessary measures at the national level aimed at achieving the full realisation of the rights recognized in the Convention'.[21]

The CERD is much less clear in this regard. There are, however, some scattered statements on the Committee's role. In its General Recommendation No 35 on Combating Racist Hate Speech, the CERD makes the following statement regarding the requirement of expediency of proceedings against alleged racist hate speech offenders: 'In this and other respects under the Convention, the Committee recalls that it is not its function to review the interpretation of facts and national law made by domestic authorities, unless the decisions are

[18] See, eg, CRC-Com, 'General Comment No 11', para 26.

[19] See further 6.3.2.

[20] CEDAW-Com, 'General Recommendation No 28', para 23.

[21] ibid; see also CEDAW-Com, 'General Recommendation No 31', para 31: 'States parties must, however, be able to demonstrate the direct relevance and appropriateness of the measures that have been taken, ensuring first and foremost that the human rights of women are not violated, and demonstrate whether such measures will achieve the desired effect and result.'

manifestly absurd or unreasonable.'[22] It becomes clear that the CERD does not see itself as a court of fourth instance and assumes a degree of deference towards the decisions of the State party. The standard of unreasonableness established in this context is also applied in the CERD's Individual Communications and will be further examined below.[23]

6.2.4. The HRC

The question whether and in which way the HRC applies the margin of appreciation doctrine has been subject to considerable discussion by literary commentators. According to many investigations into this issue, the HRC has been 'speaking silently the language of the margin', to use the often-cited words of James Crawford.[24] The discussion as a whole is beyond the scope of this study. For the purposes of this book, only those instances of the application of the margin are relevant which indicate that leeway was given in the context of obligations of conduct pursuant to a progressive notion of realisation.

There is one decision in the jurisprudence of the HRC where the margin of appreciation is explicitly mentioned: *Hertzberg v Finland*. In this case, the experts hold that 'public morals differ widely' and that '[t]here is no universally applicable moral standard. Consequently, in this respect, a certain margin of discretion must be accorded to the responsible national authorities.'[25] However, this case does not concern leeway in the implementation of a right but rather normative flexibility regarding the end result to be reached by States parties and thus does not point at the concept of progressive realisation.

Although the experts later explicitly rejected the margin of appreciation doctrine,[26] the HRC now implicitly grants a margin of appreciation in other cases where the application of this principle points at a progressive understanding of rights. This is the case, for example, in the individual concurring opinion in *Oulajin and Kaiss v the Netherlands* by Kurt Herndl, Rein Müllerson, Birame N'Diaye and Waleed Sadi. After referencing and reiterating parts of the individual opinion in *Sprenger v the Netherlands*, the experts add that

> social security legislation … necessarily must make distinctions. It is for the legislature of each country, which best knows the socio-economic needs of the society concerned, to try to achieve social justice in the concrete context. Unless the distinctions made are manifestly discriminatory or arbitrary, it is not for the Committee to

[22] CERD, 'General Recommendation No 35', para 17.
[23] See further 6.3.3.
[24] See James Crawford's Preface in Y Arai-Takahashi, *The Margin of Appreciation Doctrine and the Principle of Proportionality in the Jurisprudence of the ECHR* (Antwerpen, Intersentia, 2002) 2–3; see also Legg, 'The Margin of Appreciation', 6 with further references; see also McGoldrick, 'A Defence of the Margin of Appreciation', 55–56.
[25] See HRC, *Hertzberg v Finland*, para 10.3.
[26] HRC, 'General Comment No 34: Article 19: Freedoms of Opinion and Expression' (2011) CCPR/C/GC/34, para 36.

> re-evaluate the complex socio-economic data and substitute its judgement for that of the legislatures of States parties.[27]

It has been argued above that the Committee members in this individual opinion present a progressive notion of Article 26 of the ICCPR.[28] It is logically consistent to grant States parties a margin of appreciation for choosing the exact policy in this regard. A similar approach is chosen regarding the rights of children under Article 24 of the ICCPR, which are also perceived in a progressive way by the Committee.[29] In General Comment No 17 on this provision, the experts declare that, '[i]n most cases, however, the measures to be adopted are not specified in the Covenant and it is for each State to determine them in the light of the protection needs of children in its territory and within its jurisdiction'.[30]

6.3. REASONABLENESS

There is also evidence in the jurisprudence of the Committees that they are applying a standard of review similar to the reasonableness standard in the context of civil and political rights. Keeping in mind that this standard was included in the Optional Protocols to the ICESCR, CRPD and CRC only for socio-economic rights and specifically to establish a standard of review for progressively realisable rights,[31] the application of the reasonableness standard further breaks down the barriers between the categories of rights.[32] It must be noted, however, that not all of the Committees are equally far along in adopting a standard of reasonableness. While the CRPD-Com (6.3.1) and the CRC-Com (6.3.2) are more clear in this regard, it will be seen that some of the Committees, particularly the CEDAW-Com and CERD (6.3.3) and the HRC (6.3.4), are very unclear concerning the standard of review they apply and, in part, still adhere to a deferential standard of 'unreasonableness'.

6.3.1. The CRPD-Com

The closest resemblance to the reasonableness standard can be found in the jurisprudence of the CRPD-Com. The duty to provide reasonable accommodation

[27] HRC, *Oulajin and Kaiss v the Netherlands*, individual concurring opinion by Kurt Herndl, Rein Müllerson, Birame N'Diaye, and Waleed Sadi.

[28] See further 4.5.4.

[29] See 4.5.3.

[30] HRC, 'General Comment No 17', para 3.

[31] Regarding the CRC-OP3, see G de Beco, 'The Optional Protocol to the Convention on the Rights of the Child on a Communications Procedure: Good News?' (2013) 13 *Human Rights Law Review* 367, 378.

[32] The Constitutional Court of South Africa also applied this concept to all rights regardless of their category, see Fowkes, 'Normal Rights, Just New', 734; see also, generally, S Liebenberg, *Socio-economic Rights: Adjudication Under a Transformative Constitution* (Claremont, Juta, 2010).

under Articles 5 and 2 of the CRPD introduces the word reasonable into the CRPD, and a closer look at the jurisprudence of the CRPD-Com reveals that the Committee utilises these provisions to establish a concept very similar to the standard of reasonableness developed in the ICESCR regime. Reasonable accommodation is then applied to all rights in the CRPD, including those traditionally considered civil and political.

General Comment No 6 on Equality and Non-discrimination provides detailed guidance regarding the concepts of reasonable accommodation and disproportionate or undue burdens. The word reasonable as set out in Articles 2 and 5 of the CRPD, according to the Committee,

> should not act as a distinct qualifier or modifier of the duty. It is not a means by which the costs of accommodation or the availability of resources can be assessed – this occurs at a later stage, when the 'disproportionate or undue burden' assessment is undertaken.[33]

Rather, reasonableness is interpreted to refer only to the benefits of an accommodation measure, namely its 'relevance, appropriateness and effectiveness for the person with a disability' and therefore its aptness to achieve the 'purpose (or purposes) for which it is being made, and is tailored to meet the requirements'.[34] Resource considerations are thus only relevant for the determination of a disproportionate or undue burden which 'sets the limit of the duty to provide reasonable accommodation' by filtering out 'excessive or unjustifiable burden[s] on the accommodating party'.[35]

The concept of reasonableness under Articles 5 (3) and 2 of the CRPD, at first, appears to be interpreted more narrowly than in the context of Article 8 (4) of the ICESCR-OP where the term reasonableness itself is read to include both sides of the proportionality assessment.[36] However, even though the word reasonable is interpreted narrowly, it must be read in context of the whole concept of reasonable accommodation which always includes testing for a disproportionate or undue burden and therefore also contains the second half of the proportionality assessment. Keeping this in mind, reasonable accommodation as a whole is largely analogous to the reasonableness standard of the CESCR. In the context of both treaties, reasonableness is a contextual standard of evaluation regarding the positive measures taken or not taken by States parties. Accordingly, many commentators consider the two concepts to perform the same function.[37]

[33] CRPD-Com, 'General Comment No 6', para 25 (a); this is contrary to what many commentators read into the Convention before this General Comment was adopted, see, eg, Nilsson, 'Article 2', 79–80.

[34] CRPD-Com, 'General Comment No 6', para 25 (a).

[35] ibid, para 25 (b).

[36] See further 2.6.2.

[37] See, eg, JE Lord and R Brown, 'The Role of Reasonable Accommodation in Securing Substantive Equality For Persons with Disabilities: The UN Convention on the Rights of Persons with Disabilities' in MH Rioux, LA Basser, and M Jones (eds), *Critical Perspectives on Human Rights and Disability Law* (Leiden, Nijhoff, 2011) 304; see also Nilsson, 'Article 2', 78; B Porter,

The CRPD-Com also does not always uphold the differentiation between the tests for reasonableness and a disproportionate and undue burden but rather mixes the two. In *JH v Australia*, the CRPD-Com determines that that 'the State party failed to analyze the "reasonableness" of the accommodation requested for the author, which refers to its relevance, appropriateness and effectiveness'.[38] After clarifying that they are now talking about reasonableness, the experts again argue that the use of sign language interpreters is a common accommodation.[39] The Committee then states that the State party's arguments are 'therefore' insufficient regarding the establishment of an undue burden, thereby intermingling aspects of reasonableness and the disproportionate or undue burden. It also remains unclear whether the argument of a special oath as a possibility to ensure the confidentiality of jury deliberation concerns the reasonableness of the measure or the existence of an undue burden.[40]

The parallels between reasonableness and reasonable accommodation can be confirmed by inspecting the '[k]ey elements that guide the implementation of the duty to provide reasonable accommodation' as provided in the CRPD-Com's General Comment No 6. The CRPD-Com lists, for example, the evaluation of the proportional relationship between the means employed and the aim pursued. Financial costs are considered to play a role in this regard, more precisely 'overall assets rather than just the resources of a unit or department within an organizational structure must be considered'.[41] These elements are also present in the CESCR's interpretation of reasonableness as a standard of review regarding progressively realisable rights.[42] Another typical element of reasonableness is the requirement of involving stakeholders in the process. According to the CRPD-Com '[i]t is important that the review and adoption of these laws and regulations are carried out in close consultation with persons with disabilities and their representative organizations'.[43]

6.3.2. The CRC-Com

The CRC-Com uses the concept of 'appropriate measures' under Article 2 (2) of the CRC and other provisions in the Convention in a way similar to the standard of reasonableness and applies these concepts also to civil and political rights. One example is the CRC-Com's jurisprudence concerning the right to freedom from all forms of violence under Article 19 of the CRC. As laid out above, the

'The Reasonableness of Article 8(4): Adjudicating Claims from the Margins' (2009) 27 *Nordisk Tidsskrift for Menneskerettigheter* 39, 52; Porter, 'Reasonableness and Article 8(4)', 201.

[38] CRPD-Com, *JH v Australia*, para 7.5.

[39] ibid.

[40] ibid.

[41] CRPD-Com, 'General Comment No 6', paras 26 (d), (e).

[42] See further 2.6.2.

[43] CRPD-Com, 'General Comment No 2', para 28.

realisation of this right is conceived in a progressive way.[44] In General Comment No 13 on this provision, the CRC-Com engages in detail with what is appropriate in this context,[45] stressing the need for an 'integrated, cohesive, interdisciplinary and coordinated system' which must effectively be targeted towards the realisation of children's rights.[46] The insistence on effectiveness bears resemblance to the requirement of taking 'deliberate, concrete and targeted' measures as set out by the CESCR and appears again and again in the CRC-Com's jurisprudence. For example, in its General Comment No 19 on Public Budgeting, the experts hold that '[m]easures are considered appropriate when they are relevant to directly or indirectly advancing children's rights in a given context, including that of public budgets'.[47]

Another feature of 'appropriateness' identified by the CRC-Com is that the measures taken must be in compliance with international human rights standards, just as the CESCR repeatedly stresses for measures in the context of socio-economic rights. Regarding the treatment of unaccompanied and separated children outside their country of origin, the CRC-Com states in General Comment No 6 that the obligation to take appropriate measures under Article 22 of the CRC requires States parties to 'to set up a functioning asylum system … and to build capacities necessary to realize this treatment in accordance with applicable rights codified in the Convention and ... other international human rights'.[48] The CRC-Com also speaks of the need for participatory processes and the engagement of 'all sectors of society and, of course, children themselves' regarding the conception and implementation of child-protection policies,[49] reflecting the requirement of transparency and participation set out by the CESCR.

According to the CRC-Com, the burden of providing evidence for the reasonableness (or appropriateness) of measures lies with the States parties. This becomes clear when the CRC-Com holds that 'States parties must … be able to demonstrate the direct relevance and appropriateness of the measures that have been taken … and demonstrate whether such measures will achieve the desired effect and result'.[50] In the context of 'advancing' children's right by means of public budgeting, the States parties must likewise 'show how the public budget-related measures they choose to take result in improvements in children's rights'.[51]

[44] See further 4.3.3.
[45] CRC-Com, 'General Comment No 13', paras 38–44.
[46] ibid, para 39.
[47] CRC-Com, 'General Comment No 19', para 22.
[48] CRC-Com, 'General Comment No 6', para 64.
[49] CRC-Com, 'General Comment No 5', para 1; see also CRC-Com, 'General Comment No 13', para 42 (b) (i).
[50] CRC-Com, 'General Comment No 18', para 31.
[51] CRC-Com, 'General Comment No 19', para 24.

6.3.3. The CEDAW-Com and CERD

In the jurisprudence of the CEDAW-Com and CERD, the standards of review are less clear than in the findings of the CRPD-Com and CRC-Com. However, the concepts of 'appropriateness', 'appropriate measures', and 'due diligence' show similarities to reasonableness. The CEDAW-Com stresses that measures by States parties must 'address all aspects of their general obligations under the Convention to respect, protect, promote and fulfil women's right to non-discrimination and to the enjoyment of equality with men'.[52] Subsequently, the experts reiterate the requirements they set out for the substantive obligations under Article 2 of the CEDAW.[53] The jurisprudence of the CEDAW-Com also shows that States parties are the ones burdened with establishing the reasonableness (or appropriateness) of measures: 'Each State party must be able to justify the appropriateness of the particular means it has chosen and demonstrate whether it will achieve the intended effect and result.'[54] In this statement it also becomes clear that appropriateness must be understood as referring to the ability of the measure in achieving the intended result, namely its effectiveness.

The CEDAW-Com's Individual Communications provide some insight into the meaning the Committee affords the concept of 'due diligence' and its parallels to reasonableness. In *JI v Finland*, the experts are confronted with the question 'whether the State party fulfilled its duty of due diligence in connection with the protection of the author from, and investigation of, incidents of domestic violence'.[55] The role of the Committee and the consequent standard of review is constructed as follows: 'The Committee's task is to review, in the light of the Convention, decisions taken by the national authorities within their purview and to determine whether, in making those decisions, they took into account the obligations arising from the Convention.'[56] Consequently, the experts set out to determine whether the State party, in this case, 'applied principles of due diligence and took reasonable steps to ensure … the protection of the author and her son'.[57] Here, the CEDAW-Com explicitly mentions a standard of reasonableness. Accordingly, the experts continue to engage in great detail with the steps taken by the State party, both on a general level and in relation to the specific case of the author.[58]

[52] CEDAW-Com, 'General Recommendation No 28', para 37.
[53] ibid, paras 37, 38.
[54] ibid, para 23; see also CEDAW-Com, 'General Recommendation No 31', para 31: 'States parties must, however, be able to demonstrate the direct relevance and appropriateness of the measures that have been taken, ensuring first and foremost that the human rights of women are not violated, and demonstrate whether such measures will achieve the desired effect and result.'
[55] CEDAW-Com, *JI v Finland* [Adoption of Views] (5 March 2018) CEDAW/C/69/D/103/2016, para 8.2.
[56] ibid.
[57] ibid.
[58] ibid, paras 3-8.10.

The CERD is much less clear about what standard must be applied regarding the review of possible Convention violations. From its General Recommendations, no information regarding the precise standard of review can be derived. The CERD's decisions on Individual Communications, however, provide some clues in this regard. In *Er v Denmark*, the CERD determines that the author's claim regarding the ineffectiveness of Denmark's legislation in protecting victims of ethnic discrimination as required by Article 2 (1) (d) of the ICERD has not been sufficiently substantiated. In this regard, the experts reiterate that it is not the Committee's role 'to review the interpretation of national law made by national courts unless the decisions were manifestly arbitrary or otherwise amounted to a denial of justice'.[59] In light of judgments by the State party's courts in this case, the experts hold that

> the petitioner's claims were examined in accordance with the law that specifically regulates and penalises acts of racial or ethnic discrimination and that the decisions were reasoned and based on that law. The Committee therefore considers that this claim has not been sufficiently substantiated.[60]

With this approach, the Committee completely defers to the State party's decisions without scrutinising these decisions and their compliance with the Convention. The same approach is chosen in *Zentralrat Deutscher Sinti und Roma et al v Germany*, where the CERD, with reference to the standard established in *Er v Denmark*, simply determines that '[t]he material before the Committee does not reveal that the decisions' of the State party's authorities and courts 'were manifestly arbitrary or amounted to denial of justice', not conducting any inquiry into the compliance of State actions and omissions with standards derived from the ICERD.[61]

A completely different picture emerges when analysing two of the CERD's later decisions: *Dawas and Shava v Denmark* and *Belemvire v Republic of Moldova*. In both cases, the Committee answers the question whether the State party fulfilled its positive obligations regarding effective protection before and effective remedies after racially motivated assaults on the authors.[62] In both decisions, the CERD recalls the same standard of review mentioned above, stressing that 'it is not its role to review the interpretation of facts and national law made by domestic courts, unless the decisions were manifestly arbitrary, or otherwise amounted to a denial of justice'.[63]

[59] CERD, *Er v Denmark* [Adoption of Views] (8 August 2007) CERD/C/71/D/40/2007, para 7.2.

[60] ibid.

[61] CERD, *Zentralrat Deutscher Sinti und Roma et al v Germany* [Adoption of Views] (22 February 2008) CERD/C/72/D/38/2006, para 7.7.

[62] CERD, *Dawas and Shava v Denmark* [Adoption of Views] (6 March 2012) CERD/C/80/D/46/2009, para 7.2; CERD, *Belemvire v Republic of Moldova* [Adoption of Views] (24 November 2017) CERD/C/94/D/57/2015, para 7.2.

[63] CERD, *Dawas and Shava v Denmark*, para 7.2; CERD, *Belemvire v Republic of Moldova*, para 7.2.

However, the experts add that 'when threats of violence are made … it is incumbent upon the State party to investigate with due diligence and expedition',[64] thereby supplementing the deferential standard of arbitrariness (which amounts to a standard of 'unreasonableness') with the substantive requirement of 'due diligence'. The experts then continue with a detailed contextual inquiry into the reasonableness of the measures taken by the State parties and find violations of the Convention in both cases.[65] Some of the arguments made refer to the substantive requirements set out in the Committee's General Recommendations.[66] Elements of a proportionality analysis appear when the Committee holds that 'circumstances as serious as those in this case [warrant] a thorough investigation by public authorities into the possible racist nature of the attack against the family'.[67] Furthermore, the CERD clearly burdens the State party with providing the information regarding the reasonableness of its conduct.[68]

This more substantive standard of review has also been incorporated into one of the Committee's most recent decisions, *VS v Slovakia*. In this case, the experts engage with the question 'whether the State party fulfilled its obligations to take effective action in response to the allegations of the petitioner that she was discriminated against'.[69] Concerning the alleged violation of Article 6 of the ICERD, the experts reiterate the standard set out in *Er v Denmark* above but then add: 'However, the Committee has to examine whether the decisions of domestic courts deprived the petitioner of her right to effective protection and effective remedy against racial discrimination.'[70] This can be understood as an affirmation of the Committee's role as a court of final instance regarding the question whether States parties' conduct conforms with the Convention. And indeed, the experts continue with a contextual inquiry into the question whether the State party has done enough.[71]

It appears that the CERD, faced with the evaluation of compliance regarding positive obligations of conduct, developed an approach which bears resemblance to the reasonableness standard as applied in the context of socio-economic rights. However, this standard still remains without any explicit recognition and, therefore, is subject to considerable uncertainty.

[64] CERD, *Dawas and Shava v Denmark*, para 7.4; cited in CERD, *Belemvire v Republic of Moldova*, para 7.2.

[65] CERD, *Dawas and Shava v Denmark*, paras 7.2–7.4; CERD, *Belemvire v Republic of Moldova*, para 7.2–7.3.

[66] CERD, *Belemvire v Republic of Moldova*, para 7.3.

[67] CERD, *Dawas and Shava v Denmark*, para 7.4.

[68] ibid, para 7.3.

[69] CERD, *VS v Slovakia* [Adoption of Views] (4 December 2015) CERD/C/88/D/56/2014, para 7.2.

[70] ibid, para 7.4.

[71] ibid.

6.3.4. The HRC

The HRC engages extensively with a concept of reasonableness in the context of negative obligations, determining whether States' active interferences in certain areas are unreasonable. This is unsurprising as the ICCPR explicitly uses the term reasonable in two provisions. Article 9 (3) of the ICCPR sets out the entitlement of a criminal trial 'within a reasonable time', thereby prohibiting unreasonably long remand detention, and Article 25 of the ICCPR prohibits unreasonable restrictions on the participation in public affairs, voting, and public service.

In these contexts, the HRC interprets reasonableness to include elements of necessity and proportionality,[72] which can be seen as a first parallel to the concept of reasonableness in the context of socio-economic rights. More relevant for the present study are those cases, however, in which the HRC utilises reasonableness to specify positive obligations of States parties. The question is whether the HRC limits the inevitable leeway of States parties in deciding on the precise policy to implement its obligations of conduct by means of a standard similar to reasonableness. There are some signs in the jurisprudence of the Committee indicating that such a standard is implicitly adopted. However, there are still some remaining differences between reasonableness in the context of socio-economic rights and the approach of the HRC.

The HRC's jurisprudence in the context of the right to life under Article 6 of the ICCPR provides the clearest illustration regarding the Committee's standard of review regarding positive obligations. According to General Comment No 36 on this right, 'States parties are … under a due diligence obligation to take reasonable, positive measures that do not impose disproportionate burdens on them'.[73] Clearly, the HRC acknowledges that States parties can and must take reasonable measures within the limits of their available resources, which, in rough terms, is the same standard as in the context of socio-economic rights, as established above.

As to what 'reasonable' measures or 'due diligence' are meant to be precisely, details are hard to find. It is interesting to note, however, that the statement regarding reasonableness and disproportionality cited above is followed by a footnote referring to the IACtHR decision in *Sawhoyamaxa Indigenous Community v Paraguay*. This decision, in turn, references the ECtHR cases of *Kiliç v Turkey* and *Osman v the United Kingdom*.[74] The latter decision provides further guidance as to the standard of review regarding positive obligations in this context. According to the ECtHR, the applicant must show, in order to substantiate a violation of the right, that the State party 'did not do all that

[72] For an overview, see Conte and Burchill, *Defining Civil and Political Rights*, 52.

[73] HRC, 'General Comment No 36', para 21.

[74] IACtHR, *Sawhoyamaxa Indigenous Community v Paraguay*, para 155 with reference to ECtHR, *Osman v the United Kingdom* ECHR 1998-VIII 3124 (1998) 29 EHRR 245; ECtHR, *Kiliç v Turkey* ECHR 2000-III 75 (2000) 33 EHRR 1357.

could be reasonably expected', which is 'a question which can only be answered in light of all the circumstances of any particular case'.[75] This standard of review is similar to the contextual inquiry required by the reasonableness review of socio-economic rights violations.[76] Admittedly, this parallel is rather indirect; the terms 'reasonable', 'adequate', 'due diligence', and 'appropriate measures'[77] are not defined in General Comment No 36.

There is, however, one positive aspect of the right to life which has been extensively applied and interpreted by the HRC: the duty to investigate the disappearance or the suspicious deaths of persons.[78] In this context, the Committee declares that '[i]nvestigations into allegations of violations of article 6 must always be independent, impartial, prompt, thorough, effective, credible and transparent',[79] which is reminiscent of the CESCR's standard of 'deliberate, concrete and targeted' measures.[80] The HRC's decisions in Individual Communications, however, show that the standard of review regarding the appropriateness of investigative measures is heavily contested. In *Carrero et al v Venezuela*, the experts stress that the duty to investigate suspicious deaths is 'an obligation of means – or of due diligence – and not an obligation of result' and that 'it is not for the Committee to determine the usefulness of specific investigative measures unless the failure to take them is contrary to objective standards, or is manifestly unreasonable' which leads the experts to defer to the State party's decision and conclude that there was no violation of the author's rights in this case.[81]

This result is criticised by Committee members in a joint dissenting opinion in *Carrero et al v Venezuela*. The dissenting members stress that the steps taken by the State party to investigate the disappearance of the victim seem 'to have fallen short of what is required' and that there is an 'absence of any explanation from the State party regarding the lack of progress in the investigation'.[82] Clearly, the experts are of the opinion that the State party should bear the burden of actively establishing the reasonableness of its conduct instead of the author bearing the burden of establishing the 'unreasonableness' of the steps taken.

The deferential standard of 'unreasonableness' reappears in *Castillo v Venezuela*. In this case, the majority of the Committee members defer to the finding of the IACtHR in the same matter which declares that the domestic

[75] ECtHR, *Osman v the United Kingdom*, para 116.
[76] See further 2.6.2.
[77] See, eg, HRC, 'General Comment No 36', para 22.
[78] ibid, para 27.
[79] HRC, 'General Comment No 36', para 28 (fn omitted).
[80] *cf* 2.4.1.
[81] HRC, *Carrero et al v Venezuela* [Adoption of Views] (11 March 2020) CCPR/C/128/D/3018/2017, para 9.6.
[82] ibid, joint opinion of José Manuel Santos Pais and Gentian Zyberi (partially dissenting) para 2.

investigation into the death of the victim 'had been conducted in a reasonable manner'.[83] Based on the rules that 'the Committee gives considerable weight to the findings of international courts' and the finding that 'the information provided to the Committee by the parties does not contain sufficient elements to contradict those findings', the Committee find no violation of Covenant rights.[84] In substance, the experts put the burden of proving the 'unreasonableness' of investigations on the author of the Communication.

This approach is criticised by dissenting members, again, this time in more detail.[85] In her individual dissenting opinion, Sarah Cleveland argues that the majority's 'deference is particularly concerning', criticising the Committee for not 'independently analys[ing] or explain[ing] how the investigation satisfies the Committee's own standards for an adequate investigation under article 6'.[86] According to Cleveland, the rest of the Committee fails to determine whether the requirement of an 'independent, impartial, prompt, thorough, effective, credible and transparent' investigation was fulfilled.[87] Furthermore, the decision of the IACtHR, which the Committee deferred to, in turn defers to the decision of the Bolivarian Republic of Venezuela by applying a standard of 'unreasonableness' which led to the result that neither the IACtHR nor the HRC engaged with the question 'whether the investigation was adequate in the light of its full potential scope'.[88] Committee member Cleveland closes with the statement that, while it is 'correct that human rights commissions and courts are often better positioned to determine facts', 'this does not relieve the Committee of responsibility to independently examine a properly presented claim against the legal standards established by the Covenant'.[89]

In spite of these two contentious examples, there are instances in the Committee's jurisprudence where a stricter standard of review regarding the obligation to investigate violations of the right to life under Article 6 of the ICCPR is unanimously adopted. One such example are the views in *Bhandari v Nepal*. Here, the Committee finds that the State party 'has failed to explain the effectiveness and adequacy of … investigations and the concrete steps taken to clarify' the circumstances of the victim's death and that, therefore, 'the Committee considers that the State party has failed to conduct a thorough and effective investigation', finding a violation of Article 6 of the ICCPR and other provisions.[90]

[83] HRC, *Castillo v Venezuela* [Adoption of Views] (10 November 2017) CCPR/C/121/D/2610/2015, para 9.4.

[84] ibid, para 9.6.

[85] ibid, individual opinion of Committee member Sarah Cleveland (partly concurring, partly dissenting).

[86] ibid, para 5.

[87] ibid, para 11.

[88] ibid, paras 13–15.

[89] ibid, para 16.

[90] HRC, *Bhandari v Nepal* [Adoption of Views] (29 October 2014) CCPR/C/112/D/2031/2011, para 8.9.

In general, this struggle of the Committee (and, similarly, the CERD) in finding a suitable standard to review the 'appropriateness' of States parties' measures to fulfil obligations of conduct is reminiscent of the discussion during the drafting of the ICESCR-OP.[91] Some drafting parties proposed to include reference to 'a broad margin of appreciation' or a standard of 'unreasonableness' into Article 8 (4) of the ICESCR-OP in order to safeguard the freedom of States parties to decide what is most 'appropriate' in accordance with their domestic priorities.[92] These proposals were rejected for the more substantial standard of reasonableness, partly because focusing on 'unreasonableness' would place an insurmountable burden of proof on the author.[93] It appears that the HRC is still in the process of finding its own approach to this issue. An acknowledgment of the parallels to reasonableness in the context of socio-economic rights could help in guiding the standard of review of the HRC in a direction more beneficial to rights holders.

6.4. CONCLUSION

In their civil and political rights jurisprudence, the Committees often construct their own role and the corresponding standard of review in a way similar to what Article 8 (4) of the ICESCR-OP sets out for progressively realisable rights. Even when addressing the realisation of (positive aspects of) civil and political rights, the Committees acknowledge that it is not their role to replace policy decisions made by States parties with what they consider superior. Instead, the application of a contextual inquiry like reasonableness can be observed in many instances. This is particularly visible in the Committees' decisions on Individual Communications. The necessity of granting a certain leeway when realising rights and of limiting this leeway by means of the standard of reasonableness arises because the Committees implicitly interpret civil and political rights as, first and foremost, creating a positive obligation of conduct instead of focusing on the immediate creation of some form of end result. This is in line with the concept of progressive realisation.

Overall, the analysis in part III has confirmed the hypothesis that the standards of progressive and immediate realisation converge in practice. Regarding civil and political rights, the experts clearly accept that there are positive obligations of result which cannot be fulfilled immediately and instead construct

[91] See, generally, Porter, 'Reasonableness and Article 8(4)', 178–84.

[92] See UNHRC, 'Report of the Open-ended Working Group on an Optional Protocol to the International Covenant on Economic, Social and Cultural Rights on its 4th Session' (30 August 2007) A/HRC/6/8, paras 95–98.

[93] See UNHRC, 'Report of the Open-ended Working Group on an Optional Protocol to the International Covenant on Economic, Social and Cultural Rights on its 5th Session' (6 May 2008) A/HRC/8/7, para 171.

immediate obligations of conduct subject to available resources. On the review side, a margin of appreciation is granted and a standard similar to reasonableness is applied in the evaluation of compliance with the treaties regarding those obligations of conduct. It appears as if the experts decided to circumvent the contradictions between the alleged immediacy of civil and political rights and the resource constraints created by positive obligations by rhetorically rejecting progressive realisation while reintroducing its content through the backdoor.[94]

This discrepancy between the claim of differential treatment and the de facto uniform standard of review is also an illustration of the kind of misunderstandings which arise because of the ambiguity of the term progressive realisation. The Committees only reject a notion of progressive realisation in the context of civil and political rights which allows the postponement of taking action and thus reject only the narrow version of the concept. The experts want it understood that States parties may not drag their feet with regards to civil and political rights but also acknowledge that full realisation may take time. This conceptualisation coincides with the umbrella meaning of progressive realisation which goes unnoticed because the Committees focus on the narrow meaning of progressiveness instead.

The convergence of both standards is most advanced in the jurisprudence of the CRPD-Com, which is unsurprising for two reasons. Firstly, the CRPD can be described as the most 'modern' of the human rights treaties inspected here because it includes a range of mixed provisions and also the concept of reasonable accommodation with its built-in acknowledgment of resource limitations. The treaty also sets the focus on factual enjoyment more clearly than the other treaties.[95] Furthermore, positive obligations regarding a marginalised group such as persons with disabilities may appear less disruptive than positive obligations in the context of a more 'traditional' treaty like the ICCPR. Frédéric Mégret accordingly argues that the CRPD 'may be in a better position to recapture … the sense of unity and interdependence of rights which otherwise seems to elude the human rights project'.[96]

But even at the other end of the spectrum, the HRC's jurisprudence reveals signs of a unified approach to both categories. While an engagement with positive obligations in the fulfil dimension of rights is still rare in this context,[97] there is a notable trend in the HRC's newer jurisprudence towards recognising State duties concerning systemic issues like poverty, homelessness, etc. This modern understanding of the ICCPR necessarily entails the acceptance of a certain

[94] Similarly, regarding the CRPD, Uerpmann-Wittzack, 'Die UN-Behindertenrechtskonvention', 198–199.

[95] See also de Beco, 'The Indivisibility of Human Rights', 157.

[96] Mégret, 'The Disabilities Convention', 278; see also A Dhanda, 'Constructing a New Human Rights Lexicon: Convention on the Rights of Persons with Disabilities' (2008) 8 *Sur International Journal on Human Rights* 43, 49.

[97] See also Riedel, 'The Right to Life and the Right to Health', 353–54; T Antkowiak, 'A "Dignified Life" and the Resurgence of Social Rights' (2020) 18 *Northwestern Journal of Human Rights* 1, 11.

progressiveness of obligations under this treaty,[98] and this is what the jurisprudence of the HRC has shown.

The remaining question now is whether this unified approach is in line with what the treaties prescribe. In other words: do the Committees go beyond the limits of treaty interpretation by applying a uniform standard of realisation and review for all rights? The following part III will engage with this question, arguing that the sentiment of universality deserves agreement from a normative standpoint.

[98] Schabas, *Nowak's CCPR Commentary*, 62, 396, 893.

Part III

Treaty Interpretation

7

The Applicable Rules of Treaty Interpretation, Ordinary Meaning, and Context

7.1. INTRODUCTION

THE PREVIOUS PARTS have shown that the standards of immediate and progressive realisation converge in practice. This result makes sense from a conceptual perspective, considering that it is now generally accepted that all rights create positive as well as negative obligations regardless of the right's category.[1] From a normative perspective, however, the question remains whether the Committees' approach is contrary to what the treaties prescribe. A suitable approach to answering this question is to apply the rules of treaty interpretation pursuant to Articles 31 and 32 of the VCLT. On the basis of these rules, this part will determine whether the treaties can (or must) be interpreted to allow the application of a uniform standard of implementation to all rights.

Most arguments for differentiated standards refer to the wording of the treaties. It is particularly common to point to the fact that progressive realisation is explicitly prescribed for socio-economic rights while no mention of this standard is made in civil and political rights provisions. From this argument, commentators and practitioners deduce that civil and political rights must be immediate while progressive realisation must remain limited to socio-economic rights. In the context of the progressive realisation of socio-economic rights, the combination of immediate and progressive obligations is not debated. The critical question for this part is whether the standard applied to civil and political rights may also be constructed in such an umbrella sense, particularly whether it may include progressive elements. Thus, this part will determine whether the treaties allow interpreting civil and political rights to create obligations which are progressive in the narrow sense, ie, obligations which must not be realised to their full extent immediately.

The methods of interpretation under Articles 31 and 32 of the VCLT are distributed over the next three chapters. This chapter will address the preliminary

[1] See further 1.4.

question whether these methods of interpretation can be applied to human rights treaties (7.2) and then continue with the texts of the treaties themselves as a first source of interpretative guidance. The second section of this chapter shows that the ordinary meaning of the words in the treaties' general obligation provisions is open regarding the timeframe of realisation of civil and political rights; there is no prescription of strict immediacy for civil and political rights (7.3). The argument will then turn to the broader context of the treaties. It must be conceded that a contextual interpretation leaves some ambiguity regarding the immediacy or progressiveness of civil and political rights, but several aspects support the notion of convergent standards (7.4). This chapter will end with a conclusion (7.5).

7.2. THE RULES OF INTERPRETATION APPLICABLE TO HUMAN RIGHTS TREATIES

There exists considerable debate about the question whether and to what extent the rules of general international law apply in the field of international human rights law. At the centre of this discussion stands the debate about the applicability of the rules of interpretation under the VCLT. Naturally, this issue must be addressed before engaging in the interpretation of general obligation provisions under the UN human rights instruments. The following subsections will show that, while there are valid arguments for the position that human rights treaties are different compared to other international treaties (7.2.1), the idiosyncrasies of human rights treaties do not necessitate a departure from the rules of the VCLT. Rather, the crucible approach reflected in Articles 31 and 32 of the VCLT is sufficiently flexible to accommodate the specific nature of human rights treaties which means that the rules of the VCLT are suitable to be applied for this inquiry (7.2.2).

7.2.1. The Special Nature of Human Rights Treaties

It is a widespread and valid argument that human rights treaties have specific characteristics not exhibited by other international treaties. The relevant common feature of human rights treaties, according to this argument, is their 'non-reciprocal' or 'constitutional' nature which, in turn, is founded on the treaties' subject matter. Instead of giving effect to the will of the States parties, human rights treaties have the purpose of protecting the inherent rights of individuals.[2] Human rights treaties are neither the result of nor subject to a

[2] G Letsas, 'Intentionalism and the Interpretation of the ECHR' in M Fitzmaurice, O Elias and P Merkouris (eds), *Treaty Interpretation and the Vienna Convention on the Law of Treaties: 30 Years On*, Queen Mary Studies in International Law 1 (Leiden, Nijhoff, 2010) 272.

bargaining process between States parties but instead reflect rights which individuals possess by virtue of being human.[3] In other words, human rights treaties do not create new ideals out of thin air but instead put into writing moral obligations which existed before.[4] Accordingly, they should be understood as 'a series of unilateral adoptions of a common standard, a statement of intent'.[5] This makes them different from ordinary treaties which are characterised by a contractual approach.

The non-contractual nature of human rights treaties is not only reflected in their preambles,[6] but also supported by international jurisprudence. A similar argument is made, for example, by the ICJ in its Advisory Opinion regarding reservations to the Genocide Convention.[7] According to this decision, the Genocide Convention 'was manifestly adopted for a purely humanitarian and civilizing purpose' and therefore 'the contracting States do not have any interests of their own; they merely have, one and all, a common interest, namely, the accomplishment of those high purposes which are the raison d'être of the convention'.[8]

This specific nature of human rights treaties is then said to reduce the relevance of the will of States parties for their interpretation and to increase the relevance of teleological considerations.[9] Thus, while others declare it to be a general rule of treaty interpretation that object and purpose may not be given greater weight than the text and context of a treaty,[10] the object and purpose of human rights treaties is often accorded a predominant position among these methods of interpretation.[11] The fact that human rights result from the inherent dignity of the person instead of the will of States parties is taken to mean that the intention of the drafters, as set out in the text of the treaty or as discerned

[3] See R Higgins, 'Human Rights: Some Questions of Integrity' (1989) 15 *Commonwealth Law Bulletin* 598, 607.

[4] See G Letsas, 'Strasbourg's Interpretive Ethic: Lessons for the International Lawyer' (2010) 21 *European Journal of International Law* 509, 540.

[5] J Watson, 'The Limited Utility of International Law in the Protection of Human Rights' (1980) 74 *Proceedings of the American Society of International Law* 1, 4.

[6] See also N Maisley, 'The International Right of Rights?: Article 25(a) of the ICCPR as a Human Right to Take Part in International Law-Making' (2017) 28 *European Journal of International Law* 89, 103.

[7] ICJ, *Reservations to the Convention on the Prevention and Punishment of the Crime of Genocide* (Advisory Opinion) [1951] ICJ Rep 15.

[8] ibid, 23.

[9] See M Fitzmaurice, 'Interpretation of Human Rights Treaties' in D Shelton (ed), *The Oxford Handbook of International Human Rights Law* (Oxford, Oxford University Press, 2013) 742.

[10] See, eg, A Aust, *Modern Treaty Law and Practice*, 3rd edn (Cambridge, Cambridge University Press, 2006) 185.

[11] See B Schlütter, 'Aspects of Human Rights Interpretation by the UN Treaty Bodies' in H Keller and G Ulfstein (eds), *UN Human Rights Treaty Bodies: Law and Legitimacy* (Cambridge, Cambridge University Press, 2012) 278; M Nowak, *Introduction to the International Human Rights Regime*, The Raoul Wallenberg Institute Human Rights Library 14 (Leiden, Nijhoff, 2003) 65.

from the circumstances of treaty conclusion, carries less significance than their object and purpose.[12]

According to this approach, human rights treaties must be interpreted in a manner which gives sufficient weight to the interests of individuals in receiving effective protection of their rights, freedom, and dignity.[13] Thus, the interpretation of human rights treaties must be guided by the effectiveness of individual rights' protection instead of trying to find the meaning which least restricts national sovereignty, which is often considered to be a governing principle in the interpretation of classical treaties.[14]

7.2.2. Reconciling the Teleological Approach with the Crucible of Interpretation

One could think that the ultimate consequence of a strict teleological approach to human rights treaties would be to ignore the intention of States parties altogether, simply determining the content of rights through abstract considerations of effectiveness without respect to the text of the treaty or the *travaux préparatoires*. In this sense, it is sometimes argued that international human rights law must be considered a 'self-contained regime' which should be subject to its own *lex specialis* without regard to the traditional principles of international law and treaty interpretation.[15]

However, taking into account the special nature of human rights does not require discounting the intent of the States parties altogether. Adopting a teleological perspective and considering States' intentions are not mutually exclusive approaches. On the contrary, it is impossible to completely separate object and purpose from the intentions of the States parties. Determining the object and purpose of a treaty in itself is a process of treaty interpretation requiring the interpreter to take recourse to the treaty text and, therefore, to the intention of the States parties.[16] Thus, it would be contradictory to disregard the treaty text

[12] See W Kälin and J Künzli, *The Law of International Human Rights Protection*, 2nd edn (Oxford, Oxford University Press, 2019) 34–35; A Broderick, *The Long and Winding Road to Equality and Inclusion for Persons with Disabilities: The United Nations Convention on the Rights of Persons with Disabilities*, School of Human Rights Research Series Volume 74 (Cambridge, Intersentia, 2015) 8; see also Letsas, 'Strasbourg's Interpretive Ethic', 535.

[13] See K Mechlem, 'Treaty Bodies and the Interpretation of Human Rights' (2009) 42 *Vanderbilt Journal of Transnational Law* 905, 912; Nowak, *Introduction*, 65.

[14] The latter principle is usually called *in dubio pro mitius*, see Maisley, 'The International Right of Rights?',103.

[15] See, eg, DF Vagts, 'Treaty Interpretation and the New American Ways of Law Reading' (1993) 4 *European Journal of International Law* 472.

[16] See the separate opinion of Gerald Fitzmaurice in ECtHR, *National Union of Belgian Police v Belgium* Series A No 19 (1975) 1 EHRR 578, para 9 (i): 'The objects and purposes of a treaty are not something that exist in abstracto: they follow from and are closely bound up with the intentions of the parties, as expressed in the text of the treaty, or as properly to be inferred from it, these intentions being the sole sources of those objects and purposes'; see also Schlütter, 'Human Rights

and the *travaux préparatoires* altogether in favour of an interpretation focused on object and purpose which in turn are deduced from the elements which were rejected as irrelevant before.[17]

In essence, this idea also underlies the approach of the so-called teleological school of interpretation. There appears to be agreement among the representatives of this approach that the treaty texts are still relevant, if less so than the more abstract object and purpose. This can be seen, eg, in the ECtHR's *Airey* decision where the justices hold that '[t]he Convention is intended to guarantee rights that are not theoretical or illusory, but rights that are practical and effective'.[18] The justices explicitly refer to the 'intent' of the drafters and implicitly demand that sincerity is attributed to these original intentions.[19]

On a different note, a practical argument speaks for this approach. As Tobin has noted, interpreting treaties means more than simply finding or communicating a meaning, but, instead, interpretation constitutes an 'act of persuasion'.[20] This is true not only in human rights law but in international law in general. Because there is no comprehensive system of sanctions for non-compliance with obligations resulting from international law, the persuasiveness and legitimacy of a certain interpretation is crucial in ensuring the factual compliance of States parties and, therefore, the implementation of the treaty.[21] In other words, one is more likely to convince States to comply with a certain interpretation of human rights obligations when this interpretation is at least partially based on traditional legitimacy considerations. This further supports the notion that some form of respect to the text and the drafting parties' intentions is necessary.

It appears that, even though there is a widespread insistence upon the special nature of human rights treaties, arguments advocating a complete rejection of the rules of interpretation under Articles 31 et seq VCLT have not prevailed.[22] It is now generally accepted that, in some form, the VCLT and its rules on interpretation apply to human rights treaties.[23] The discussion centres around a question of degree rather than the categorical (non-)applicability of general rules of international law to the regime of human rights.[24] On the one hand,

Interpretation', 278: 'The determination of the object and purpose itself is closely related to the individual theory scholars follow when interpreting a treaty.'

[17] See also the approach of Letsas, 'Strasbourg's Interpretive Ethic'.

[18] ECtHR, *Airey v Ireland* Series A No 32 (1979) 2 EHRR 305, para 24.

[19] B Çalı, 'Specialized Rules of Treaty Interpretation: Human Rights' in DB Hollis (ed), *The Oxford Guide to Treaties*, 2nd edn (Oxford, Oxford University Press, 2020) 513.

[20] J Tobin, 'Seeking to Persuade: A Constructive Approach to Human Rights Treaty Interpretation' (2010) 23 *Harvard Human Rights Journal* 1, 7.

[21] See McGrogan, 'Interpretation of Human Rights Treaties', 350.

[22] See also Çalı, 'Specialized Rules', 505–11.

[23] See McGrogan, 'Interpretation of Human Rights Treaties', 350; Fitzmaurice, 'Interpretation of Human Rights Treaties', 739–43; J Christoffersen, 'Impact on General Principles of Treaty Interpretation' in MT Kamminga and M Scheinin (eds), *The Impact of Human Rights Law on General International Law* (Oxford, Oxford University Press, 2009); Çalı, 'Specialized Rules'.

[24] As Fitzmaurice notes, even the ECtHR with its liberal approach does not argue for a complete irrelevance of general international law in the context of human rights, Fitzmaurice, 'Interpretation of Human Rights Treaties', 741–42.

there are different approaches which argue for a modification of the rules of interpretation in this area of international law.[25] On the other hand, there are authors who reject the classification of human rights treaties as fundamentally non-reciprocal to begin with and therefore insist upon the relevance of the intent of the parties and the contractually agreed upon text.[26] One of the latter is Bruno Simma, who argues that reciprocity will always remain 'the principal leitmotif' for international law, also in the subject area of human rights.[27] Gardiner similarly stresses that arguments derived from the object and purpose cannot override the text of the treaty.[28]

Beyond more liberal arguments that textual considerations are less relevant, and more orthodox arguments that reciprocity and State intent must remain in focus, no commentator has suggested a universal and conclusive strategy of interpretation. It can be concluded that the truth lies somewhere in the middle. The relevance and priority of treaty interpretation methods must be decided on a case by case basis and founded on a balanced approach not disregarding any aspect altogether.[29] This insight is not limited to international human rights law but instead coincides with what has, for a long time now, been called the crucible approach inherent to the VCLT: due to the ambiguous wording of Article 31 of the VCLT, there exists considerable flexibility regarding the methods of interpretation and their hierarchy.[30] Applying the canon of interpretative methods cannot be understood as an algorithm-like application of hierarchically organised processes but instead must be conducted as a 'single combined operation', as remarked by the ILC in its Commentaries on the draft VCLT.[31]

Because of this inherent flexibility of the crucible approach, the discussion about allegedly different schools of interpretation can be considered to be 'somewhat unreal';[32] if the disagreement is one about degree, the crucible approach of the VCLT is suitable to accommodate human rights treaties, regardless of whether the focus must lie on textual or teleological features.[33] As Başak Çalı noted, this approach is simply 'too abstract not to be applicable to human rights treaties'.[34]

[25] See, for example, M Craven, 'Legal Differentiation and the Concept of the Human Rights Treaty in International Law' (2000) 11 *European Journal of International Law* 489; see also Fitzmaurice, 'Interpretation of Human Rights Treaties', 759.

[26] See, eg, ILC, 'Second Report on Reservations to Treaties by Alain Pellet, Special Rapporteur' (13 June 1996) A/CN.4/477/ADD.1, para 85.

[27] B Simma as cited in M Fitzmaurice, 'Interpretation of the European Convention on Human Rights: Lessons from the Naït-Liman Case' in S Forlati and P Franzina (eds), *Universal Civil Jurisdiction: Which Way Forward?* (Leiden, Brill, 2020) 61–62.

[28] RK Gardiner, *Treaty Interpretation* (Oxford, Oxford University Press, 2008) 211.

[29] See also Fitzmaurice, 'Interpretation of the European Convention on Human Rights', 62.

[30] See Gardiner, *Treaty Interpretation*, 9–12.

[31] ILC, 'Draft Articles on the Law of Treaties with Commentaries' (1966) *Yearbook of the International Law Commission* 187, 219.

[32] I Sinclair, *The Vienna Convention on the Law of Treaties*, 2nd edn (Manchester, Manchester University Press, 1984) 116–17.

[33] See Çalı, 'Specialized Rules', 505–11.

[34] ibid, 522.

For this study, these results mean that no abstract categorical decision regarding the 'correct' approach is necessary because the approaches to human rights treaty interpretation set out above are not mutually exclusive but exist along a sliding scale. This means that, a priori, all methods of interpretation are applicable. A decision as to the hierarchy or relevance of interpretative methods must be made only if there are contradictory results, eg, when the treaty text cannot be brought in line with findings based on the object and purpose of the instrument. Reversely, no such arguments are necessary where all methods of interpretation lead to the same result. After answering this preliminary question, it is then appropriate to proceed with the entire canon of interpretation in the following sections.

7.3. ORDINARY MEANING, ARTICLE 31 (1) OF THE VCLT

Article 31 (1) of the VCLT prescribes that '[a] treaty shall be interpreted in good faith in accordance with the ordinary meaning to be given to the terms of the treaty in their context and in the light of its object and purpose'. There is no one true objective meaning of a term to be discovered by the interpreter. Instead, this meaning shall be 'given' by the interpreter to the words which means that, out of a number of possible ordinary meanings, '*that* particular ordinary meaning will be established which is the common intention of the parties'.[35] It is thus clear that the assessment of the ordinary meaning of a word or phrase cannot be conducted in the abstract, separate from a consideration of the context and object and purpose of the treaty. Rather, all those factors interact when determining the meaning of a provision.[36] This is in line with the ILC interpretation of the rules of interpretation as a crucible.[37]

According to a traditional understanding, however, the ordinary meaning, or rather, the range of possible ordinary meanings of words, fulfil the function of limiting the interpretation of treaties.[38] An interpretation which is irreconcilable with *all* of the possible ordinary meanings of the words in question is not in line with the limits set out by the VCLT and would constitute impermissible legislation or revision of the treaty instead of interpretation.[39] Adherents

[35] ME Villiger, 'The Rules on Interpretation: Misgivings, Misunderstandings, Miscarriage? The 'Crucible' Intended by the International Law Commission' in E Cannizzaro (ed), *The Law of Treaties Beyond the Vienna Convention* (Oxford, Oxford University Press, 2011) 109.

[36] Gardiner, *Treaty Interpretation*, 181; see also ME Villiger, *Commentary on the 1969 Vienna Convention on the Law of Treaties* (Leiden, Nijhoff, 2009) 427.

[37] See Villiger, 'The Rules on Interpretation', 118.

[38] See ICJ, *Interpretation of Peace Treaties with Bulgaria, Hungary and Romania* (Second Phase, Advisory Opinion) [1950] ICJ Rep 221, 229: 'The principle of interpretation expressed in the maxim: *Ut res magis valeat quam pereat*, often referred to as the rule of effectiveness, cannot justify the Court in attributing to the provisions for the settlement of disputes in the Peace Treaties a meaning which, as stated above, would be contrary to their letter and spirit.'

[39] See Villiger, *Commentary on the VCLT*, 427; Villiger, 'The Rules on Interpretation', 110.

to a teleological approach, on the other hand, argue that one should not cling to a dictionary meaning of the words used in the treaty.[40] A decision as to the relevance of dictionary meanings is only necessary, however, if the analysis determines that the interpretation in question cannot be reconciled with any conceivable ordinary meaning.

Consequently, the question at hand is whether the Committees have stayed within this limit when applying a de facto uniform standard of realisation to all rights in the treaties. In other words, can the general obligation provisions be interpreted to imply a progressive obligation of full realisation combined with an immediate obligation to take steps, or does the ordinary meaning of the terms only permit the construction of an immediate obligation of result regarding civil and political rights? It is submitted here that the wording of the relevant provisions does not prescribe such an interpretation. There is nothing in the relevant provisions of the ICCPR (7.3.1), the CRC and CRPD (7.3.2) or the CEDAW and ICERD (7.3.3) which would logically preclude the notion of progressive elements.

7.3.1. Article 2 of the ICCPR

Article 2 (1) of the ICCPR sets out that '[e]ach State Party to the present Covenant undertakes to respect and to ensure … the rights recognized in the present Covenant'. Article 2 (2) of the ICCPR further elaborates that 'each State Party to the present Covenant undertakes to take the necessary steps … to adopt such laws or other measures as may be necessary to give effect to the rights recognized in the present Covenant'. The terms 'undertake to respect' and 'undertake to take the necessary steps' represent the core of these general obligation provisions.

None of the meanings for the word 'undertake' provided in common English dictionaries indicate that the task or obligation undertaken must be fulfilled at an instant. The word instead is taken to refer to, on the one hand, making the promise of doing something and, on the other hand, commencing on a certain task.[41] In the context of international treaties, the ICJ adheres to the former meaning, holding that '[t]he ordinary meaning of the word "undertake" is to give a formal promise, to bind or engage oneself, to give a pledge or promise, to agree, to accept an obligation'.[42] There is no indication in this wording, however,

[40] See, eg, the approach of the ECtHR as described in Letsas, 'Strasbourg's Interpretive Ethic'.

[41] 'undertake, v.' in *Merriam-Webster* online, www.merriam-webster.com/dictionary/undertake; 'undertake, v.' in *Oxford English Dictionary* online, www.oed.com/view/Entry/212141.

[42] ICJ, *Application of the Convention on the Prevention and Punishment of the Crime of Genocide (Bosnia and Herzegovina v Serbia and Montenegro)* (Merits, Judgment) [2007] ICJ Rep 43, para 162.

as to the timeframe in which the obligation must be performed.[43] Interestingly, the meaning provided by the *Cambridge Dictionary* even refers to a prolonged timeframe in finishing the task undertaken; according to this source, to undertake means 'to do or begin to do something, especially something that will take a long time or be difficult'.[44]

The wording of Article 2 (2) of the ICCPR furthermore shows that the taking of steps must be the object of States parties' undertaking. The provision does not focus on the result here but rather on the process of moving towards a result. The ordinary meaning of the phrase 'to take the necessary steps … to adopt such laws or other measures as may be necessary to give effect to the rights recognized in the present Covenant' thus can be read to allow progressive elements.[45]

7.3.2. Articles 2 and 4 of the CRC and Article 4 (1) of the CRPD

Article 2 (1) of the CRC sets out that 'States Parties shall respect and ensure the rights set forth in the present Convention to each child within their jurisdiction without discrimination of any kind'. This provision not only establishes a rule of non-discrimination but also clarifies the type of obligations which the Convention entails by setting out the duties to respect and ensure.[46] Article 4 of the CRC determines that 'States Parties shall undertake all appropriate legislative, administrative, and other measures for the implementation of the rights recognized in the present Convention'. This serves as a concretisation of the general obligations to respect and fulfil under Article 2 of the CRC.[47]

Neither of these provisions contain wording which indicates any temporal frame of realisation. Not unlike the word 'undertake', the term 'shall', according to *Merriam-Webster*, is 'used in laws, regulations, or directives to express what is mandatory'.[48] Thus, the wording only sheds light on the degree of commitment of the States parties but not on the timeframe of realisation.

Article 4 (1) of the CRPD addresses both aspects at once: 'States Parties undertake to ensure and promote the full realization of all human rights and

[43] See also O Schachter, 'The Obligation to Implement the Covenant in Domestic Law' in L Henkin (ed), *The International Bill of Rights: The Covenant on Civil and Political Rights* (New York, Columbia University Press, 1981) 322.

[44] 'undertake, v.' in *Cambridge English Dictionary* online, www.dictionary.cambridge.org/dictionary/english/undertake.

[45] See Schabas, *Nowak's CCPR Commentary*, 60–62; Seibert-Fohr, 'Domestic Implementation', 406–07; Künnemann, 'A Coherent Approach', 331.

[46] See Schmahl, *CRC-Commentary*, 45; see also S Besson and E Kleber, 'Article 2: The Right to Non-Discrimination' in John Tobin (ed), *The UN Convention on the Rights of the Child: A Commentary* (Oxford, Oxford University Press, 2019) 50.

[47] See Schmahl, *CRC-Commentary*, 47; Besson and Kleber 'Article 2', 50.

[48] 'shall, v.' in *Merriam-Webster* online, www.merriam-webster.com/dictionary/shall.

fundamental freedoms for all persons with disabilities without discrimination of any kind on the basis of disability.' The provision goes on to concretise that, '[t]o this end, States Parties undertake … [t]o adopt all appropriate legislative, administrative and other measures for the implementation of the rights recognized in the present Convention', afterwards continuing with a list of further measures to be taken. Again, the word 'undertake' leaves the timeframe of realisation open.

7.3.3. Article 2 of the CEDAW and Article 2 (1) of the ICERD

Article 2 of the CEDAW prescribes that 'States Parties … agree to pursue by all appropriate means and without delay a policy of eliminating discrimination against women and, to this end, undertake' to take a number of measures. Similarly, Article 2 (1) of the ICERD reads: 'States Parties … undertake to pursue by all appropriate means and without delay a policy of eliminating racial discrimination in all its forms and promoting understanding among all races'. This wording is also not in conflict with a standard of realisation which entails immediate obligations of conduct and progressive obligations of result.

The phrase 'without delay' refers not to the achievement of substantive equality but rather to the pursuit of a policy towards that goal. Consequently, States parties are under an obligation to take steps towards the complete elimination of racial discrimination. This is in line with the immediate obligation to take steps identified as a part of progressive realisation in part I. Furthermore, the word 'pursue', particularly in connection to the word 'policy', indicates a progressive rather than immediate notion of realisation.[49] Regarding the word 'pursue', the *Cambridge Dictionary* explains that it represents the efforts to achieve a plan, activity or situation 'usually over a long period of time'.[50] This clearly indicates a progressive notion of achievement. A similar result also follows from inspecting the words of Article 24 of the CEDAW, which reads: 'States Parties undertake to adopt all necessary measures at the national level aimed at achieving the full realization of the rights recognized in the present Convention.' The word 'undertake' leaves open the timeframe of realisation, while the phrase 'aimed at achieving the full realization' implies that the measures taken must not immediately lead to full realisation but instead must be tailored towards achieving this goal in the future.

[49] See R Cera, 'Article 5: Equality and Non-Discrimination' in V Della Fina, R Cera and G Palmisano (eds), *The United Nations Convention on the Rights of Persons with Disabilities: A Commentary* (Cham, Springer, 2017) 165.

[50] 'pursue, v.' in *Cambridge English Dictionary* online, www.dictionary.cambridge.org/dictionary/english/pursue.

7.4. CONTEXT, ARTICLE 31 (1) OF THE VCLT

According to Article 31 (1) of the VCLT, the ordinary meaning shall be given to the terms of the treaty in their context. This context encompasses 'the text, including its preamble and annexes'. Because treaties are drafted as one cohesive legal entity, it makes sense for them to follow a coherent linguistic and grammatical logic. Accordingly, interpreting a treaty requires reading it as a whole. There is no way to determine the meaning of a singular article, section or part of the treaty in abstraction from the rest of the text.[51] Furthermore, the VCLT, in Article 31 (2) (b), sets out as part of the context 'any instrument which was made by one or more parties in connection with the conclusion of the treaty and accepted by the other parties as an instrument related to the treaty'.

This section will first engage with one of the arguments most frequently made for the 'immediacy' of civil and political rights: civil and political rights are immediate because progressive realisation is prescribed explicitly only for socio-economic rights. It must be conceded that there is some undeniable logic to this reading of the treaties (7.4.1). There are several other clues in the treaties, however, which support the conclusion that civil and political rights create both immediate and progressive obligations. Firstly, and most importantly, all treaties contain provisions which obligate States parties to report on progress regarding the realisation of human rights (7.4.2). Furthermore, the regimes of special measures in the CEDAW, ICERD and CRPD imply that the creation of de facto equality will take time (7.4.3). Lastly, the concept of reasonable accommodation under the CRPD clearly introduces resource considerations and, therefore, the notion of progressive elements to all rights into this Convention (7.4.4).

7.4.1. Prescription of Progressive Realisation Only for Socio-economic Rights

The argument perhaps most frequently put forward for the 'immediacy and unconditionality' of civil and political rights is a contextual one; it draws a comparison between the provisions relating to socio-economic and civil and political rights respectively. While the former expressly set out progressive realisation, the latter do not. Accordingly, it is argued, progressive elements do not exist in the context of civil and political rights. Because progressive realisation is expressly set out for socio-economic rights, the omission of this standard in the context of civil and political rights means that it is not applicable there. This kind of inverted argument is often called *expressio unius exclusio alterius* (saying one means excluding the other) or *argumentum e contrario* (argument from the contrary).[52]

[51] Sinclair, *The VCLT*, 127.

[52] See F Jhabvala, 'The Practice of the Covenant's Human Rights Committee, 1976-82: Review of State Party Reports' (1984) 6 *Human Rights Quarterly* 81, 96–99; Schwelb, 'The Nature of the Obligations', 309.

On the one hand, this argument is made for treaties which contain both traditionally civil and political and socio-economic rights and explicitly set out progressive realisation and the relevance of limited resources only for the latter category, namely the CRPD and the CRC. Here, the comparative interpretation takes place inside the confines of the respective treaties. Article 4 (2) of the CRPD explicitly sets out progressive realisation on the basis of limited resources only for socio-economic rights. Sentence two of Article 4 of the CRC similarly mentions limited resources only in the context of socio-economic rights.[53] These textual differences between the two sets of rights as regards their implementation and the applicable standard of review are commonly used to draw a line between immediate and absolute rights on the one hand and progressive and relative rights on the other. When the CRPD-Com and the CRC-Com argue for the 'immediacy' of civil and political rights, the experts often do so with reference to the non-applicability of Article 4 (2) of the CRPD and sentence two of Article 4 of the CRC respectively.[54] There are many instances in the literature where such a comparative argument is made.[55]

The ICCPR, CEDAW and ICERD do not contain any reference to progressive realisation or limited resources. Here, the *argumentum e contrario* is commonly based on a comparison between the ICCPR, CEDAW and ICERD on the one hand and the ICESCR on the other. The HRC and the CEDAW-Com both declare that the general obligation provisions contained in their respective treaties are 'unqualified' and, therefore, 'immediate'. Delays or a failure to comply with these obligations, according to the experts, cannot be justified by reference to political, social, cultural, religious, economic, resource, or other considerations.[56] Although no explicit reference is made to Article 2 (1) of the ICESCR, the experts obviously centre their argument around the absence of any language similar to this provision. This follows from the word 'unqualified' which implies that the relevant provisions do not set out any qualifying factors which may influence the implementation of rights. Also, the Committees explicitly reject the relevance of resource considerations for the implementation of rights, which is what the ICESCR explicitly recognises for socio-economic rights. The CESCR is more explicit regarding this question and the comparison across treaties, holding that the obligation under Article 2 (1) of the ICESCR 'differs significantly from that contained in Article 2 of the

[53] For the inextricable link between limited resources and progressive realisation, see 2.5.

[54] See, eg, CRPD-Com, 'General Comment No 1', para 30; CRC-Com, 'General Comment No 19', para 25.

[55] Regarding the CRC, see Todres, 'Emerging Limitations', 178; W Vandenhole, GE Türkelli and S Lembrechts, *Children's Rights: A Commentary on the Convention on the Rights of the Child and its Protocols* (Cheltenham, Elgar, 2019) 75–76 and Schmahl, *CRC-Commentary*, 100 with further references; regarding the CRPD, see Della Fina, 'Article 4', 147.

[56] HRC, 'General Comment No 31', para 14; CEDAW-Com, 'General Recommendation No 28', para 29.

International Covenant on Civil and Political Rights which embodies an immediate obligation to respect and ensure all of the relevant rights'.[57]

Literary commentators also refer to the ICESCR as a point of comparison when establishing the immediate nature of obligations under the other treaties. Anja Seibert-Fohr, for example, remarks that comparing the ICCPR to the ICESCR leads to the conclusion that the ICCPR 'creates immediate and stringent (i.e. unconditional) obligations'.[58] Similarly, Christian Tomuschat declares that such a comparison supports the argument that the ICCPR 'contains strict obligations' which must be 'secured immediately from the time of ratification'.[59] Egon Schwelb explicitly holds that the ICESCR and, particularly, Article 2 (1) of the ICESCR are part of the 'context' of the ICCPR as envisioned in Article 31 of the VCLT and continues to argue that an '*argumentum a contrario* confirms the proposition' that the ICCPR, in contrast to the ICESCR, 'is not a "promotional" instrument' but instead creates the obligation of 'immediate application'.[60] Similar arguments are made in the context of the CEDAW.[61]

What must be noted in this context, however, is that these commentators use the *a contrario* reading (and other arguments) to reject only a narrow reading of progressive realisation for civil and political rights. In fact, they continue to set out a standard of realisation analogous to the umbrella concept of progressive realisation, as will be illustrated later in this book.[62] It becomes clear that the discussion about immediate and progressive realisation of civil and political rights rests upon the ambiguity of terminology. In substance, both sides propose a notion of realisation which includes both immediate obligations of conduct and obligations of result which are progressive in the narrow sense of the term.

Regarding the contextual argument itself, the question arises whether a contextual interpretation also allows drawing parallels or highlighting differences in relation to other treaties rather than the text of the treaty itself. The ICJ regularly refers to other treaties when establishing the meaning of a certain provision.[63] In *Land, Island and Maritime Frontier Dispute (El Salvador v Honduras, Nicaragua intervening)*, the ICJ remarks that the provision in question must be 'considered in the wider context' which includes not only the treaty itself but also a separate treaty which contains the 'same contrast of wording'.[64]

[57] CESCR, 'General Comment No 3', para 5.

[58] Seibert-Fohr, 'Domestic Implementation', 405 (fn omitted); see also AW Heringa, 'Judicial Enforcement of Article 26 of the International Covenant on Civil and Political Rights in the Netherlands' (1993) 24 *Netherlands Yearbook of International Law* 139, 150.

[59] Tomuschat, 'National Implementation', 35.

[60] Schwelb, 'The Nature of the Obligations', 309.

[61] See MA Freeman, CM Chinkin and B Rudolf, 'Article 3' in MA Freeman, CM Chinkin and B Rudolf (eds), *The UN Convention on the Elimination of All Forms of Discrimination against Women: A Commentary*, 1st edn (Oxford, Oxford University Press, 2012) 108.

[62] See further 8.3.2.1. and 9.3.1.1.

[63] See, eg, ICJ, *Maritime Delimitation in the Indian Ocean (Somalia v Kenya)* (Preliminary Objections, Judgment) [2017] ICJ Rep 3, para 91.

[64] ICJ, *Land, Island and Maritime Frontier Dispute (El Salvador v Honduras, Nicaragua intervening)* (Merits, Judgment) [1992] ICJ Rep 351, para 374.

In view of the VCLT's structure, it appears more sensible to consider other treaties not as context in the more narrow sense of the word but to treat them as 'relevant rules of international law applicable in the relations between the parties' which must be taken into account 'together with the context', according to Article 31 (3) (c) of the VCLT.[65] Be that as it may, it is generally accepted that these relevant rules include at least those treaties which are in force between the parties at the time of interpretation and 'relevant' for the question at hand, ie, those treaties which concern the same subject-matter.[66] It appears convincing to assume such a relationship between all the UN human rights treaties, particularly between the ICCPR and the ICESCR, as they were created with the same object and purpose.

In general, the ICJ considers an *a contrario* reading of treaty provisions to be a valid argument, for example in *Territorial and Maritime Dispute (Nicaragua v Colombia)*,[67] as did the Permanent Court of International Justice (PCIJ) in the *Wimbledon* case. The latter decision provides a suitable explanation for the rationale behind an *a contrario* reading of treaty provisions. If one provision is read as setting out the same rule as another treaty provision, even though they are different in their wording, one of them

> would lose their 'raison d'être', such repetitions as are found in them would be superfluous and there would be every justification for surprise at the fact that … the authors of the Treaty should have taken the trouble to repeat their terms or re-produce their substance.[68]

In the context of the CRC and the CRPD, one could thus ask: why should progressive realisation and the relevance of limited resources be set out explicitly for socio-economic rights when these concepts are also read to be implied by provisions applicable to all rights? There is some validity in this reading. After all, there would be no discernible reason for the additional inclusion of progressive realisation for socio-economic rights if this principle was to be applied regardless of category on the basis of the general obligation provisions not limited to any group of rights.

[65] See also O Dörr and K Schmalenbach, *Vienna Convention on the Law of Treaties: A Commentary*, 2nd edn (Berlin, Springer, 2018) 584.

[66] Villiger, *Commentary on the VCLT*, 433 with reference to ICJ, *Certain Questions of Mutual Assistance in Criminal Matters (Djibouti v France)* (Merits, Judgment) [2008] ICJ Rep 177, para 112; see also ICJ, *Legal Consequences for States of the Continued Presence of South Africa in Namibia (South West Africa) notwithstanding Security Council Resolution 276 (1970)* (Advisory Opinion) [1971] ICJ Rep 16, para 53; Dörr and Schmalenbach, *VCLT*, 605 with reference to ICJ, *Maritime Delimitation in the Indian Ocean (Somalia v Kenya)*, para 89; it is unclear, however, whether this mode of interpretation requires that the parties to the treaty taken into account for interpretation must be identical to the parties to the treaty currently being interpreted, see Gardiner, *Treaty Interpretation*, 302–04.

[67] ICJ, *Territorial and Maritime Dispute (Nicaragua v Colombia)* (Application by Honduras for Permission to Intervene, Judgment) [2011] ICJ Rep 420, para 29.

[68] PCIJ, *Case of the SS 'Wimbledon'* [1923] Series A No 1, 24.

7.4.2. Reporting Procedure in All Treaties

But there is a number of contextual clues in the treaties which do support a gradual approach to the full realisation of all rights, the most important being the reporting obligations set out in all treaties. The general idea of these provisions is to provide for a way to encourage and supervise the implementation of human rights in the States parties by prescribing the submission of reports. Usually, the treaties demand a first report one or two years after their entry into force and, thereafter, either upon the request of the competent Committee or in regular intervals of several years. The notion of submitting a regular report in itself indicates that there may be changes over time. Also, most of the treaties explicitly speak of a report on the 'progress' regarding the implementation of human rights in the State party.

In the context of the ICCPR, the issue of reporting and immediate or progressive realisation has been discussed extensively.[69] Article 40 of the ICCPR regulates the reporting procedure to the HRC. The first paragraph of this provision requires the States parties to 'submit reports on the measures they have adopted which give effect to the rights recognized herein and on the progress made in the enjoyment of those rights'. This provision explicitly refers to the 'progress made' regarding the enjoyment of rights by rights holders. States parties' reports, according to Article 40 (1) (a), (b) of the ICCPR, must be provided within one year after the entry into force of the treaty but also 'thereafter whenever the Committee so requests'.

This reporting procedure clearly corresponds with the modern interpretation of progressive realisation. It recognises a gradual improvement of the actual enjoyment of rights, ie, a gradual nature of the obligation of result regarding full realisation ('progress made in the enjoyment'), but at the same time indicates that there is an immediate obligation of conduct to pursue this goal ('measures they have adopted'). Accordingly, Article 40 of the ICCPR has been interpreted to indicate a progressive nature of obligations under the Covenant.[70] Article 40 (2) of the CRPD further supports this interpretation of realisation as a process over time determined by a number of factors as it requires that States parties' reports 'shall indicate the factors and difficulties, if any, affecting the implementation of the present Covenant'.[71]

A number of literary commentators reject this argument and try to uphold the differentiation between immediate civil and political and progressive socio-economic rights by pointing out that the term 'progress made' only refers to the result of the measures taken but not to the measures themselves.[72] These

[69] For the discussions during the drafting of the Covenant see 9.3.1.1.

[70] See Jhabvala, 'Domestic Implementation', 471; Schabas, *Nowak's CCPR Commentary*, 61–62.

[71] See Jhabvala, 'Domestic Implementation', 471.

[72] See Seibert-Fohr, 'Domestic Implementation', 407; Schwelb, 'The Nature of the Obligations', 308.

arguments are mostly also based on the drafting history of this provision which will be explored in more detail below.[73] However, many of these arguments are based on a misunderstanding of progressive realisation as being diametrically opposed to immediate obligations. The relevant commentators fail to see that progressive realisation is also used as an umbrella term which includes immediate as well as progressive obligations in the narrow sense. For example, when Seibert-Fohr points out that 'progress' cannot be understood to refer to the measures but only to the results of those measures, she fails to recognise that this is precisely how the umbrella concept of progressive realisation is interpreted in the context of socio-economic rights.

A related systematic argument is made by Christian Tomuschat, who compares Article 40 (1) of the ICCPR to Article 16 of the ICESCR. The latter provision prescribes that States parties prepare reports 'on the measures which they have adopted and the progress made in achieving the observance of the rights'; the former demands reports about measures 'which give effect' to the rights under the ICCPR 'and on the progress made in the enjoyment of those rights'. Tomuschat, presumably focusing on the difference between the words 'observance' and 'enjoyment', declares that '[t]he divergence speaks for itself' and that the ICCPR imposes upon States parties 'an obligation to achieve a specific result'.[74] He goes on to declare that 'States are duty-bound not only to strive in good faith for the attainment of certain aims, but to secure that the relevant rights be effective'.[75]

In light of the tripartite structure of obligations and the understanding of progressive realisation as it exists today, this argument cannot be upheld. Implicit in Tomuschat's statements is the idea that the 'enjoyment' of rights, which is subject to a progressive notion under the ICCPR, is not part of the 'observance' of rights which takes its place in the formulation of the ICESCR. It appears that Tomuschat is arguing that the actual enjoyment of human rights is not subject to States parties' obligations under the ICCPR and that, therefore, the notion of 'progress' is not connected to the duties of States parties. In other words, States parties can 'observe' the rights in the ICCPR without ensuring their enjoyment. However, in light of the fact that Article 2 of the ICCPR obliges States parties not only to respect rights under the Covenant but also to ensure them, there is no reason to draw such a distinction: establishing the actual enjoyment of human rights is what the observance of human rights treaties demands. Thus, the notion of progressiveness established through the reporting procedure does refer to a legal obligation of States parties, namely the obligation to ensure the enjoyment of rights.

Underlying Tomuschat's argument is furthermore the notion that there can only be either immediate obligations or long-term non-committal programmatic

[73] See further 9.3.1.1.
[74] Tomuschat, 'National Implementation', 41.
[75] ibid.

aims. However, Article 40 (1) of the ICCPR can also be interpreted to establish both an immediate obligation of conduct, namely to take measures 'which give effect to' the rights under the ICCPR, combined with a progressive obligation of establishing the full enjoyment of rights. In other words, Tomuschat also only rejects the narrow understanding of progressive realisation while not considering that the term is also used to refer to a combination of immediate and progressive obligations.

The CEDAW, CRPD and CRC all contain reporting obligations which set out that States parties must report on measures they have taken 'to give effect' to the rights under the respective treaties and 'on the progress made' either 'in this respect', 'in that regard', or 'on the enjoyment of those rights'.[76] These provisions, like Article 40 (1) of the ICCPR, explicitly contain the word 'progress'. Thus, they can be interpreted to relate to an immediate obligation to take steps combined with a gradual obligation of ensuring the full positive enjoyment of rights. Another aspect relevant here is that Article 44 (1) of the CRC and Article 35 (1) of the CRPD prescribe one form of reporting obligation without differentiating between socio-economic and civil and political rights even though they do so in their general obligations provisions. The CRC provision does so utilising wording similar to Article 40 (1) of the ICCPR (reporting on measures 'to give effect' to rights and 'on the progress made on the enjoyment of those rights'). Tomuschat's argument that this wording is clearly only linked to immediately realisable civil and political rights can thus not be upheld.

Article 9 of the ICERD is the only reporting provision inspected here which does not contain an obligation regarding reports on the 'progress'. According to this provision, States parties must submit 'a report on the … measures which they have adopted and which give effect to the provisions of this Convention'. However, this absence of an explicit reference to 'progress' is not overly relevant. This is because the concept of regular reporting in itself already implies a progress over time.

7.4.3. Special Measures in the CEDAW, ICERD and CRPD

As the analysis in part II has shown, the CEDAW-Com's and CERD's application of the special measures regime reveals the recognition that de facto equality must be considered a long-term goal which must be accelerated by special measures where necessary.[77] Such an interpretation is inherent in the structure of the treaties. Both treaties contain provisions setting out the duty or admissibility of undertaking 'temporary', 'special', and 'concrete' measures aimed at 'accelerating de facto equality' or ensuring 'adequate development' of groups of the population. As long as these measures do not lead to the 'maintenance of

[76] Article 18 of the CEDAW; Article 35 (1) of the CRPD; Article 44 (1) of the CRC.
[77] See further 4.4.2.

unequal or separate' rights or standards, they are not to be considered discriminatory (even though they privilege a certain group).[78] The CRPD contains a similar provision mentioning special measures which are necessary to 'accelerate or achieve de facto equality'.[79] These provisions imply that there is a process of gradual improvement over time regarding de facto equality which can (and must) be accelerated by certain measures benefitting particular groups. As none of the provisions are limited to socio-economic rights, this gradual notion of realisation clearly applies to substantive equality regarding all rights no matter their category. This also clarifies that the claim of immediacy of non-discrimination can only be understood to refer to de jure equality but not de facto equality.

7.4.4. Reasonable Accommodation in the CRPD

The CRPD arguably is the most 'modern' of the UN human rights treaties, and it challenges the divide between socio-economic and civil and political rights in several ways.[80] Not only do many of the rights in the Convention evade categorisation into these classical categories, the treaty also introduces resource considerations to all rights by way of the concept of reasonable accommodation. Article 5 (3) of the CRPD determines that, '[i]n order to promote equality and eliminate discrimination, States Parties shall take all appropriate steps to ensure that reasonable accommodation is provided'. The concept of reasonable accommodation, according to a definition provided in Article 2 of the CRPD, 'means necessary and appropriate modification and adjustments not imposing a disproportionate or undue burden'.[81]

The concept of 'disproportionate and undue burden' is inextricably linked to the notion of progressive elements. Reasonable accommodation simply represents the individual-oriented perspective of progressive realisation. Consequently, the introduction of resource considerations through reasonable accommodation necessarily entails the acceptance of a standard for all rights

[78] Article 4 (1) of the CEDAW: 'Adoption by States Parties of temporary special measures aimed at accelerating de facto equality between men and women shall not be considered discrimination as defined in the present Convention, but shall in no way entail as a consequence the maintenance of unequal or separate standards; these measures shall be discontinued when the objectives of equality of opportunity and treatment have been achieved.' Article 2 (2) of the CERD: 'States Parties shall, when the circumstances so warrant, take, in the social, economic, cultural and other fields, special and concrete measures to ensure the adequate development and protection of certain racial groups or individuals belonging to them, for the purpose of guaranteeing them the full and equal enjoyment of human rights and fundamental freedoms.' See also Article 1 (4) of the CERD.

[79] Article 5 (4) of the CRPD: 'Specific measures which are necessary to accelerate or achieve de facto equality of persons with disabilities shall not be considered discrimination under the terms of the present Convention.'

[80] See further 1.3.1.3.

[81] This provision also provides a definition of discrimination which reiterates that a 'denial of reasonable accommodation' falls into the scope of this definition.

which is analogous to progressive realisation. The terms 'reasonableness' and 'disproportionate or undue burden' under Articles 5 (3) and 2 of the CRPD introduce a notion of progressive realisation into the obligation of reasonable accommodation under the CRPD because these concepts take into account the variable nature of circumstances in the State party which have an influence on the ability to perform the obligations in question.[82] This extends the notion of resource dependence and progressiveness to all rights in the Convention, as States are obligated to provide reasonable accommodation in all areas covered by the Convention.[83]

7.5. CONCLUSION

It seems that many literary commentators as well as the Committees consider the wording and context of the treaties to clearly require the differentiation between immediate and progressive realisation. Even though it must be conceded that the explicit provision of progressive realisation only in the context of socio-economic rights is a reflection of this old thinking, other linguistic and contextual clues point into the opposite direction. The wording of relevant civil and political rights provisions does not demand immediacy in the sense that all aspects must be provided at once. From a contextual perspective, the reporting procedures set out in every treaty also require consideration of a progressive improvement for this category of rights. The following chapters will provide even more support from sources of interpretation outside the text of the treaties.

[82] See also Lawson, *Disability and Equality Law in Britain*, 32.
[83] See Broderick, *The Long and Winding Road*, 155; Ferri, 'Reasonable Accommodation', 42; Lord and Brown, 'The Role of Reasonable Accommodation', 279.

8

External Sources of Treaty Interpretation

8.1. INTRODUCTION

MOST ARGUMENTS FOR the immediacy of civil and political rights pivot on the wording of the treaties, either in isolation or in contrast to other provisions. However, the regime under Articles 31 and 32 of the VCLT sets out many other sources of interpretation. If one takes seriously the conception of a crucible of interpretation, arguments based on the wording of treaty provisions cannot stand in isolation without a consideration of all other relevant factors. Thus, the text of the treaties must be viewed before the background of external factors which aid in the finding of its meaning.

Again, the question is whether these external sources of interpretation indicate that civil and political rights must really be purely immediate or whether there is support for a standard of realisation analogous to progressive realisation, ie, a standard which includes not only strictly immediate but also progressive obligations. This chapter will address the external sources of treaty interpretation mentioned in Article 31 of the VCLT, starting with relevant rules of international law (8.2), continuing with the object and purpose of the treaties (8.3), and finally inspecting the subsequent practice of States parties (8.4), before ending with a conclusion (8.5).

8.2. RELEVANT RULES OF INTERNATIONAL LAW, ARTICLE 31 (3) (c) OF THE VCLT

According to Article 31 (3) (c) of the VCLT, 'together with the context', any relevant rules of international law applicable in the relations between the parties shall be taken into account. These relevant rules include general principles of international law in the sense of Article 38 (1) (c) of the ICJ Statute.[1] Two

[1] See Dörr and Schmalenbach, *VCLT*, 608; Sinclair, *The VCLT*, 76. It must be noted that, in this context, no particular relevance is to be accorded to the differentiation between 'rules' and 'principles'. The ICJ uses both terms interchangeably in the context of Article 38 (1) (c) of the ICJ Statute, see A Pellet and D Müller, 'Article 38' in A Zimmermann, CJ Tams, K Oellers-Frahm

general principles of this type are relevant here and support the application of a uniform standard of realisation and review.

Firstly, the principle of legal certainty prescribes that treaties must be interpreted in a way which leads to clear and unambiguous obligations. Attaching legal consequences to the categorisation of rights conflicts with this principle because there is no authoritative way of undertaking such a division (8.2.1). Secondly, it is a generally accepted principle of international law that a treaty cannot prescribe obligations for States parties which are materially impossible. In the present context, this principle prohibits an interpretation of the treaties which puts on States parties extensive positive obligations under civil and political rights which are immediate in the strict sense of the word because the realisation of such obligations would be materially impossibly (8.2.2). Together, these principles lead to the conclusion that a uniform standard of realisation must be applied to all rights and that this standard cannot be one of immediate implementation in the strict sense of the word.

8.2.1. Legal Certainty

Treaty interpretation in line with Articles 31 et seq of the VCLT requires taking into account the principle of legal certainty as a relevant rule of international law. Articles 31–33 of the VCLT and their customary law counterparts are aimed at creating legal certainty as the main goal of legal science.[2] In 2004, a report by the UN Secretary-General set out legal certainty as an integral part of the rule of law which is described as 'a concept at the very heart of the [UN's] mission', not only in the relation between State and individual but also concerning the rules governing State conduct.[3] The concept of legal certainty, according to *Black's Law Dictionary*, describes 'clarity, unambiguity, and stability in a system of law allowing those within the system to regulate their conduct according to the law's dictates'.[4] In the context of treaty interpretation, this requires choosing the meaning which leads to the least ambiguity in application when faced with several options of interpreting the treaty.

and C Tomuschat (eds), *The Statute of the International Court of Justice: A Commentary*, 3rd edn (Oxford, Oxford University Press, 2019) 925.

[2] See P Merkouris, 'Introduction: Interpretation is a Science, is an Art, is a Science' in M Fitzmaurice, O Elias and P Merkouris (eds), *Treaty Interpretation and the Vienna Convention on the Law of Treaties: 30 Years On*, Queen Mary Studies in International Law 1 (Leiden, Nijhoff, 2010) 10–11; see also P Merkouris, '"Third Party" Considerations and "Corrective Interpretation" in the Interpretative Use of Travaux Préparatoires: Is it Fahrenheit 451 for Preparatory Work?' in M Fitzmaurice, O Elias and P Merkouris (eds), *Treaty Interpretation and the Vienna Convention on the Law of Treaties: 30 Years On*, Queen Mary Studies in International Law 1 (Leiden, Nijhoff, 2010) 79.

[3] UNSC, 'Report of the Secretary-General on the Rule of Law and Transitional Justice in Conflict and Post-Conflict Societies' (23 August 2004) S/2004/616, para 6.

[4] 'Legal certainty' in BA Garner and HC Black, *Black's Law Dictionary*, 10th edn (St Paul, Thomson Reuters, 2014).

Differentiating between immediately realisable civil and political and progressively realisable socio-economic rights conflicts with this principle because attaching legal consequences to an uncertain differentiation produces legal uncertainty. It has already been shown in the previous part of this book that the Committees struggle to establish a coherent differentiation between the categories of socio-economic and civil and political rights.[5] Not only do these issues exist in practice, the following arguments will show that, also in theory, there is no coherent method of differentiation.

Originally, the bifurcation of the Covenants gave proponents of the divide a seemingly simple way to delimit the categories: socio-economic rights are those in the ICESCR, while civil and political rights are those in the ICCPR.[6] However, even at the time of the bifurcation decision, it was already noted that there was no clear way of differentiating between the categories.[7] This issue of uncertainty particularly concerns those treaties which combine rights from both categories and explicitly prescribe a legal differentiation, ie, the CRPD and the CRC (8.2.1.1). Neither of these treaties provide a list of which right belongs in which category or a set of criteria to decide this question.[8] Similar issues also arise in the context of non-discrimination and equality under the CEDAW and ICERD (8.2.1.2), as well as the ICCPR (8.2.1.3), since these treaties forbid discrimination in all areas of life.

8.2.1.1. *The CRPD and the CRC*

The reason why the CRPD-Com and CRC-Com fail to provide a consistent way of categorising rights is that the treaties do not permit such a division. No guidance is provided by the treaty texts regarding the question what makes a right civil and political or socio-economic. A common approach in literature, also proposed by Philip Alston, is to look for parallels of rights to those in the ICCPR and ICESCR respectively.[9] The same method is applied unsuccessfully by the Committees.[10] The structure of the CRPD and CRC thwarts any attempts at creating a clear and consistent categorisation along these lines.[11] This is so because the treaties combine aspects of life into singular provisions which, in

[5] See further ch 3.

[6] See, eg, P Alston, 'The Legal Framework of the Convention on the Rights of the Child' (1992) 91 *Bulletin of Human Rights* 1.

[7] See UNGA, 'Draft International Covenants on Human Rights', ch II para 8.

[8] This was also noted by Todres, 'Emerging Limitations', 179; while the creation of such a list was attempted during the drafting of the CRPD, this undertaking eventually failed, see BG Flóvenz, 'The Implementation of the UN Convention and the Development of Economical and Social Rights as Human Rights' in OM Arnardóttir and G Quinn (eds), *The UN Convention on the Rights of Persons with Disabilities: European and Scandinavian Perspectives*, International Studies in Human Rights 100 (Leiden, Nijhoff, 2009) 265–66.

[9] See Alston, 'The Legal Framework of the CRC', 11.

[10] See further 3.2.

[11] See Todres, 'Emerging Limitations', 179.

light of the respective subject areas of the ICESCR and ICCPR, fall on different sides of the division between socio-economic and civil and political rights. Both treaties contain provisions which are combined from elements of both the ICCPR and ICESCR and, therefore, cannot easily be ascribed to a category by way of this method.[12]

One such example is the right to independent living under Article 19 of the CRPD which combines aspects connected to, on the one hand, the rights to freedom of movement and liberty and the prohibition of torture, which are similar to rights in the ICCPR, and, on the other hand, traditionally socio-economic topics of social security and housing.[13] Another example is the traditionally civil and political right of freedom of expression under Article 21 of the CRPD which also includes the obligation to accept, facilitate, recognise, and promote the use of sign language.[14]

The CRC similarly restates and integrates a number of rights from the ICESCR and ICCPR and places them in the context of the special situation of children. Many of those rights can be understood to combine elements from both categories or to exhibit no discernible features of either category.[15] The CRC contains many provisions which focus on certain life situations of children and the measures necessary to ensure their rights instead of directly restating traditional civil and political or socio-economic rights. Examples include the situations of extra-familial care (Article 20 of the CRC), adoption (Article 21 of the CRC), and children seeking refuge (Article 22 of the CRC). Similarly, the rights to be protected from abduction and sale (Article 35 of the CRC) and against all forms of exploitation (Article 36 of the CRC) are new and not easily ascribable to either category.[16] Another example is the obligation to 'take all effective and appropriate measures with a view to abolishing traditional practices prejudicial to the health of children' under Article 24 (3) of the CRC. The corresponding right could be placed either in the (traditionally socio-economic) context of the right to health or ascribed to the prohibition of torture and therefore categorised as civil and political.[17] One must also ask whether the special protection obligations regarding child labour under Article 32 of the CRC fall into the category of socio-economic rights due to their relation to the right to

[12] See de Beco, 'The Indivisibility of Human Rights', 144–45; Rishmawi, *Article 4*, 17–18; Lord and Brown, 'The Role of Reasonable Accommodation', 274; Broderick, 'Article 4', 131; S Trömel, 'A Personal Perspective on the Drafting History of the United Nations Convention on the Rights of Persons with Disabilities' (2009) 1 *European Yearbook of Disability Law* 115, 119; Flóvenz, 'The Implementation of the UN Convention', 265–66.

[13] See de Beco, 'The Indivisibility of Human Rights', 150–51; see also Dhanda, 'Constructing a New Human Rights Lexicon', 48–50.

[14] See Mégret, 'The Disabilities Convention', 267.

[15] See Z Vaghri, J Zermatten, G Lansdown and R Ruggiero, *Monitoring State Compliance with the UN Convention on the Rights of the Child*, Children's Well-Being: Indicators and Research 25 (Cham, Springer, 2022) 415; Rishmawi, *Article 4*, 16–17.

[16] See Rishmawi, *Article 4*, 17.

[17] Vandenhole, Türkelli and Lembrechts, *Children's Rights*, 76.

work, or whether child labour must be considered to, at least in some cases, violate civil and political rights.[18]

The CRPD and CRC can thus be considered to 'move seamlessly between both categories of rights'.[19] Consequently, as Gauthier de Beco found in relation to the CRPD, these treaties do more than blend socio-economic and civil and political rights. They dissolve the borders between the categories altogether, which means that there is no way of sorting the rights in the Convention into the two categories.[20] This statement reflects the indistinguishability of rights which has already been observed in the jurisprudence of the Committees: not only are rights interdependent and indivisible in the sense that they are important for each other, but they have become indistinguishable.[21] There is no way to ascribe a certain State obligation to a certain right and therefore no way to clearly distinguish immediate and progressive obligations.

8.2.1.2. The CEDAW and the ICERD

Considerable legal uncertainty also arises in the context of the CEDAW and the ICERD. While none of the treaties in the UN system set out a legal differentiation between the two categories of rights in the context of non-discrimination, the HRC repeatedly saw the need to attempt such a differentiation in cases concerning social security systems.[22] This attempt inevitably failed, which can be explained by the unclear categorisation of rights in the treaties.

While the CEDAW and ICERD undoubtedly cover non-discrimination in all areas of life, neither of the treaties explicitly states which rights covered in the text are civil and political and which are socio-economic. If one wanted to apply the traditional bifurcation of rights to the CEDAW and the ICERD, two possible approaches are conceivable. On the one hand, one could focus on the right to non-discrimination as such, asking the question which category of rights it belongs into. Many commentators in literature consider non-discrimination to be a civil and political right,[23] which would mean that the CEDAW and the ICERD have an exclusively civil and political scope. However, this approach is bound to run into considerable difficulties as all UN human rights treaties

[18] See Todres, 'Emerging Limitations', 179.

[19] Mégret, 'The Disabilities Convention', 267.

[20] De Beco, 'The Indivisibility of Human Rights', 150; Flóvenz, 'The Implementation of the UN Convention', 265–66.

[21] See further 3.5.

[22] See further 4.5.4.

[23] See, eg, in the context of the CRPD, Cera 'Article 5', 164–65; A Lawson, 'The UN Convention on the Rights of Persons with Disabilities and European Disability Law: A Catalyst for Cohesion?' in OM Arnardóttir and G Quinn (eds), *The UN Convention on the Rights of Persons with Disabilities: European and Scandinavian Perspectives*, International Studies in Human Rights 100 (Leiden, Nijhoff, 2009) 103–04.

contain some form of prohibition of discrimination, including the ICESCR.[24] In a traditional understanding, the ICESCR exclusively covers socio-economic rights, which logically would also extend to the non-discrimination provision contained therein. The second possible method of categorisation centres around the rights which the obligation of non-discrimination refers to.[25] This approach, at a first glance, appears more feasible, as the ICCPR and ICESCR are structured at least roughly around the traditional categories.

There is, however, no consistent separation into the categories of socio-economic and civil and political rights in the ICCPR, CEDAW or ICERD. In Article 5 of the CERD, a list of rights is provided in relation to which States parties are obligated to provide equal enjoyment. This provision lists 'the right to equal treatment before tribunals and all other organs administering justice', 'the right to security of person' including the freedom from violence and bodily harm, 'political rights', and '[o]ther civil rights'. The latter group contains traditional civil and political rights also contained in the ICCPR. The list then continues with '[e]conomic, social and cultural rights' including a number of traditional socio-economic rights. As a last point, the list refers to the 'right of access to any place or service intended for use by the general public'. When conducting the classical bifurcation based on this list, it remains unclear in which category the rights to equal treatment before the law, security and inviolability of the person, and access to public places belong.

The CEDAW does not explicitly contain such a categorisation, but divides rights into 'Parts' roughly, but not consistently, corresponding with the traditional bifurcation. 'Part II' of the CEDAW contains the prohibition of discrimination in political and public life (Article 7 of the CEDAW), the right to participate in political representation (Article 8 of the CEDAW) and rights related to nationality (Article 9 of the CEDAW). 'Part III' continues with the rights to education (Article 10 of the CEDAW), employment (Article 11 of the CEDAW), health care (Article 12 of the CEDAW), rights in 'other areas of economic and social life' (Article 13 of the CEDAW) and the rights of rural women (Article 14 of the CEDAW). 'Part IV' then sets out the right to equality before the law (Article 15 of the CEDAW) and the prohibition of discrimination relating to marriage and family relations (Article 16 of the CEDAW). If one wanted to divide the rights into categories on the basis of this structure, 'Part II' could be interpreted to cover civil and political rights while 'Part III' could be read to refer to socio-economic rights. It would remain unclear, however, to which category Articles 15 and 16 of the CEDAW should be ascribed.

[24] See, eg, Article 3 of the ICESCR: 'The States Parties to the present Covenant undertake to ensure the equal right of men and women to the enjoyment of all economic, social and cultural rights set forth in the present Covenant.'

[25] This approach is taken, eg, by experts of the HRC in an individual concurring opinion in the case of *Sprenger v the Netherlands*.

8.2.1.3. The ICCPR

When proceeding from the notion that civil and political rights are simply those contained in the ICCPR, the issue of categorisation, and thus also the issue of legal certainty, appear to be non-existent for that treaty. However, it has already been noted by the Limburg Principles that the ICESCR and the ICCPR are 'related' to each other and that

> [a]lthough most rights can clearly be delineated as falling within the framework of one or other Covenant, there are several rights and provisions referred to in both instruments which are not susceptible to clear differentiation. Both Covenants moreover share common provisions and articles.[26]

The same issue has been recognised by the often-cited *Airey* decision of the ECtHR which confirms that 'there is no water-tight division separating' the sphere of socio-economic rights from the field covered by the ECHR which, according to the Court, 'sets forth what are essentially civil and political rights'.[27]

Furthermore, even if the substantive rights contained in the ICCPR could all be categorised as civil and political, the principle of non-discrimination – laid down, for example, in Articles 3 and 26 of the ICCPR – extends to all areas of life. This is why there have been attempts by the HRC to conduct a differentiation between socio-economic and civil and political rights in the context of non-discrimination.[28] The HRC is faced with the same issues of delineation which are also experienced by the CEDAW-Com and CERD. There is no way of creating a conceptualisation of the right to non-discrimination which hinges upon the divide between categories of rights without creating considerable legal uncertainty.[29]

8.2.2. No Impossible Obligations

The notion that impossible obligations cannot exist is frequently described as a (general) principle of international law.[30] It represents the axiom that States parties are not bound by duties which are impossible to perform. Often, this principle is called *impossibilium nulla est obligatio* (what is impossible is not an obligation) or *ultra posse nemo obligatur* (no one is obliged beyond

[26] UNCHR, 'Limburg Principles', para 98.

[27] ECtHR, *Airey v Ireland*, para 26.

[28] See further 4.5.4.

[29] See also Leckie, 'Another Step Towards Indivisibility', 104.

[30] See, eg, ICJ, *Pulp Mills on the River Uruguay (Argentina v Uruguay)* (Merits, Judgment) [2010] ICJ Rep 14, separate opinion Torres Bernárdez, para 65; Dörr and Schmalenbach, *VCLT*, 1197; Sinclair, *The VCLT*, 191; M Szabo, 'General Principles of Law in the Practice of International Courts and the European Court of Justice' (2016) 4 *Hungarian Yearbook of International Law and European Law* 135, 139.

their capabilities).[31] Reflections of this notion can also be found in the VCLT, for example in Article 61 which governs the supervening impossibility of performance of treaty obligations.[32] When applying this principle as a tool of treaty interpretation via Article 31 (3) (c) of the VCLT, it commands interpreting treaty provisions in a way which does not create obligations impossible to fulfil. This has major implications for the interpretation of treaty obligations under the UN human rights treaties, particularly regarding positive obligations. The immediate realisation of civil and political rights – in the strict sense of the term – is materially impossible if meaningful positive obligations are attached to them.[33] Of course, one could object to a positive reading of civil and political rights altogether in order to avoid this issue. It appears, however, that such a restrictive reading of the treaties has now been overcome.[34] In any case, the argument for positive obligations under civil and political rights is not the subject of the current inquiry.

Proceeding from the positive conception of all rights, the impossibility of immediate realisation results not only from economic constraints but also from the necessity of social and cultural transformation.[35] The full realisation of civil and political rights and the pace at which States parties may achieve this goal depends on the amount of resources available as well as on the development of societal structures.[36] The latter is particularly obvious in light of the fact that all treaties discussed here are geared towards the de facto full and equal enjoyment of human rights instead of mere formal guarantees.[37] While it may

[31] See also 'Impossibilium nulla obligatio est' in B Garner (ed), *Black's Law Dictionary*, 11th edn (St Paul, Thomson Reuters, 2019).

[32] See Sinclair, *The VCLT*, 191; C Binder, *Die Grenzen der Vertragstreue im Völkerrecht: Am Beispiel der nachträglichen Änderung der Umstände*, Beiträge zum ausländischen öffentlichen Recht und Völkerrecht (Heidelberg, Springer, 2013) 182.

[33] It must be stressed again here that the recognition of these factual difficulties does not mean that they should be used as an excuse for inaction. Rather, staying in line with the approach chosen by the CESCR, progressive realisation must be interpreted to demand immediate action to the maximum extent possible to enact change, as quickly as possible, towards the full realisation of rights and complete equality in their enjoyment.

[34] See further 1.3.1.

[35] See Jhabvala, 'Domestic Implementation', 473–74; Brems, 'Minimum and Maximum Perspectives', 366.

[36] See also Alston and Quinn, 'Obligations under the ICESCR', 172.

[37] Articles 2 and 5 (3) of the CRPD contain a strong variant of the principle of non-discrimination which is aimed at enabling the enjoyment of human rights by persons with disabilities 'on an equal basis with others' and prescribe the positive duty of actively removing barriers by providing reasonable accommodation; the preamble of the CEDAW explicitly recognises that 'a change in the traditional role of men as well as the role of women in society and in the family is needed to achieve full equality between men and women'; the regime of special measures pursuant to Articles 1 (4) and 2 (2) of the ICERD is likewise targeted towards the notion of full and equal enjoyment or exercise of human rights and fundamental freedoms instead of mere formal equality; the actual enjoyment of human rights (as opposed to formal guarantees) is also the goal underlying the ICCPR, as the preamble shows: 'freedom from fear and want can only be achieved if conditions are created whereby everyone may enjoy his civil and political rights'.

be realistic to demand immediate legislative action by States parties in order to establish the necessary formal guarantees, the creation of de facto equal enjoyment of rights demands positive measures aimed at transforming attitudes and systems which require significant resources.[38]

In the context of the ICERD, Joshua Castellino makes the same argument: the complete elimination of all forms of racial discrimination cannot be an immediate obligation of result but instead must be seen as a universal and legally binding standard which States parties must work towards. Demanding an immediate elimination of discrimination 'potentially dooms any analysis of its effectiveness to failure' which is why, as Castellino realises, the language of progressive realisation is more suitable here than utopian demands of instant de facto equality, even though the latter may seem more desirable.[39]

It is only logical to conclude that the same applies to the obligations under the ICCPR and that the obligation of result regarding the complete realisation of the rights under the Covenant can only be understood as progressive.[40] Eva Brems, when setting out progressive realisation as the correct standard for the non-discrimination treaties, aptly speaks of a 'horizon line' of full realisation which must be constantly pursued.[41] She furthermore provides an interesting example of an international treaty which explicitly recognises this issue.[42] The Inter-American Convention on the Prevention, Punishment and Eradication of Violence against Women (Convention of Belém Do Pará)[43] distinguishes between duties to be performed 'without delay' and measures which States must 'undertake progressively'.[44] The latter group contains (among others) the obligation to modify social and cultural patterns of conduct regarding the roles of women and men by adopting educational programmes, counteracting prejudice, customs, etc.[45] Notably, this treaty does not distinguish between categories of rights but instead between immediate and progressive *obligations*, which apply across all rights.

8.3. OBJECT AND PURPOSE, ARTICLE 31 (1) OF THE VCLT

The final method of interpretation mentioned in the first paragraph of Article 31 of the VCLT relates to the treaty's 'object and purpose'. According

[38] See also S Ratjen and M Satija, 'Realizing Economic, Social, and Cultural Rights for All' in E Riedel, G Giacca and C Golay (eds), *Economic, Social, and Cultural Rights in International Law: Contemporary Issues and Challenges* (Oxford, Oxford University Press, 2014) 116.

[39] Castellino, 'Protecting Minorities', 233.

[40] The same conclusion is drawn by Jhabvala, 'Domestic Implementation', 475.

[41] Brems, 'Minimum and Maximum Perspectives', 355.

[42] See ibid, 367–68.

[43] Inter-American Convention on the Prevention, Punishment and Eradication of Violence against Women (Convention of Belém Do Pará), www.oas.org/juridico/english/treaties/a-61.html.

[44] ibid, Articles 7 and 8.

[45] ibid, Article 8 (b).

to this provision, the ordinary meaning of the treaty text shall be interpreted not only having respect to its context but also 'in the light of its object and purpose'. Here, the VCLT introduces the teleological element of treaty interpretation which also allows consideration of the principle of effectiveness, ie, the notion that treaty provisions shall be interpreted in a way which advances the aims of the treaty.[46] This section will lay out how the convergence of standards in the jurisprudence of the Committees is not detrimental but beneficial in light of the object and purpose of human rights treaties. The main focus will be on the normative effectiveness of this interpretation, which requires not an empirical ex post evaluation but instead an exploration of the potential effectiveness of human rights treaties and certain interpretations.[47] Thus, this chapter will not address concerns about a potential abuse of a certain standard of realisation by States parties but rather focus on its doctrinal soundness.

Part II has shown that the standard of realisation applied to civil and political rights has been aligned with progressive realisation. But because this alignment has yet to be noticed by others, criticism regarding progressive realisation has centred around the approach to socio-economic rights. Accordingly, this section will focus on the arguments extended in this context. The reputation of progressive realisation has always suffered under the perception that it is a weak standard which provides States parties with excuses for not taking any action towards the fulfilment of their obligations. Accordingly, some would argue that the alignment of the standard applicable to civil and political rights with progressive realisation weakens the protection of this category which would contradict the object and purpose of human rights treaties. This section asks the question whether it really is detrimental to the effective protection of human rights when the Committees accept that all rights entail not only strictly immediate but also progressive obligations.

In a first step, this section will determine that the equal de facto enjoyment of human rights, ie, effective human rights protection, is the central objective of the relevant treaties (8.3.1). In a second step, it will be argued that the application of an umbrella understanding of progressive realisation, contrary to common concerns, is not detrimental to human rights protection because, correctly interpreted, it is not a weak standard of realisation (8.3.2). Instead, as the third subsection will show, the identification of progressive elements in any right additionally strengthens protection more so than an insistence upon strict immediacy (8.3.3).

[46] See Gardiner, *Treaty Interpretation*, 211.

[47] Regarding the terms of normative and potential effectiveness, see A Vandenbogaerde and W Vandenhole, 'The Optional Protocol to the International Covenant on Economic, Social and Cultural Rights: An Ex Ante Assessment of its Effectiveness in Light of the Drafting Process' (2010) 10 *Human Rights Law Review* 207, 231; see also Letsas, 'Strasbourg's Interpretive Ethic', 535; Maisley, 'The International Right of Rights?', 102.

8.3.1. Full and Equal De Facto Enjoyment of Human Rights as Object and Purpose

Determining the object and purpose of a treaty is no mechanical exercise separate from the other methods of treaty interpretation. Instead, it is itself an interpretive question and therefore an integral part of the overall interpretative process.[48] This is also why there cannot be a clear differentiation between the teleological and textual approaches to interpretation.[49] The object and purpose of international treaties is commonly derived from their preambles,[50] although the substantive provisions of the instruments, of course, also play a role in this regard. Inspecting the preambular text of the treaties instead of the totality of substantive provisions has the advantage that, in the former context, the objective of the treaty is often formulated in a more concise manner.

All of the treaties covered here start out their preambular paragraphs with a recognition of the inherent dignity of human beings and the inalienable human rights of every person, which is in accordance with the principles proclaimed in the Charter of the United Nations.[51] The ICCPR continues to clarify 'that these rights derive from the inherent dignity of the human person'.[52] Another aspect common to all treaty preambles is the insistence upon the entitlement to the equal enjoyment of human rights. It becomes clear that the promotion of this ideal of equal enjoyment of human rights is the central aim of the treaties. The ICCPR's preambular paragraphs, in connection with this, mention 'the obligation of States under the Charter of the United Nations to promote universal respect for, and observance of, human rights and freedoms'.[53] The ICERD is prefaced by the preamble: 'Resolved to adopt all necessary measures for speedily eliminating racial discrimination.'[54] Similarly, the CEDAW's preambles contain the following statement: 'Determined to implement the principles set forth in the Declaration on the Elimination of Discrimination against Women and, for that purpose, to adopt the measures required for the elimination of such discrimination in all its forms and manifestations.'[55]

[48] Letsas, 'Strasbourg's Interpretive Ethic', 533.

[49] See further 7.2.2.

[50] See Sinclair, *The VCLT*, 127–28; B Slocum and J Wong, 'The Vienna Convention and Ordinary Meaning in International Law' (2021) 46 *Yale Journal of International Law* 191, 199; EJ Kakoullis and Y Ikehara, 'Article 1: Purpose' in I Bantekas, MA Stein and D Anastasiou (eds), *The UN Convention on the Rights of Persons with Disabilities: A Commentary* (Oxford, Oxford University Press, 2018) 48; see also Gardiner, *Treaty Interpretation*, 217–18 urging for a cautious approach to the interpretation of preambles in this context.

[51] See preamble 1 of the ICCPR, preamble 1 of the ICESCR, preamble 1 of the CRC, preamble (a) of the CRPD, preamble 2 of the CEDAW, preamble 1 of the ICERD.

[52] Preamble 2 of the ICCPR.

[53] Preamble 4 of the ICCPR.

[54] Preamble 1 of the ICERD.

[55] Preamble 14 of the CEDAW.

In this respect, the CRPD takes a more broad approach (as it often does) by explicitly setting out the purpose of the Convention in Article 1 of the CRPD, which is an approach remaining unique in the core UN human rights instruments:[56] 'The purpose of the present Convention is to promote, protect and ensure the full and equal enjoyment of all human rights and fundamental freedoms by all persons with disabilities, and to promote respect for their inherent dignity.'

Furthermore, and this is particularly important for the following analysis, the preambles of each treaty clearly envision the factual enjoyment of human rights instead of mere formal equality as being at the centre of their objective. The CRPD's preambles, again, are rather extensive and clear-cut in this respect by stressing that, despite various human rights instruments and other undertakings, 'persons with disabilities continue to face barriers in their participation as equal members of society'.[57] The ICCPR also makes reference to the notion of factual enjoyment requiring positive State action by holding that

> the ideal of free human beings enjoying civil and political freedom and freedom from fear and want can only be achieved if conditions are created whereby everyone may enjoy his civil and political rights, as well as his economic, social and cultural rights.[58]

The titles of the treaties can serve as another clear indication of their object and purpose. All treaties declare themselves to be Covenants or Conventions 'of rights' or 'on the elimination of discrimination'. Lastly, the substantive provisions of the treaties support the above conclusion: most of the provisions in the human rights treaties refer to individual rights and the obligations parties undertake. Clearly, effective human rights protection is the object and purpose of all treaties covered here. Regarding the general obligation provisions in the UN human rights treaties, a teleological interpretation thus requires determining which of their conceivable meanings benefits most the full and equal protection of rights.

8.3.2. Progressive Realisation does not Weaken Rights Protection

In light of this object and purpose, a range of critical arguments are extended regarding the concept of progressive realisation (and, thus, indirectly against the application of an analogous standard to civil and political rights). In short, stakeholders, actors and commentators were and are concerned that progressive realisation weakens the effectiveness of human rights. Criticism of progressive realisation as a weak standard was and is being extended in a number of contexts. This includes, firstly, sceptical comments regarding the introduction

[56] See Kakoullis and Ikehara, 'Article 1', 48.
[57] Preamble (k) of the CRPD.
[58] Preamble 3 of the ICCPR.

of progressive realisation for socio-economic rights during and after the drafting of the treaties.[59] Secondly, drafting parties and literary commentators argue that progressive realisation would weaken the protection of civil and political rights when faced with the idea of extending the application of this concept either during the drafting phase or in the process of interpretation.[60] Thirdly, progressive realisation is described as weak in the context of comments about the alleged aspirational or programmatic nature of socio-economic rights; it is assumed that progressive realisation is a natural reflection of those idiosyncrasies.[61]

In substance, the arguments are the same in all three contexts and may thus be addressed together. The scepticism towards progressive realisation, in all these contexts, refers to two major points. Firstly, it is claimed that progressive realisation gives States parties an excuse for indefinitely postponing their realisation by declaring that resources are limited or by pointing to the overall progressive nature of implementation (8.3.2.1). Secondly, progressively realisable rights are often said to be unsuitable for judicial enforcement due a perceived lack of clear obligations and a consequent impossibility of establishing treaty violations (8.3.2.2). The following subsections will engage with this criticism and show that it is based upon a defeatist reading of the concept of progressive realisation which is not in line with the interpretation of the Committees today. In other words, what the commentators criticise with reference to the object and purpose of the treaties is not the de facto uniform standard that is applied by the Committees.

8.3.2.1. No Justification for Indefinite Postponement

There is a common misconception that declaring rights to be progressively realisable puts them under a 'limitation' by creating a legal defence for States parties to not fulfil or work towards the goals of the rights.[62] In this context, commentators often voice their concern that progressive realisation acts as an 'escape hatch' for States parties looking to avoid their human rights obligations.[63] The assumption that progressive realisation might act as an 'escape hatch', in turn, is based in two interconnected concerns. Firstly, commentators are concerned that States could point to the progressive nature of realisation in general in order to indefinitely postpone any action towards the realisation of the right.[64] Secondly, it is argued that accepting the relevance of limited resources would encourage States to reject taking action with reference to budget issues.

[59] See, eg, the arguments exchanged during the drafting of the ICESCR explored in 9.3.1.

[60] See, eg, the arguments exchanged during the drafting of the CRC explored in 9.3.4.

[61] See, eg, Felner, 'Closing the Escape Hatch', 406; Dennis and Stewart 'Justiciability of Economic, Social, and Cultural Rights', 465; Todres, 'Emerging Limitations', 178.

[62] See, eg, KG Young, *Constituting Economic and Social Rights* (Oxford, Oxford University Press, 2012) 101–04.

[63] See Leckie, 'Another Step Towards Indivisibility', 94; Felner, 'Closing the Escape Hatch'.

[64] See Felner, 'Closing the Escape Hatch', 407–08.

In general, critics of progressive realisation are concerned that this concept would provide States parties with some sort of temporal loophole which renders all obligations pointless.[65] Tomuschat, for example, argues that progressive realisation cannot apply to civil and political rights because there must not be a margin of discretion regarding the time-limits in which States parties must bring about full compliance with their obligations under the ICCPR.[66] He even fears that not insisting upon immediate realisation would entail a 'transitory period' which would allow States parties to arbitrarily interfere with the rights guaranteed in the treaty.[67] Ahcene Boulesbaa similarly rejects the application of progressive realisation to civil and political rights, stating that '[s]uch an interpretation would enable states to delay the implementation as they did with regard to' the ICESCR.[68] On the basis of these alleged shortcomings, the ICESCR has been described as a 'relatively weak international human rights treaty' with reference to its general obligations provision and its recognition of the relevance of limited resources and progressive realisation.[69]

There can be no doubt that, from a perspective of effective human rights protection, States parties must not be provided with a blanket excuse for doing nothing. However, as the concept of progressive realisation is filled out with more and more concrete legal obligations, the risk of States parties abusing this concept becomes less and less of a problem.[70] Langford and King likewise argue that concerns about the vague or aspirational nature of obligations under the ICESCR have been losing their impetus as the CESCR continues to flesh out the concepts of 'maximum of available resources', progressive realisation, 'appropriate means', and 'legislative measures'.[71]

It is this coherent understanding of progressive realisation and its components which alleviates the above-mentioned concerns of it being a weak standard. Progressive realisation, as it is understood today, does not provide States parties with an excuse for inaction or indefinite postponement of fulfilment.[72] The CESCR in particular does not allow the concept of progressive realisation to be abused as a 'let-out clause'; instead, its interpretation obligates States parties to do as much as possible and chose those measures which are suitable to bring about full realisation in the shortest possible time.[73] It has been stressed again

[65] Such concerns already existed during the drafting of the ICESCR, see UNGA, 'Draft International Covenants on Human Rights', ch V paras 23–24; see also Jhabvala, 'Domestic Implementation', 475 with reference to UNGA, 'Draft International Covenants on Human Rights: Observations by Governments' (13 October 1955) A/2910/Add.6.

[66] Tomuschat, 'National Implementation', 42.

[67] ibid, 41.

[68] A Boulesbaa, 'The Nature of the Obligations Incurred by States under Article 2 of the UN Convention against Torture' (1990) 12 *Human Rights Quarterly* 53, 80.

[69] See, eg, Todres, 'Emerging Limitations', 178.

[70] See also Leckie, 'Another Step Towards Indivisibility', 94.

[71] Langford and King, 'CESCR', 482.

[72] See Tobin, 'Article 4', 111.

[73] Craven, *The ICESCR*, 131.

and again by the experts of the CESCR that progressive realisation should not be misinterpreted as depriving obligations of all meaningful content.[74]

An indefinite postponement of realisation is not tolerated in the context of progressive realisation under any circumstances because this concept demands immediate action to the largest extent possible. The CESCR is clear about the fact that the duty to 'take steps' requires States parties to do as much as available resources allow them at any point in time in order to move towards the realisation of the right as expeditiously as possible. The flexibility of progressive realisation is based only on factual and demonstrable limitations; there is no moment in the timeframe of realisation which would allow States parties to lose their focus on the goal of full realisation. At no point in time may States parties 'drag their feet'.[75] In this context, it is useful to recall that progressiveness implied by the concept of progressive realisation is not understood to refer to the concrete obligations States parties are facing but instead to the overall implementation of the right in its fullest form: States parties have an immediate obligation of conduct which requires them to take steps to their best ability while the full realisation is an obligation of result which will necessarily take time.[76]

The same has been stressed in the Limburg Principles:

> The obligation 'to achieve progressively the full realization of the rights' requires States parties to move as expeditiously as possible towards the realization of the rights. Under no circumstances shall this be interpreted as implying for States the right to defer indefinitely efforts to ensure full realization. On the contrary all States parties have the obligation to begin immediately to take steps to fulfil their obligations under the Covenant.[77]

It is also an untenable presumption that the reference to available resources as an integral part of progressive realisation would provide States parties with an 'escape hatch'. Resource constraints, according to the understanding of progressive realisation submitted here, cannot justify inaction.[78] Furthermore, resource excuses become truly difficult to make if States parties are required to – as an immediate obligation – provide a detailed plan of action including resource planning.[79]

There is also no leeway in the concept of progressive realisation providing States parties with the legal excuse to actively interfere with human rights guarantees on the basis of limited resources. Clearly, the obligation to respect is not

[74] See, eg, CESCR, 'General Comment No 3', para 9; the CESCR's conception is usually transferred to the other treaty regimes, see Broderick, 'Article 4', 131.

[75] Chenwi, 'Unpacking Progressive Realisation', 744.

[76] See also Langford and King, 'CESCR', 487.

[77] UNCHR, 'Limburg Principles', para 21.

[78] See Porter, 'Reasonableness and Article 8(4)', 182.

[79] See M Langford, 'Substantive Obligations' in M Langford, B Porter, R Brown and J Rossi (eds), *The Optional Protocol to the International Covenant on Economic, Social and Cultural Rights: A Commentary* (Pretoria, Pretoria University Law Press, 2016) 232.

construed as being subject to available resources. A good example for this is the insistence by the CESCR that forced evictions are prima facie violations of the treaty.[80] As a matter of mere logic, it is difficult to construe limited resources as a reason for the active interference with human rights.[81] The burden of proof in this matter, in any case, would rest with the State party.[82] When the available resources phrase is read in this way, ie, as demanding all possible investments instead of providing an excuse, this suddenly aligns with what many critics implicitly recognise themselves, namely that civil and political rights cannot be absolute in the sense that they cannot demand a certain result of States parties regardless of their actual capabilities.[83]

Ultimately, the criticism that progressive realisation is a weak standard is based upon a misunderstanding created by the ambiguity of the term. Critics are concerned about a blanket application of the narrow understanding of the term, while the other side insists that progressive realisation is an umbrella concept which includes both immediate and progressive obligations. This coexistence between immediate and progressive obligations is often overlooked by critics of progressive realisation; there is a common misunderstanding that progressive realisation and immediate obligations are mutually exclusive. Schabas, for example, declares that general international law prescribes that States parties 'are obliged to observe and implement the duties contained in the treaty as of the date on which it entered into force .... This principle does not apply when a treaty itself provides only for a duty of progressive implementation.'[84] Clearly, Schabas does not take into account that progressive realisation does in fact entail immediate obligations which apply at the date on which the treaty enters into force, namely the obligation to take steps and to ensure de jure equality.

The misunderstanding becomes even more apparent when inspecting Schabas' conception of civil and political rights realisation. He sets out a combination of immediate obligations of conduct and progressive obligations of result which coincides with the umbrella concept of progressive realisation. Schabas finds that a modern conception of civil and political rights which includes negative as well as positive aspects allows the coexistence of the immediate obligation to respect human rights and the progressive obligation to ensure these rights.[85] Interestingly, however, Schabas still upholds that civil and political rights are immediate as opposed to progressively realisable,[86] seemingly unaware that the structure of obligations he so aptly sets out is precisely what the modern interpretation of progressive realisation entails.

[80] See, eg, CESCR, 'General Comment No 7: The Right to Adequate Housing (art. 11 (1) of the Covenant): Forced Evictions' (1997) HRI/GEN/1/Rev.7, para 2.
[81] See also Künnemann, 'A Coherent Approach', 330–31.
[82] See further 2.4.3.
[83] See, eg, Boulesbaa 'The Nature of the Obligations under Article 2 UNCAT', 62.
[84] Schabas, *Nowak's CCPR Commentary*, 61.
[85] ibid, 62, 892–93.
[86] ibid, 62.

8.3.2.2. No Conflict with Adjudication

The rejection of progressive realisation is also often motivated by the perception that this standard would not allow manageable standards for judicial review.[87] This second dimension of apprehension towards progressive realisation is even more intertwined with the discussion about the nature of socio-economic rights than the first. Socio-economic rights are said to be unfit for (quasi-)judicial review due to their nature as progressively realisable. It is a common concern that 'the principle of progressive realization of these [socio-economic] rights creates special difficulties regarding accountability'.[88] Such concerns were also extended during the drafting phase of the ICESCR-OP when discussing the individual complaints mechanism of the CESCR. According to the Canadian representative, '[p]rogressive realization is not a concept which easily lends itself to adjudication'.[89]

It is often perceived that the necessarily variable nature of progressively realisable obligations complicates their monitoring. After all, the treaties do not specify precisely which steps States parties must take and what the concepts 'progressively' and 'available resources' mean. Therefore, it is argued, setting out only a vague obligation of result regarding the full realisation of the right some day in the future would leave 'little basis upon which to judge whether or not [States parties] were acting in good faith'.[90] Because the ICESCR does not provide any information on what States parties have to do precisely and instead 'only' requires that States parties take steps toward the realisation of socio-economic rights, it is perceived as difficult to establish violations or compliance with the treaties.[91] Tomuschat, when rejecting progressive realisation as a standard for civil and political rights, maintained that a strict standard of immediate realisation is necessary in order to enable findings of the HRC on the violation of specific provisions.[92] According to his argument, if rights are interpreted to create 'purely promotional obligations' then there is no way for individuals to bring successful claims about the violation of these rights.[93]

On further inspection, there is no support for the claim that progressive realisation produces unworkable difficulties for the adjudication of rights. The Limburg Principles provide some useful guidance in this respect by setting

[87] See, eg, Heringa, 'Judicial Enforcement', 150–51; Felner, 'Closing the Escape Hatch', 408; see also Humphrey, 'Letter to the Editor', 539.

[88] UNHCHR, 'Plan of Action Submitted by the United Nations High Commissioner for Human Rights, Louise Arbour' (26 May 2005) A/59/2005/Add.3, para 78.

[89] UNCHR, 'Status of the International Covenants on Human Rights: Report of the Secretary General on the Draft Optional Protocol to the International Covenant on Economic, Social and Cultural Rights' (16 March 1998) E/CN.4/1998/84/Add.1, para 3.

[90] Craven, *The ICESCR*, 107.

[91] See Todres, 'Emerging Limitations', 178.

[92] See Tomuschat, 'National Implementation', 42.

[93] ibid, 41.

out a section about 'Violations of Economic, Social and Cultural Rights'. This section includes, amongst others, the cases of failing to take steps required by the Covenant, 'wilfully' failing to meet minimum requirements, and deliberately halting or retarding the progressive realisation of a right under the ICESCR unless the reason is a lack of available resources.[94] This document is in line with the idea that progressive realisation entails the immediate obligation to do as much as possible combined with the progressive obligation to fully realise the right.

Regarding the immediate obligation to take steps, the determination of violations raises no particular difficulties. State duties concerning strategies, plans of action, and the implementation of a monitoring system are not limited by available resources. If States parties fail to engage with these immediate obligations, there is an identifiable breach of the treaty.[95] There are also ways to determine cases where States have violated their progressive obligation to move towards complete fulfilment 'as expeditiously as possible'. In order to deal with this, admittedly more difficile, question, the CESCR has repeatedly endorsed the utilisation of indicators and benchmarks. A number of tools are available in this context, for example the OHCHR's guide on the measurement and implementation of human rights in 2012 or the Social and Economic Rights Fulfilment Index (SERF Index).[96] It is important to note that progressive realisation puts a burden on the State party to actively document and show their progress.[97]

Another point in this context concerns the recognition in Article 8 (4) of the ICESCR-OP and Article 10 (4) of the CRC-OP3 that States parties 'may adopt a range of possible policy measures' for the implementation of the rights set forth in the treaties. During the drafting of Article 8 (4) of the ICESCR-OP, there were concerns that this recognition of what is commonly called the margin of appreciation would mean an abdication of the role of the CESCR as a supervisory body.[98] However, the Committees repeatedly stress that they adopt a strong reading of the margin according to which they still ultimately decide on what is reasonable and what is not.[99] Furthermore, allowing States parties a certain leeway instead of prescribing specific steps to be taken may lead to Committees providing States parties with more 'guidance and explanatory reasoning'.[100]

[94] UNCHR, 'Limburg Principles', para 72.
[95] Langford and King, 'CESCR', 489.
[96] OHCHR, 'Human Rights Indicators: A Guide to Measurement and Implementation' (2012) HR/PUB/12/5; see also Heymann, McNeill and Raub, 'Rights Monitoring and Assessment'.
[97] See Leckie, 'Another Step Towards Indivisibility', 93–94.
[98] See Porter, 'Reasonableness and Article 8(4)', 184–87.
[99] See further 2.6.
[100] McGoldrick, 'A Defence of the Margin of Appreciation', 56.

8.3.3. Progressive Realisation Additionally Strengthens Rights Protection

While the previous arguments have shown that progressive realisation does not deserve its reputation as an excuse for States parties to do nothing, one could still argue that demands for a strict immediacy of rights would provide a *more* stringent standard of realisation and therefore benefit rights holders more. Thus, one could oppose the convergence of standards, arguing that civil and political rights should retain a strict standard of immediacy because this would be even more effective in rights protection. However, this argument would disregard the fact that the recognition of progressive elements has some undeniable benefits compared to an insistence upon the immediacy of rights, particularly with a view to making positive obligations manageable. In other words, focusing on the immediate implementation of civil and political rights might obstruct the view for long-term positive measures which aim at the de facto enjoyment of those rights.[101]

Firstly, and most importantly, a combination of immediate and progressive obligations enables an engagement with positive measures and their sufficiency in light of treaty requirements, which is an aspect that often comes up short when the immediacy of obligations is in focus (8.3.3.1). Secondly, the traditional conception of immediate and progressive categories of rights inadvertently places the latter on a lower level in a hierarchy of rights, which is incompatible with the interdependence and indivisibility of human rights (8.3.3.2). Lastly, accepting progressive elements is necessary to resolve the contradiction between immediacy and (extensive) positivity of obligations, which heightens the potential acceptability of human rights obligations. Acknowledging that the treaties do not demand impossible measures can help foster States parties' acceptance of the treaties and may increase the chances of more States acceding to these instruments (8.3.3.3).

8.3.3.1. Revealing Positive Obligations and Adding a Layer of Scrutiny

Insisting upon the 'immediacy and unconditionality' of civil and political rights prevents the engagement with some positive aspects of civil and political rights. While immediacy is the appropriate standard for some positive obligations, such as those relating to formal equality and minimum core duties, this standard fails to provide guidance for long-term policy issues. A standard like progressive realisation reveals new dimensions of positive obligations, gives the Committees the doctrinal tools to deal with them, and thereby strengthens rights protection.[102] Even though it may not be trivial to assess whether the

[101] See also de Beco, 'The Indivisibility of Human Rights', 156.

[102] A similar argument is made by Jhabvala, 'Domestic Implementation', 475 and de Beco, 'The Indivisibility of Human Rights', 157.

maximum of available resources has been used and whether the State party has done enough to implement a process of gradual realisation, a complicated standard of realisation and review for these positive aspects is better than no standard at all. If there are no criteria developed to address the issue of long-term goals, then there will be no supervision of this aspect of rights. In particular, progressive realisation allows an engagement with positive obligations so onerous that they can realistically only be realised over time.

Correctly applied, a standard analogous to progressive realisation does not 'limit' the scope of rights which before were unlimited under the ICCPR, but instead allows engagement with positive obligations unexplored before due to a lack of tools to deal with the inevitable difficulties such positive aspects create. A gradual notion of realisation enables the addressing of general policy issues which are undoubtedly relevant for the protection of the right. Progressive realisation furthermore allows a differentiation as regards to the degree of good vs bad human rights compliance, instead of merely finding States in violation of their obligations when they have not immediately and completely realised the relevant human rights.[103] It is much more useful to demand justification from a State party that everything in its power has been done than to simply state that the State party is in continuous violation because full realisation has not been achieved immediately. While the latter option may also have the effect of motivating the State party to take action, the former option has the advantage of giving guidance as to what to do in which order.

In order to provide illustration and evidence for this claim, the following subsections present Committee decisions on Individual Communications. Firstly, the Committees' socio-economic rights jurisprudence shows that progressive realisation is not utilised as a legal excuse for State parties, but instead as a way to add a layer of scrutiny regarding general policy issues. Secondly, examples from the Committees' civil and political rights jurisprudence are presented to illustrate how a refusal to engage with progressive elements leaves opportunities for heightened scrutiny on the table.

Examples of Progressive Realisation Increasing Scrutiny

Several examples from the Committees' views in Individual Communications concerning socio-economic rights can serve to illustrate the point made above. From a critical perspective on progressive realisation, one might fear that the Committees simply accept the argument of resource constraints or progressiveness invoked by States parties to justify their inaction or even active interference with rights, with no questions asked. However, the opposite becomes apparent from the Committees' views in Individual Communications. Not only do the

[103] See Brems, 'Minimum and Maximum Perspectives', 356.

experts not allow progressive realisation as a blanket excuse, they furthermore utilise this concept as a means to engage with general policy issues as an additional layer of scrutiny.

This can be illustrated, firstly, by the case of *Djazia and Bellili v Spain*. Here, the CESCR refers to the general housing policy of the city of Madrid, criticising the city government's sale of public housing units. The experts make it clear that the authors' rights were violated, not only because of the State party's failure to provide emergency housing in the case at hand, but also due to inadequacies in the general housing policy of the city.[104] Regarding the issue of general policy, the CESCR finds that the State party could not convincingly explain why it was necessary to sell public housing and that, therefore, these retrogressive measures could not be justified.

Accordingly, the concept of progressive realisation and the pursuant prohibition of retrogressive steps is employed to scrutinise the overall progress towards realising the right to housing for all rights holders in Spain. If the Committee had insisted upon the immediacy of the rights in question, as demanded for civil and political rights, this larger group-oriented context would likely not have been subject to the experts' review. Because then it would have sufficed to state that, in the case at hand, the individual was not provided with housing and, thus, their rights were violated. Furthermore, Spain would not have been compelled to provide justification for its lack of progress if the right to housing was interpreted as unconditional. The application of progressive realisation allows taking into account the overall gradual process of providing social housing for those in need.

Similar tendencies can be observed in the CRPD-Com's jurisprudence on socio-economic rights. In *Gröninger v Germany*, the CRPD-Com scrutinises in detail the State party's social legislation aimed at bringing persons with disabilities into the labour market and finds that '[t]he policy is not consistent with the general principles set forth in article 3 of the Convention, read together with paragraphs (i) and (j) of the preamble' and that 'the existing model for the provision of integration subsidies does not effectively promote the employment of persons with disabilities'. Consequently, the State party's integration subsidies scheme 'as applied in the case of the author's son' is in violation of the obligations under the Convention.[105] The insufficiency of Germany's general policy is used as a basis for finding a violation of Convention rights. Notably, this is in addition to finding violations of the rights of the author's son due to an insufficiency of measures taken in the specific case.[106]

In *Calleja Loma and Calleja Lucas v Spain*, the CRPD-Com refers to its findings in its Concluding Observations and its inquiry under Article 6 of

[104] CESCR, *Djazia and Bellili v Spain*, paras 17.5, 17.6.
[105] CRPD-Com, *Gröninger v Germany*, para 6.2.
[106] See ibid, para 6.3.

the CRPD-OP, recalling that those findings 'indicate grave or systematic violations', criticising the 'limited progress made by the State party with regard to inclusive education, including the lack of a clear policy and action plan for the promotion of inclusive education'.[107] These general findings are used as a basis for the Committee's General Recommendations in this case,[108] thereby giving substance to the requirement of preventing similar violations in the future.

A further example can be found in the jurisprudence of the CEDAW-Com. In *OG v Russia*, the applicant argues that the State party violated her rights under the Convention because authorities did not conduct timely and effective investigations into domestic abuse and threats due to gender stereotypes.[109] Furthermore, the complainant refers to the lack of 'contemporary and comprehensive legislation on domestic violence' in Russia, asserting that the State party consequently failed to fully implement the Convention.[110] The experts follow this combination of individual and collective aspects in its arguments on the merits. Firstly, Russia is found to be in violation of the treaty because, in the author's case, the authorities failed to act in a timely and adequate manner and were being influenced by gender stereotypes.[111] Secondly, the experts declare that Russia failed to sufficiently amend its legislation in the field of domestic violence, which 'directly affected the possibility of the author being able to claim justice and to have access to efficient remedies and protection'. Thirdly, this omission is also found to constitute 'a failure by the State party in its duty to take all appropriate measures to modify the social and cultural patterns of conduct' incompatible with the Convention.[112] The CEDAW-Com also combines immediate individual and long-term collective aspects, clearly signalling that Russia must intensify its efforts to abolish gender stereotypes in society.

Missed Opportunities to Engage with General Policy Issues

Even though there are convergent tendencies, the Committees do not always apply a standard analogous to progressive realisation when addressing civil and political rights. Progressive elements and the aspect of general policy are often ignored in civil and political rights cases. This reduces the range of positive obligations which can be scrutinised by the Committees and therefore weakens the protection of the rights in question. The argument here is not that the

[107] CRPD-Com, *Calleja Loma and Calleja Lucas v Spain* [Adoption of Views] (28 August 2020) CRPD/C/23/D/41/2017, paras 8.5, 8.6.
[108] ibid, para 9 (b).
[109] CEDAW-Com, *OG v Russian Federation* [Adoption of Views] (6 November 2017) CEDAW/C/68/D/91/2015, paras 3.2–3.6.
[110] ibid, para 3.1.
[111] ibid, para 7.6.
[112] ibid, paras 7.7.–7.8.

Committees are necessarily wrong in finding a violation of an individual's rights in the following examples. It of course helps the applicant to demand immediate fulfilment of aspects relevant to their individual case. However, progressive realisation would allow taking into account the group-oriented dimension in addition to this individual aspect. Perhaps the State party violated human rights not only because it did not take sufficient measures for the individual author but also, additionally, because it failed to make sufficient progress in the fulfilment of the right for all persons concerned. The examples in the previous subsection show that progressive realisation is suitable to address both of these dimensions, while the following examples illustrate that an insistence upon immediacy and unconditionality limits review to the individual-oriented aspect.

This contrast becomes particularly apparent in the jurisprudence of the CRPD-Com. It appears that the Committee, in civil and political rights issues, limits itself by assuming the non-applicability of Article 4 (2) of the CRPD and progressive realisation. Issues of general policy are largely ignored even though the applicants and all other rights holders could benefit from guidance in this respect. This is even more surprising in light of the fact that the Committee itself developed the standard of gradual implementation of accessibility,[113] which could be used to engage with the topic in wider policy circumstances. But in the CRPD-Com's Individual Communications, there is no attempt to give life to the principle of gradual implementation as introduced by General Comment No 2.[114] Instead, the experts prefer to frame civil and political positive duty cases in terms of a denial of reasonable accommodation. Again, it is not wrong to criticise the State party for failing to take action for the authors in these individual cases, but ignoring the larger policy context constitutes a missed opportunity.

This tendency is illustrated by what Maria Liisberg calls the 'fairly absolutist approach'[115] of the CRPD-Com towards accessibility in the cases of *Nyusti and Takács v Hungary* as well as two of its jury duty cases, namely *Beasley v Australia* and *Lockrey v Australia*. Although these cases, according to the CRPD-Com's interpretation of Article 9 of the CRPD, should concern the gradual implementation of accessibility to already existing objects,[116] the Committee finds violations of the authors' rights simply because there was no accessibility in their particular case.[117] The Committee applies only the individual-oriented perspective of reasonable accommodation, whereas it could

[113] See further 4.2.1.2.

[114] Lawson, 'Article 9', 260–61, 271–72.

[115] MV Liisberg, 'Accessibility of Services and Discrimination: Concentricity, Consequence, and the Concept of Anticipatory Reasonable Adjustment' (2015) 15 *International Journal of Discrimination and the Law* 123, 129.

[116] *cf* 4.2.1.2.

[117] CRPD-Com, *Beasley v Australia*, para 8.6; CRPD-Com, *Lockrey v Australia*, para 8.6.

also have added scrutiny regarding the gradual realisation of accessibility as a group-oriented right.

In *Nyusti and Takács v Hungary*, two authors complain about the inaccessibility of ATMs for persons with visual impairments. The CRPD-Com focuses on the authors' claim under Article 9 of the CRPD, asking the question 'whether the State party has taken appropriate measures to ensure the accessibility of the banking card services provided by the entire network of ATMs operated by OTP for persons with visual impairments'.[118] According to the CRPD-Com's interpretation of Article 9 of the CRPD, this case should concern a gradually realisable duty to provide accessibility to existing objects, since the ATMs existed before the treaty came into force.[119] At first, it seems that the Committee plans to engage with the appropriateness of measures taken by the Hungarian State. The experts acknowledge 'the gradual achievability of such comprehensive accessibility due to costs involved' and the efforts made by the government, which include promises to retrofit the ATMs as well as concrete government recommendations regarding accessibility of financial services.[120]

While the decision could be read to contain an implicit finding that Hungary's steps were not sufficient to fulfil a standard of gradual realisation,[121] the experts undertake no explicit evaluation of the appropriateness of these steps and thus provide the State party with no guidance regarding general policy. Even though the experts claim to have given 'due regard to the measures',[122] there is no analysis in the decision as to why they were insufficient. Instead, they hold that 'none of these measures *have ensured* the accessibility to the banking card services provided by the ATMs operated by OTP for the authors or other persons in a similar situation' (emphasis added), thus finding a violation of the right to accessibility.[123] The experts convincingly argue that Hungary had no excuse for denying reasonable accommodation in this specific case but miss the chance to *additionally* engage with the requirement of more general measures of accessibility for visually impaired persons.[124]

In the CRPD-Com's jury duty cases, the Committee likewise focuses on an individual absence of accessibility and ignore the larger context of accessibility policy.[125] When engaging with the alleged violation of the right to accessibility under Article 9 of the CRPD, the experts treat this right as immediate and unconditional. While the State party submits that it 'devotes significant efforts

[118] CRPD-Com, *Nyusti and Takács v Hungary* [Adoption of Views] (16 April 2013) CRPD/C/9/D/1/2010, para 9.2.
[119] See Lawson, 'Article 9', 272.
[120] CRPD-Com, *Nyusti and Takács v Hungary*, para 9.5.
[121] See Lawson, 'Accessibility Obligations in the CRPD', 386.
[122] CRPD-Com, *Nyusti and Takács v Hungary*, para 9.6.
[123] ibid.
[124] See ibid.
[125] For more detail on these cases, see 5.2.2.

and resources to ensuring that persons with disabilities are able to enjoy all human rights fully on an equal basis with others', the experts counter that 'the obligation to implement accessibility is unconditional' and that 'the denial of access should be considered to constitute a discriminatory act'.[126] Consequently, by failing to take the necessary measures in the present cases, 'the State party did not take the appropriate measures to enable the author to perform jury duty', thereby violating the authors' rights under Article 9 of the CRPD and other provisions.[127] Not only does this approach lead to contradictions in the Committee's own systematisation of obligations,[128] the experts also miss out on engaging with Australia's general policy of including persons with disabilities in the justice system. Even though Australia sets out an argument regarding its 10-year plan to produce inclusion,[129] there is no scrutiny by the experts as to whether this constitutes a sufficient effort in light of the duty to gradually realise accessibility.

A similar approach was chosen by the CRPD-Com in *Given v Australia*, where the author complains about the inaccessibility of voting options to persons with physical disabilities. In this case, the State party provides extensive arguments as to its general legislative and administrative framework for disabled persons in the voting system.[130] However, the Committee sweeps aside the State party's reference to gradual implementation and focuses on the fact that the author, in this individual case, was not provided with sufficient support. The Committee finds that the State party did not provide information that would 'justify the claim that the use of such an electronic voting option would have constituted a disproportionate burden … for the author *and for all persons requiring such accommodation*' (emphasis added).[131] Perhaps the Committee was aware of the fact that the underlying question was whether the State party had done enough in general. Closer scrutiny of Australia's policy, however, is missing and could have added valuable information as to the State party's general level of fulfilment regarding accessibility in the context of political rights.

[126] CRPD-Com, *Beasley v Australia*, para 8.6; CRPD-Com, *Lockrey v Australia*, para 8.6.

[127] CRPD-Com, *Beasley v Australia*, para 8.6; CRPD-Com, *Lockrey v Australia*, para 8.6.

[128] The Committee de facto applies the individual perspective of reasonable accommodation without (explicitly) testing for a disproportionate or undue burden. The resulting legal question ('was it in violation of the Convention to deny certain positive measures?') is the same question asked in the context of reasonable accommodation. This leads to the paradoxical result that the concrete lack of access will only be in violation of Article 5 (3) of the CRPD if the existence of a disproportionate or undue burden is rejected, but will always be in violation of Article 9 (and Article 5 (2)) of the CRPD since, according to the Committee, this obligation is 'unconditional'. It is contradictory to assess the proportionality of measures in the context of reasonable accommodation while ignoring resource considerations completely when asking the same question in the context of other rights. Reasonable accommodation would be superfluous if the same test is conducted in the context of other rights but without the limit of a disproportionate or undue burden.

[129] See Australia's own arguments regarding this policy, CRPD-Com, *Beasley v Australia*, para 4.1; CRPD-Com, *Lockrey v Australia*, para 4.1.

[130] See further 5.2.3.

[131] CRPD-Com, *Given v Australia*, para 8.9.

8.3.3.2. Preventing an Unjustified Hierarchy

It has been argued in detail in the preceding subsections that applying an umbrella concept of realisation to all rights does not reduce but increase human rights protection. A connected argument is that giving up the differentiation between immediate and progressive rights will also benefit socio-economic rights because the traditional approach creates an artificial hierarchy between both categories and therefore devalues socio-economic rights.[132] Alston also acknowledges this fact, stating that this artificial hierarchy is 'fundamentally incompatible with international human rights law'.[133]

Prioritising civil and political rights by calling them 'unlimited' contradicts the idea of the indivisibility and interdependence of rights and hurts the overall objective of the human rights project.[134] This is so because States parties need to make decisions regarding the allocation of resources when faced with a number of positive obligations. If, however, civil and political rights obligations are immediate and not subject to available resources, while socio-economic rights must be fulfilled progressively and to the maximum of available resources, logic would dictate that States parties must always prioritise the implementation of civil and political rights.[135] Similar arguments were also extended concerning the inclusion of a provision analogous to Article 8 (4) of the ICESCR-OP during the drafting of the CRC-OP3 by experts and NGOs.[136]

8.3.3.3. Fostering State Acceptance by Applying a Realistic Standard

Accepting the existence of progressive elements in all rights will also likely increase the legitimacy of the UN human rights treaties amongst States which are already party to the Covenants and Conventions, and States which are considering ratification. This argument is closely connected to the principle that impossible obligations cannot exist. It is reasonable to assume that States will be more hesitant to join a treaty regime which puts on them immediate and unconditional positive obligations which are, in reality, impossible to fulfil all at once. Because if they do so, they will risk being accused of continuous rights violations. Accordingly, making human rights obligations more realistic and

[132] See de Beco, 'The Indivisibility of Human Rights', 158 and Flóvenz, 'The Implementation of the UN Convention', 262, who correctly identify this hierarchy to be a remnant of the historical division between positive and negative rights.

[133] P Alston, 'Phantom Rights: The Systemic Marginalization of Economic and Social Rights' (Open Global Rights, 4 August 2016), www.openglobalrights.org/phantom-rights-systemic-marginalization-of-economic-and-social-rights/.

[134] See also Brems, 'Minimum and Maximum Perspectives', 366; see also, regarding the CAT, M Nowak and E McArthur, *The United Nations Convention Against Torture: A Commentary* (Oxford, Oxford University Press, 2008) 116.

[135] Brems, 'Minimum and Maximum Perspectives', 366.

[136] UNHRC, 'Report of the Open-ended Working Group on an Optional Protocol to the Convention on the Rights of the Child to Provide a Communications Procedure on its 2nd Session' (24 May 2011) A/HRC/17/36, para 74.

approachable will reduce the risk of States parties evading them altogether.[137] This is particularly true for the instruments focused on non-discrimination and equality such as the CEDAW and ICERD.

This aspect was implicitly recognised during the drafting of the ICCPR when delegates argued that demanding complete compliance with the Covenant would delay accession to the treaty until domestic legislation has been adapted.[138] Accepting the progressive nature of extensive positive duties, resulting from, for example, the right to life will likely encourage States parties to accede to the ICCPR and other treaties containing civil and political rights.[139] This logic also applies to the rights compliance of those States already party to the treaties. As will be seen later in this part, States parties clearly envision their obligations to refer to realistic evolving policies when positive human rights dimensions are concerned.[140]

A similar argument can be made with a view to legal certainty. Further to the impossibility of immediately realising all positive obligations, uncertainties regarding the categorisation of socio-economic and civil and political rights also jeopardise State acceptance. As has been argued above, attaching a legal consequence to an uncertain differentiation between categories of rights clashes with the principle of legal certainty.[141] However, norm determinacy and legal certainty are important factors of legitimacy.[142] It can be suspected that States parties are less accepting of a system of human rights obligations when the determination of their pace of realisation is arbitrary and unpredictable.

8.4. SUBSEQUENT AGREEMENTS AND SUBSEQUENT PRACTICE, ARTICLE 31 (3) (a), (b) OF THE VCLT

Pursuant to Article 31 (3) (a) and (b) of the VCLT, 'any subsequent agreement between the parties regarding the interpretation of the treaty or the application of its provisions' and 'any subsequent practice in the application of the treaty which establishes the agreement of the parties regarding its interpretation' shall be taken into account in addition to the context when interpreting the treaty. This section will focus on subsequent practice under Article 31 (3) (b) of the VCLT. While subsequent agreements might be interesting when discussing the aspect of positive obligations under civil and political rights, there is no indication that there are any relevant instruments concerning the specific aspect of progressive realisation. The question remains the same: does subsequent practice support an understanding of civil and political rights which includes

[137] See Brems, 'Minimum and Maximum Perspectives', 367.
[138] See UNCHR, 'Summary Record of the 125th Meeting' (13 June 1949) E/CN.4/SR.125, 3–4.
[139] See Jhabvala, 'The Practice of the HRC', 99.
[140] See further 8.4.3.
[141] See further 8.2.1.
[142] See TM Franck, *The Power of Legitimacy Among Nations* (Oxford, Oxford University Press, 1990) 50.

progressive elements, or does it require an interpretation of those rights as strictly immediate?

Regarding subsequent practice, there are several conceivable sources of interpretative guidance. Firstly, there is 'primary' practice by States parties which supports the notion of progressive realisation of civil and political rights. 'Primary' in this context means that the conduct is independent of any Committee jurisprudence (8.4.1). Secondly, it is sometimes argued that Committee practice itself can constitute subsequent practice in the sense of the VCLT. There are good reasons to reject this approach, however, and to consider Committee practice only as supplementary means of interpretation under Article 32 of the VCLT (8.4.2). The Committees' pronouncements may, however, give rise to subsequent practice of States parties, particularly in the drafting process of General Comments. States parties' feedback during these discussions provides evidence for their endorsement of progressive realisation as a uniform standard of obligations (8.4.3).

8.4.1. 'Primary' State Practice

Traditionally, treaty interpretation according to Article 31 (3) (b) of the VCLT entails an engagement with States parties' domestic legislative, administrative, judicial and other practice. It would theoretically be possible to inspect these areas of practice to determine whether States parties apply a standard to civil and political rights which includes progressive obligations.[143] However, a detailed analysis in this regard would be beyond the scope of this book.[144] A brief reference to the findings of other commentators will suffice at this point. Alston and Quinn have determined that States parties in fact apply a standard of progressive realisation to the rights in the ICCPR which is implicitly accepted by the HRC.[145] According to Jhabvala, State parties' reports have shown that the implementation of positive aspects of rights (beyond legislative action) under the ICCPR was not and is not being achieved immediately.[146] According to former British representative in the HRC, Sir Vincent Evans, it has become 'abundantly clear from reports submitted by States parties, as also from oral presentations', that the full implementation of the Covenant would 'most certainly depend on the material resources available'.[147]

[143] Although such an undertaking would be complicated by the fact that there are many inconsistencies in terminology.

[144] Furthermore, States parties' reactions to Committee practice, particularly to their General Comments, are more useful to determine their position regarding the Committees' conceptions of immediate and progressive realisation which is why these sources will be explored later on in this analysis, see 8.4.3.

[145] Alston and Quinn 'Obligations under the ICESCR', 173.

[146] Jhabvala, 'Domestic Implementation', 471–72.

[147] HRC, 'Summary Record of the Meeting Held on 27 July 1982' (27 July 1982) CCPR/C/SR.378/Add.1, para 1.

8.4.2. The Relevance of Committee Pronouncements

While the legal relevance of Committee findings is hotly debated,[148] there is general agreement amongst commentators, States parties, and international judicial institutions that Committee pronouncements must carry *some* legal effect. Often, the jurisprudence of the Committees is simply described as 'authoritative' without going into detail regarding its legal relevance in terms of the VCLT.[149] This approach was also taken by the ICJ in relation to the HRC in *Ahmadou Sadio Diallo (Republic of Guinea v Democratic Republic of the Congo)*. Here, the Court declares that

> [a]lthough the Court is in no way obliged, in the exercise of its judicial functions, to model its own interpretation of the Covenant on that of the Committee, it believes that it should ascribe great weight to the interpretation adopted by this independent body that was established specifically to supervise the application of that treaty.[150]

There are three main assertions in this statement which are relevant here. Firstly, the ICJ clarifies that Committee pronouncements are not formally legally binding. Secondly, it is asserted that, nevertheless, Committee jurisprudence should be accorded some authority without explicitly stating the nature of this authority. Thirdly, it appears that the ICJ bases this conclusion on the fact that the HRC is an 'independent body' which has been specifically established by the States parties to supervise the application of the ICCPR. There are also other cases in which the ICJ relies on Committee pronouncements, again without clarifying which kind of legal relevance these sources have.[151]

It is sometimes claimed that, for the interpretation of the UN human rights treaties, Committee pronouncements assume the role of subsequent practice under Article 31 (3) (b) of the VCLT. Birgit Schlütter even declares that the Committees' General Comments are a 'prime example' of subsequent practice in the sense of the VCLT.[152] This approach rests on the fact that Article 31 (3) (b)

[148] See, generally, R van Alebeek and A Nollkaemper, 'The Legal Status of Decisions by Human Rights Treaty Bodies in International Law' in H Keller and G Ulfstein (eds), *UN Human Rights Treaty Bodies: Law and Legitimacy* (Cambridge, Cambridge University Press, 2012); for a good summary see ILC, 'Fourth Report on Subsequent Agreements and Subsequent Practice in Relation to the Interpretation of Treaties by Georg Nolte, Special Rapporteur' (7 March 2016) A/CN.4/694; see also G Ulfstein, 'Treaty Bodies and Regimes' in DB Hollis (ed), *The Oxford Guide to Treaties*, 2nd edn (Oxford, Oxford University Press, 2020) 425–26 with further references.

[149] This was also noted by van Alebeek and Nollkaemper, 'The Legal Status', 408.

[150] ICJ, *Ahmadou Sadio Diallo (Republic of Guinea v Democratic Republic of the Congo)* (Merits, Judgment) [2010] ICJ Rep 639, para 66.

[151] See ICJ, *Application of the International Convention on the Elimination of All Forms of Racial Discrimination (Qatar v United Arab Emirates)* (Preliminary Objections, Judgment) [2021] ICJ Rep 71, para 77; ICJ, *Questions relating to the Obligation to Prosecute or Extradite (Belgium v Senegal)* (Merits, Judgment) [2012] ICJ Rep 422, para 101; ICJ, *Legal Consequences of the Construction of a Wall in the Occupied Palestinian Territory* (Advisory Opinion) [2004] ICJ Rep 136, para 109; see also D Azaria, 'The Legal Significance of Expert Treaty Bodies Pronouncements for the Purpose of the Interpretation of Treaties' (2020) 22 *International Community Law Review* 33.

[152] Schlütter, 'Human Rights Interpretation', 289.

of the VCLT is silent on whose practice is relevant as long as it establishes the agreement of the States parties.[153] Some arguments also refer to the special nature of human rights treaties, arguing that it would be self-defeating to rely on State conduct to determine the normative content of human rights while this conduct, by nature, always falls short of the ideals that must be considered to be enshrined in the relevant norms.[154] A related argument is that the national institutions of States parties (which are the traditional source of subsequent practice) have a vested interest to interpret human rights obligations restrictively in order to gain flexibility for domestic policy decisions.[155] Furthermore, it is sometimes held that the practice of the Committees constitutes a 'devolved or delegated form of subsequent practice' which can be traced back to the intentional creation of the human rights bodies by the States parties via the Covenants/Conventions and their optional protocols.[156]

However, the UN human rights treaties themselves establish that Committee output is not formally legally binding.[157] Granting Committee practice the normative weight of subsequent practice under Article 31 (3) (b) of the VCLT would mean that the decisions become legally binding through the backdoor, which would conflict with this common assessment.[158] Furthermore, this approach would also ignore the fact that Article 31 (3) (b) of the VCLT demands the agreement of States parties. The Committees are expert bodies, with the experts acting in their 'personal capacity' instead of being representatives of States parties.[159] The output of those treaty bodies is not generally attributable to a State party and, therefore, does not constitute a form of subsequent practice because it cannot establish the agreement of States parties.[160] Accordingly, the role of States parties in creating subsequent practice is not handed off to the Committees, and some more direct connection to their agreement must be established.[161]

These concerns cannot be alleviated by speaking of a combination of Committee practice and State parties' agreement, as, for example, Schlütter does.[162] It is true that the *travaux préparatoires* of the VCLT imply that tacit agreement of States parties suffices in order to establish agreement in the sense of Article 31 (3) (b) of the VCLT.[163] If, however, inaction by States parties is

[153] See McGrogan, 'Interpretation of Human Rights Treaties', 353.
[154] ibid, 363.
[155] See Mechlem, 'Treaty Bodies', 919–20.
[156] McGrogan, 'Interpretation of Human Rights Treaties', 353.
[157] See ILC, 'Report on Subsequent Agreements and Subsequent Practice', para 15 with further references; ILA, 'Final Report on the Impact of Findings of the United Nations Human Rights Treaty Bodies', para 15, www.ila-hq.org/en_GB/documents/conference-report-berlin-2004-9.
[158] Van Alebeek and Nollkaemper, 'The Legal Status', 409.
[159] See, eg, Article 28 (3) of the ICCPR.
[160] See ILC, 'Report on Subsequent Agreements and Subsequent Practice', para 42.
[161] See Mechlem, 'Treaty Bodies', 920.
[162] See Schlütter, 'Human Rights Interpretation', 289–92.
[163] See M Scheinin, 'Impact on the Law of Treaties' in MT Kamminga and M Scheinin (eds), *The Impact of Human Rights Law on General International Law* (Oxford, Oxford University

sufficient in this context, then Committee pronouncements by themselves carry normative weight which, again, circumvents the agreed-upon fact that they are not legally binding.

It must also be noted that the HRC attempted to assert its own role as an originator of subsequent practice in its draft General Comment No 33 but backtracked after significant pushback from a number of States parties.[164] Originally, this document argued that the Committees' jurisprudence may serve as subsequent practice in the sense of the VCLT.[165] Many States parties disagreed with this idea and explicitly rejected the notion that General Comments would carry such legal authority. Particularly critical in this regard has been the United States. The US noted that it 'strongly disagrees with this extraordinary assertion', firstly arguing that neither Articles 31 and 32 of the VCLT nor the underlying rules of customary international law can include human rights bodies' jurisprudence as subsequent practice because the experts serve in their personal capacity.[166] Many other States parties were also critical of this notion, particularly concerning the idea that Committee jurisprudence in itself can be subsequent practice.[167]

Furthermore, most States parties agreed that their silent acquiescence cannot be considered subsequent practice or agreement thereto, thus rejecting the idea that a combination of Committee pronouncements and non-opposition of States parties may serve as subsequent practice.[168] Similar statements can be found in relation to the HRC's draft General Comment No 36,[169] as well as the CRC-Com's draft General Comment No 26.[170]

Accordingly, the more convincing conclusion is that the Committees' jurisprudence may only 'reflect or give rise to a subsequent agreement or a

Press, 2009) 33; Dörr and Schmalenbach, *VCLT*, 599–602; see also Villiger, *Commentary on the VCLT*, 432 with further references.

164 See Azaria, 'Expert Treaty Bodies Pronouncements', 35–36.

165 HRC, 'Draft General Comment No 33: The Obligations of States Parties under the Optional Protocol to the International Covenant on Civil and Political Rights, 2nd Version' (25 August 2008) CCPR/C/GC/33/CRP.3, paras 12–21.

166 Input statement by the USA for HRC draft General Comment No 33, 6. All input statements for this draft General Comment are available at www.ohchr.org/en/calls-for-input/general-comment-no-33-obligations-states-parties-under-optional-protocol.

167 See, for example, input statements by the UK for HRC draft General Comment No 33; input statement by Belgium for HRC draft General Comment No 33, 2–3; input statement by Japan for HRC draft General Comment No 33, para 10; all available at the URL cited in n 166.

168 See, eg, input statement by the USA for HRC draft General Comment No 33, 6; input statement by the UK for HRC draft General Comment No 33, 2–3; both available at the URL cited in n 166.

169 Input statement by the USA for HRC draft General Comment No 36, paras 4, 5; input statement by Canada for HRC draft General Comment No 36, paras 2, 3. All input statements for this draft General Comment are available at www.ohchr.org/en/calls-for-input/general-comment-no-36-article-6-right-life.

170 See, eg, input statement by Denmark for CRC-Com draft General Comment No 26, www.ohchr.org/sites/default/files/documents/hrbodies/crc/gcomments/gc26/2023/states/GC26-states-denmark-2023-03-01.doc: 'Where no specific comments are provided on issues discussed in the draft General Comment, this should not be interpreted as either agreement or disagreement with the substance of the draft General Comment.'

subsequent practice by the parties themselves' without being subsequent practice as such.[171] The Committee pronouncements themselves, however, may serve as supplementary means of interpretation under Article 32 of the VCLT.[172] If Committee practice cannot be subsequent practice in isolation and if silent acquiescence of the States parties does not suffice, then it is necessary to find explicit statements or actions by States parties in order to establish subsequent practice. Relevant statements often arise in the context of the feedback rounds for draft General Comments. Some examples are discussed in the following subsection.

8.4.3. State Practice in Response to Committee Pronouncements

The reactions of States parties to Committee pronouncements illustrate that they implicitly endorse a standard of realisation for civil and political rights which includes progressive obligations. This tendency is clear almost consistently across the State parties' feedback statements to the Committees' draft General Comments and Recommendations. It is appropriate to speak of subsequent State practice in the sense of Article 32 (3) (b) of the VCLT in this regard. States parties are primarily concerned about overburdening or even impossible positive obligations (8.4.3.1). Because of this concern, it is unsurprising that States consider civil and political rights obligations to be neither strictly immediate (8.4.3.2) nor independent from resource considerations (8.4.3.3).

8.4.3.1. Extensive Positive Obligations as the Central Concern of States Parties

When examining the States parties' statements, it becomes clear that they are primarily concerned about an overburdening extension of positive obligations. A particularly illustrative example can be found in the input statements received by the HRC during the drafting of General Comment No 36 on the Right to Life under Article 6 of the ICCPR. This General Comment sets out extensive positive obligations under the right to life but, at the same time, claims that these obligations are not unconditional.[173]

Regarding the draft General Comment prepared by the HRC, many statements criticise the experts' framing of the right to life in an 'overly broad' manner.[174] According to the Canadian statement, 'Canada disagrees with the

[171] ILC, 'Report on Subsequent Agreements and Subsequent Practice', para 43; see also, with further references, ILA, 'Final Report on the Impact of Findings of the United Nations Human Rights Treaty Bodies', para 21, available at the URL cited in n 157.

[172] ILC, 'Report on Subsequent Agreements and Subsequent Practice', paras 49–65.

[173] See further 5.5.1.

[174] Input statement by Australia for HRC draft General Comment No 36, para 4 (only 'arbitrary deprivation of life or a failure to protect the right to life by law'); see also input statement by

Committee's assertion that the right to life includes a right to a life with dignity to the extent that this could be read to encompass certain socio-economic entitlements'.[175] This statement further asserts that the HRC is not permitted to 'expand the scope of measures required by the Covenant to prevent violations of the right to life'.[176] The British government finds that the references to 'extreme poverty and homelessness' and measures of education are examples where the draft is too broad because it thereby intermingles quality of life considerations with the right to life under the ICCPR.[177] The Australian statement argues that General Comment No 36 in its draft form 'extend[s] the obligations of States Parties beyond the law of State responsibility', criticising, for example, the inclusion of obligations regarding the prevention of suicide or general conditions in society that may give rise to threats to life.[178]

Similar concerns were voiced regarding draft General Comment No 21 by the CRC-Com. This General Comment also provides an extensive scope for the right to life under Article 6 of the CRC, which was criticised by States parties. Australia, for example, was

> concerned that the Committee seeks to significantly expand the scope of this right in the draft General Comment by indicating that exposure to a wide range of life threatening circumstances, such as traffic deaths or deaths as a result of unsafe sexual practices, fall within the scope of Article 6(1).[179]

While the issue of positive obligations is not the subject of this inquiry, it is important to note that the disagreement in this context does not automatically render a positive reading by the Committees incompatible with Articles 31 et seq of the VCLT. Rather, due to the specific nature of human rights treaties, the disagreement of States parties and any subsequent practice derived therefrom cannot surpass readings which are clearly in line with object and purpose as well

Denmark for HRC draft General Comment No 36, 1: 'we do find that the drafting at times is too wide and the use of terms too general'; input statement by the UK for HRC draft General comment No 36, para 3: 'too general or too broad terms', see also ibid, para 22; all available at the URL cited in n 169.

[175] Input statement by Canada for HRC draft General Comment No 36, para 20; see also ibid, para 14; available at the URL cited in n 169.

[176] ibid, para 5.

[177] Input statement by the UK for HRC draft General Comment No 36, para 23, available at the URL cited in n 169.

[178] Input statement by Australia for HRC draft General Comment No 36, para 5, available at the URL cited in n 169.

[179] Input statement by Australia for CRC-Com draft General Comment No 21, para 6. Australia also references HRC General Comment No 36: 'the Committee seeks to support its proposed broadening of the obligations by referring to the Human Rights Committee's draft General Comment 36 on the right to life. This draft General Comment has been the subject of much discussion by the Committee with National Human Rights Institutions, civil society and academia but has remained unfinalised over a number of years.' All input statements for CRC-Com draft General Comment No 21 are available at www.ohchr.org/en/documents/general-comments-and-recommendations/general-comment-no-21-2017-children-street.

as the ordinary meaning of the treaty.[180] While the precise extent of positive obligations, of course, is subject to reasonable debate, the triad of respect, protect, fulfil and its applicability to all rights appears to be commonly accepted.[181] In any event, this issue must be (and already has been) subject to separate inquiries.

8.4.3.2. Agreement Regarding Progressiveness

If States parties were concerned about overly broad obligations under civil and political rights provisions, the implicit acceptance of the progressiveness of those obligations appears to be in line with what States parties demand: a realistic standard not subjecting States parties to an undue burden. The statements of States parties in several input procedures show that there is indeed implicit support for progressive elements in civil and political rights.

One such example is the input statement from Denmark concerning CRPD-Com General Comment No 7 on the Participation of Persons with Disabilities under Articles 4 (3) and 33 (3) of the CRPD. This Comment, according to the CRPD-Com, concerns the civil and political right of participation.[182] Denmark's statement reiterates that, according to the draft Comment, '[t]he civil and political rights' obligations of States parties are immediately applicable' and goes on to declare that, '[g]iven the exact scope and content of this sentence may be subject to some doubt, Denmark recommends that the sentence is removed, thereby leaving the paragraph to focus on participation and consultation'.[183]

Further relevant statements were made during the feedback round for draft General Comment No 5 on the Right to Independent Living under Article 19 of the CRPD. In the final form of this Comment, the CRPD-Com declares that 'Article 19 (a), the right to choose one's residence and where, how and with whom to live, is immediately applicable as it is a civil and political right'.[184] In substance, however, the Committee establishes a progressive mode of implementation.[185] Germany disagrees with the professed immediacy and, therefore, agrees with the implicit progressiveness of this obligation: 'Germany does not share the view that the right to choose one's residence and to decide freely, where, how and with whom to live, is immediately applicable.'[186]

[180] See also McGrogan, 'Interpretation of Human Rights Treaties', 374.
[181] See further 1.3.1.
[182] CRPD-Com, 'General Comment No 7', para 28.
[183] Input statement by Denmark for CRPD-Com draft General Comment No 7. All input statements for this draft General Comment are available at www.ohchr.org/en/documents/general-comments-and-recommendations/general-comment-no7-article-43-and-333-participation.
[184] CRPD-Com, 'General Comment No 5', para 39.
[185] See further 4.2.4.
[186] Input statement by Germany for CRPD-Com draft General Comment No 5, 4. All input statements for this draft General Comment are available at www.ohchr.org/en/documents/general-comments-and-recommendations/general-comment-no5-article-19-right-live.

Clearly, Germany wants to say that the obligation of result regarding the complete realisation of independent living is not immediately realisable. This becomes more apparent later on when the text turns to the obligation of deinstitutionalisation. Regarding the part of the draft General Comment which demands that the 'misallocation' of funds to institutional housing must be ended by immediate steps, Germany declares the following:

> As a States Party Germany does not share this view as this would mean that all [institutional homes] would have to be closed. Against the background of the long tradition of institutions for persons with disabilities and the efforts undertaken by the [the German government], the situation can only change gradually. It is not possible to immediately replace all existing institutions for persons with disabilities as the loss for the persons with disabilities affected by such a decision would be experienced as very dramatic and would also lead to irreparable collateral damages.[187]

Colombia also clearly understands Article 19 of the CRPD as a whole to entail an obligation of a progressive nature. Colombia's statement declares that independent living in the sense of Article 19 of the CRPD requires a change of attitudes and cultural paradigms which takes time and cannot be produced at an instant by laws or political decisions.[188] Later on, the text uses the term 'realización progresiva' for the whole of Article 19 of the CRPD, which can be translated to progressive realisation.[189] Colombia considers the essence of Article 19 of the CRPD to be the development of equality. While the input statement recognises that equality requires immediate compliance and enforceability ('inmediato cumplimiento y exigibilidad'), it continues to declare that, due to the requirement of positive measures and diverging levels of development, this right must be realised progressively.[190]

States parties also provided statements during the drafting of the CRPD-Com's General Comment No 6 on Equality and Non-discrimination under Article 5 of the CRPD. It has been discussed above how the language in this General Comment implies a gradual nature of realisation even though the right to non-discrimination is considered to be civil and political and immediate.[191] The input documents reveal that States parties are, in fact, also taking a progressive approach to the realisation of de facto equality.[192] The Dutch input statement on this Comment explicitly supports such an interpretation. According to this document, '[t]he Netherlands is of the opinion

[187] ibid, 4–5.

[188] Input statement by Colombia for CRPD-Com draft General Comment No 5, 1, available at the URL cited in n 186.

[189] ibid, 2.

[190] ibid, 2–3.

[191] See further 4.2.2.

[192] See, for example, the input statements by Colombia, Spain, and Turkey for CRPD-Com draft General Comment No 6. All input statements for this General Comment are available at www.ohchr.org/en/documents/general-comments-and-recommendations/general-comment-no6-equality-and-non-discrimination.

that the majority of the provisions of the Convention … are of a programmatic nature'.[193] The statement continues to declare that '[i]n light of this, the Netherlands has chosen to gradually implement the Convention in the existing policies at the national level that aim at the inclusion of persons with a disability'.[194] In the same paragraph of their statement, the Dutch representatives even explicitly refer to the traditional civil and political right of participation in public and political life under Article 29 of the CRPD.[195] Colombia likewise declares that it is appropriate to continue efforts to move progressively towards a rights-based approach to the concept of disability.[196]

The Maltese statement makes a similar point when arguing for 'reasonable transitional periods, in which States Parties are to bring their legislation and policies in line with the UN CRPD'. The next paragraph then goes on to read:

> Thus, any claim of progressive realisation would only be imputable to necessary administrative mechanisms towards change, and not to a *voluntary* progressive realisation arbitrarily adopted by States Parties, or motivated by, ex. financial reasons, or arguments linked to changing social mores. (emphasis added)[197]

This statement clarifies that States parties shall be granted the 'necessary' time to bring their systems in line with the requirements of the Convention but shall not be allowed 'voluntary' delays based on financial or social grounds. This coincides with the notion of the CESCR that implementation may take time but that resource considerations do not justify inaction.

8.4.3.3. Agreement Regarding Relevance of Resource Considerations

It also becomes clear that States parties reject the immediacy of positive civil and political rights duties because of resource considerations, thereby implicitly supporting the concept of 'maximum of available resources'. This point is illustrated by the Dutch input statement received during the drafting of HRC General Comment No 36 which recommends including into the Comment references to the ECtHR's jurisprudence regarding the obligation of States parties to actively counteract threats to the right to life. According to the statement, 'this positive obligation only exists under certain, strict circumstances. Leaving out these criteria, conditions and limitations would render this obligation unworkable and unrealistic.'[198] The HRC followed this proposition by

[193] Input statement by the Netherlands for CRPD-Com draft General Comment No 6, para 2, available at the URL cited in n 192.

[194] ibid.

[195] ibid.

[196] Input statement by Colombia for CRPD-Com draft General Comment No 6, 4, available at the URL cited in n 192.

[197] Input statement by Malta for CRPD-Com draft General Comment No 6, 1, available at the URL cited in n 192.

[198] Input statement by the Netherlands for HRC draft General Comment No 36, para 5, available at the URL cited in n 169.

including a reference to ECtHR jurisprudence in the General Comment's final version, which introduced the notion of 'undue burdens' and therefore counteracts an absolute understanding of civil and political rights from a perspective of resources.[199]

Interestingly, the Dutch statement goes on to explicitly declare that 'the Netherlands also prefers deleting the suggested reference to progressive realization, as this fits more within the sphere of economic and social rights'.[200] However, it is important not to cling to the terminology in this context. This rejection of progressiveness must be seen in light of the statements mentioned above which clearly reject an absolutist reading of civil and political rights. The Dutch representatives also do not elaborate upon the concept of progressive realisation they reference. Instead, the statement continues to hold that '[i]t seems more logical to approach the right to life from the perspective of positive obligations of States in this respect'.[201] This sentence implies that the Dutch government bases its statement on the notion that progressive realisation and a 'perspective of positive obligations' are somehow mutually exclusive ('instead'). It appears that, like the Committees, the Dutch government only rejects a weak reading of progressive realisation which does not entail immediate obligations of conduct but only vague and 'aspirational' long-term goals. The representatives do so without realising that the acceptance of the limit of 'disproportionate or undue burdens' necessarily entails the acceptance of progressive elements.[202]

A request to recognise resource limitations was also extended by the UK input for CRPD-Com General Comment No 7 on the Participation of Persons with Disabilities under Articles 4 (3) and 33 (3) of the CRPD:

> The UK Government agrees with the importance of engaging civil society organisations in the periodic reporting process under the CRPD. We respectfully observe, however, that State resources are not unlimited. State budgets need to strike a balance between competing priorities each year, and State expenditure must ultimately be accountable to Parliament and to the taxpayer. The Committee may therefore wish to consider qualifying its view on funding by, for example, adding the words 'as appropriate' to (and deleting the words 'non-conditional' from) the relevant paragraphs.[203]

[199] See further 5.5.1.

[200] Input statement by the Netherlands for HRC draft General Comment No 36, para 21; the draft contained the phrase 'given their wide ranging implications some of the obligations relating to the general conditions necessary for full enjoyment of the right to life can only be realised progressively', as cited by Tobin and Peleg, 'Article 6', 203; Canada likewise mentions that 'the ICESCR imposes a different standard of implementation of States Parties' obligations, which is progressive realization, as described in article 2(1) of ICESCR', see input statement by Canada for HRC draft General Comment No 36, para 20; both available at the URL cited in n 169.

[201] Input statement by the Netherlands for HRC draft General Comment No 36, para 21, available at the URL cited in n 169.

[202] *cf* 2.5.

[203] Input statement by the UK for CRPD-Com draft General Comment No 7, available at the URL cited in n 183.

A similar discussion took place in the context of CRPD-Com General Comment No 6 on Equality and Non-discrimination, namely regarding the concept of reasonable accommodation. Even though reasonable accommodation applies to all aspects of the Convention, the Committee interprets it (and the 'disproportionate burden' limit) to introduce resource considerations to all rights no matter their category.[204] While the final version of the Comment clarifies that the cost of accommodations is not relevant for their reasonableness,[205] it is very clear regarding the fact that cost plays a role when determining the existence of an undue burden and, therefore, is relevant for reasonable accommodation as a whole.[206] States parties, in substance, agree with this idea, but locate resource considerations already in the concept of reasonableness. Finland proposed 'to remove the part in square brackets on the cost of the accommodation not playing a role in deciding whether the accommodation is reasonable'.[207] The same was proposed by Switzerland.[208]

Resources as a relevant factor are also mentioned in the feedback round to the same CRPD-Com General Comment regarding Article 12 (3) of the CRPD which lays down the positive dimension of the (civil and political) right of equal recognition before the law, setting out the positive obligation of States to provide the necessary support for the exercise of legal capacity. The Swiss input document also clarifies that the obligations under this provision must not be understood to be unlimited.[209] Switzerland voiced similar concerns regarding resources in its input statement during the drafting of CRC-Com General Comment No 21 on Children in Street Situations. Regarding the phrase 'States are urged to adopt holistic and long term strategies, with budget allocation', the Swiss statement criticised that such a requirement is demanding and difficult, particularly for countries with limited resources.[210]

8.5. CONCLUSION

External sources of treaty interpretation provide ample support for the introduction of progressive elements into civil and political rights. Legal certainty requires giving up the differentiation between immediately and progressively realisable categories, while the principle of *impossibilium nulla est obligatio*

[204] See further 5.2.
[205] CRPD-Com, 'General Comment No 6', para 25 (a).
[206] ibid, para 26 (e).
[207] Input statement by Finland for CRPD-Com draft General Comment No 6, 3, available at the URL cited in n 192.
[208] Input statement by Switzerland for CRPD-Com draft General Comment No 6, 2, available at the URL cited in n 192.
[209] ibid.
[210] Input statement by Switzerland for CRC-Com draft General Comment No 21, 1, available at the URL cited in n 179.

clearly demands that the uniform standard applicable to all rights must allow for temporal delay where complete realisation at an instance is materially impossible. A standard like progressive realisation which combines immediate and progressive elements also does not conflict with the object and purpose of human rights treaties because it does not weaken rights protection but instead strengthens the scrutiny of positive obligations. It has also become clear that the subsequent practice of States parties supports the inclusion of progressive elements and the acceptance of resource dependency also on the side of civil and political rights. This concludes the interpretation according to the primary sources of interpretation under Article 31 of the VCLT. The next chapter will engage with supplementary means under Article 32 of the VCLT.

9

Supplementary Means and Result of Interpretation

9.1. INTRODUCTION

ACCORDING TO ARTICLE 32 of the VCLT, 'supplementary means of interpretation' may be utilised to either 'confirm the meaning resulting from the application of article 31' of the VCLT, or to establish a meaning when the interpretation on the basis of Article 31 of the VCLT 'leaves the meaning ambiguous or obscure' or 'leads to a result which is manifestly absurd or unreasonable'. Supplementary means under this provision include, but are not limited to,[1] 'the preparatory work of the treaty and the circumstances of its conclusion', the former commonly being referred to as *travaux préparatoires*. Arguments for the 'immediate and unlimited' nature of civil and political rights are sometimes made on the basis of the *travaux préparatoires*.[2]

This chapter will argue that supplementary means of interpretation are generally admissible in this context (9.2) and that the *travaux préparatoires* do not support the idea that civil and political rights are immediate in the strict sense of the word (9.3). Other supplementary means of interpretation further suggest that civil and political rights must include progressive elements (9.4). Lastly, a synopsis of the results will show that contextual ambiguities found in chapter 7 are not decisive in light of the overwhelming evidence gathered by the other methods of interpretation and that, consequently, the convergence of standards is reconcilable with the treaties (9.5). A conclusion will be drawn in the last section (9.6).

9.2. THE ADMISSIBILITY OF UTILISING SUPPLEMENTARY MEANS OF INTERPRETATION

Article 32 of the VCLT, like the second and third paragraphs of Article 31 of the VCLT, refers to materials extrinsic to the treaty text but accords them

[1] Villiger, *Commentary on the VCLT*, 445.
[2] See, eg, Schachter, 'The Obligation to Implement'.

(at least at a first glance)[3] only secondary relevance by utilising the term 'supplementary' and by setting out a certain frame of application of these means of interpretation.[4] Furthermore, unlike the general rule under Article 31 of the VCLT, the utilisation of interpretative measures under Article 32 of the VCLT is optional ('[r]ecourse may be had').[5]

It follows from the text of Article 32 of the VCLT that recourse to supplementary means of interpretation is allowed only under certain circumstances. This design element of the VCLT is a reflection of the textual approach and is supported by a well-placed hesitance towards relying on, first and foremost, the *travaux préparatoires*.[6] The provision sets out three scenarios in which supplementary means may play a role: the confirmation of the result found by applying Article 31 of the VCLT or the determination of a different meaning either when the inquiry under Article 31 of the VCLT leaves an 'ambiguous or obscure' result or when this result is 'manifestly absurd or unreasonable'. However, these three scenarios are present in most, if not all, cases. Inspecting supplementary materials in itself is an open-ended exercise. If there is no confirmation to be gained through the supplementary materials, the interpreter may be inspired to find an ambiguity or contradiction in the original meaning which they did not notice before. Consequently, the confirmatory approach transforms into the determination of a different meaning.[7] This means that, in substance, the interpretation pursuant to Article 32 of the VCLT becomes an integral part of the general rule of interpretation and operates on a similar level.[8]

There are several ways in which the supplementary means of interpretation can be utilised in supporting the result reached in the two previous chapters. Firstly, the *travaux préparatoires* reveal that the drafting parties envisioned a very similar timeframe of realisation for civil and political rights as for socio-economic rights. Thus, this supplementary method of interpretation 'confirms' the interpretation of the Committees, namely the convergence of standards. At the same time, the result that all positive obligations are immediate in the strict sense of the word is 'manifestly absurd' and 'unreasonable' because it demands impossible things of States parties.[9] Therefore, the *travaux préparatoires* may also be invoked in order to 'determine the [correct] meaning' which, according

[3] See also Gardiner, *Treaty Interpretation*, 347–48.

[4] See Dörr and Schmalenbach, *VCLT*, 617.

[5] See ICJ, *Application of the International Convention on the Elimination of All Forms of Racial Discrimination (Georgia v Russian Federation)* (Preliminary Objections, Judgment) [2011] ICJ Rep 70, para 142.

[6] Dörr and Schmalenbach, *VCLT*, 618; for further details see 9.3.

[7] See Gardiner, *Treaty Interpretation*, 355.

[8] Dörr and Schmalenbach, *VCLT*, 629; see also Villiger, *Commentary on the VCLT*, 447.

[9] According to Egon Schwelb, '[i]t is certainly neither absurd or unreasonable to hold that a treaty creates immediately applicable obligations', Schwelb, 'The Nature of the Obligations', 313. However, the immediacy proposed by Schwelb also allows a certain degree of flexibility; he does not propose an immediate realisation of all positive aspects of rights in the strict sense of the word.

to the argument made here, is a notion of progressiveness for all rights. One could also argue that the *argumentum a contrario* creates some doubt regarding the issue of immediacy or progressiveness, leading to an 'ambiguous or obscure' meaning in the sense of Article 32 (a) of the VCLT. This opens the door for a utilisation of the *travaux préparatoires* in order to determine the 'correct' reading which, as said before, is a uniform standard of realisation which also includes progressive obligations.

9.3. PREPARATORY WORK AND CIRCUMSTANCES OF TREATY CONCLUSION, ARTICLE 32 OF THE VCLT

Interpreting a treaty on the basis of the *travaux préparatoires* is an exercise which must be approached with appropriate carefulness. There are good reasons to be sceptical of the value these materials can have for interpretation. The search for a subjective intent of the States parties has rightfully been compared to the 'search for the pot of gold at the end of a rainbow'.[10] More often than not, the preparatory materials are a combination of overlapping and differing opinions and thus do not allow the deduction of a singular will of the drafters.[11] There may also be contradictory statements by a single State party in different documents and/or at different times.[12] The same is true for the *travaux préparatoires* of the human rights treaties examined here.

It is not the purpose of this section to determine the one common conception of the drafting parties regarding the pace of realisation. Instead, it will be shown that, while there was reasonable disagreement about the precise nature of obligations, no representative argued for immediacy of positive obligations in the strict sense of the word. All parties agreed that there must be some degree of flexibility even for civil and political rights.

The best illustration of this claim can be found in the *travaux préparatoires* for the ICESCR and ICCPR (9.3.1). During the drafting of these treaties, the issue of immediate and progressive realisation was discussed at length. Interesting aspects can also be found in the preparatory materials for the ICERD (9.3.2), CEDAW (9.3.3), CRC (9.3.4.) and CRPD (9.3.5). However, it appears that during the drafting of these treaties, the issue of progressive or immediate realisation was not discussed to any great extent. This might be so because, after the adoption of the ICCPR and ICESCR, the different nature of socio-economic and civil and political rights had been accepted as a given rule of international law.

[10] Sinclair, *The VCLT*, 130.

[11] See Y Le Bouthillier, 'Article 32' in O Corten and P Klein (eds), *The Vienna Conventions on the Law of Treaties: A Commentary* (Oxford, Oxford University Press, 2011) 857.

[12] Villiger, *Commentary on the VCLT*, 446.

9.3.1. ICESCR and ICCPR

After the bifurcation decision,[13] the ICCPR and ICESCR were drafted together by the Drafting Committee, a sub-organ of the Commission on Human Rights, and later discussed together in the Third Committee of the UN General Assembly.[14] Hence, the general obligation provisions of both Covenants were frequently compared side to side, and the preparatory materials give some insight into the opinions of the drafting parties as to the legal difference between the two categories of rights.

There are instances in the *travaux préparatoires* where drafting parties declare socio-economic and civil and political rights to be inherently different. The summary reports of the discussions in the Third Committee relay the statements of UK representative Goodhard as follows:

> His Government had always believed that the rights set forth in the two draft Covenants respectively were fundamentally different in nature: economic, social and cultural rights were capable of almost indefinite expansion and were therefore suitable for progressive implementation, whereas civil and political rights were capable of precise formulation and, generally speaking, of immediate implementation.[15]

A similar position was taken by the French representative Bouquin during an earlier meeting of the Third Committee.[16] However, there were also representatives who disagreed with this strict legal divide. Israeli representative Najar, during an earlier Third Committee meeting, doubted the traditional perception of civil and political rights as immediately realisable because 'the effective implementation of those rights called for a highly developed judiciary organization, which could not be achieved at short notice'.[17] Accordingly, an Israeli memorandum instead suggested differentiating between '[r]ights which are capable of effectively becoming a reality through immediate legislative or administrative action' and '[r]ights which ... cannot effectively come into existence in law until after the execution of programmes ... which may vary in duration and feasibility'.[18]

[13] See further 1.2.1.

[14] For a brief and concise summary, see MJ Bossuyt, *Guide to the 'travaux préparatoires' of the International Covenant on Civil and Political Rights* (Leiden, Martinus Nijhoff Publishers, 1987) XIX–XX.

[15] UNGA Third Committee, 'Summary Record of the 1257th Meeting' (8 November 1963) A/C.3/SR.1257, para 6; see also the remarks of his colleague Glover during an earlier meeting of the Third Committee: 'It was a mistake to introduce the idea of progressive application into an article concerning civil and political rights. Those rights were capable of precise formulation and immediate application', UNGA Third Committee, 'Summary Record of the 1181st meeting' (13 November 1962) A/C.3/SR.1181, para 2.

[16] UNGA Third Committee, 'Summary Record of the 1181st Meeting', para 23.

[17] UNGA Third Committee, 'Summary Record of the 410th Meeting' (29 January 1952) A/C.3/SR.410, para 54.

[18] UNGA Third Committee, 'Draft International Declaration of Human Rights and Measures of Implementation: Memorandum Presented by Israel' (8 January 1952) A/C.3/565, para 9.

While such a categorisation was not accommodated in the Covenant, statements of the other drafting parties show that, in substance, such a notion was also underlying their arguments. Just as the Israeli proposal did explicitly, most other drafting parties implicitly recognised that civil and political rights also require a certain flexibility regarding those aspects which simply are not, in the words of the Israeli proposal, 'capable of effectively becoming a reality through immediate legislative or administrative action'.[19] In other words, the term 'immediate', again, is not interpreted to mean complete realisation all at once. At the same time, parties arguing for the immediacy of rights rejected the applicability of only a very weak reading of progressive realisation in the realm of the ICCPR.

Evidence for these claims will be provided in the following subsection (9.3.1.1) Additionally, the parties also did not envision progressive realisation as set out for socio-economic rights to be a standard of indefinite postponement (9.3.1.2). Accordingly, both standards converge: if 'immediate' realisation is not really immediate but allows a 'certain flexibility', and progressive realisation also entails the obligation to immediately take action, then the concepts meet each other in the middle without the drafters realising. Here, too, misunderstandings about the term progressive realisation are the reason why this de facto uniform standard of realisation went unnoticed. As a last point regarding the ICESCR and ICCPR, it will be argued that the perceived difference between socio-economic and civil and political rights arose because the drafting parties were still influenced by the perception that civil and political rights are at least less positive than socio-economic rights (9.3.1.3). In the end it becomes clear that both sets of rights are not perceived as categorically different, even though the drafters' rhetoric might evoke that impression.

9.3.1.1. Immediate is not Immediate (Certain Flexibility)

Article 2 (2) of the ICCPR,[20] the subject of the main debate about immediate and progressive realisation, set out the following provision:

> Where not already provided for by existing legislative or other measures, each State undertakes to take the necessary steps, in accordance with its constitutional processes and with the provisions of this Covenant, to adopt such legislative or other measures as may be necessary to give effect to the rights recognized in this Covenant.

The ordinary meaning of the phrase 'undertake[s] to take … steps' arguably leaves open the timeframe of realisation, as has been argued above.[21] Accordingly,

[19] ibid; see also the statements of Danish representative Sørensen, UNCHR, 'Summary Record of the 125th Meeting', 2–3.

[20] Articles mentioned in this section are those in the present text if not explicitly denoted as provisions of the draft texts.

[21] See further 7.3.1.

discussions regarding the immediacy of civil and political rights centred around this particular provision of the draft. The reporting procedure laid down in what is now Article 40 of the ICCPR was another common point of attachment for general discussions about the implementation of the Covenant. Usually, arguments centred around the notion of reporting on the 'progress' which must be subject to the reports and whether this wording implies a progressive mode of implementation.

If inspected closely, the statements of State representatives reveal that the drafting parties in substance agreed that there are positive aspects of civil and political rights which will take some time to realise. The Rapporteur of the Third Committee, when reporting to the General Assembly on the draft Covenants, noted the following: 'The Committee sincerely hopes that as States consolidate their progress, they will assume increasingly great obligations as they attain the levels necessary to permit full implementation of the provisions of the Covenant.'[22] This clearly implies a progressive and, more importantly, uniform standard of realisation for both Covenants.[23]

In reality, the discussion was not about the timeframe of realisation itself but rather about the way in which the need for a certain flexibility could be balanced with the concerns about indefinite postponement. In other words, the drafters implicitly agreed upon a standard of implementation analogous to the umbrella concept of progressive realisation, while not being in agreement about the way in which a purely narrow reading of progressiveness could be prevented. Generally speaking, there were three approaches to this issue, as was summarised by the report of the Third Committee on its 18th session to the General Assembly:[24] A first group, centred around the representatives of the UK, proposed to delete Article 2 (2) of the ICCPR because this provision would encourage States parties to evade their obligations. The second approach was to retain this provision but to add the requirement that measures be adopted 'within a reasonable time'. The third group of representatives wanted to retain Article 2 (2) of the draft unchanged, arguing that '[t]he notion of implementation at the earliest possible moment was implicit in article 2 as a whole' and that 'the reporting requirement stipulated in article 49 would indeed serve as an effective curb on undue delay'.[25]

A statement by Italian representative Capotorti during the discussions in the Third Committee shows how all three of these approaches really proceeded from the same notion of realisation:

> Previous debates on paragraph 2 of the article had not disclosed any disagreement on the fundamental notion that the provisions of the draft Covenant should be implemented immediately, or at least within a very short period after ratification.

[22] UNGA, 'Summary Record of the 1495th Plenary Meeting' (16 December 1966) A/PV.1495, para 78.

[23] See also Jhabvala, 'Domestic Implementation', 471.

[24] UNGA Third Committee, 'Report on the 18th Session' (10 December 1963) A/5655.

[25] ibid, paras 21–23.

> Nevertheless, three conflicting views had been expressed concerning the existing text: some delegations had proposed its complete deletion, lest it should seem to authorize delays in the adoption of the necessary legislation; others had argued that States must be allowed a reasonable time in which to take action, and that it should be expressly so stated; and a third group had felt that the notion of implementation within a reasonable time was implicit in the text.[26]

Capotorti preferred the third approach mentioned above and considered the text of Article 2 in conjunction with Article 49 of the draft to be 'flexible enough to … meet the dual requirement of rapid implementation and the granting of reasonable time to States which could not adjust their legislation overnight'.[27] His statement shows that the notion of immediacy, which all parties generally agreed upon, must be understood as requiring 'rapid implementation' while recognising that some changes cannot take place overnight, requiring the acknowledgment of a 'reasonable time' for implementation. States parties were simply in disagreement about how to achieve this without leaving States parties too much leeway for implementation.

While it may seem that the representatives adhering to the first approach might oppose a notion of progressiveness, two things must be considered. Firstly, they interpreted Article 2 (2) of the draft to introduce progressiveness but, later on, still agreed to the provision. Secondly, and much more importantly, their statements reveal that they did not argue for the deletion of this provision in order to establish an immediate realisation in the strict sense of the word. Instead, they tried to ensure, like their colleagues, that there was no indefinite postponement of obligations. As the Secretary-General's Annotations of the draft Conventions summarise, the proponents of a deletion of Article 2 (2) of the draft were concerned that it introduced into the ICCPR 'the notion of progressiveness'. The term progressiveness, however, was understood as a concept which would render 'Covenant ratification … no more than a vague promise to be fulfilled by some unspecified date'.[28] This means that these critical representatives did not reject the umbrella meaning of progressive realisation but instead only the narrow meaning, again showing a misunderstanding about the nature of this concept.

This conclusion is further supported by inspecting the statements of the UK representatives who introduced the proposal to remove Article 2 (2) from the draft and were particularly vocal about the problems with a 'progressive' notion of realisation.[29] UK representative Glover was concerned that paragraph 2 of Article 2 in the draft would introduce the idea of progressive realisation to civil and political rights which he considered to be a mistake.[30] Glover declared that,

[26] UNGA Third Committee, 'Summary Record of the 1257th Meeting', para 12.
[27] ibid.
[28] UNGA, 'Draft International Covenants on Human Rights', ch V para 10.
[29] See UNGA Third Committee, 'United Kingdom: Amendments to Article 2 of the Draft Covenant on Civil and Political Rights' (7 November 1963) A/C.3/L.1167.
[30] UNGA Third Committee, 'Summary Record of the 1181st Meeting', para 2.

in contrast to socio-economic rights, civil and political rights were 'capable of precise formulation and immediate application'. Accordingly, a State becoming a party to the Covenant 'should ensure that, in almost all respects, its legislation was, or would almost immediately be, in conformity with the principles set forth in the Covenant'.[31]

Two aspects of these statements are relevant. Firstly, Glover refers only to the need for immediate legislative action, which is also part of progressive realisation as understood by the CESCR. Furthermore, he accepts that there may be aspects even in the legislative dimension which, realistically, cannot be implemented at once. In order to provide some flexibility for these aspects, Glover suggests 'a well-drafted article on reservations', which would account for the fact that the parliaments of States parties would not be able to 'bring their legislation, even in its smallest details, into alignment with the principles set forth in the Covenants'.[32] Even without taking into account other areas of State action, Glover recognises that there may be a certain delay. He simply disagrees about the way in which this fact should be taken into consideration in the Covenant without providing States with too much leeway. Accordingly, Glover sets out a combination of an immediate obligation to take steps and a progressive obligation of full realisation which is analogous to the umbrella meaning of progressive realisation.

Glover's colleague, UK representative Goodhart, took a similar position during a later discussion in the Third Committee, again arguing for the deletion of the provision on the grounds that it 'introduced an element of progressive implementation'.[33] Goodhart, like Glover, only speaks of the immediate adoption of appropriate legislation, declaring that, regarding civil and political rights, a State party should undertake that, 'in nearly all respects, its legislation was, or would be almost immediately, in conformity with the requirements of the Covenant'.[34] His rejection of a progressive notion of implementation is based on the idea that it would 'provid[e] a major loop-hole … since the obligation to take steps to adopt the necessary measures, being subject to no time-limit, was meaningless'.[35] Clearly, Goodhart also only disagrees with a form of implementation which allows State parties to avoid their obligations altogether, ie, with only a narrow understanding of progressive realisation.

Support for a progressive element under an umbrella concept of realising civil and political rights can also be deduced from the statements of delegates which argued for the inclusion of the phrase 'within a reasonable time'. Unlike the UK delegation, French representative Combal considered that Article 2 (2) of the draft 'could be interpreted in two diametrically opposite

[31] ibid.
[32] ibid, para 3.
[33] UNGA Third Committee, 'Summary Record of the 1257th Meeting', para 6.
[34] ibid.
[35] ibid, para 7.

ways'. Firstly, according to his statement, it could be interpreted to mean either that 'steps to bring legislation into harmony with the Covenant should be taken immediately' or that 'an indefinite period was allowed for such adjustments'.[36] According to Combal,

> [b]oth interpretations would be most unfortunate – the former because it imposed a totally unrealistic requirement, and the latter because it would be contrary to the spirit of the Covenant, for it could not be admitted that the fundamental rights to which the draft Covenant related should be subject to a principle of progressiveness.[37]

Combal's further statement shows that he understands 'progressiveness' to entail 'an indefinite postponement of legislative adjustments'.[38] Combal thus implies that the preferable interpretation lies somewhere in the middle between 'unrealistic' immediacy and meaningless 'indefinite postponement'. While he believed that the reporting requirement under Article 40 (1) of the ICCPR 'made it quite clear that the Covenant did not permit an indefinite postponement of legislative adjustments', he argued that 'the idea would gain from being explicitly spelt out in article 2'.[39] In his perception, an explicit formulation of this idea can be achieved by reintroducing the phrase 'within a reasonable time', which had previously been deleted during the Commission proceedings.[40] In simple terms, Combal argues that Article 2 (2) of the ICCPR leaves open the timeframe of realisation but should be read to imply neither strict immediacy nor indefinite postponement of obligations, thus arguing for a standard analogous to the umbrella concept of progressive realisation.

The same sentiment is apparent in the statements of Combal's colleague, French representative Bouquin, which were made during an earlier meeting of the Third Committee. According to his arguments, the UK representatives were correct to speak of the 'almost immediate application' of civil and political rights 'rather than of their immediate application'.[41] While a strictly immediate conception of implementation may be appropriate for 'technical agreements' with a very specific scope, 'in the case of a Covenant of vast scope like the Covenant on Civil and Political Rights, a certain delay was bound to occur during which States would continue to apply their constitutional procedures'.[42]

Bouquin also argued for the reintroduction of 'within a reasonable time' in order to prevent a reading of Article 2 (2) of the draft as either 'unrealistically' immediate or as allowing 'States to delay indefinitely'.[43] From this proposition, the Chilean representative Diaz Casanueva 'gathered that the French

[36] ibid, para 21.
[37] ibid.
[38] ibid.
[39] ibid.
[40] ibid.
[41] UNGA Third Committee, 'Summary Record of the 1181st Meeting', para 23.
[42] ibid.
[43] ibid, para 24.

representative wished to weaken the provisions of article 2 of the two draft Covenants by introducing the idea of a "reasonable" time-limit'. According to his argument, the phrase was previously deleted in order to 'avoid giving a weapon to states which did not sincerely desire to guarantee the exercise of the rights set out there'.[44] Bouquin, however, made clear that with this phrase 'he sought to strengthen the text, not to weaken it, [as] the article provided ... no time-limit for' the steps it requires.[45] This exchange shows how the delegates agreed that there should not be an excuse for inaction in the Covenant. They disagreed only on the way in which this goal should be achieved.

Lastly, there were also representatives who believed that the treaty already provided for a sufficient flexibility with sufficient safeguards against indefinite postponement without any clarification. This position even more clearly supports the interpretation of the ICCPR as providing for a progressive notion of realisation. One example for this has already been mentioned above. The Italian representative Capotorti envisioned the text of the draft to already account for a balanced approach which neither demanded strict immediacy nor allowed undue delays.[46]

As mentioned above, the reporting procedure under what is now Article 40 (1) of the ICCPR, and particularly the phrase 'progress made', evoked a debate between the drafting parties. Again, the critical parties were concerned that the progressive notion introduced by this formulation would allow any State to 'invoke that principle as an excuse for inaction'.[47] Others, for example the Iraqi representative Afnan, were in favour of this phrase and argued that 'it was impossible for any State to claim that its legislation fully conformed to all the provisions of a Covenant which covered so enormous a field as that of civil and political rights'.[48] In this context, too, the sceptical representatives were concerned not about the umbrella concept of progressive realisation but instead about an understanding which would allow States parties indefinite postponement.

US representative Harris, who argued for her country's proposal to remove the words 'progress made', still acknowledged that the necessary measures for implementation 'might not be taken at once', thus welcoming the fact that the draft foresaw a one-year timeframe for submitting the first report.[49] UK representative Gaitskell, who supported the US proposal, argued that, although 'civil and political rights could be accorded much more rapidly' than socio-economic rights, they also require 'further legislative and administrative measures as might

[44] ibid, para 27.

[45] ibid, para 28.

[46] UNGA Third Committee, 'Summary Record of the 1257th Meeting', para 12.

[47] UNGA Third Committee, 'Report on the 21st Session' (13 December 1966) A/6546, para 382.

[48] UNGA Third Committee, 'Summary Record of the 1427th Meeting' (18 November 1966) A/C.3/SR.1427, para 3.

[49] ibid, para 27.

be necessary to ensure that civil and political rights were accorded in practice as well as in law'.[50] Gaitskell implicitly refers to the difference between formal and de facto enjoyment of rights which strongly corresponds with the modern understanding of progressive realisation.

What further supports this conclusion is the fact that the wording of the reporting provision was changed from 'the progress made in *giving effect* to the rights' to 'the progress made in the *enjoyment* of those rights' (emphasis added).[51] With this change, the drafting parties made clear that the notion of progressiveness refers not to the action taken by the States parties but rather to the enjoyment of rights holders. The representative of Upper Volta, Sanon, pointed out that the French version of the proposal discussed during the respective meeting 'made it clearer that what was meant was the progress made as a result of the measures adopted'.[52] Accordingly, the sponsors of the amendment in question agreed to change the wording in the aforementioned way, which was welcomed by many representatives.[53]

After this adjustment, the Malagasy representative Ramaholimihaso, who previously had been critical of the phrase 'progress made',[54] declared that she 'would not press her earlier request for a separate vote on the words "the progress made" if it was clearly understood that they meant the progress which had been made as a result of the measures adopted by States'.[55] It becomes clear that Ramaholimihaso was only content after clarifying that the progressiveness implied by the relevant phrase was to be understood in the sense that it allows postponement only in relation to the obligation of result, ie, the facilitation of complete enjoyment, while the obligation of conduct, ie, 'giving effect to' or taking steps, must be understood as immediate. Supporting this conclusion is the fact that the drafting parties intended the reporting procedure to, on the one hand, prevent inappropriate delays in implementation and, on the other hand, bring States parties to adopt positive measures necessary for the full realisation of rights.[56]

This flexible understanding of immediacy also carries over into the arguments made by literary commentators on the basis of the *travaux préparatoires*. Oscar Schachter deduces from the legislative history and the reporting requirement under Article 40 of the draft that this one-year period reflects the amount of 'elasticity' to be granted under Article 2 of the ICCPR. He continues to note that this timeframe may be extended depending on the particular circumstances in the concrete case, taking into account the steps already taken

[50] ibid, paras 21–22.

[51] UNGA Third Committee, 'Report on the 21st Session', paras 372–97.

[52] UNGA Third Committee, 'Summary Record of the 1427th Meeting', para 35.

[53] See the statements of the representatives of Nigeria, New Zealand, the USA, and Ireland, ibid, paras 36–39.

[54] ibid, paras 28–30.

[55] ibid, para 45.

[56] See ibid, paras 22, 27; see also Seibert-Fohr, 'Domestic Implementation', 407–10.

by the State party and the likelihood of these steps leading to the realisation of the right.[57] This statement is very similar to the requirements set out in the context of reasonableness.[58] Boulesbaa, who insists on the immediacy of obligations under Article 2 of the ICCPR, agrees with Schachter's argument for flexibility.[59] He notes that States parties must gradually improve their legislative and other measures in order to respond to newly emerging issues in practice. However, Boulesbaa cautions that this exceptional extension should not reach the level of 'progressive implementation' because this would enable States parties to 'delay the implementation as they did with respect to' the ICESCR.[60] Boulesbaa thus argues for a continuous improvement, stretching the term 'immediate', while discouraging the interpretation of the general obligation provision as allowing a deliberate delay by States parties. Again, this statement reveals a misunderstanding about the nature of progressive realisation which cannot be interpreted to allow for a 'deliberate delay' in a State party's efforts to realise the right.

Schabas similarly recognises the duality between immediate and progressive elements, at least implicitly. He declares that the State representatives, while insisting on the immediate and direct nature of the ICCPR, introduced certain phrases into the text which indicate 'a dynamic element of progressive realization'. He goes on to remark that only an 'extremely one-sided, static' reading of civil and political rights based on the outdated positive/negative or subjective/programmatic rights divide would connote a contradiction between the immediacy of rights and this dynamic element.[61] Particularly appropriate is Schabas' acknowledgment that the acceptance of positive obligations necessarily entails 'a relative or dynamic element in the realization of human rights'.[62] Schabas even utilises the term 'progressive implementation' when referring to the positive dimension of the triad of obligations, namely the obligation to fulfil rights.[63] Anja Seibert-Fohr likewise recognises the necessarily progressive nature of positive aspects, declaring that there is no contradiction between the progressiveness of these positive aspects and the immediacy of obligations under the ICCPR in general.[64]

Although these observations are most apposite, both Schabas and Seibert-Fohr fail to see that they implicitly endorse a standard analogous to progressive realisation in its umbrella meaning. Like most other commentators, they appear to be blinded by deeply entrenched perceptions of the words 'progressive' and 'immediate'.

[57] Schachter, 'The Obligation to Implement', 324.
[58] *cf* 2.6.2.
[59] Boulesbaa transfers arguments made in the context of the ICCPR to the obligations under the CAT, see Boulesbaa 'The Nature of the Obligations under Article 2 UNCAT', 76–80.
[60] ibid, 80.
[61] Schabas, *Nowak's CCPR Commentary*, 892–93.
[62] ibid, 893.
[63] ibid, 62.
[64] Seibert-Fohr, 'Domestic Implementation', 415.

9.3.1.2. Progressive Realisation is not Indefinite Postponement

The previous subsection has shown that the drafting parties only rejected a narrow understanding of progressiveness for civil and political rights while implicitly endorsing a standard which combines immediate and progressive obligations. This subsection will illustrate that the same umbrella understanding is not only the common conception of progressive realisation today but was also envisioned for socio-economic rights during the drafting process. The drafting parties did not envision progressive realisation in the context of socio-economic rights as allowing an indefinite postponement of obligations but instead set out a combination of immediate obligations of conduct and a progressive notion only for the full realisation of the right. This means that the drafting parties supported the same understanding of realisation for both categories and implicitly endorsed a uniform standard of obligations analogous to what is now called progressive realisation. Alston and Quinn summarise that the supporters of progressive realisation envisioned this concept as a necessity which could accommodate the various levels of economic development in different states. The *travaux préparatoires*, Alston and Quinn argue, show that the representatives supportive of progressive realisation did not construct it as an 'escape hatch' for States parties who were not willing to match their efforts to their abilities for the purposes of the Convention.[65]

The sentiment that progressive realisation is no excuse for States parties is best represented by the statements of Australian representative Whitlam. As reported by the secretariat,

> [w]ith regard to the idea of progressive realization provided for in article 1, he did not think it limited the rights to which it applied; it merely took into account the existing situation and ensured that the realization of those rights did not stop at a given level.[66]

US representative Roosevelt, according to the Secretariat's summary records, 'failed to see any danger in the use of the word "progressively"'. According to her conception, 'it merely specified what was implicit in several of the draft articles, namely that some of the economic, social and cultural rights could not be enacted into law immediately'.[67] French representative Juvigny is reported to have said that, while progressive realisation in itself is a limitation,

> care should be taken not to distort its meaning. The progressive realization of the rights set forth in the covenant should depend entirely on the resources available to a State, and should not be invoked by States as grounds for failing to implement a right when resources were available.[68]

[65] Alston and Quinn, 'Obligations under the ICESCR', 175. The analysis conducted by Alston and Quinn further provides a number of useful examples, see ibid, 172–81, some of which are also referenced in the following paragraphs.

[66] UNCHR, 'Summary Record of the 308th Meeting' (6 June 1952) E/CN.4/SR.308, 5.

[67] UNCHR, 'Summary Record of the 271st Meeting' (14 May 1952) E/CN.4/SR.271, 12.

[68] UNCHR, 'Summary Record of the 307th Meeting' (9 June 1952) E/CN.4/SR.307, 5.

During the discussion in the Third Committee of the General Assembly, French representative Bouquin similarly considered that progressive realisation was a necessary part of the ICESCR 'since the real enforcement of the provisions of the Covenant involved first of all a thorough revision of certain systems and then the mobilization of all the financial resources of the State'.[69]

What is more, the concept was perceived to strengthen the realisation of rights. According to French representative Cassin, replacing the phrase 'the progressive implementation' with the phrase 'progressively the full realization' was undertaken to serve to 'strengthen rather than to weaken the objective set before future contracting parties'.[70] Egyptian representative Bey similarly declared that 'the word "progressive" was preferred to the phrase "by stages", in order to stress that the implementation of the rights in question should be pursued without respite'.[71] The Secretariat's annotation on the draft Covenants reported that '[i]t was also claimed that the use of the word "progressively" in fact placed upon signatories a duty to achieve ever higher and higher levels of fulfilment of rights'.[72]

There were also drafting parties more sceptical of the concept of progressive realisation. A number of representatives were concerned that the inclusion of progressive realisation would weaken rights by providing an excuse to States parties. It must be stressed, however, that these sceptics did not argue that including progressive realisation would, from a normative point of view, weaken rights. Instead, the critical representatives were concerned about a misappropriation of the concept from a practical perspective. This concern shows that they did not consider socio-economic rights to be a category of rights which is subject to a 'weaker' form of realisation. What the sceptical representatives rejected was a form of progressive realisation which in no way resembles the concept as it is understood today.

The Lebanese representative, for example, considered that the concept of progressive realisation should be deleted from the Covenant. According to his argument, the phrase in Article 2 of the ICESCR 'added nothing' because progressive realisation was implicit in the Covenant's substantive provisions. Including it 'might be interpreted as discouraging immediate implementation even in cases where such implementation was possible'.[73] The Congolese representative Sita was concerned that 'the principle of progressive implementation was so elastic that it left room for deliberate misinterpretation'. Therefore, he argued, it was essential to include the idea of a reasonable time-limit in article 2 of the draft Covenant'.[74] Interestingly, this is reminiscent of the discussion about

[69] UNGA Third Committee, 'Summary Record of the 1181st Meeting', para 25.
[70] UNCHR, 'Summary Record of the 233rd Meeting' (2 July 1951) E/CN.4/SR.233, 8.
[71] ibid, 4–5.
[72] UNGA, 'Draft International Covenants on Human Rights', ch V para 24.
[73] UNCHR, 'Summary Record of the 271st Meeting', 5.
[74] UNGA Third Committee, 'Summary Record of the 1181st Meeting', para 29.

reasonable time-limits regarding the ICCPR.[75] A more extreme argument was made by the Soviet representative. According to Morozov, the inclusion of the word 'progressively' would mean that 'colonial powers and States unwilling to grant their people the rights to which they were entitled could use that adverb as an excuse for progress so slow to be imperceptible'.[76]

Accordingly, there was agreement on the normative level that socio-economic rights shall not be limited by a conception of progressive realisation which allows States parties to delay measures as they wish. Instead, the drafting parties generally agreed that socio-economic rights must be realised 'as quickly as possible', as Costa Rican representative Volio noted.[77] Matthew Craven correctly observes that this coincides with the notion of implementation 'at the earliest possible moment' which was thought to be appropriate for the ICCPR.[78] Whether it is true, as the Soviet representative claimed, that the 'so-called advanced countries' secretly intended to include progressive realisation merely 'to continue to hold many under-developed countries in economic slavery to them',[79] can at least not be determined by analysing the *travaux préparatoires*. The analysed documents do, however, not support the claim that the drafters envisioned progressive realisation as a 'mere promotional type of commitment to enhance certain objectives set by the Covenant without requiring the attainment of specific results'.[80]

9.3.1.3. Influence of the Positive/Negative Rights Divide

The two previous subsections have shown that the drafting parties only envisioned a differentiation between 'immediate' and 'progressive' realisation on a surface level but, in substance, argued for a very similar form of implementation for both categories of rights. A good explanation for this miscommunication is that the parties were influenced by the positive/negative rights divide, at least to a degree.[81] The consensus between the parties was that civil and political rights entail a number of positive obligations, as the formulation in Article 2 (2) of the ICCPR ('legislative or other measures') demonstrates. Yet, the representatives arguing for a differential standard of implementation appear to have ignored a wide range of positive measures when doing so and focused mainly on legislative action. It must be stressed, however, that the *travaux préparatoires* do not show

[75] See further 9.3.1.1.

[76] UNCHR, 'Summary Record of the 271st Meeting', 8.

[77] UNGA Third Committee, 'Summary Record of the 1202nd Meeting' (5 December 1962) A/C.3/SR.1202, para 26.

[78] Craven, *The ICESCR*, 130.

[79] UNCHR, 'Summary Record of the 273rd Meeting' E/CN.4/SR.273, 7.

[80] This was claimed by E Riedel, G Giacca and C Golay, 'The Development of Economic, Social, and Cultural Rights in International Law' in E Riedel, G Giacca and C Golay (eds), *Economic, Social, and Cultural Rights in International Law: Contemporary Issues and Challenges* (Oxford, Oxford University Press, 2014) 12(fn).

[81] See also Jhabvala, 'Domestic Implementation', 467–68 and Schabas, *Nowak's CCPR Commentary*, 61.

that representatives actively argued against a wide range of positive measures in order to uphold their claim of immediacy of civil and political rights. They simply declared that legislation must be adopted immediately.

An example of this is a statement by Chilean representative Diaz Casanueva. During discussions in the Third Committee, he stated that

> the guarantee of economic, social and cultural rights raised problems of a material nature, which the guarantee of civil and political rights did not. The former group of rights could not be ensured simply by enacting legislation and providing for enforcement, but depended on the level and rate of economic development.[82]

In a later meeting of the Third Committee, Greek representative Mantzoulinos agreed with the criticism by the UK delegation regarding concerns about a progressive notion of implementation being introduced by Article 2 (2) of the draft. Mantzoulinos argued the following:

> The enjoyment of civil and political rights, however, was not dependent on economic considerations, and a State becoming a party to the draft Covenant under discussion should satisfy itself that its legislation conformed to the provisions of that instrument or, subject to the requirements of its legislative procedure, would be adjusted in the very near future.[83]

It seems that the drafting parties were actively ignoring the fact that the consensus included a range of positive obligations in order to avoid the logical conclusion that these measures might take time to take effect. By focusing on the formal enjoyment of rights, the parties arguing for immediacy of civil and political rights did not engage with the question of de facto enjoyment and its timeframe of realisation. In this respect, one could speak of a 'blind spot' in the treaties, ie, a regulatory gap that was overlooked or unanticipated during the drafting process.[84] However, even if one found that the parties set out civil and political rights as only requiring legislative action, it must be remembered that, even regarding this aspect, the drafting parties agreed that States parties would need a certain degree of flexibility analogous to the umbrella understanding of progressive realisation. After acknowledging this general fact, the further argument for progressiveness is simply one of degree.

9.3.2. ICERD

The *travaux préparatoires* of the ICERD reveal that the complete elimination of racial discrimination and the creation of full de facto equality was perceived by the drafting parties as a long-term goal which requires immediate action from

[82] UNGA Third Committee, 'Summary Record of the 1203rd Meeting' (5 December 1962) A/C.3/SR.1203, para 12.

[83] UNGA Third Committee, 'Summary Record of the 1257th Meeting', para 2.

[84] See also Tobin, 'Seeking to Persuade', 44.

the States parties. Accordingly, the drafting parties implicitly endorsed progressive elements for this treaty.

UK representative Hoare noted that, while the chapeau of Article 2 of the ICERD requires States parties to condemn racism and to undertake to pursue a policy of eliminating such discrimination, Article 2 (1) (d) of the ICERD demands bringing it to an end. However, 'to arrive at that goal, it would be necessary to undertake action which would inevitably require time'.[85] Accordingly, his delegation proposed to introduce a formulation according to which States parties undertake 'to adopt all necessary measures, including legislation if appropriate, for the purpose of bringing to an end all discrimination by any person, group or organization'.[86] This amendment was strongly criticised by the representative of the USSR, Morozov. He found that the proposed amendment 'was totally unacceptable and ran counter to the essential purposes of the Convention' because

> [i]f a State party refused to prohibit racial discrimination and proposed instead a very vague undertaking to bring it to an end within an unspecified period of time, the purpose for which the convention had been drafted would never be attained.[87]

The previous quote illustrates that Morozov misunderstood the approach of the UK representative. Morozov was concerned that States parties to the Convention would be allowed by the text proposed in the amendment to refuse taking any action. As such, Morozov declared that the text 'would prolong the struggle against discrimination indefinitely and would provide a number of loopholes by means of which compliance with various provisions of the convention could be evaded'.[88] Clearly, his wish was that the immediacy of obligations regarding legislation be upheld, as he stated that '[t]he question was whether the State party should begin by prohibiting discrimination'.[89] In other words, Morozov rejected a narrow understanding of progressive realisation while endorsing a combination of immediate obligations of conduct aimed at the long-term goal of eliminating racial discrimination.

The criticism of the UK amendment by the USSR and other States was obviously provoked by the proposed deletion of the phrase 'to prohibit'. The Polish representative, Resich, explicitly criticised this move,[90] as did the Lebanese representative Hakim. The latter went on to state that

> [t]he United Kingdom representative thought that the elimination of racial discrimination would take time and that it was accordingly not possible to stipulate a prohibition. Yet such a prohibition was in the spirit of the Universal Declaration

[85] UNCHR, 'Summary Record of the 787th Meeting' (21 April 1964) E/CN.4/SR.787, 10.
[86] UNCHR, 'United Kingdom: Amendments to Article 2 of the Draft Convention on the Elimination of All Forms of Racial Discrimination' (1 January 1964) E/CN.4/L.689 contained in E/3873, para 108.
[87] UNCHR, 'Summary Record of the 787th Meeting', 11.
[88] ibid.
[89] ibid.
[90] See ibid, 12.

itself. It was not the prohibition which would take time but the measures for its application referred to in the second part of sub-paragraph (c).[91]

However, this exact interpretation arguably was what the UK representative proposed. During the next meeting of the Commission, Hoare declared that 'he was grateful to the representative of Lebanon for clarifying the issues on that sub-paragraph'.[92] Upon closer examination, the immediate obligation of taking steps was never called into question by the UK proposal or by the accompanying arguments by Hoare. Only the obligation of result, ie, of fully eliminating racial discrimination de facto, was deemed to be a matter of gradual realisation. When he declared that 'to arrive at that goal … would inevitably require time', the goal referenced was not the prohibition of discrimination, but the goal of the policy mentioned in the previous sentence, namely 'eliminating such discrimination'.[93]

During the next session, it became clear that the proposition to delete the words 'shall prohibit' was only motivated by the concern that it would impose upon States parties a specific obligation to adopt new legislation where sufficient laws were already present.[94] The Canadian representative Aitken agreed with this concern, questioning the need for an explicit requirement of prohibition, because '[i]f the intention was to place upon States the obligation to abolish racial discrimination, the Convention should emphasize positive measures to that end'.[95] The drafting parties were not really in disagreement about the timeframe of realisation but rather about the degree of precision regarding the measures prescribed by the Convention. A statement by the Ecuadorian representative illustrates this point: '[t]he prohibition of racial discrimination could be accomplished either through the courts or through legislation.'[96] In the end, the drafting parties agreed unanimously upon the final form of Article 2 (1) (d) of the ICERD as a compromise which took into account different approaches to the prohibition and eradication of discrimination.[97]

9.3.3. CEDAW

Before the Commission on the Status of Women (CSW), which was tasked with drafting the CEDAW, were proposals brought by Egypt and Denmark which set out the obligation to take measures or establish procedures 'aimed

[91] ibid.

[92] UNCHR, 'Summary Record of the 788th Meeting' (21 April 1964) E/CN.4/SR.788, 4.

[93] See UNCHR, 'Summary Record of the 787th Meeting', 10.

[94] See UNCHR, 'Summary Record of the 788th Meeting', 4–5; see also the comments by French representative Bouquin, ibid, 6–7.

[95] ibid, 5.

[96] ibid, 8.

[97] See ibid, 10; see also the statement by Costa Rican representative Volio: 'the Turkish amendment actually improved the Sub-Commission's text because it emphasized that states were to prohibit racial discrimination "by all appropriate means", that was to say means within the law, and it did not commit them to enact new legislation unless it was necessary', ibid, 9.

at achieving progressively the full realisation of the rights recognized in the present Convention'. Subsequently, the sponsors of these amendments deleted the term 'progressively'.[98] Some literary commentators argue that, because the term 'progressively' was removed from Article 24 of the CEDAW, the obligations pursuant to the CEDAW are 'immediate'.[99] However, there are no statements in the *travaux préparatoires* indicating that this was the intention of the drafting parties. Rather, there was no in-depth discussion of this issue at all.[100] There seemed to be something of an agreement that even the necessary legislative measures would need time, as Rehof recounts: the drafters felt that the Convention should be seen as a challenge for States parties to bring their legislation into conformity with the provisions 'in course of time'.[101]

It becomes clear again that the term 'progressively' was not deleted because the drafters rejected a standard like progressive realisation in its umbrella sense but instead only to prevent an unjustified postponement of obligations. The States parties accepted that the full realisation of the CEDAW's goals would take time. The same is apparent from the arguments of literary commentators which insist upon the immediacy of the rights under the CEDAW. They recognise that there is only an immediate obligation to adopt measures with the goal of realising the rights but no 'obligation of immediate realization of the goals set out', meaning no obligation to immediately establish complete equality.[102]

9.3.4. CRC

During the drafting process of the CRC, the provision which is now laid down in Article 4 of the CRC was initially proposed without the differentiation between categories of rights. The version adopted by the Working Group at first reading in 1988 read:

> The States Parties to the Present Convention shall undertake all appropriate administrative and legislative measures, in accordance with their available resources and,

[98] CSW, 'Report on the 26th and Resumed 26th Sessions' (1 January 1977) E/CN.6/608, paras 190–92; see also LA Rehof, *Guide to the Travaux Préparatoires of the United Nations Convention on the Elimination of all Forms of Discrimination against Women*, International Studies in Human Rights 29 (Leiden, Nijhoff, 1993) 224–25.

[99] See MA Freeman, CM Chinkin and B Rudolf, 'Article 24' in MA Freeman, CM Chinkin and B Rudolf (eds), *The UN Convention on the Elimination of All Forms of Discrimination against Women: A Commentary*, 1st edn (Oxford, Oxford University Press, 2012) 541.

[100] The issue of progressive or immediate realisation has not been discussed in the context of Article 21 of the draft CEDAW during the 661st, 662nd, 665th, 666th, 667th, and 672nd meetings of the CSW, see the CSW's summary records of these meetings under the following symbols: E/CN.6/SR.661, E/CN.6/SR.662, E/CN.6/SR.665, E/CN.6/SR.666, E/CN.6/SR.667, and E/CN.6/SR.672. It appears that this issue was only discussed in a separate working group which did not provide written recordings. In contrast to the rest of the provision, paragraph 1 of draft Article 21 was later adopted without any discussion, see CSW, 'Summary Record of the 673rd Meeting' (16 December 1976) E/CN.6/SR.673, paras 2–3.

[101] Rehof, *Guide to the Travaux Préparatoires*, 224.

[102] Freeman, Chinkin and Rudolf, 'Article 24', 541.

> where needed, within the framework of international co-operation, for the implementation of the rights recognized in this Convention.[103]

The inclusion of the phrase 'in accordance with their available resources' and its application to civil and political rights was heavily criticised. During technical review, UNICEF argued that the applicability of the 'available resources' phrase should be limited to socio-economic rights in light of the fact that the ICCPR, CEDAW and ICERD did not contain such a provision. UNICEF based its argument on the idea that

> [i]n this respect, article 5 of the draft convention would achieve a radical diminution of the standards contained in existing instruments and would run counter to all of the assumptions that have hitherto governed the recognition of civil and political rights in international law.[104]

In the following discussions, the total deletion of the phrase was proposed by the delegations of Canada, Sweden, New Zealand, Argentina, Portugal and the United Kingdom. They followed the argument of UNICEF and, according to the report of the Working Group, argued that the ICCPR does not subject rights to the availability of resources and that 'the Covenant's standards should not be weakened in the child's convention'.[105] Others (Brazil, India, Venezuela, Libya and Algeria) disagreed, arguing that resource constraints concerned all rights.[106] Finally, the concept of 'maximum extent of their available resources' was included only for socio-economic rights.

While the available *travaux préparatoires* do not provide a conclusive discussion of the concept, the above statements do illustrate that the criticism extended was entirely based on the conception that the ICCPR and the ICESCR established dramatically different levels of protection, ie, that the concept of progressive realisation entails a considerably lower standard of obligations. It appears that the parties never discussed what precisely the concept of 'available resources' would entail and instead clung to the notion that socio-economic rights protection under the UN human rights treaties is inherently weaker. This means that the parties were not generally opposed to the idea of a uniform standard of obligations but rather wanted to prevent a diminution of the standard applicable to civil and political rights. Accordingly, the *travaux préparatoires* reveal no attitudes inconsistent with the argument proposed in this book.

More definite support for a uniform standard of obligations – and, particularly, of review – can be found in the drafting history of the CRC-OP3.

[103] UNCHR, 'Draft Convention on the Rights of the Child: Text of the Draft Convention as Adopted by the Working Group' (24 February 1988) E/CN.4/1988/WG.1/WP.1/Rev.1, 7.

[104] UNCHR, 'Technical Review of the Text of the Draft Convention on the Rights of the Child' (20 October 1988) E/CN.4/1989/WG.1/CRP.1, 19.

[105] UNCHR, 'Report of the Working Group on a Draft Convention on the Rights of the Child on its 11th Session' (2 March 1989) E/CN.4/1989/48, para 172.

[106] See ibid, para 173.

Article 10 (4) of the CRC-OP3 establishes that a standard of reasonableness shall be applied by the Committee when alleged violations of socio-economic rights are claimed in Individual Communications. This provision was also not adopted without debate in the Working Group. According to the Report of the Open-ended Working Group on the Optional Protocol, some delegations argued that the restriction of reasonableness to socio-economic rights 'would undermine the holistic nature of the Convention, the fact that, for all rights, there were obligations to respect, protect and fulfil and the principle that all rights covered in a treaty should be protected to the same degree'.[107]

Delegations critical of the draft further argued that '[c]ommunications may involve multiple violations arising out of the same situation – violations of civil and political rights as well as of economic social and cultural rights'.[108] By extension, this means not only that one and the same action by the State party may illegitimately restrict more than one Convention right, but also that one and the same omission may be in conflict with several rights under the CRC. Consequently, one and the same positive duty may be the counterpart to both socio-economic and civil and political rights. Because of this fact, there is no way to ascribe a positive duty to one or the other category of rights in order to determine whether it must be fulfilled immediately or progressively. Hence, as the critical voices found, '[t]he Convention rights were not severable from one another'.[109] This point is of particular interest for this study; including the reasonableness standard only for socio-economic rights is argued to undermine the fact that all rights entail obligations to respect, protect and ensure.

9.3.5. CRPD

The discussions regarding the immediacy or progressiveness of rights during the drafting of the CRPD are far less extensive compared to those during the drafting of the Covenants. Presumably, this is due to the conviction of the drafting parties that the question has been settled before and that the divide is consistent with existing international human rights law.[110] Furthermore, the drafters of the CRPD agreed to take Article 4 of the CRC as a model for Article 4 of the CRPD and, therefore, somewhat evaded engaging with the basic question whether such a differentiation is appropriate in the first place.[111] And yet, there

[107] UNHRC, 'Report of the Open-ended Working Group on an Optional Protocol to the Convention on the Rights of the Child to Provide a Communications Procedure on its 2nd Session', para 75.
[108] ibid.
[109] ibid; see also S Egan, 'The New Complaints Mechanism for the Convention on the Rights of the Child' (2014) 22 *The International Journal of Children's Rights* 205, 220.
[110] Della Fina, 'Article 4', 148.
[111] See UNGA, 'Report of the Ad Hoc Committee on a Comprehensive and Integral International Convention on the Protection and Promotion of the Rights and Dignity of Persons with Disabilities on its 4th Session' (14 September 2004) A/59/360, Annex IV para 7.

are some valuable insights to be gained from the *travaux préparatoires* which support the idea of a uniform standard of realisation. In particular, it becomes clear that the drafting parties were aware of the issue that there is no way of drawing clear boundaries between the categories of rights.

The first relevant aspect in the drafting history of the CRPD is the fact that the drafting parties were proceeding from a strong reading of progressive realisation which also manifested itself in the formulation of Article 4 (2) of the CRPD as it stands today. According to the report of the competent Ad Hoc Committee to the General Assembly, '[d]raft article 4 should include the concept of progressive realisation of economic, social and cultural rights, balanced by the need to implement immediately those obligations that are capable of immediate implementation'.[112] The drafting parties decided to add the phrase 'without prejudice to those obligations contained in the present Convention that are immediately applicable according to international law' to Article 4 (2) of the draft even though they were convinced that this aspect is already implicit in the concept of 'maximum of available resources'.[113] During the discussions in the Ad Hoc Committee, '[t]he Coordinator indicated his understanding that what is being discussed here is not an "escape clause" for States Parties'.[114]

Another interesting part of the *travaux préparatoires* concerns the discussion about the implementation of accessibility. Regarding this right, the drafting parties were in agreement that progressive realisation is applicable, although there was disagreement about whether this should explicitly be included in the provision.[115] The Chair of the Ad Hoc Committee noted that

> the idea of progressive implementation had been brought up again. Accessibility is an economic, social, and cultural right, and so progressive realization would be appropriate; however, there are also elements of a civil and political right, freedom of expression; therefore Article 19 is something of a hybrid.[116]

While this statement reflects a traditional conjunction of progressive realisation with the category of socio-economic rights, the Chair also acknowledged that accessibility extends beyond the boundaries of this category. Thus, he implicitly accepts that progressive realisation also applies to the civil and political aspects of the right. Further discussions arose around the characterisation of denials of accessibility as discrimination. The drafting parties recognised that there is a contradiction between the progressive realisation of accessibility, on the one hand, and the immediacy of non-discrimination, on the other.[117] No solution

[112] ibid.
[113] Ad Hoc Committee on the CRPD, 'Daily Summary of Discussion at the Fourth Session: 30 August 2004', www.un.org/esa/socdev/enable/rights/ahc4sum30aug.htm.
[114] ibid.
[115] See also Lawson, 'Article 9', 266–68.
[116] Ad Hoc Committee on the CRPD, 'Daily Summary of Discussion at the Sixth Session: 05 August 2005', www.un.org/esa/socdev/enable/rights/ahc6sum5aug.htm.
[117] See ibid.

was found for this issue and the Chair declared that there was need for further discussion.[118] As has been seen above, the only way out of this dilemma is to recognise that substantive enjoyment of accessibility can only be achieved over time while some immediate measures are possible and required.

A third important lesson to be learned from the *travaux préparatoires* is that the drafting parties, while generally insisting on the traditional divide,[119] were quite uncertain about how to differentiate socio-economic from civil and political rights.[120] The Israeli representative held that

> [t]here is uncertainty regarding what would be considered economic, social and cultural rights. Thus Israel reiterates its proposal from AHC3 to 'identify those articles where the economic implications are major' in a non-exhaustive list in Article 4 .... This will give guidance on what rights should be subject to progressive realization.[121]

Even though none of the other representatives denied that there was such uncertainty, Israel's proposal was widely rejected. The delegate of New Zealand, for example, declared that '[s]pecific articles should not be mentioned' and that they are 'very unhappy' with the list of provisions that were proposed by Israel to be included in this list. They particularly disagreed with the categorisation of draft Articles 9d and 13.[122] The Canadian representative called Israel's idea a 'very dangerous approach' and said that '[t]here is no need to further distinguish civil and political rights, as this is not done in CRC Article 4' without proposing an alternative solution for the obvious uncertainty in the current draft.[123] Liechtenstein at least acknowledged the source of the difficulties. The summary record reports the following stance by this drafting party:

> Specific enumeration of articles subject to progressive realization is not useful as 'almost all the articles in such a convention are somewhat heterogeneous in themselves,' and there is also no clear distinction between civil and political rights and economic, social and cultural rights. A listing would risk including some aspects of rights that do not belong.[124]

The Dutch delegation likewise found that '[s]uch a list would be "a dangerous path to follow" as many draft articles contain both civil and political, and

[118] Ad Hoc Committee on the CRPD, 'Daily Summary of Discussion at the Seventh Session: 17 January 2006', www.un.org/esa/socdev/enable/rights/ahc7sum17jan.htm.

[119] An exception can be seen in the statements by the Chinese representative: 'there has always been an "argument" whether civil and political rights or economic, social and cultural rights, are more important and pressing. There is a need to balance both categories of rights. ... Progressive realization of both kinds of rights is equally important', see Ad Hoc Committee on the CRPD, 'Daily Summary of Discussion at the Fourth Session: 30 August 2004', available at the URL cited in n 113.

[120] See also Flóvenz, 'The Implementation of the UN Convention', 271.

[121] Ad Hoc Committee on the CRPD, 'Daily Summary of Discussion at the Fourth Session: 30 August 2004', available at the URL cited in n 113.

[122] ibid.

[123] See ibid.

[124] ibid.

economic, social and cultural rights'.[125] The problem was also seen by Japan. According to the report, Japan's representatives agreed that the approach of Israel would be dangerous and, although they were 'opposed to further differentiation between categories of rights', they 'would appreciate further discussion of these issues to foster a common understanding regarding what aspects of articles would be subject to progressive realization'.[126]

The solution for the Committee, apparently, was to ignore and circumvent the issue. This becomes clear from a letter by the Chairman to all members of the Committee which declared that the agreed upon progressiveness of socio-economic rights cannot be introduced into each substantive rights provision but instead should be delegated to a general Article because the 'hybrid nature' of rights in the Convention would make such an approach 'both messy and complex'.[127] Clearly, the drafting parties were faced with the same insurmountable uncertainties that practitioners are faced with today when they insist upon the immediacy of civil and political rights.

9.4. FURTHER SUPPLEMENTARY MEANS OF INTERPRETATION

As Article 32 of the VCLT does not provide an exhaustive list of sources, there are other supplementary means of interpretation besides the preparatory work of the treaty and the circumstances of its conclusion.[128] Firstly, Article 32 of the VCLT includes subsequent practice which does not fulfil the requirements of Article 31 (3) (b) of the VCLT, for example, because it cannot be ascribed to the parties, does not relate to the application of the treaty, or does not establish an agreement of the States parties.[129] Often, the inclusion of this material is supported by a reference to Article 38 (1) (d) of the ICJ Statute which determines 'judicial decisions and the teachings of the most highly qualified publicists of the various nations' to constitute subsidiary means for determining the rules of law.[130] This means that all pronouncements of the Committees (regardless of State reactions) may serve as supplementary means of interpretation.[131] This includes not only the General Comments and Recommendations but also the views adopted in Individual Communication procedures, as far as the pronouncements in question are aimed at the interpretation of treaty terms and provide a consistent pattern.[132] The convergence of standards of realisation

[125] ibid.

[126] ibid.

[127] Ad Hoc Committee on the CRPD, 'Letter dated 2005/10/07 from the Chairman to all members of the Committee' (14 October 2005) A/AC.265/2006/1, paras 23–24.

[128] Villiger, *Commentary on the VCLT*, 445.

[129] Dörr and Schmalenbach, *VCLT*, 627; Sinclair, *The VCLT*, 138.

[130] See van Alebeek and Nollkaemper, 'The Legal Status', 410–11.

[131] ILC, 'Report on Subsequent Agreements and Subsequent Practice', paras 49–65; see also Pellet, 'Article 38', 859–60.

[132] Villiger, *Commentary on the VCLT*, 446.

identified in the previous part of this book constitutes such a consistent pattern and may thus be utilised as a supplementary means of interpretation.

Furthermore, Article 32 of the VCLT introduces the possibility of referring to the pronouncements of literary commentators. As discussed earlier in book, there are some authors who support the idea of a common standard of realisation for all rights.[133] But even those who appear to be critical of the idea of progressive elements for all rights, in substance, only reject the narrow reading of progressiveness while implicitly endorsing a uniform standard which coincides with the umbrella reading of the term.[134] Another point to mention here are the Maastricht Guidelines on Violations of Economic, Social and Cultural Rights which were the result of extensive discussions amongst experts from various nations brought together in the framework of the International Commission of Jurists (IComJ).[135] This document declares that '[t]he fact that the full realisation of most economic, social and cultural rights can only be achieved progressively ... in fact also applies to most civil and political rights'.[136]

It is also commonly accepted that the jurisprudence of international as well as national courts is part of the unlisted supplementary sources. For reasons of succinctness, this jurisprudence will only be discussed briefly. These materials could, however, constitute interesting areas of further research. On the international level, there is jurisprudence by the ECtHR and the IACtHR supporting the idea of a uniform standard of realisation including progressive elements for all rights. One example from the ECtHR has already been mentioned above. In *Airey v Ireland*, the Court finds that 'there is no water-tight division separating that sphere [ie, socio-economic rights] from the field covered by the Convention',[137] implying that such an uncertain differentiation might not be suitable to use as a point of reference for legal differentiations. Another decision by the ECtHR further supports the thesis of this book. In *Frăsilă and Ciocîrlan v Romania*, the Court finds that

> in determining whether or not a positive obligation exists, regard must be had to the fair balance that has to be struck between the general interest of the community and the interests of the individual, the search for which is inherent throughout the Convention. The scope of this obligation will inevitably vary, having regard to the diversity of situations obtaining in Contracting States, the difficulties involved in policing modern societies and the choices which must be made in terms of priorities and resources. Nor must such an obligation be interpreted in such a way as to impose an impossible or disproportionate burden on the authorities (see, among other authorities, Özgür Gündem v. Turkey, no. 23144/93, § 43, ECHR 2000-III).[138]

[133] See further 1.4.
[134] See, eg, 8.3.2.1. and 9.3.1.1.
[135] See IComJ, 'Maastricht Guidelines'.
[136] ibid, para 8.
[137] ECtHR, *Airey v Ireland*, para 26.
[138] ECtHR, *Frăsilă and Ciocîrlan v Romania* (2012) App No 25329/03, para 55.

With this argument, the Court establishes that the positive obligations of all rights are dependent on the availability of resources and the conditions in each specific State party generally. A progressive notion also underlies the ECtHR's approach to non-discrimination regarding gender. In *Petrovic v Austria*, the Court notes that '[o]nly gradually, as society has moved towards a more equal sharing between men and women of responsibilities for the bringing up of their children, have the Contracting States introduced measures extending to fathers, like entitlement to parental leave'.[139]

The IACtHR adopts a very similar approach in *Sawhoyamaxa Indigenous Community v Paraguay*, finding that

> a State cannot be responsible for all situations in which the right to life is at risk. … Taking into account the difficulties involved in the planning and adoption of public policies and the operative choices that have to be made in view of the priorities and the resources available, the positive obligations of the State must be interpreted so that an impossible or disproportionate burden is not imposed upon the authorities.[140]

It is particularly relevant to remember that the HRC referred to this jurisprudence when establishing its concept of 'disproportionate burdens' in the context of the right to life under Article 6 of the ICCPR.[141]

On this basis, the justices argue that the State party was not in violation of the ECHR due to the fact that it 'appears difficult to criticise the Austrian legislature for having introduced in a gradual manner … legislation which is, all things considered, very progressive in Europe'.[142] Further comparison could be made to the jurisprudence of the African Commission on Human and Peoples' Rights (ACHPR). In the case of *Zimbabwe Human Rights NGO Forum v Zimbabwe*, the Commission clearly envisions a uniform standard of positive obligations for civil and political as well as socio-economic rights.[143]

Lastly, domestic jurisprudence may also be of interest. Because this source is beyond the scope of this book, two brief examples will suffice in order to illustrate that a uniform standard of progressive realisation of human rights is not foreign to national legal orders. One interesting example is the jurisprudence of the South African Constitutional Court. The South African conception of reasonableness has served as a model for Article 8 (4) of the ICESCR-OP.[144] In the context of the UN human rights system, reasonableness has since been inextricably linked to the progressive realisation of socio-economic rights. Yet, this concept has never been limited to socio-economic rights in South African jurisprudence. Instead, the Constitutional Court of South Africa explicitly linked

[139] ECtHR, *Petrovic v Austria* ECHR 1998-I 21 (1998) 33 EHRR 14, para 40.

[140] IACtHR, *Sawhoyamaxa Indigenous Community v Paraguay*, para 155; both Courts also reference each other's jurisprudence in this context.

[141] See further 5.5.1.

[142] ECtHR , *Petrovic v Austria*, para 41.

[143] See ACHPR, *Zimbabwe Human Rights NGO Forum v Zimbabwe* (2006) Comm No 245/02.

[144] See Porter, 'Reasonableness and Article 8(4)', 178–84.

this standard of review to positive obligations, regardless of their category.[145] An interesting point of comparison is also the jurisprudence of the Supreme Court of India and its doctrine of progressive realisation (of all rights).[146]

9.5. THE RESULT OF THE INTERPRETATION

For the question initially posed, the treaty analysis has yielded the following results. Most methods of interpretation clearly support the idea that civil and political rights must not be immediate in the strict sense of the word and that, instead, a uniform standard of realisation should apply to all rights which includes not only immediate but also progressive obligations. The only aspect which leads to some degree of ambiguity is the fact that the treaties set out progressive realisation explicitly only for socio-economic rights. There is some validity to the *argumentum e contrario* derived from this contextual circumstance. To find a definitive result of the interpretation, it is necessary to determine the relative weight and the interrelationship of interpretational methods. There are several good arguments why an *a contrario* reading in itself cannot determine the correct interpretation of a treaty provision.

Firstly, this instrument of treaty interpretation is usually not accorded sufficient independent weight in the 'crucible of interpretation' to warrant an interpretational result which is not supported by other methods. Even from a rather orthodox perspective with a clear focus on the treaty text, this aspect is usually not perceived as automatically dictating a certain result.[147] A recent case before the ICJ illustrates this. In *Alleged Violations of Sovereign Rights and Maritime Spaces in the Caribbean Sea (Nicaragua v Colombia)*, the ICJ argues that, while '[a]n a contrario reading of a treaty provision ... has been employed by both the present Court ... and the Permanent Court of International Justice', it must be stressed that '[s]uch an interpretation is only warranted ... when it is appropriate in light of the text of all the provisions concerned, their context and the object and purpose of the treaty'.[148]

Other commentators even consider the *a contrario* reading to be a line of argumentation which falls not into the category of contextual interpretation but rather of supplementary means of interpretation under Article 32 of the VCLT,[149]

[145] See Fowkes, 'Normal Rights, Just New', 734 (fn) with reference to South African Constitutional Court, *Rail Commuters Action Grp. v Transnet Ltd. t/a Metrorail* 2005 (2) SA 359 (CC), paras 84, 86–88.

[146] See, eg, Supreme Court of India, *Navtej Singh Johar and Others v Union of India through Secretary Ministry of Law and Justice*, Writ Petition No 76 of 2016, paras 178–90.

[147] See A Senegacnik, 'Expressio Unius (Est) Exclusio Alterius', Max Planck Encyclopaedia of International Law, opil.ouplaw.com/display/10.1093/law-mpeipro/e3383.013.3383/law-mpeipro-e3383?prd=MPIL%2F1000, paras 35, 36.

[148] ICJ, *Alleged Violations of Sovereign Rights and Maritime Spaces in the Caribbean Sea (Nicaragua v Colombia)* (Preliminary Objections, Judgment) [2016] ICJ Rep 3, para 37.

[149] See, eg, Villiger, *Commentary on the VCLT*, 445.

which further indicates its inability to be a sufficient argument by itself. The contextual interpretation above has shown that the text of the treaties as a whole provides ample evidence against an *a contrario* reading of the general obligation provisions, as do explorations of the object and purpose and all other methods of interpretation.

Secondly, the insistence upon the relevance of wording and context usually represents the effort to give effect to the intent of the drafting parties. This argument would assume that socio-economic and civil and political rights require a differential treatment because this was the will of the drafting parties. This means that the *travaux préparatoires* assume a particularly important role in determining the weight of an *a contrario* reading because they provide information about the true intent of the drafters. However, as has become clear in this chapter, the original intent as deduced from the *travaux préparatoires* does not indicate such a conclusion. The drafters did not want to establish an obligation of immediate realisation in the strict sense of the word for civil and political rights and also did not envision progressive realisation as an indeterminate standard. The different formulation of general obligation provisions is rooted in a misunderstanding. It is a mistake in drafting rather than a reflection of the true intentions of States parties.

Thirdly, there is a good argument for prioritising effectiveness considerations rather than the wording of the general obligation provisions in this specific case. This argument flows from the special nature of human rights treaties. George Letsas convincingly differentiates between the concrete and abstract will of the drafting States or their 'intentions of detail' and their 'intentions of principle', determining that the latter shall be at the centre of interpretation in the form of an objective determination of the object and purpose of human rights treaties.[150] He explains that the abstract intention of the drafting parties to establish an international system of human rights protection should be prioritised over their concrete intentions regarding the precise elaboration of human rights and the pursuant obligations.[151] This is so, Letsas argues, because the States parties undoubtedly intended to 'give effect to the more abstract moral truths rather than to their own imperfect understanding of what these moral truths are'.[152]

Hence, it is not the goal of the treaties, as discernible from the abstract intention of the parties, to give effect to some specific original delineation of rights and obligations but rather to give effect to the general goal of creating a functioning and, above all, effective human rights regime. A predominant weight of object and purpose is furthermore necessitated by the requirement to interpret treaties according to good faith.[153] It can also be argued that this focus on the abstract intentions of State parties is not something inherent to the special

[150] See Letsas, 'Strasbourg's Interpretive Ethic', 532–41.
[151] ibid, 538.
[152] ibid, 540.
[153] See Alston and Quinn, 'Obligations under the ICESCR', 160–61.

nature of human rights treaties but rather a consequence of the general issue that provisions in international treaties often are formulated in a vague manner out of necessity.[154] Regardless of the subject matter at hand, the abstract intent of parties, ie, the object and purpose of the treaty, becomes more relevant the less clarity the interpreted norms exhibit. This has been recognised even by more traditionally minded commentators such as Arnold McNair.[155]

As a last point, another reference to the now familiar misunderstanding is in order. A thorough inspection of the arguments extended in this regard has revealed that the *argumentum e contrario* is utilised only to reject the idea that States parties may take their time when realising civil and political rights. In substance, critics make a teleological argument: it is not argued that categories of rights must be different as a matter of principle, but instead that civil and political rights cannot be 'weakened' by a standard which includes progressive obligations. One such example can be found in the work of Egon Schwelb who generally argues for the immediate and not progressive implementation of the ICCPR. Schwelb, after employing the *argumentum e contrario*, argues that States parties would be in violation of the principle of good faith in the interpretation and application of the ICCPR if they delayed the establishment of the necessary legislation by several years.[156] It appears that he argues not for an immediate realisation of all positive aspects of civil and political rights but instead against a postponement of those obligations which are considered to be immediately realisable in the context of progressive realisation, as well.

Anja Seibert-Fohr, likewise on the basis of an *a contrario* reading, perceives progressive realisation as 'a mere promotional type of commitment', contrasting it with the 'stringent' obligations under the ICCPR. She argues that only the latter apply from the point in time where a State becomes a party to the Covenant.[157] Like Schwelb, she does not reject the idea that States parties must take immediate action while substantive fulfilment will take time, but instead only asserts that civil and political rights cannot be read as establishing only 'promotional' obligations. In the context of the CRC, Jonathan Todres adheres to the traditional differentiation between immediately and progressively realisable rights with reference to Article 4 of the CRC.[158] He also proceeds from a very weak reading of progressive realisation in general, considering that this concept provides States parties with a loophole which reflects the nature of the ICESCR as a 'relatively weak international human rights treaty'. The ICESCR, in Todres' interpretation, does not require States parties to actually ensure rights but instead only demands that they '"take steps" toward ensuring' those rights.[159]

[154] See Çalı, 'Specialized Rules', 508.
[155] See AD McNair, *The Law of Treaties* (Oxford, Oxford University Press, 1961).
[156] Schwelb, 'The Nature of the Obligations', 310.
[157] Seibert-Fohr, 'Domestic Implementation', 405.
[158] Todres, 'Emerging Limitations', 178.
[159] ibid.

With this statement, Todres shows that he does not take into consideration the concrete and immediate obligations flowing from progressive realisation according to the interpretation which the CESCR has been applying for decades now.

9.6. CONCLUSION

This part has shown that the treaties allow an interpretation of civil and political rights which includes progressive obligations. This means that the convergent tendencies discovered in part II are in accordance with international human rights law. It has become clear that the drafting parties envisioned standards of realisation for both categories that are quite similar to each other, which, upon a closer look, turns out to be reflected in the treaty texts. The fact that progressive realisation was explicitly included only for socio-economic rights can be considered a misguided reflection of the artificial dichotomy between positive and negative rights and, therefore, a mistake in drafting rather than a conscious decision to establish different methods of implementation.[160] An interpretation of the treaty texts reveals that a standard analogous to progressive realisation is already implicit for civil and political rights. In accordance with the legal principle that repetitious clauses are harmless,[161] the superfluous prescription of progressive realisation for socio-economic rights can be ignored.

The only way to accord any legal relevance to this textual feature would be to return to the notion that civil and political rights are purely negative. Only then it would be possible to treat civil and political rights as immediate in the strict sense of the word. This, however, is not an option in line with the principles of treaty interpretation. The drafting parties were clearly proceeding from a positive conception of all rights, which is also reflected in the text of the treaties, for example in the phrase 'respect and … ensure' in Article 2 of the ICCPR. The notion of a tripartite structure of obligations has long been widely accepted in international human rights law.[162] With the divide between positive and negative rights surpassed and the tripartite structure of obligations generally acknowledged, there is no reasonable argument for clinging to the divide between immediately and progressively realisable rights.

What remains is a discussion about degree, namely about the extent of positive obligations pursuant to civil and political rights. It is, of course, subject to reasonable debate how far the positive duties of States parties should go, eg, in the context of the right to life under Article 6 of the ICCPR. Whether there is (or should be) a *gradual* difference regarding the timeline of realisation between the

[160] See also Dhanda, 'Constructing a New Human Rights Lexicon', 48; Brems, 'Minimum and Maximum Perspectives', 365.

[161] This principle is also often termed *superflua non nocent*, see 'Superflua non nocent' in BA Garner (ed), *Black's Law Dictionary*, 11th edn (St Paul, Thomson Reuters, 2019).

[162] See further 1.3.1.

two categories of rights due to a *gradual* difference regarding the extent of positive obligations is a good question but also a question which does not need to be addressed here. This is so because it suffices to establish that the treaties do not warrant a *categorical* differentiation between those rights in order to argue that both categories should be subject to the same flexible conception of realisation. It is, for example, very much possible to apply the concept of progressive realisation to a conservative reading of the right to life under Article 6 of the ICCPR without depriving the right of its impact. Progressive realisation demands that States parties extend the maximum effort at any point in time. If the right to life is read to entail only limited positive action and resource expenditure, States parties could rarely point to any restricting factors to prolong the period of realisation. The right would entail mostly obligations which are immediate in the strict sense of the word. Thus, progressive realisation can exist as a uniform standard even when the precise extent of positive civil and political rights obligations remains under debate.

Just as in the jurisprudence of the Committees, most arguments for an immediate realisation of civil and political rights – be it in literature or the *travaux préparatoires* – in fact set out immediacy mostly for obligations of conduct. This means that, upon a closer look, most commentators accept that, while States must immediately take action, there are long-term goals which are not immediate in the strict sense of the word. The few proponents of a uniform standard, however, endorse the application of the umbrella concept of progressive realisation which also includes immediate obligations. After clearing up this terminological misunderstanding, it becomes clear that both modes of realisation converge and that there never has been a real argument for a differential treatment of socio-economic and civil and political rights.

Conclusion, Recommendations, and Outlook

SUMMARY OF RESULTS

THE MOST IMPORTANT conclusions of this book are the following. A differentiation between immediately and progressively realisable categories of rights is inconsistent from a theoretical perspective, does not happen in practice, and is not required by law. Accordingly, it is time to abandon this last stubborn dichotomy between socio-economic and civil and political rights and to accept a uniform standard of obligations for all rights. Instead, literary commentators and practitioners should embrace the methodology developed under the term of progressive realisation, ie, a combination of an immediate obligation to take steps with the long-term obligation of full realisation. It is this methodology which underlies the de facto uniform standard of realisation of the Committees.

While this means that both categories shall be equal from a legal point of view, it does not necessarily entail giving up the categories altogether. As suggested by James Fowkes, it would be perfectly reasonable to employ the categories for purely 'taxonomical' purposes.[1] But this is where the relevance of these categories must end, not only because there are no differences in the nature of the categories which would warrant a legal differentiation but also because no clear boundary between them can be established.

COORDINATION, CROSS-REFERENCING, AND A JOINT GENERAL COMMENT

The Committees must resolve the contradiction between the alleged immediate/progressive rights divide and the fact that they apply a uniform standard to all rights. Their jurisprudence enjoys less credibility, and it cannot fulfil its function as legally sound guidance for the States parties when there are doctrinal inconsistencies. It is inappropriate to ignore the fact that the Committees, in fact, already apply a uniform standard of realisation in many instances even though the experts claim that they do not. This issue is clearly not going away and the Committees must deal with it. Accordingly, it is proposed that the Committees embrace the concept of a uniform standard of realisation explicitly.

[1] Fowkes, 'Normal Rights, Just New', 725.

Furthermore, cases where the Committees do apply a strict understanding of immediacy to civil and political rights constitute missed opportunities because this prevents the Committees from engaging with broader policy issues, particularly in the context of Individual Communications. Recognising the contextual variability of positive obligations, furthermore, might promote the acceptability of human rights obligations.

In practice, the Committees must align their doctrinal approaches to the nature of States parties' obligations and also communicate this to the States parties in a way which does not leave room for misunderstandings. Early on after the adoption of the ICESCR-OP, it was noted that the HRC and the CESCR have points of intersection regarding their mandate which require 'consultative arrangements'[2] between the treaty bodies in order to promote inter-Committee 'cross-fertilization'.[3] This aspect remains important to this day and also applies to the inter-relationship between the HRC, CESCR and the rest of the Committees. Cooperation is particularly important regarding points which are of such a general nature that all Committees cannot avoid dealing with them. One such point is the nature of States parties' obligations, particularly when considering the fact that the Committees are moving towards a de facto uniform standard of realisation across all regimes.

Cooperation between the Committees has taken place in different forms for some time now. Annual meetings of chairpersons were established in 1983 in response to a General Assembly Resolution in order to discuss how to enhance the work of the treaty bodies.[4] These meetings still take place to this day.[5] Additionally, from 2002 to 2011, inter-committee meetings took place which included additional members from the Committees. This format was abolished at the Chairpersons' 23rd session in 2011 in favour of a more specific approach founded on ad hoc working groups which should discuss common challenges and promote the harmonisation of working methods and jurisprudence.[6]

[2] UNCHR, 'Limburg Principles', para 98.

[3] See Scott, 'Interdependence and Permeability', 849 who borrows the term 'cross-fertilization' from T Meron, *Human Rights Law-Making in the United Nations: A Critique of Instruments and Process* (Oxford, Oxford University Press, 1986) 242.

[4] See UNGA Res 38/117 'Reporting Obligations of the States Parties to the International Covenants on Human Rights' (16 December 1983) A/RES/38/117; the General Assembly referred back to a corresponding recommendation by the HRC, see HRC, 'Report on the 19th Session' (15 September 1963) A/38/40(SUPP), para 32. In 1995, the UNGA adopted a resolution which called for an annual rhythm of the Chairpersons' meetings, see UNGA Res 49/178 'Effective Implementation of International Instruments on Human Rights, including Reporting Obligations under International Instruments on Human Rights' (23 December 1994) A/RES/49/178.

[5] For information on the most recent and previous meetings, see www.ohchr.org/en/treaty-bodies/annual-meeting-chairpersons-human-rights-treaty-bodies.

[6] UNGA, 'Report of the Chairs of the Human Rights Treaty Bodies on their 23rd Meeting' (22 July 2011) A/66/175, para 25: 'The Chairs agreed that the inter-committee meeting in its current format should be abolished and transformed, for instance, into ad hoc thematic working groups to be established at the request of the Chairs. Such working groups could discuss issues of common interest, including the harmonization of treaty body jurisprudence.'

At the same meeting, the Chairpersons decided to discuss at their 24th session joint statements and joint General Comments and Recommendations as ways to increase coordination.[7]

The Chairpersons' annual meetings have mostly focused on a harmonisation of working methods.[8] There is also no information available suggesting that ad hoc working groups have been established which are concerned with the dogmatic alignment of States parties' obligations between the treaty bodies. This framework would, however, be the logical point of departure for such an alignment regarding the timeframe of realisation for the rights in the treaties. Thus, the first recommendation issued here is that the Committees should utilise their annual meetings format in order to harmonise their approach to the timeframe of realisation, ideally by establishing an ad hoc working group regarding a universal standard of realisation as suggested in the previous section.

In a second step, the alignment of doctrinal approaches must find its way to the States parties through the various ways in which the Committees present their legal views. Specifically, this means introducing the universal standard of realisation into Concluding Observations, views on Individual Communications, and, most importantly, into General Comments and Recommendations. When doing so, the Committees should increase cross-referencing between the treaty regimes. It is not unusual that the Committees reference the work of their 'sister human rights bodies' when drafting General Comments and Recommendations.[9] It is rare, however, that they cross-reference Committee jurisprudence on socio-economic rights when they are concerned with States parties' obligations resulting from civil and political rights.[10] It is precisely this approach which should be strengthened.

The Committees should take into account the guidance regarding progressive realisation developed in the context of socio-economic rights when engaging with civil and political rights. For example, when updating its General Comment on the Right to Life, the HRC should not hesitate to draw from the CESCR's General Comment No 3 on States Parties' Obligations in order to clarify the relationship of immediate obligations of conduct and progressive obligations of result.

Another more direct way of signifying the unity of States parties' obligations would be to adopt a joint General Comment/Recommendation on this matter.[11]

[7] See ibid, para 23.

[8] See, for example, UNGA, 'Report of the Chairs of the Human Rights Treaty Bodies on their 31st Annual Meeting' (30 July 2019) A/74/256; UNGA, 'Report of the Chairs of the Human Rights Treaty Bodies on their 32nd Annual Meeting' (14 September 2020) A/75/346 and UNGA, 'Report of the Chairs of the Human Rights Treaty Bodies on their 33rd Annual Meeting' (30 July 2021) A/76/254.

[9] This term was used by CERD, 'General Recommendation No 35', para 4.

[10] Some rare examples have been examined above as evidence for the application of a uniform standard of obligations.

[11] This has also been suggested by Brems, 'Minimum and Maximum Perspectives', 369.

Until now, joint General Comments and Recommendations have been adopted on issues at the intersection of two different treaty regimes.[12] There is not yet any such joint document by more than two treaty bodies. Even though it might present a challenge to coordinate work on a joint General Comment/Recommendation by all treaty bodies, the methods of cooperation set out above make this a viable approach. This is illustrated by the fact that, in 2021, the CEDAW-Com, CED, CMW, CRC-Com, CRPD-Com, and the Subcommittee on Prevention of Torture and other Cruel, Inhuman or Degrading Treatment or Punishment (SPT) adopted a joint statement on corruption and human rights.[13] This statement, similar to a General Comment or Recommendation, includes a section on the obligations of States parties to respect, protect, and fulfil human rights in the context of corruption.

Because of the political volatility of the issue, however, it would be useful to ensure some sort of dialogue with States parties and other stakeholders when drafting the joint General Comment/Recommendation. For that purpose, the Committees should organise a collective Day of General Discussion on the nature of States parties' obligations. Most Committees in the UN system hold such events in order to allow States parties, NGOs, intergovernmental organisations, and individuals to partake in the discussion about a certain topic pertinent to the treaty regime in question.[14] The Days of General Discussion also serve to provide the basis for future General Comments or Recommendations. As such, the HRC received numerous input statements regarding its then draft General Comment No 36 on the Right to Life.[15] This type of dialogical approach would enable the Committees to respond to States parties and other stakeholders and thereby prevent misunderstandings about the uniform standard of obligations. In particular, the experts could stress that the standard of realisation regarding civil and political rights is not weakened by recognising that some positive aspects of these rights will require time to realise.

[12] See, eg, CRC-Com, 'General Comment No 18 on Harmful Practices' and CEDAW-Com, 'General Recommendation No 31 on Harmful Practices'.

[13] www.ohchr.org/sites/default/files/Documents/HRBodies/TB/AnnualMeeting/JointStatementonCorruptionandHR20May2021.docx.

[14] Days of General Discussion have been held on a biannual basis by the CESCR since 1989; information and reports on these days of discussion are available at www.ohchr.org/en/treaty-bodies/cescr/days-general-discussion; see also CESCR, 'Report on the 44th and 45th Sessions' (3 May 2011) E/2011/22, para 49. The CRC-Com has utilised this concept since 1992, see www.ohchr.org/en/treaty-bodies/crc/days-general-discussion; this measure has been based on what is now Rule 79 of the CRC-Com's rules of procedure, see CRC-Com, 'Rules of Procedure' (1 March 2019) CRC/C/4/Rev.5. The CEDAW started to utilise this format in 2011, see www.ohchr.org/en/treaty-bodies/cedaw/general-discussion-days. The CRPD has done so since 2013, see www.ohchr.org/en/treaty-bodies/crpd/days-general-discussion. Since 2000, the CERD holds regular 'thematic discussions', which effectively have the same purpose, see www.ohchr.org/en/treaty-bodies/cerd/thematic-discussions. The HRC also holds irregular (half) days of general discussion; reference to this is made in HRC, 'The Relationship of the Human Rights Committee with Nongovernmental Organizations' (4 June 2012) CCPR/C/104/3, para 14.

[15] See the input statements available at the URL cited in ch 8, n 169.

OUTLOOK AND FURTHER AVENUES OF RESEARCH

The issue of positive civil and political rights obligations and their standard of realisation becomes more pressing as this category of rights is interpreted more extensively. There is a trend in the jurisprudence of the HRC towards the extension of the scope of rights under the ICCPR. This has been particularly clear in the context of the right to life under Article 6 of the ICCPR.[16] It is thus only a matter of time until other commentators and, more significantly, States parties note the inconsistencies in the jurisprudence of the Committees. This is why it is necessary to take action as soon as possible.

The extensive interpretation or 'permeability' of civil and political rights has not remained without criticism.[17] One aspect which certainly warrants closer examination is the fact that this approach leads to the blurring of lines between the scopes of different rights. This was criticised, for example, during the drafting of HRC General Comment No 36 on the Right to Life. The relevant US statement contained the following assessment: 'Although the United States agrees that human rights treaties may be mutually reinforcing, this does not mean that the contents of obligations contained within one human rights treaty can be imputed or read into other human rights treaties.'[18]

It is a valid point of criticism that complicating the demarcation of different rights might create difficulties and, ultimately, might weaken their protection. To be clear, this concern exists not because such a mixing of rights transcends the boundaries of the categories of socio-economic and civil and political rights. As has been argued extensively, this delimitation is of no legal value. It is still questionable, however, if it benefits rights protection when separating the scopes of different rights becomes increasingly difficult and, ultimately, arbitrary. Others do not see this as an issue but rather as a chance to promote greater unity or even a 'partial fusion' of the treaties.[19] Whatever the result, it is necessary to further engage with this question.

Another potential area of research would be a comparative assessment of the nature of States parties' obligations in other international treaty regimes, such as the ECHR and the European Social Charter (ESC).[20] A similar issue might exist in this context, considering the differences in the treaty texts. Part I of the ESC holds that '[t]he Parties accept as the aim of their policy, to be pursued by all appropriate means both national and international in character, the attainment of conditions in which the following rights and principles may be effectively

[16] See further 4.5.2.

[17] See, eg, Schmahl, *CRC-Commentary*, 127, regarding the right to life in the CRC.

[18] Input statement by the USA for HRC for draft General Comment No 36, available at the URL cited in ch 8, n 169.

[19] See, eg, Scott, 'Interdependence and Permeability'.

[20] European Convention of Human Rights (adopted 4 November 1950, entered into force 3 September 1953) ETS 5; European Social Charter (adopted 3 May 1996, entered into force 1 July 1999) ETS 163.

realised'. The ECHR, in contrast, declares that '[t]he High Contracting Parties shall secure to everyone within their jurisdiction the rights and freedoms defined in Section I of this Convention'. The European system furthermore establishes two different implementation mechanisms: the ECtHR which is mandated to adopt legally binding decisions on civil and political rights violations, and the European Committee of Social Rights (ECSR) which is responsible for a reporting mechanism leading only to non-binding conclusions and, in some cases, recommendations by the Council of Europe's Committee of Ministers. Thus, the European implementation regime displays a differentiation similar to the one which used to exist in the UN system.

The findings of this book must also be viewed in the context of the ongoing discussion about strengthening the UN human rights treaty body system. Since 1988, there have been efforts to improve the effectiveness of the Committees' work, mainly by establishing common and streamlined working methods such as the simplified reporting procedure.[21] But this process also brought forth proposals for structural reforms. One such proposal was Louise Arbour's idea of a unified standing treaty body.[22] In 2006, Arbour's concept paper argued that a single treaty body would solve issues of duplication as well as procedural inconsistencies – particularly in the reporting procedure – and would make the system more accessible, transparent, and visible for outsiders. But she also presented arguments from a substantive viewpoint, declaring that a unified treaty body would be 'more likely to produce consistent and authoritative jurisprudence'.[23] She rightfully recognised that the boundaries of treaty regimes are relevant neither for States parties nor for individuals exercising their human rights.[24] Accordingly, a unified treaty body could, for example, adopt General Comments

[21] The process started with Philip Alston proposing, inter alia, consolidated State reports for the six treaty bodies existing at that time, see UNCHR, 'Final Report on Enhancing the Long-term Effectiveness of the United Nations Human Rights Treaty System by the Independent Expert Philip Alston' (27 March 1997) E/CN.4/1997/74, and continued under the auspices of UNHCHR Navi Pillay and Louise Arbour, see UNHCHR, 'Report of UN High Commissioner for Human Rights Navi Pillay on the Strengthening of Human Rights Treaty Bodies Pursuant to General Assembly Resolution 66/254' (26 June 2012) A/66/860 and UNHCHR, 'Concept Paper on the High Commissioner's Proposal for a Unified Standing Treaty Body' (22 March 2006) HRI/MC/2006/2. Navi Pillay's report of 2012 inspired the GA to adopt a Resolution in 2014 which called for 'strengthening and enhancing the effective functioning of the human rights treaty body system' and an overall review of the system in 2020, see UNGA Res 68/268 'Strengthening and Enhancing the Effective Functioning of the Human Rights Treaty Body System' (9 April 2014) A/RES/68/268. In 2020, the corresponding report was adopted, see UNGA, 'Report on the Process of the Consideration of the State of the United Nations Human Rights Treaty Body System' (17 November 2020) A/75/601. Most recently, the Chairpersons of the treaty bodies addressed the results of the 2020 report in their 34th meeting in 2022, see UNGA, 'Report of the Chairs of the Human Rights Treaty Bodies on their 34th Meeting' (26 July 2022) A/77/228.

[22] See UNHCHR, 'Concept Paper on the High Commissioner's Proposal for a Unified Standing Treaty Body'.

[23] ibid, para 27.

[24] ibid, para 28.

or Recommendations which would represent a 'holistic approach to overlapping obligations in the treaties'.[25]

Arbour's proposal has not led to a reform of the UN treaty system, at least not regarding the creation of a uniform treaty body. However, the findings of this book suggest reconsidering this issue. The Committees are implicitly applying a very similar standard of realisation to all rights regardless of their category or treaty regime. As set out above, coordinating this de facto uniform approach is necessary to ensure the consistency and legitimacy of the Committees' jurisprudence. Such coordination would be improved considerably if a single treaty body were to adopt uniform General Comments/Recommendations. Such a structural reform would also alleviate the problems created by the fact that there is no consistent way of differentiating between categories of rights and, therefore, to delineate treaty regimes.

In any case, it would be useful to pay consideration to the de facto uniform standard of realisation when establishing new frameworks of cooperation between the Committees, for example during the 37th meeting of Chairpersons. Increasing coordination regarding the standard of States parties' obligations will be an important part of ensuring that the treaty bodies can live up to their role as 'one of the greatest achievements in the history of the global struggle for human rights'.[26]

[25] ibid, para 51.

[26] See the foreword by then Secretary-General Ban Ki-moon in UNHCHR, 'Report of UN High Commissioner for Human Rights Navi Pillay on the Strengthening of Human Rights Treaty Bodies', 7.

Bibliography

Albuquerque, C de, 'Chronicle of an Announced Birth: The Coming into Life of the Optional Protocol to the International Covenant on Economic, Social and Cultural Rights – the Missing Piece of the International Bill of Human Rights' (2010) 32 *Human Rights Quarterly* 144.

Alebeek, R van, and Nollkaemper, A, 'The Legal Status of Decisions by Human Rights Treaty Bodies in International Law' in H Keller and G Ulfstein (eds), *UN Human Rights Treaty Bodies: Law and Legitimacy* (Cambridge, Cambridge University Press, 2012) 356–413.

Alexy, R and Rivers, J, (trans) *A Theory of Constitutional Rights* (Oxford, Oxford University Press, 2010).

Alston, P, 'International Law and the Human Right to Food' in P Alston and K Tomaševski (eds), *The Right to Food*, International Studies in Human Rights 4 (Boston, Nijhoff, 1984) 9–68.

—— 'Out of the Abyss: The Challenges Confronting the New U. N. Committee on Economic, Social and Cultural Rights' (1987) 9 *Human Rights Quarterly* 332.

—— 'No Right to Complain About Being Poor: The Need for an Optional Protocol to the Economic Rights Covenant' in A Eide and J Helgesen (eds), *The Future of Human Rights Protection in a Changing World: 50 Years since the Four Freedoms Address. Essays in Honour of Torkel Opsahl* (Oslo, Norwegian University Press, 1991) 79–100.

—— 'The Legal Framework of the Convention on the Rights of the Child' (1992) 91 *Bulletin of Human Rights* 1.

Alston, P and Quinn, G, 'The Nature and Scope of States Parties' Obligations under the International Covenant on Economic, Social and Cultural Rights' (1987) 9 *Human Rights Quarterly* 156.

Antkowiak, T, 'A "Dignified Life" and the Resurgence of Social Rights' (2020) 18 *Northwestern Journal of Human Rights* 1.

Arai-Takahashi, Y, *The Margin of Appreciation Doctrine and the Principle of Proportionality in the Jurisprudence of the ECHR* (Antwerpen, Intersentia, 2002).

Aust, A, *Modern Treaty Law and Practice*, 3rd edn (Cambridge, Cambridge University Press, 2006).

Azaria, D, 'The Legal Significance of Expert Treaty Bodies Pronouncements for the Purpose of the Interpretation of Treaties' (2020) 22 *International Community Law Review* 33.

Baderin, MA and McCorquodale, R, 'The International Covenant on Economic, Social and Cultural Rights: Forty Years of Development' in M Baderin and R McCorquodale (eds), *Economic, Social, and Cultural Rights in Action* (Oxford, Oxford University Press, 2007).

Bandes, S, 'The Negative Constitution: A Critique' (1990) 88 *Michigan Law Review* 2271.

Bantekas, I, Stein, MA and Anastasiou, D (eds), *The UN Convention on the Rights of Persons with Disabilities: A Commentary* (Oxford, Oxford University Press, 2018).

Beco, G de, 'The Optional Protocol to the Convention on the Rights of the Child on a Communications Procedure: Good News?' (2013) 13 *Human Rights Law Review* 367.

—— 'The Indivisibility of Human Rights and the Convention on the Rights of Persons with Disabilities' (2019) 68 *International and Comparative Law Quarterly* 141.

Berlin, I, *Four Essays on Liberty* (Oxford, Oxford University Press, 1969).

Besson, S and Kleber, E, 'Article 2: The Right to Non-Discrimination' in J Tobin (ed), *The UN Convention on the Rights of the Child: A Commentary* (Oxford, Oxford University Press, 2019) 41–72.

Bilchitz, D, *Poverty and Fundamental Rights: The Justification and Enforcement of Socio-economic Rights* (Oxford, Oxford University Press, 2007).

Binder, C, *Die Grenzen der Vertragstreue im Völkerrecht: Am Beispiel der nachträglichen Änderung der Umstände*, Beiträge zum ausländischen öffentlichen Recht und Völkerrecht 245 (Heidelberg, Springer, 2013).

Bossuyt, MJ, *Guide to the 'travaux préparatoires' of the International Covenant on Civil and Political Rights* (Dordrecht, Martinus Nijhoff Publishers, 1987).

Boulesbaa, A, 'The Nature of the Obligations Incurred by States under Article 2 of the UN Convention against Torture' (1990) 12 *Human Rights Quarterly* 53.

Brems, E, 'Accommodating Diversity in International Human Rights: Legal Techniques' in Paul Meerts (ed), *Culture and International Law*, From Peace to Justice Series 2 (The Hague, Hague Academic Press, 2008) 63–81.

—— 'Human Rights: Minimum and Maximum Perspectives' (2009) 9 *Human Rights Law Review* 349.

Broderick, A, *The Long and Winding Road to Equality and Inclusion for Persons with Disabilities: The United Nations Convention on the Rights of Persons with Disabilities*, School of Human Rights Research Series Volume 74 (Cambridge, Intersentia, 2015).

—— 'Article 4: General Obligations' in I Bantekas, MA Stein and D Anastasiou (eds), *The UN Convention on the Rights of Persons with Disabilities: A Commentary* (Oxford, Oxford University Press, 2018) 106–39.

Brown, R, Chenwi, L and Stein, MA, 'Equality and Non-Discrimination' in M Langford, B Porter, R Brown and J Rossi (eds), *The Optional Protocol to the International Covenant on Economic, Social and Cultural Rights: A Commentary* (Pretoria, Pretoria University Law Press, 2016) 253–92.

Byrne, S, 'Reclaiming Progressive Realisation: A Children's Rights Analysis' (2020) 28 *International Journal of Children's Rights* 748.

Byrnes, AC, 'Article 2' in MA Freeman, CM Chinkin and B Rudolf (eds), *The UN Convention on the Elimination of All Forms of Discrimination against Women: A Commentary*, 1st edn (Oxford, Oxford University Press, 2012) 71–100.

Çalı, B, 'Specialized Rules of Treaty Interpretation: Human Rights' in DB Hollis (ed), *The Oxford Guide to Treaties*, 2nd edn (Oxford, Oxford University Press, 2020) 504–23.

Çalı, B and Koch, A, 'Explaining Compliance: Lessons Learned from Civil and Political Rights' in M Langford, C Rodríguez-Garavito, and J Rossi (eds), *Social Rights Judgements and the Politics of Compliance: Making it Stick* (Cambridge, Cambridge University Press, 2017) 43–74.

Castellino, J, 'How Effective has CERD been in Protecting Minorities?' in D Keane and A Waughray (eds), *Fifty Years of the International Convention on the Elimination of All Forms of Racial Discrimination: A Living Instrument* (Manchester, Manchester University Press, 2017) 227–45.

Cavallaro, J and Schaffer, E, 'Less as More: Rethinking Supernational Litigation of Economic and Social Rights in the Americas' (2004) 56 *Hastings Law Journal* 217.

Cera, R, 'Article 5: Equality and Non-Discrimination' in V Della Fina, R Cera and G Palmisano (eds), *The United Nations Convention on the Rights of Persons with Disabilities: A Commentary* (Cham, Springer, 2017) 157–74.

Chapman, A, 'A Violations Approach for Monitoring the International Covenant on Economic, Social and Cultural Rights' (1996) 18 *Human Rights Quarterly* 23.

Chapman, A and Russell, S (eds), *Core Obligations: Building a Framework for Economic, Social and Cultural Rights* (Antwerp, Intersentia, 2002).

—— 'Introduction' in A Chapman and S Russell (eds), *Core Obligations: Building a Framework for Economic, Social and Cultural Rights* (Antwerp, Intersentia, 2002).

Chenwi, L, 'Correcting the Historical Asymmetry Between Rights: The Optional Protocol to the International Covenant on Economic, Social and Cultural Rights' (2009) 9 *African Human Rights Law Journal* 23.

—— 'Unpacking "Progressive Realisation", its Relation to Resources, Minimum Core and Reasonableness, and Some Methodological Considerations for Assessing Compliance' (2013) 46 *De Jure* 742.

Christoffersen, J, 'Impact on General Principles of Treaty Interpretation' in MT Kamminga and M Scheinin (eds), *The Impact of Human Rights Law on General International Law* (Oxford, Oxford University Press, 2009) 37–62.
Conte, A and Burchill, R, *Defining Civil and Political Rights: The Jurisprudence of the United Nations Human Rights Committee*, 2nd edn (London, Routledge, 2016).
Coomans, F (ed), *Justiciability of Economic and Social Rights: Experiences from Domestic Systems* (Antwerp, Intersentia, 2006).
Cox, A, 'Foreword: Constitutional Adjudication and the Promotion of Human Rights' (1966) 80 *Harvard Law Review* 91.
Cranston, MW, *Human Rights To-day* (London, Ampersand, 1962).
Craven, M, *The International Covenant on Economic, Social, and Cultural Rights: A Perspective on Its Development* (Oxford, Clarendon, 1995).
—— 'Legal Differentiation and the Concept of the Human Rights Treaty in International Law' (2000) 11 *European Journal of International Law* 489.
Cross, FB, 'The Error of Positive Rights' (2001) 48 *UCLA Law Review* 857.
Currie, DP, 'Positive and Negative Constitutional Rights' (1986) 53 *University of Chicago Law Review* 864.
Della Fina, V, 'Article 4: General Obligations' in V Della Fina, R Cera, and G Palmisano (eds), *The United Nations Convention on the Rights of Persons with Disabilities: A Commentary* (Cham, Springer, 2017) 137–56.
Dennis, MJ and Stewart, DP, 'Justiciability of Economic, Social, and Cultural Rights: Should There Be an International Complaints Mechanism to Adjudicate the Rights to Food, Water, Housing, and Health?' (2004) 98 *American Journal of International Law* 462.
Dhanda, A, 'Constructing a New Human Rights Lexicon: Convention on the Rights of Persons with Disabilities' (2008) 8 *Sur International Journal on Human Rights* 43.
Dörr, O and Schmalenbach, K, *Vienna Convention on the Law of Treaties: A Commentary*, 2nd edn (Berlin, Springer, 2018).
Egan, S, 'The New Complaints Mechanism for the Convention on the Rights of the Child' (2014) 22 *The International Journal of Children's Rights* 205.
Eide, A, 'Realization of Social and Economic Rights – the Minimum Threshold Approach' (1989) 43 *ICJ Review* 40.
—— 'The Four Freedoms and Human Rights in the New International Order' in A Eide and J Helgesen (eds), *The Future of Human Rights Protection in a Changing World: 50 Years since the Four Freedoms Address. Essays in Honour of Torkel Opsahl* (Oslo, Norwegian University Press, 1991) 1–8.
Felner, E, 'Closing the "Escape Hatch": A Toolkit to Monitor the Progressive Realization of Economic, Social, and Cultural Rights' (2009) 1 *Journal of Human Rights Practice* 402.
Ferri, D, 'Reasonable Accommodation as a Gateway to the Equal Enjoyment of Human Rights: From New York to Strasbourg' (2018) 6 *Social Inclusion* 40.
Fiss, O, 'Foreword: The Forms of Justice' (1979) 93 *Harvard Law Review* 1.
Fitzmaurice, M, 'Interpretation of Human Rights Treaties' in D Shelton (ed), *The Oxford Handbook of International Human Rights Law* (Oxford, Oxford University Press, 2013) 739–71.
—— 'Interpretation of the European Convention on Human Rights: Lessons from the Naït-Liman Case' in S Forlati and P Franzina (eds), *Universal Civil Jurisdiction: Which Way Forward?* (Leiden, Brill, 2020).
Flóvenz, BG, 'The Implementation of the UN Convention and the Development of Economical and Social Rights as Human Rights' in OM Arnardóttir and G Quinn (eds), *The UN Convention on the Rights of Persons with Disabilities: European and Scandinavian Perspectives*, International Studies in Human Rights 100 (Leiden, Nijhoff, 2009) 257–77.
Fowkes, J, *Building the Constitution: The Practice of Constitutional Interpretation in Post-Apartheid South Africa*, Cambridge Studies in Constitutional Law 16 (Cambridge, Cambridge University Press, 2016).

—— 'Normal Rights, Just New: Understanding the Judicial Enforcement of Socioeconomic Rights' (2020) 68 *American Journal of Comparative Law* 722.

Franck, TM, *The Power of Legitimacy Among Nations* (Oxford, Oxford University Press, 1990).

Fredman, S, *Human Rights Transformed: Positive Rights and Positive Duties* (Oxford, Oxford University Press 2008).

—— *Comparative Human Rights Law* (Oxford, Oxford University Press, 2018).

Freeman, MA, Chinkin, CM and Rudolf, B, 'Article 24' in MA Freeman, CM Chinkin and B Rudolf (eds), *The UN Convention on the Elimination of All Forms of Discrimination against Women: A Commentary*, 1st edn (Oxford, Oxford University Press, 2012) 539–46.

—— 'Article 3' in MA Freeman, CM Chinkin and B Rudolf (eds), *The UN Convention on the Elimination of All Forms of Discrimination against Women: A Commentary*, 1st edn (Oxford, Oxford University Press, 2012) 101–22.

Fried, C, *Right and Wrong* (Cambridge, Harvard University Press, 1978).

Fuller, LL, 'The Forms and Limits of Adjudication' (1978) 92 *Harvard Law Review* 353.

Gardiner, RK, *Treaty Interpretation*, 2nd edn (Oxford, Oxford University Press, 2015).

Garner, BA (ed), *Black's Law Dictionary*, 11th edn (St. Paul, Thomson Reuters, 2019).

Garner, BA and Black, HC, *Black's Law Dictionary*, 10th edn (St. Paul, Thomson Reuters, 2014).

Gearty, CA and Mantouvalou, V, *Debating Social Rights*, Debating Law 2 (Oxford, Hart Publishing, 2011).

Goodwin-Gill, GS, 'Obligations of Conduct and Result' in P Alston and K Tomaševski (eds), *The Right to Food*, International Studies in Human Rights 4 (Boston, Nijhoff, 1984) 111–18.

Green, M, 'What We Talk About When We Talk About Indicators: Current Approaches to Human Rights Measurement' (2001) 23 *Human Rights Quarterly* 1062.

Hayek, FA and Hamowy, R (ed), *The Constitution of Liberty: The Definitive Edition*, The Collected Works of F.A. Hayek 17 (London, Routledge, 2012).

Henkin, L, 'Introduction' in L Henkin (ed), *The International Bill of Rights: The Covenant on Civil and Political Rights* (New York, Columbia University Press, 1981) 1–31.

Heringa, AW, 'Judicial Enforcement of Article 26 of the International Covenant on Civil and Political Rights in the Netherlands' (1993) 24 *Netherlands Yearbook of International Law* 139.

Heymann, J, McNeill, K and Raub, A, 'Rights Monitoring and Assessment Using Quantitative Indicators of Law and Policy: International Covenant on Economic, Social and Cultural Rights' (2015) 37 *Human Rights Quarterly* 1071.

Higgins, R, 'Human Rights: Some Questions of Integrity' (1989) 15 *Commonwealth Law Bulletin* 598.

Holmes, S and Sunstein, CR, *The Cost of Rights: Why Liberty Depends on Taxes* (New York, Norton, 2000).

Hoof, GJH van, 'The Legal Nature of Economic, Social and Cultural Rights: A Rebuttal of Some Traditional Views' in P Alston and K Tomaševski (eds), *The Right to Food*, International Studies in Human Rights 4 (Boston, Nijhoff, 1984) 97–111.

Humphrey, JP, 'Letter to the Editor' (1984) 6 *Human Rights Quarterly* 539.

IComJ, 'Maastricht Guidelines on Violations of Economic, Social and Cultural Rights' (1998) 20 *Human Rights Quarterly* 691

ILC, 'Draft Articles on the Law of Treaties with Commentaries' (1966) *Yearbook of the International Law Commission* 187.

Jhabvala, F, 'On Human Rights and the Socio-Economic Context' (1984) 31 *Netherlands International Law Review* 149.

—— 'The Practice of the Covenant's Human Rights Committee, 1976-82: Review of State Party Reports' (1984) 6 *Human Rights Quarterly* 81.

—— 'Domestic Implementation of the Covenant on Civil and Political Rights' (1985) 32 *Netherlands International Law Review* 461.

Kakoullis, EJ and Ikehara, Y, 'Article 1: Purpose' in I Bantekas, MA Stein and D Anastasiou (eds), *The UN Convention on the Rights of Persons with Disabilities: A Commentary* (Oxford, Oxford University Press, 2018) 35–62.

Kälin, W and Künzli, J, *The Law of International Human Rights Protection*, 2nd edn (Oxford, Oxford University Press, 2019).
Kelley, D, *A Life of One's Own: Individual Rights and the Welfare State* (Washington, Cato Institute, 1998).
Kilcommins, S, 'Doctrinal Legal Method (Black Letterism): Assumptions, Commitments and Shortcomings' in L Cahillane and J Schweppe (eds), *Legal Research Methods: Principles and Practicalities* (Dublin, Clarus Press, 2016) 5–19.
King, JA, 'The Pervasiveness of Polycentricity' (2008) 53 *Public Law* 101.
—— *Judging Social Rights* (Cambridge, Cambridge University Press, 2012).
Koch, IE, 'The Justiciability of Indivisible Rights' (2003) 72 *Nordic Journal of International Law* 3.
—— 'Dichotomies, Trichotomies or Waves of Duties?' (2005) 5 *Human Rights Law Review* 81.
Künnemann, R, 'A Coherent Approach to Human Rights' (1995) 17 *Human Rights Quarterly* 323.
Langford, M (ed), *Social Rights Jurisprudence: Emerging Trends in International and Comparative Law* (Cambridge, Cambridge University Press, 2009).
—— 'The Justiciability of Social Rights: From Practice to Theory' in M Langford (ed), *Social Rights Jurisprudence: Emerging Trends in International and Comparative Law* (Cambridge, Cambridge University Press, 2009) 3–45.
—— 'Substantive Obligations' in M Langford, B Porter, R Brown and J Rossi (eds), *The Optional Protocol to the International Covenant on Economic, Social and Cultural Rights: A Commentary* (Pretoria, Pretoria University Law Press, 2016) 203–52.
Langford, M and King, JA, 'Committee on Economic, Social and Cultural Rights: Past, Present and Future' in M Langford (ed), *Social Rights Jurisprudence: Emerging Trends in International and Comparative Law* (Cambridge, Cambridge University Press, 2009) 477–516.
Lawson, A, *Disability and Equality Law in Britain: The Role of Reasonable Adjustment* (Oxford, Hart, 2008).
—— 'The UN Convention on the Rights of Persons with Disabilities and European Disability Law: A Catalyst for Cohesion?' in OM Arnardóttir and G Quinn (eds), *The UN Convention on the Rights of Persons with Disabilities: European and Scandinavian Perspectives*, International Studies in Human Rights 100 (Leiden, Nijhoff, 2009) 81–110.
—— 'Accessibility Obligations in the UN Convention on the Rights of Persons with Disabilities: Nyusti & Takács v. Hungary' (2014) 30 *South African Journal on Human Rights* 380.
—— 'Article 9: Accessibility' in I Bantekas, MA Stein and D Anastasiou (eds), *The UN Convention on the Rights of Persons with Disabilities: A Commentary* (Oxford, Oxford University Press, 2018) 258–86.
Bouthillier, Y Le, 'Article 32' in O Corten and P Klein (eds), *The Vienna Conventions on the Law of Treaties: A Commentary* (Oxford, Oxford University Press, 2011).
Leckie, S, 'Another Step Towards Indivisibility: Identifying the Key Features of Violations of Economic, Social and Cultural Rights' (1998) 20 *Human Rights Quarterly* 81.
Legg, A, *The Margin of Appreciation in International Human Rights Law: Deference and Proportionality*, (Oxford, Oxford University Press 2012).
Lerner, N, *The UN Convention on the Elimination of All Forms of Racial Discrimination*, Nijhoff Classics in International Law 3 (Leiden, Nijhoff, 2015).
Letsas, G, 'Intentionalism and The Interpretation of the ECHR' in M Fitzmaurice, O Elias and P Merkouris (eds), *Treaty Interpretation and the Vienna Convention on the Law of Treaties: 30 Years On*, Queen Mary Studies in International Law 1 (Leiden, Nijhoff, 2010) 255–72.
—— 'Strasbourg's Interpretive Ethic: Lessons for the International Lawyer' (2010) 21 *European Journal of International Law* 509.
Liebenberg, S, 'The International Covenant on Economic, Social and Cultural Rights and its Implications for South Africa' (1995) 11 *South African Journal on Human Rights* 359.
—— 'The Protection of Economic and Social Rights in Domestic Legal Systems' in A Eide, A Rosas and C Krause (eds), *Economic, Social, and Cultural Rights: A Textbook*, 2nd edn, (Leiden, Nijhoff, 2001) 55–84.

—— *Socio-economic Rights: Adjudication Under a Transformative Constitution* (Claremont, Juta, 2010).

Liisberg, MV, 'Accessibility of Services and Discrimination: Concentricity, Consequence, and the Concept of Anticipatory Reasonable Adjustment' (2015) 15 *International Journal of Discrimination and the Law* 123.

Lord, JE and Brown, R, 'The Role of Reasonable Accommodation in Securing Substantive Equality for Persons with Disabilities: The UN Convention on the Rights of Persons with Disabilities' in MH Rioux, LA Basser and M Jones (eds), *Critical Perspectives on Human Rights and Disability Law* (Leiden, Nijhoff, 2011).

Maisley, N, 'The International Right of Rights?: Article 25(a) of the ICCPR as a Human Right to Take Part in International Law-Making' (2017) 28 *European Journal of International Law* 89.

Marcus, D, 'The Normative Development of Socioeconomic Rights Through Supranational Adjudication' (2006) 42 *Stanford Journal of International Law* 53.

Marks, SP, 'Emerging Human Rights: A New Generation for the 1980s?' (1981) 33 *Rutgers Law Review* 435.

McGoldrick, D, *The Human Rights Committee: Its Role in the Development of the International Covenant on Civil and Political Rights* (Oxford, Clarendon Press, 1991).

—— 'A Defence of the Margin of Appreciation and an Argument for its Application by the Human Rights Committee' (2016) 65 *International and Comparative Law Quarterly* 21.

McGrogan, D, 'On the Interpretation of Human Rights Treaties and Subsequent Practice' (2014) 32 *Netherlands Quarterly of Human Rights* 347.

McNair, AD, *The Law of Treaties* (Oxford, Oxford University Press, 1961).

Mechlem, K, 'Treaty Bodies and the Interpretation of Human Rights' (2009) 42 *Vanderbilt Journal of Transnational Law* 905.

Mégret, F, 'The Disabilities Convention: Towards a Holistic Concept of Rights' (2008) 12 *The International Journal of Human Rights* 261.

Merkouris, P, 'Introduction: Interpretation is a Science, is an Art, is a Science' in M Fitzmaurice, O Elias and P Merkouris (eds), *Treaty Interpretation and the Vienna Convention on the Law of Treaties: 30 Years On*, Queen Mary Studies in International Law 1 (Leiden, Nijhoff, 2010) 1–13.

—— '"Third Party" Considerations and "Corrective Interpretation" in the Interpretative Use of Travaux Préparatoires: Is it Fahrenheit 451 for Preparatory Work?' in M Fitzmaurice, O Elias and P Merkouris (eds), *Treaty Interpretation and the Vienna Convention on the Law of Treaties: 30 Years On*, Queen Mary Studies in International Law 1 (Leiden, Nijhoff, 2010) 75–95.

Meron, T, *Human Rights Law-Making in the United Nations: A Critique of Instruments and Process* (Oxford, Oxford University Press, 1986).

Mureinik, E, 'Beyond a Charter of Luxuries: Economic Rights in the Constitution' (1992) 8 *South African Journal on Human Rights* 464.

Neumann F, *The Democratic and the Authoritarian State: Essays in Political and Legal Theory* (Glencoe, Free Press, 1957).

Nilsson, A, 'Article 2: Definitions' in I Bantekas, MA Stein and D Anastasiou (eds), *The UN Convention on the Rights of Persons with Disabilities: A Commentary* (Oxford, Oxford University Press, 2018) 63–83.

Nolan, A, 'Two Steps Forward, No Steps Back?: Evolving Criteria on the Prohibition of Retrogression in Economic and Social Rights' in A Nolan (ed), *Economic and Social Rights after the Global Financial Crisis* (Cambridge, Cambridge University Press, 2014) 121–45.

Nolan, A, Porter, B and Langford, M, 'The Justiciability of Social and Economic Rights: An Updated Appraisal' in MT Kamminga (ed), *Challenges in International Human Rights Law Volume III* (London, Routledge, 2014) 89–126.

Nowak, M, *Introduction to the International Human Rights Regime*, The Raoul Wallenberg Institute Human Rights Library 14 (Leiden, Nijhoff, 2003).

—— *Article 6: The Right to Life, Survival and Development*, A Commentary on the United Nations Convention on the Rights of the Child Series 6 (Leiden, Nijhoff, 2005).

Nowak, M and McArthur, E, *The United Nations Convention Against Torture: A Commentary* (Oxford, Oxford University Press, 2008).

Nussbaum, M, *Women and Human Development: The Capabilities Approach*, The Seeley Lectures 3 (Cambridge, Cambridge University Press, 2000).

O'Connell, R, Nolan, A, Harvey, C, Dutschke, M and Rooney, E, *Applying an International Human Rights Framework to State Budget Allocations: Rights and Resources* (London, Routledge, 2014).

Orakhelashvili, A, *The Interpretation of Acts and Rules in Public International Law* (Oxford University Press 2008).

Pellet, A and Müller, D, 'Article 38' in A Zimmermann, CJ Tams, K Oellers-Frahm and C Tomuschat (eds), *The Statute of the International Court of Justice: A Commentary*, 3rd edn, (Oxford, Oxford University Press, 2019) 819–70.

Pieterse, M, 'Coming to Terms with Judicial Enforcement of Socio-economic Rights' (2004) 20 *South African Journal on Human Rights* 383.

Polanyi, M, *The Logic of Liberty: Reflections and Rejoinders*, The International Library of Sociology, Political Sociology 11 (London, Routledge, 1951).

Porter, B, 'The Reasonableness of Article 8(4): Adjudicating Claims from the Margins' (2009) 27 *Nordisk Tidsskrift for Menneskerettigheter* 39.

—— 'Reasonableness and Article 8(4)' in M Langford, B Porter, R Brown and J Rossi (eds), *The Optional Protocol to the International Covenant on Economic, Social and Cultural Rights: A Commentary* (Pretoria, Pretoria University Law Press, 2016) 173–202.

Ratjen, S and Satija, M, 'Realizing Economic, Social, and Cultural Rights for All' in E Riedel, G Giacca and C Golay (eds), *Economic, Social, and Cultural Rights in International Law: Contemporary Issues and Challenges* (Oxford, Oxford University Press, 2014) 111–33.

Rehof, LA, *Guide to the Travaux Préparatoires of the United Nations Convention on the Elimination of all Forms of Discrimination against Women*, International Studies in Human Rights 29 (Leiden, Nijhoff, 1993).

Riedel, E, 'The Right to Life and the Right to Health, in Particular the Obligation to Reduce Child Mortality' in C Tomuschat, E Lagrange and S Oeter (eds), *The Right to Life* (Leiden, Nijhoff, 2010) 351–69.

Riedel, E, Giacca, G and Golay, C, 'The Development of Economic, Social, and Cultural Rights in International Law' in E Riedel, G Giacca and C Golay (eds), *Economic, Social, and Cultural Rights in International Law: Contemporary Issues and Challenges* (Oxford, Oxford University Press, 2014) 3–48.

Ringel, W, 'Non-discrimination, Accommodation, and Intersectionality under the CRPD: New Trends and Challenges for the UN Human Rights System' (2017) 20 *Max Planck Yearbook of United Nations Law* 98.

Rishmawi, M, *Article 4: The Nature of States Parties' Obligations*, A Commentary on the United Nations Convention on the Rights of the Child Series 4 (Leiden, Nijhoff, 2005).

Robertson, RE, 'Measuring State Compliance with the Obligation to Devote the "Maximum Available Resources" to Realizing Economic, Social, and Cultural Rights' (1994) 16 *Human Rights Quarterly* 693.

Saul, B, Kinley, DH and Mowbray, J, *The International Covenant on Economic, Social and Cultural Rights: Commentary, Cases, and Materials* (Oxford, Oxford University Press, 2016).

Schabas, WA, 'Introduction Essay: The Drafting and Significance of the Universal Declaration of Human Rights' in WA Schabas (ed), *The Universal Declaration of Human Rights: The Travaux Préparatoires* (Cambridge, Cambridge University Press, 2013) lxxi–cxxv.

—— *U.N. International Covenant on Civil and Political Rights: Nowak's CCPR Commentary*, 3rd edn (Kehl, NP Engel, 2019).

Schachter, O, 'The Obligation to Implement the Covenant in Domestic Law' in L Henkin (ed), *The International Bill of Rights: The Covenant on Civil and Political Rights* (New York, Columbia University Press, 1981) 311–31.

—— 'Human Dignity as a Normative Concept' (1983) 77 *American Journal of International Law* 848.
Scheinin, M, 'Justiciability and the Indivisibility of Rights' in J Squires, M Langford and B Thiele (eds), *The Road to a Remedy: Current Issues in the Litigation of Economic, Social and Cultural Rights* (Sydney, Australian Human Rights Centre, 2005).
—— 'Impact on the Law of Treaties' in MT Kamminga and M Scheinin (eds), *The Impact of Human Rights Law on General International Law* (Oxford, Oxford University Press, 2009) 23–36.
Schlütter, B, 'Aspects of Human Rights Interpretation by the UN Treaty Bodies' in H Keller and G Ulfstein (eds), *UN Human Rights Treaty Bodies: Law and Legitimacy* (Cambridge, Cambridge University Press, 2012) 261–319.
Schmahl, S, *Convention on the Rights of the Child: Article-by-Article Commentary* (Baden-Baden, Nomos, 2021).
Schwelb, E, 'The Nature of the Obligations of the States Parties to the International Covenant on Civil and Political Rights' in R Cassin (ed), *Amicorum Discipulorumque Liber: Problèmes de Protection Internationale des Droits de l'Homme* (Paris, Pédone, 1969) 301–24.
Scott, C, 'The Interdependence and Permeability of Human Rights Norms: Towards a Partial Fusion of the International Covenants on Human Rights' (1989) 27 *Osgoode Hall Law Journal* 769.
Scott, C and Macklem, P, 'Constitutional Ropes of Sand or Justiciable Guarantees? Social Rights in a New South African Constitution' (1992) 141 *University of Pennsylvania Law Review* 1.
Seibert-Fohr, A, 'Domestic Implementation of the International Covenant on Civil and Political Rights Pursuant to its Article 2 Para. 2' in JA Frowein, R Wolfrum and CE Philipp (eds), *Max Planck Yearbook of United Nations Law Volume* 5 (The Hague, Kluwer Law International, 2001) 399–72.
Sen, A, *Development as Freedom* (New York, Knopf, 1999).
—— *Inequality Reexamined* (Oxford, Oxford University Press, 1995).
Sepúlveda, MM, *The Nature of the Obligations Under the International Covenant on Economic, Social and Cultural Rights* (Antwerp, Intersentia, 2003).
Shany, Y, 'Toward a General Margin of Appreciation Doctrine in International Law?' (2005) 16 *European Journal of International Law* 907.
Shue, H, 'The Interdependence of Duties' in P Alston and K Tomaševski (eds), *The Right to Food*, International Studies in Human Rights 4 (Boston, Nijhoff, 1984) 83–95.
—— *Basic Rights: Subsistence, Affluence, and U.S. Foreign Policy*, 40th Anniversary edn (Princeton, Princeton University Press, 2020).
Sinclair, I, *The Vienna Convention on the Law of Treaties*, 2nd edn (Manchester, Manchester University Press, 1984).
Slocum, B and Wong, J, 'The Vienna Convention and Ordinary Meaning in International Law' (2021) 46 *Yale Journal of International Law* 191.
Steiner, HJ, Alston, P and Goodman, R, *International Human Rights in Context: Law, Politics, Morals; Text and Materials*, 3rd edn (Oxford, Oxford University Press, 2008).
Sunstein, CR, 'Lochner's Legacy' (1987) 87 *Columbia Law Review* 873.
Szabo, M, 'General Principles of Law in the Practice of International Courts and the European Court of Justice' (2016) 4 *Hungarian Yearbook of International Law and European Law* 135.
Tobin, J, 'Article 4: A State's General Obligation of Implementation' in J Tobin (ed), *The UN Convention on the Rights of the Child: A Commentary* (Oxford, Oxford University Press, 2019) 108–58.
—— 'Seeking to Persuade: A Constructive Approach to Human Rights Treaty Interpretation' (2010) 23 *Harvard Human Rights Journal* 1.
Tobin, J and Cashmore, J, 'Article 19: The Right to Protection against All Forms of Violence' in J Tobin (ed), *The UN Convention on the Rights of the Child: A Commentary* (Oxford, Oxford University Press, 2019) 687–724.
Tobin, J and Peleg, N, 'Article 6: The Rights to Life, Survival, and Development' in J Tobin (ed), *The UN Convention on the Rights of the Child: A Commentary* (Oxford, Oxford University Press, 2019) 186–236.

Todres, J, 'Emerging Limitations on the Rights of the Child: The U. N. Convention on the Rights of Child and its Early Case Law' (1998) 30 *Columbia Human Rights Law Review* 159.

Tomaševski, K, 'Justiciability of Economic, Social and Cultural Rights' (1995) 55 *ICJ Review* 203.

Tomuschat, C, 'National Implementation of International Standards on Human Rights' (1984–1985) 31 *Canadian Human Rights Yearbook* 31.

Trömel, S, 'A Personal Perspective on the Drafting History of the United Nations Convention on the Rights of Persons with Disabilities' (2009) 1 *European Yearbook of Disability Law* 115.

Tushnet, M, 'Social Welfare Rights and the Forms of Judicial Review' (2004) 82 *Texas Law Review* 1895.

Tyagi, Y, *The UN Human Rights Committee: Practice and Procedure* (Cambridge, Cambridge University Press, 2011).

Uerpmann-Wittzack, R, 'Die UN-Behindertenrechtskonvention in der Praxis des Ausschusses für die Rechte von Menschen mit Behinderungen' (2016) 54 *Archiv des Völkerrechts* 181.

Ulfstein, G, 'Treaty Bodies and Regimes' in DB Hollis (ed), *The Oxford Guide to Treaties*, 2nd edn (Oxford, Oxford University Press, 2020) 414–31.

Vaghri, Z, Zermatten, J, Lansdown, G and Ruggiero, R, *Monitoring State Compliance with the UN Convention on the Rights of the Child*, Children's Well-Being: Indicators and Research 25 (Cham, Springer, 2022).

Vagts, DF, 'Treaty Interpretation and the New American Ways of Law Reading' (1993) 4 *European Journal of International Law* 472.

Vandenbogaerde, A and Vandenhole, W, 'The Optional Protocol to the International Covenant on Economic, Social and Cultural Rights: An Ex Ante Assessment of its Effectiveness in Light of the Drafting Process' (2010) 10 *Human Rights Law Review* 207.

Vandenhole, W, Türkelli, GE and Lembrechts, S, *Children's Rights: A Commentary on the Convention on the Rights of the Child and its Protocols* (Cheltenham, Elgar, 2019).

Villiger, ME, *Commentary on the 1969 Vienna Convention on the Law of Treaties* (Leiden, Nijhoff, 2009).

—— 'The Rules on Interpretation: Misgivings, Misunderstandings, Miscarriage? The 'Crucible' Intended by the International Law Commission' in E Cannizzaro (ed), *The Law of Treaties Beyond the Vienna Convention* (Oxford, Oxford University Press, 2011) 105–22.

Watson, J, 'The Limited Utility of International Law in the Protection of Human Rights' (1980) 74 *Proceedings of the American Society of International Law* 1.

Whelan, DJ and Donnelley, J, 'The West, Economic and Social Rights, and the Global Human Rights Regime: Setting the Record Straight' (2007) 29 *Human Rights Quarterly* 908.

Wills, J and Warwick, B, 'Contesting Austerity: The Potential and Pitfalls of Socioeconomic Rights Discourse' (2016) 23 *Indiana Journal of Global Legal Studies* 629.

Young, KG, *Constituting Economic and Social Rights* (Oxford, Oxford University Press, 2012).

—— 'Proportionality, Reasonableness, and Economic and Social Rights' in VC Jackson and M Tushnet (eds), *Proportionality: New Frontiers, New Challenges*, Comparative Constitutional Law and Policy (Cambridge, Cambridge University Press, 2017).

—— 'Waiting for Rights: Progressive Realization and Lost Time' in KG Young (ed), *The Future of Economic and Social Rights* (Cambridge, Cambridge University Press, 2019) 654–83.

Yourow, HC, *The Margin of Appreciation Doctrine in the Dynamics of European Human Rights Jurisprudence*, International Studies in Human Rights 28 (Dordrecht, Nijhoff, 1996).

Index

www.ingramcontent.com/pod-product-compliance
Ingram Content Group UK Ltd.
Pitfield, Milton Keynes, MK11 3LW, UK
UKHW020240290926
15470UKWH00002B/652